Minority Families in the United States

A Multicultural Perspective

Third Edition

Edited by
Ronald L. Taylor

Prentice
Hall

Upper Saddle River, New Jersey 07458

Library of Congress Cataloging-in-Publication Data

Minority families in the United States : a multicultural perspective / edited by Ronald L. Taylor.—3rd ed.

    p. cm.

  Includes bibliographical references and index.

  ISBN 0-13-016558-1

    1. Minorities—United States. 2. Family—United States. I. Taylor, Ronald L. (Ronald Lewis)

E184.A1 M5437 2002   *047755859*

  305.8'00973—dc21

2001036900

AVP, Publisher: Nancy Roberts
Managing editor (editorial): Sharon Chambliss
Executive managing editor (production): Ann Marie McCarthy
Production liaison: Fran Russello
Editorial/production supervision: Bruce Hobart (Pine Tree Composition)
Prepress and manufacturing buyer: Mary Ann Gloriande
Art director: Jayne Conte
Cover designer: Bruce Kenselaar
Marketing manager: Chris Barker

This book was set in 10/12 New Baskerville by Pine Tree Composition, Inc., and was printed and bound by Hamilton Printing Company
The cover was printed by Jaguar Advanced Graphics

© 2002, 1988, 1994 by Pearson Education, Inc.
Upper Saddle River, New Jersey 07458

Printed in the United States of America

10 9 8 7 6 5 4 3 2

ISBN 0-13-016558-1

Pearson Education LTD., London
Pearson Education Australia PTE, Limited, Sydney
Pearson Education Singapore, Pte. Ltd
Pearson Education North Asia Ltd, Hong Kong
Pearson Education Canada, Ltd., Toronto
Pearson Educación de Mexico, S.A. de C.V.
Pearson Education—Japan, Tokyo
Pearson Education Malaysia, Pte. Ltd
Pearson Education, Upper Saddle River, New Jersey

Contents

Contributors

HECTOR CARRASQUILLO is Associate Professor of Puerto Rican Studies and Director of the Center for Latino Studies at Brooklyn College, City University of New York. His current work focuses on the family and the Latino aged population.

EVELYN NAKANO GLENN is Professor of Women's Studies and Ethnic Studies at the University of California at Berkeley. She has written extensively on work and technology, the race and gender stratification of labor markets, and gender politics in family and household. Glenn is the author of *Issei, Nisei, War Bride: Three Generations of Japanese Women in Domestic Service* (1986), and co-editor of *Mothering: Ideology, Experience, and Agency* (1994).

NAZLI KIBRIA is Assistant Professor of Sociology at Boston University. She has written a number of articles on Vietnamese women and work. Kibria is completing a book on changes in family structure among Vietnamese refugees following migration to the United States.

MICHEL S. LAGUERRE is Professor of Social Anthropology in the Department of African American Studies and the Ph.D. Program in Ethnic Studies at the University of California at Berkeley. He has published several books on the sociology of Caribbean societies, including *American Odyssey: Haitians in New York City* (1984) and *Urban Poverty in the Caribbean* (1990).

ROBERT E. MILLETTE is former chairperson of the Division of Social Sciences and Behavioral Studies at Lincoln University in Pennsylvania and is presently U.N. Ambassador of Grenada. He is the author of *The Grenada Revolution: Why It Failed?* (1985).

PYONG GAP MIN is Professor of Sociology at Queens College and the Graduate School of the City University of New York. He has written widely on Korean families in the United States. His most recent book is titled *Caught in the Middle: Korean Communities in New York and Los Angeles* (1996).

LISANDRO PÉREZ is Associate Professor of Sociology and Anthropology and Director of the Cuban Research Center at Florida International University. He has published extensively on Cuban immigration and community and family life in the United States.

ANGELA Y. H. POK is a doctoral student in the Department of Sociology at Michigan State University. Her areas of specialization include gender, race, and immigration.

BANDANA PURKAYASTHA is Assistant Professor of Sociology at the University of Connecticut. Her research focuses on the social construction of gender and race, place-based influences on ethnic groups, and transnational networks of new immigrant groups to the United States. She is currently completing a book on second-generation Asian Indian youth and Indian women's activism.

C. MATTHEW SNIPP is Professor of Sociology at Stanford University. He has published numerous works on American Indian demography, economic development, poverty, and unemployment. He is the author of *American Indians: The First of This Land* (1989), among other works.

DANA Y. TAKAGI is Associate Professor of Sociology at the University of California, Santa Cruz. She is the author of *The Retreat from Race,* published by Rutgers University Press (1993), and has written a number of articles on Asian Americans.

RONALD L. TAYLOR is Professor of Sociology and Vice Provost for Multicultural Affairs at the University of Connecticut, Storrs. He is coauthor and editor (with Doris Y. Wilkinson) of *The Black Male in America: Perspectives on His Status in Contemporary Society* (1977) and *African American Youth: Their Social and Economic Status in the United States* (1995). He has published widely on African American families, youth, and gender.

STACEY G. H. YAP is Associate Professor of Sociology at Plymouth State College, Plymouth, New Hampshire. She is author of *Gather Your Strengths, Sister: The Emerging Role of Chinese Women Community Workers* (1989).

MICHAEL YELLOWBIRD is a Ph.D. candidate in the School of Social Welfare at the University of Wisconsin, Madison. He is an enrolled member (Arikara/Hidatsa) of the Three Affiliated Tribes on the Fort Berthold Indian Reservation in North Dakota. His research interests include federal Indian policy, the family, and the health of indigenous populations.

MAXINE BACA ZINN is Professor of Sociology and Senior Associate in the Julian Samora Research Institute at Michigan State University. She is the coauthor (with D. Stanley Eitzen) of *Diversity in Families* (3rd edition, 1993) and *In Conflict and Order: Understanding Society.* Zinn is also the coeditor of *Women of Color in U.S. Society* (1994). She received the 2000 American Sociological Association's Jessie Bernard Career Award.

Preface

American families encompass a diversity of family forms and patterns, reflecting in some measure the varied and diverse cultural histories of the nation's ethnic and racial composition, and the influence of structured social inequalities on family resources and processes. This book focuses on minority families in the United States, that is, those families that have historically experienced social, economic, and political subordination vis-à-vis other families, as a consequence of their race, ancestry, or other assumed inferior traits or characteristics. The dominant minority groups in the United States are African Americans, Hispanics, and Asian Americans. Each of these major groups is further characterized by a number of subgroups, cultures, and nationalities that contribute to even greater diversity in family patterns. Some writers prefer the term "ethnic" or "ethnic families of color" to "minority" as the identifying term for these groups and their families. However, since the term "minority" connotes the subordination of groups and their unequal access to sources of economic and political power in society, the term seems appropriate in view of the historical experiences and devalued status of African Americans, Latinos, and Asian Americans in the stratified hierarchy of American society.

This volume brings together analyses of minority families organized around a common set of issues and themes, including historical influences on the nature of family organization among these groups, contemporary trends in family structure and living arrangements, and the influence of socioeconomic factors on family organization and processes, which enable the reader to appreciate significant similarities and differences between groups, as well as the considerable diversity within each of these broad categories, which is frequently ignored or glossed over in much of the family literature. For example, there are important differences in family processes and organization between African Americans and blacks of West Indian origin that are typically minimized or obscured in more global treatments of African American families. Much the same can be said regarding the treatment of Asian American and Latino families in the literature.

The minority populations included in this volume were selected to represent the diversity of minority families, from those whose histories predate that of many of the European ethnic groups, to those of more recent origin, and to highlight the impact of historical and contemporary processes on the development of distinctive family lifestyles among these diverse groups.

ABOUT THE SECOND EDITION

To better reflect the growing diversity of minority families in the United States, new chapters on West Indian, Korean, and Asian Indian families have been added to the second edition of this volume. These groups, together with African American, Mexican American or Chicano, Puerto Rican, Cuban, Chinese, Japanese, Vietnamese, and American Indian populations included in this edition, represent more than 90 percent of the racial ethnic minority population in the United States and account for two-thirds of the 28 million people added to the United States population between 1980 and 1992. Beyond updating several chapters for which recent data were available and the addition of new chapters, the structure and the organization of the volume remain unchanged. The exception is the chapter on "Minority Families and Social Change" (Chapter 13), which has been expanded to include discussion of several emerging issues that are likely to contribute to even greater heterogeneity among and between minority families in the United States in the decades to come.

One of the major frustrations experienced in revising the first edition was the unavailability of certain data on Asian Indian and American Indian populations from the 1990 census. Although the 1990 census provides a wealth of new data on these populations as a whole, it offers far less detailed information on the various subgroups within these larger populations that would permit useful comparisons over time on certain important characteristics than does the 1980 census. In the absence of such data, some of the finer distinctions between and among groups presented in the first edition were not possible in this edition. Despite this limitation, students and instructors should find this edition more informative with the addition of new chapters and the inclusion of more recent material on minority families in the United States.

PREFACE TO THE THIRD EDITION

As the third edition of this text goes to press, results from the 2000 census are being released, which highlight the dramatic rise in the number of immigrants entering the United States during the past decade—at its highest point since 1900—creating a more racially and ethnically diverse society than ever before and more variation in the structure and form of family life. This new edition continues to reflect the diversity of family life in the United States among the so-called minority families, which include African American, Haitian, Mexican American (or Chicano), Puerto Rican, Cuban, Chinese, Japanese, Vietnamese, American Indian, West Indian, Korean, and Asian Indian or Indo-American families, and account for nearly a third of the U.S. population. Although the structure and organization of the volume remain unchanged from previous editions, we have sought to update various chapters where recent data were available. Despite a wealth of demographic data from the 2000 census, there is again a paucity of detailed information on the various subgroups within the larger minority populations that permits useful comparisons over time on certain familial characteristics than was the case when the first edition of this volume was published. This is especially the case with respect to detailed and current information on American Indian and Asian Indian or Indo-American populations. The unavailability of this information has prevented us from making some of the finer distinctions between and among groups that were possible in the first edition. Nonetheless, students and instructors will find the new edition no less informative and current than were the previous editions. In preparing this edition of the text, I was ably assisted by Danielle Currier, doctoral student in sociology at Connecticut, whose thoroughness greatly enhanced the quality of this edition. I acknowledge her help with gratitude.

Ronald L. Taylor
University of Connecticut

Minority Families in America: An Introduction

Ronald L. Taylor

The United States is a mosaic of family patterns created by a history of incorporating diverse racial and ethnic groups that came to this country at different periods and under vastly different social and economic conditions. These groups differ on a number of important attributes, including cultural histories, socioeconomic characteristics, kinship structures, intergenerational relationships, and patterns of residence (Lieberson and Waters 1988; Wilkinson 1987). Such diversity in family forms and functioning belies the popular conception of "the American family" as a monolithic unit, that is, as a fixed and uniform structure. Instead, "'the family' is experienced differently by people in different social classes, by people of different racial and ethnic backgrounds, and even by gender. And variations in families occur within a social class or ethnic group" (Baca Zinn and Eitzen 1993:xii). In short, race, ethnicity, social class, and gender are major determinants of variations in family patterns and experiences within families. Hence, to speak of *the* American family is to ignore the great diversity in form, lifestyle, and experiences of such families.

This book focuses on minority families in the United States—those families that have historically experienced social, economic, and political subordination vis-à-vis families of the dominant majority, as a consequence of their race, ancestry, and/or other characteristics that the latter holds in low esteem (Simpson and Yinger 1985). From a sociological perspective, the terms *minority* and *majority* are not used to refer to the numerical size of groups but as a status designation, that is, to the relative prestige and power of groups in the stratification hierarchy of the social order (Newman 1973; Schermerhorn 1970). The essence of minority group status is unequal access to the sources of economic and political power in society.

In the United States, the dominant minority populations are African Americans and those of Hispanic (Mexican, Puerto Rican, Cuban) and Asian (Chinese, Japanese, Filipino) ancestry (U.S. Bureau of the Census 1990a). Although smaller and less visible than the aforementioned groups, Native Americans, who numbered 1.9 million in 1990 and 2.36 million in 1998, are the oldest and one of the fastest

1

growing minority groups in the United States (U.S. Bureau of the Census 2000b). Together these groups account for more than 80 million people, whose ranks and proportion of the total population continue to grow as a result of high fertility rates and the increasing flow of immigration from Third World nations. Within each of these minority populations is found a diversity of ethnic groups linked in many cases by a shared cultural heritage, language, and collective experience of political, social, and economic subordination.

Although related, the terms *minority* and *ethnic group* are not synonymous but are analytically distinct categories (Simpson and Yinger 1985). Yinger defines an ethnic group as "a segment of a larger society whose members are thought, by themselves and/or others, to have a common origin and to share important segments of a common culture and who, in addition, participate in shared activities in which the common origin and culture are significant ingredients" (1976:200). Ethnicity thus refers to the primary ties that bind individuals into solidary groups by virtue of a shared cultural history and common symbols (Taylor 1979). Ethnic groups differ from other groups in society by some combination of race, nationality, language, or religion (Gordon 1964; Schermerhorn 1970). However, not all groups distinguished by these characteristics are minority groups. As noted before, a group's restricted access to sources of economic and political power and marginal location in the social order define it as a minority.

Some sociologist distinguish "ethnic" from "racial" minorities, reserving the former term for groups that differ on the basis of cultural criteria and the latter for groups that differ from the dominant majority in physical characteristics (Heckman 1983; Simpson and Yinger 1985). Thus, African Americans, Asians, and other "nonwhite" populations are usually regarded as racial minorities, whereas European nationalities and some religious groups are referred to as ethnic or cultural minorities (Petersen 1980). Such a distinction is warranted when the aim is to emphasize the qualitatively different experiences of groups defined by their genetic or physical characteristics and those defined by their nationality, religion, or some other cultural criteria. Indeed, as van den Berghe contends, a definition of group membership based on racial or physical criteria is far more problematic and "stigmatizing than an ethnic definition, and typically gives rise to far more rigid social hierarchies" in society (1978:xvi). In his view,

> the distinction between societies where the important criteria of group membership are physical ones and those where they are cultural—that is, the distinction between multiethnic and multiracial societies—is an important one. It is true that systems of race and systems of ethnic relations have much in common, but multiracial societies are in the nature of the case more rigidly ascriptive ones than most of the multiethnic societies. Some of the world's most rigid systems have not ostensibly been based on race, notably the Hindu caste system (which may, however, have originated in a racial system), but a disproportionate number of the world's most rigid systems of social stratification have been racial, and indeed racist, in character. (van den Berghe 1970:10)

In short, group differentiation based on physical characteristics represents an extreme case of status ascription, creating a more rigid basis of cleavage between groups than divisions based on cultural characteristics. An important feature of multiracial societies is that racial groups are invariably stratified in terms of their access to sources of prestige, wealth, and power (van den Berghe 1978). The ranked hierarchy of racial groups is also a structured system of exploitation and social discrimination, which in turn produces significant differences between racial groups in many aspects of family life, including marriage, divorce, and family structure (Baca Zinn and Eitzen 1993).

The distinction between racial and ethnic criteria of group membership, although analytically important, should not be understood to mean that the groups to which they refer are mutually exclusive. Groups defined on the basis of racial or physical characteristics are often distinguished by cultural characteristics as well (Taylor 1979). African Americans, Native Americans, and other "nonwhite" minority groups are also ethnic groups to the degree that they "differ in religion, language, or attachments to some elements of an ancestral culture" (Simpson and Yinger 1985:11). In other words, none of the criteria used to delineate the boundaries for racial and ethnic minority populations is precise enough to separate these subpopulations sharply. Nonetheless, phenotypical differences (that is, anatomical features such as skin color and body and facial shape) between groups have been far more salient in the United States as an organizing principle in social relations than cultural ones, and groups socially defined as racial ethnics have historically been at a considerable disadvantage in their treatment in American society (Lieberson and Waters 1988; Omni and Winant 1986). Moreover, family life has been profoundly affected by the experience of and responses to such structured disadvantages.

The tendency in recent works to treat the ethnicity of racial minorities and white immigrant groups as variants of the same phenomena implies a continuity in the collective experiences of these groups that obscures fundamental disparities in their social histories, treatment, and status in the United States (Steinberg 1989; Omni and Winant 1986). For this reason, and in order to highlight the fateful consequences for families that have occupied an unprecedented status in the social structure of American society, we use the term *minority families* in preference to "ethnic families" or "ethnic families of color" to refer to those racially defined minority groups.

MINORITY FAMILIES AND THE "NEW DARWINISM"

Some social scientists disagree that the historical experiences of African Americans, Asians, and other racially defined minorities in the United States have been fundamentally different from the experiences of white European immigrant groups and thus de-emphasize the legacy of racial subordination in accounting for many of the observed differences among ethnic and racial minorities in family and social life. Although acknowledging the more extreme forms of prejudice and discrimination to which racial minorities have historically been subjected, these writers credit differences in basic cultural characteristics (such as family cohesion, strong work ethic, and emphasis on education), particularly family structure, between immigrant and racial minority groups as major determinants of their respective fates in American society (Glazer and Moynihan 1970; Sowell 1981).

Nathan Glazer is prominent among those writers who assume that the experiences of white ethnics and racial minorities have been different in degree rather than in kind. He argues that differences between these groups are a consequence of a number of factors, prominent among which are

> cultural differences created in other settings and of new differences that arise in this country because of the complex interaction between the pre-existing cultural characteristics, various degrees of prejudice and discrimination, and the economic and political situation of the country and relevant parts of the country at the time of arrival and other elements. The line between white ethnics and ethnic groups of other races does not determine their fate. Racial identities can change their meaning. Italians and Jews, considered "racially" different by Americans at the turn of the century, are not so considered today . . . Neither in America nor elsewhere are race and ethnicity categories so different that the processes that affect the assimilation and integration of ethnic groups change completely when groups of a different race are involved. (1983:73)

Thus, according to Glazer and Moynihan, what matters in the long term for the successful assimilation of racial and ethnic groups into society and the achievement of high group status are the values and norms that those groups bring to bear on general social circumstances to which they are exposed. In short, they hypothesize that "ethnic groups bring different norms to bear on common circumstances with consequent different levels of success—hence group differences in status" (Glazer and Moynihan 1975:17).

The economist Thomas Sowell (1981) likewise de-emphasizes the importance of the "color" line in accounting for differential patterns of achievement and status between racial and ethnic minority families in the United States. From his review of the history and progress of such groups as the Irish, Jews, Italians, Chinese, Japanese, Puerto Ricans, and African Americans, Sowell concedes that race has been a major force in determining the trajectory of incorporation and achievement for some of these groups but contends that it has not been an insurmountable barrier, as the notable achievements and mobility of the Japanese, West Indians, Koreans, and Jews so dramatically attest. In his view, the middle-class values and orientation (for example, discipline, hard work, thrift, and self-reliance) of these groups are the keys to their success and mobility in America.

Critics of the cultural or normative explanation of group differences in mobility and achievement in American society charge that such explanations involve a deceptive form of circular reasoning in that they incorrectly infer group values from group outcomes and then point to such values as causal factors (Steinberg 1989; Omni and Winant 1986). To wit,

> Why are two or more groups different with respect to some characteristic or dependent variable? Presumably, they differ in their values or in some norm. How do we know that they differ in their values and norms? The argument then frequently involves using the behavioral attribute one is trying to explain as the indicator of the normative or value dif-

ference one is trying to use as the explanation. A pure case of circular reasoning! (Lieberson 1980:8)

An example of this is the common explanation given for the superior educational achievement of Japanese Americans. "Since 1940," writes Petersen (1971) in his study of Japanese Americans, "the Japanese have had more schooling than any other race in the American population, including whites" (p. 113). He attributes their educational success to a particular set of cultural values. But as Lieberson (1980) argues, proving the cultural thesis requires independent measures of such values and norms to justify a cultural or normative explanation.

In challenging cultural explanations of group differences in success and achievement in society, Steinberg (1989) calls attention to the affinity of such explanation with Social Darwinist theory of the nineteenth century, which provided a pseudoscientific rationale for social inequality between races or groups based on notions of biological superiority and inferiority. In his view, "nineteenth-century Social Darwinism has been replaced with a 'New Darwinism' that has simply substituted culture for genes" (p. 79). Indeed, Steinberg finds that

> Though the New Darwinists eschew such value-laden terminology as cultural "superiority" and "inferiority," they nevertheless argue that the relative socioeconomic success of each ethnic group depends upon the extent to which it exemplifies a given set of cultural values. The specific values cited are familiar to anyone who has heard Benjamin Franklin's homilies or read Horatio Alger novels—frugality, industry, foresight, perseverance, ingenuity, and the like. Though masked in pseudoscientific terminology, and obscured by an avalanche of statistics, the underlying premise of the New Darwinism is that "good" things come to those with the "right" cultural values, whereas social dishonor and a host of social problems befall those groups that are culturally aberrant. (1981:79–80)

Viewed in these terms, the New Darwinists advance what amounts to a moral interpretation of history in that they assume "that society functions as a kind of moral benefactor parceling out its rewards to the most culturally deserving . . . and that groups that are less successful in the competition are somehow deficient in character or in their cultural values" (Steinberg 1989:87).

Because the subcultures of ethnic groups are inclusive of many norms, values, and other institutional properties, finding some elements that lend support to a cultural interpretation of group success or failure is not difficult. As Jiobu observes, "if a group succeeds, then observers cull the subculture for traits that engender success. If a group fails, the observers cull the subculture for traits that engender failure. In either case . . . observers can almost always find some trait that supports the subcultural argument" (1988:218).

The cultural thesis is suspect for other reasons as well. It not only ignores significant differences in the opportunity structures available to ethnic and racial minorities upon entry to this country but also assumes that all groups started out from the bottom of the socioeconomic system. Although all groups may have started at the bottom, "the bottom," as Blauner (1972) points out, was by no means the same for all groups. Unlike their ethnic counterparts who, although mercilessly exploited in the labor market, "had a foot in the most dynamic centers of the economy and could, with time, rise to semiskilled and skilled positions" (Blauner 1972:63), racial minorities were largely excluded from the industrial sectors of the national economy until well after the flow of immigrants from Europe subsided in the 1920s. In short, concentrating as it does on the elements of group culture as sources of success or failure in society, the cultural thesis effectively rules out consideration of structural conditions or situational differences that racially defined minorities have encountered in the United States that distinguish their experiences from the experiences of European immigrants. As a result, this thesis fails to acknowledge the implications of the fact that in the United States, only Native Americans were subject to genocide and removal to reservations, only African Americans were enslaved, only Chicanos or Mexicans Americans were singled out for exclusion, and only Japanese Americans were placed in concentration camps (Blauner 1972; Takaki 1987). Recent research documents that these experiences, together with a variety of other external social constraints, were fateful for the respective destinies of racial minorities in the United States and produced historical variations in the family and social life of these groups (Glenn 1987; Lieberson 1980; Steinberg 1987).

In sum, the historical conditions under which racial and European immigrants entered American society were crucial in determining not only patterns of mobility and achievement but also the nature of family and community life. Knowledge of these conditions and of the manner of incorporation of these groups is as essential to an understanding of their contemporary position in the larger society as are cultural factors.

MINORITY FAMILIES AND THE STRUCTURE OF INEQUALITY

The earliest studies of immigrant and racially defined minority families typically assumed that such families were subject to a universal process of incorporation into society (Baca Zinn and Eitzen 1993). This assumption was key to Robert Park's (1950) now famous "race-relations cycle," a theory of racial and ethnic assimilation. According to Park, when dominant and minority groups come into contact, they enter a series of relationships characterized by competition, accommodation, and eventual assimilation. He saw this cycle as universal, progressive, and irreversible: "Customs regulations, immigration restrictions, and racial barriers may slacken the tempo of the movement; may perhaps halt it altogether for a time; but cannot change its direction, cannot, at any rate, reverse it." (1950:150) As major components of ethnic groups, families were expected to follow the same pattern of development.

For Park, assimilation was a necessary and desirable outcome of dominant-minority group interactions, and his normative theory with its strong "assimilationist bias" came to dominate much of the research and writing on minority families in the United States for more than half a century (Banton 1974; Blauner 1972). Following Park's lead, research on ethnic minority families concentrated on the conditions under which the process of assimilation of these families was hindered or facilitated. Thus, much attention was given to the alleged "handicaps" of these families, particularly those aspects of their cultural backgrounds that deviated from the norms of the dominant majority (Maldonado and Moore 1985).

From the outset, societal acceptance of racial and ethnic minority populations varied along a continuum, with groups closest to the national ideal in language (English), religion (Protestant), descent (Northern European), and physical appearance (light Caucasian) preferred over groups furthest from the norm (Lieberson 1980; Steinberg 1989); Wagley and Harris 1956). However, the need for labor and other requirements of national economic development eventually took precedence over such preferences, resulting in a more inclusive policy toward immigrant populations. Thus, as Thernstrom (1982:6) observed, "Anyone who subscribed to republican principles of liberty, equality and government by consent and who renounced allegiance to all other governments or powers could become an equal member of the national community (Any free white, that is. Barriers to the naturalization of various nonwhite groups would not be lifted until much later.)." Although at times hostile to and fearful of the growing number of immigrants from many lands, especially those from Southern-Central and Eastern Europe, the national ideological orientation toward white European immigrants was essentially assimilationist and egalitarian (Glazer 1983; Gordon 1975).

The national disposition toward the assimilation of racial minorities, however, was quite different. The race or "color" consciousness of American society was manifested early in, for example, the Naturalization Law of 1790. This legislation specified that only free "white" immigrants would be eligible for naturalized citizenship in the United States. Thus for more than 160 years (from 1790 to 1952, when the Walter-McCarran Act was passed), "the Naturalization Law while allowing various European or 'white' ethnic groups to enter the United States and acquire citizenship, specifically denied citizenship to other groups on a racial basis" (Takaki 1987:29).

Under the Naturalization Law, even Native Americans, indigenous to the United States, were ineligible for citizenship because they were regarded as members of tribal groups whose status was comparable to that of foreign nationals. As such, they could not apply for naturalized citizenship because they were not "white" (Takaki 1987). Although welcomed as immigrant laborers in the economically backward regions of the western states, Chinese and later other Asian groups were also denied naturalized citizenship because of their alien status and racial membership. And despite a history of residence that predated that of most European immigrants, African Americans were granted citizenship with the passage of the Civil Rights Act of 1866, nearly 250 years after their arrival in 1619. In short, a sharp distinction was drawn early in the United States between race and ethnicity, and it was not until the passage of the New Immigration Act of 1965 that all traces of racial and ethnic preference were expunged from immigration policy.

As research has shown, the quality of entry and labor status are key factors that distinguish the experiences of racial and ethnic minorities in the United States (Jiobu 1988; Lieberson 1980; Steinberg 1989). In his analysis of the divergent historical experiences of racial and immigrant minorities in the United States, Blauner (1972) borrowed the concept of colonialism from the former colonies of European countries to describe the manner of incorporation and labor market status of Third World (that is, African American, Asian, and Chicano) peoples. Noting that colonialism and immigration are the two principal means by which multiracial and multiethnic societies arise, each with its own chain of consequences, Blauner argued that racial groups were internally "colonized" minorities within the boundaries of the United States, whereas Europeans immigrated to this society: "The colonized became ethnic minorities en bloc, collectively, through conquest, slavery, annexation, or a racial labor policy. The European immigrant peoples became ethnic groups and minorities within the United States by the essentially voluntary movements of individuals and families" (Blauner 1972:55).

Moreover, racial and immigrant minorities were consigned to play vastly different roles in the developing economy and labor markets of the United States:

> Like European overseas colonialism, America has used African, Asian, Mexican and, to a lesser degree, Indian workers for the cheapest labor, concentrating people of color in the most unskilled jobs, the last advanced sectors of the economy and the most industrially backward regions of the nation. In an historical sense, people of color provided much of the hard labor (and the technical skills) that built up the agricultural base and the mineral-transport-communication infrastructure necessary for industrialization and modernization, whereas the Europeans worked primarily within the industrialized, modern sectors. The initial position of European ethnics, while low, was therefore strategic for movement up the economic and social pyramid. The placement of nonwhite groups, however, imposed barriers upon barriers on such mobility, freezing them for long periods of time in the least favorable segments of the economy. (Blauner 1972:62)

Given the conditions under which racial ethnic groups were incorporated into American society, and their marginal, highly circumscribed position in the economy, some social scientists question the appropriateness of such terms as *assimilation, acculturation,* and other ethnicity-based paradigms in addressing the historical experiences of these groups—distinctive experiences that included slavery, colonialization, exclusion, and in the case of Native Americans, near extermination (Moore 1973; Omni and Winant 1986; Steinberg 1989). Although European immigrants, particularly those from Southern and Eastern Europe, were disparaged for their cultural peculiarities and experienced brutal prejudice and discrimination, the aim of national policy was their rapid assimilation into American society. By contrast, the dominant aim for racial minorities was segregation and social subordination, uniquely tailored to fit the respective functions that these groups played in the national economy (Jiobu 1988; Lieberson 1980; Schermerhorn 1970; Steinberg 1989).

Thus social and economic segregation and exclusion from full participation in American life required racially defined minority groups to forge a variety of adaptive strategies to survive and surmount the hardships imposed by the larger society, and these adaptive strategies have produced historical variations in the family life of these groups. Although such variations in family patterns have often been seen as deficient and exceptions to the norm, they are patterns created by mainstream forces; that is, they are the products of the social and economic conditions with which minority families have been forced to cope (Baca Zinn and Eitzen 1993). And like their European counterparts who "used their cultural baggage to help them control and fashion their own destinies" (Early 1983:482), racial minorities used alternative family patterns to survive and create a history and a future in America.

MINORITY FAMILIES AND THE THEORY OF INTRINSIC DIFFERENCE

Drawing attention to the structural conditions under which racially defined minority families were incorporated into American society is not meant to imply that differences in background characteristics, including culture, between these families and European immigrants played no role in the historical achievements and status of these groups. Rather, it is to emphasize that differences in the quality of incorporation and opportunity structures available to racial and ethnic minority families are not to be taken lightly in accounting for the relative achievements and progress of these groups in the United States.

Scholars have identified a number of background characteristics and circumstances of ethnic and racial minorities that enabled some groups to advance faster and further than others. Such characteristics as education, experience, skills, and ability are referred to as the "human capital" of individuals and of groups, and research on the background characteristics of immigrants "indicates substantial group differences in the distribution of human capital and human-capital returns" (Model 1988:370). Immigrants who set out from more economically advanced urban societies and with relatively high levels of education and occupational skills were in a more favorable position to take advantage of labor market opportunities in the urban industrial centers of the new world than were immigrants from folk or semifeudal societies with high rates of illiteracy and few skills. Thus, the urban experience, high levels of literacy, and occupational skills of many Northern European immigrants, Jews from Eastern Europe, and East Asians were to serve these groups well in the modern industrial economy of the United States (Model 1988). Such "intrinsic differences," as Lieberson (1980) has called them, "are sufficient to explain why groups will start off occupying different socioeconomic niches" (p. 374) in the economy of their new home, if not why such differences persist over time.

In addition to differences in the distribution of human resources among immigrant groups that influenced their potential for certain employment opportunities following their arrival in the United States were other factors such as timing of arrival and demographic characteristics, including gender ratios, geographical location, and the ethnic-racial composition of local labor markets, which favored some groups over others in their pursuit of economic and social advancement (Lieberson and Waters 1988; Model 1988; Steinberg 1989).

Timing of arrival is important because groups arriving at different periods are presented with different economic and political conditions, as well as distinctive employment opportunities:

> Those Northern Europeans who arrived before the close of the frontier and before the rise of mass production could still put land to the plow or indulge in entrepreneurial craftsmanship. The Irish avoided the countryside, however, and accepted unskilled

urban laboring jobs instead. As manufacturing quickened, most urban immigrants and their children joined the Irish in becoming increasingly proletarianized . . . The urban Germans, for instance, many of whom were artisans, discovered that the markets for their skills declined. Nineteenth century economic fluctuations meant that those groups whose mass migration began earlier were more dispersed among jobs and less likely to display intergenerational persistence in those jobs than did the groups who began to arrive after industrial take-off . . . (Model 1988:372)

Time of arrival also influenced the geographical location and concentration of immigrants in certain regions of the country where employment opportunities related to background, skills, and experience were to be found. For example, the concentration of some immigrant families from Central and Eastern Europe in the industrial centers of the Northeast and Midwest reflected employment opportunities in the steel and automobile industries in those regions during the late nineteenth and early twentieth centuries, as well as the limited skills these groups possessed upon arrival in the United States. Similar processes operated for racially defined minorities as well:

The pronounced early concentration of various Asian groups on the West Coast reflects the ports of entry and the location of economic opportunities for them, just as migrant groups from Mexico, Cuba and French Canada are affected by the proximity of their countries to different parts of the United States. Special conditions operated for blacks, who were concentrated initially in the South. Groups such as Hispanos in New Mexico and elsewhere and the French in Louisiana found themselves suddenly living in territories that were either conquered or purchased as the United States extended its boundaries across the continent. This, too, helped to develop distinctive locational patterns when these areas and peoples were incorporated into the nation. (Lieberson and Waters 1988:52)

As Lieberson and Waters point out, location was no trivial matter but had important consequences for a group's "assimilation, intermarriage, political power, visibility and interaction with other groups" (1988:53), and these in turn had implications for employment patterns, family income, and social mobility.

Employment and family patterns among immigrants were also influenced by intentions either to return to their home countries or to become permanent residents in the United States. Many immigrants who came with the intent to repatriate (for example, East Asians and Southern and Eastern Europeans) were single or married men who sent portions of their earnings to their families left behind in the home country. Excluding Chinese men, who were recruited for labor gangs in the West, unmarried immigrant men were less likely to marry than native white men of native parentage, owing in part to the scarcity of women from their homelands and a desire to improve their economic status before taking on the financial responsibilities of marriage and family (Lieberson and Waters 1988; Heer 1961). Among groups whose members sought permanent residence (such as the Germans, Irish, Scandinavians, and Jews), gender ratios were more balanced because these groups came as families or individuals (Model 1988). Some writers contend that unbalanced gender ratios and delayed family formations among some groups (such as Chinese, Irish, and Eastern Europeans) retarded their economic advancement (Kessler-Harris and Yans-McLaughlin 1978; Nee and Wong 1985), but Heer's (1961) study of mobility patterns among second-generation Americans found that groups that achieved the highest socioeconomic status included greater proportions of single individuals.

In some cities and regions of the country, the occupational upgrading and economic advancement of European immigrants were facilitated by the presence in large numbers of non-European minorities who were often recruited for or confined to jobs at the bottom of the labor queue (Lieberson 1980; Bonacich 1973). As Model (1988) observes, in the local labor markets of the Northeast, European immigrants found it more difficult to escape the less desirable jobs at the bottom of the labor market than did their counterparts in other regions of the country where employment opportunities and the racial/ethnic mix were different. However, the cessation of immigration from Europe during the 1920s, followed by the movement of African Americans to the Northeast in large numbers during that period, altered this situation: "These blacks offered the white laboring classes of the North the same exemptions from undesirable employment that their counterparts in the South and West had enjoyed earlier" (Model 1988:372). Thus, the antagonisms and discrimination experienced by South-Central-Eastern European immigrants in the North were modified and redirected toward the growing number of African Americans, who were regarded as even less desirable as coworkers and neighbors than the new European groups. Lieberson (1980), among others (Olzar 1989; Steinberg 1989), views these developments as significant contributors to the differences in outcomes experienced by the new European immigrants and African Americans.

As the preceding discussion indicates, a variety of structural and historical conditions combined with the background characteristics of new European immigrants to produce ethnic variations in socioeconomic mobility and other outcomes unique to specific groups and their families. Accordingly, no explanation of the economic progress of these groups is complete without reference to the historical context and the favorable economic and social conditions that enabled these groups to utilize selected aspects of their cultural traditions to promote improvements in their economic status. Indeed, as Steinberg (1989) points out, without the congruence between culture and circumstance, it is unlikely that the new European immigrants could have sustained those values and practices often held accountable for their economic advancement. As with their European counterparts, differences among minority families are a consequence of their unique demographic and background characteristics, cultural histories, economic origins, and statuses (Wilkinson 1987). All of these factors have influenced the institutional properties of minority families as well as their relative progress in the United States.

ORGANIZATION AND FOCUS

In this volume, the family characteristics of the following racially distinct minority populations are examined: African Americans (including West Indians), Chicanos or Mexican Americans, Puerto Ricans, Cubans, Chinese, Japanese, Koreans, Asian

Indians, Vietnamese, and Native Americans. These groups were selected to represent the diversity of minority families, from those whose histories predate those of many of the European ethnic groups to those of more recent origin, and to highlight the impact of historical and contemporary processes on the development of distinctive family lifestyles among these diverse groups. African Americans numbered 33.9 million in 1996 and an estimated 35.4 million in 2000, or 12.8 percent of the nation's resident population (U.S. Bureau of the Census 2000b). Although usually perceived as a single group, they are a melange of subgroups, cultures, and nationalities, as demonstrated by the inclusion of Haitians, Jamaicans, Trinidadians, and other West Indian, African, and Latin American peoples, and by a large Native American, Hispanic, and European blend within these groups (Farley and Allen 1987; Harrison and others 1984). The experience of African Americans is unique among ethnic minorities in the United States in that they entered the country involuntarily and were subjected to more than two hundred years of slavery. Their history of servitude, followed by a prolonged period of legal discrimination, enforced segregation, and exclusion, has profoundly affected the institutional properties, integrity, and functioning of African American families and continues to influence their collective fate in the United States. As this nation's largest minority, African American families are examined first in Part I of this volume. The family relationships and household organization of Haitian Americans, one of the more recent Caribbean immigrant groups to the United States, are also examined in that section by way of illustrating the diversity in family patterns and functioning to be found among African Americans.

Americans of Hispanic or Spanish origins are among the fastest growing ethnic minority populations in the United States, totaling 28.4 million in 1996 (10.8 percent of the U.S. population) and 32.8 million in 2000 (11.9 percent of the U.S. population). The Hispanic population is projected to be the largest minority in the United States by the year 2010 (U.S. Bureau of the Census, 2000b). Like African Americans, Hispanics are a highly diverse ethnic category, including Mexican Americans or Chicanos (the largest), followed by Puerto Ricans, Cubans, and other persons from Central and South America. Given the range of physical types among Hispanic Americans, their racial classification has varied widely over time. In the 1930s, for example, Mexican Americans were relegated to a residual racial category ("other nonwhites") in the census; by 1940, they were classified as an ethnic group ("persons of Spanish mother tongue"). In 1980, Mexican Americans, Puerto Ricans, Cubans, and other Hispanics were regarded as "a kind of superethnic group, listed along with other national descent groups and also in a category by itself" (Moore 1981:276). Although it is currently acknowledged that people of Hispanic origin can be of any race, they are officially classified as "white" by the census.

Hispanic Americans have entered society under a variety of conditions. In the twentieth century, the majority of Mexican Americans have migrated to the United States voluntarily, but it was largely through military conquest and the annexation of their homelands in what is now the American Southwest that Chicanos were involuntarily incorporated into the United States, in a fashion similar to classic European colonialism. Thus, Mexican Americans are not technically immigrants in that the majority inhabit areas of the country that were once part of their native land. The experience of Puerto Ricans is similarly characterized by forced and voluntary entry into U.S. society. As a result of the Spanish-American War, Puerto Rico came under U.S. rule in 1898, and in 1917, the inhabitants of the island were granted American citizenship, which enabled them to immigrate freely to the mainland without restriction. The greatest influx of Cubans to the United States has occurred since 1960 and has been a voluntary immigration inspired by political and economic developments at home. Those who came during the 1960s and 1970s were overwhelmingly middle- and upper-class professionals and businesspeople alienated by the Castro regime. Those arriving in the late 1980s were mostly working- and lower-class persons, with thousands of criminals among them. Despite unique cultural histories and experiences, Hispanic Americans are linked by a shared language and historical experience derived from Spanish and American colonialism that have influenced the institutional character of the family. Because they are the largest elements of the Hispanic American population in the United States, Mexican American, Puerto Rican, and Cuban American families are examined in Part II.

In 2000, the designation "Asian" included approximately 30 Asian and 25 Pacific Islander subgroups (Goldsea 2000). Between 1980 and 1990, the Asian American population increased by 107 percent and accounted for 3 percent of the total U.S. population. By 1999, there were 10.9 million Asian Americans in the United States, accounting for 4.0 percent of the population (U.S. Bureau of the Census 2000a), and they are estimated to increase to 15.3 million in 2010, accounting for 5.1 percent of the population (U.S. Bureau of the Census 2000b). Chinese, Japanese, Korean, Filipino, and Vietnamese are among the largest subpopulations, representing nearly 80 percent of Asian American groups in the United States. Asians entered the United States under diverse auspices: as contract laborers for construction and agricultural work, beginning in the 1840s (for example, Chinese, Japanese, and Koreans), as foreign nationals (for example, Filipinos), and more recently as political refugees (for example, Vietnamese, Laotians, and Cambodians).

Although Chinese and Japanese American minorities have been a significant presence in the United States for more than a century, immigration and resettlement of refugees from Asia and Southeast Asia constituted the majority of population growth for Asians in the United States through the early 1980s (86 percent). As a result, a majority of the Asian American population is foreign-born. However, the rates of foreign-born Japanese, Chinese, and Vietnamese are consistently dropping, so that a larger proportion of the Asian American population has become U.S.-born over the past two decades (Goldsea 2000). As the first and largest of the Asian groups to enter the United States, the Chinese and Japanese inspired considerable antagonism and discrimination, culminating in various laws restricting their entry during the nineteenth and early twentieth centuries. Restrictive legislation and a severely unbalanced gender ratio effectively contained the growth and size of these groups for decades and influenced the structure and nature of family life. The sharpest increase in the Asian population has occurred since 1965, with the liberalization of the immigration law in that year, which brought to the United States immigrants from a wider variety of Asian societies. On the whole, these immigrants have tended to be better educated and more highly skilled than those of earlier periods, enabling many of them to accelerate their economic and social adaptation to American society. As the first and latest of the Asian minority populations to enter the United States, Chinese, Japanese, Korean, Asian Indian, and Vietnamese American families are examined in Part III of this volume.

The history of Native Americans predates the histories of all other ethnic and minority populations in the United States, extending back at least to 35,000 B.C. (Wax 1971). When Columbus landed on the shores of North America, an estimated 5 to 10 million Native Americans were organized into hundreds of nations or tribes, speaking many different languages and adhering to disparate cultural and social systems. Over time, and as a result of a national policy of genocide and containment, epidemic diseases, and chronic poverty, the Native American population declined to less than 250,000 by the beginning of the twentieth century and has since begun a slow but accelerating increase in size. Today, Native Americans are one of the smallest but fastest-growing groups in the United States, with a population of 1.42 million in 1980, 2.1 million in 1990, and 2.36 million in 1998. They currently constitute 0.9 percent of the U.S. population but are projected to increase to 1.1 percent of the population by the year 2050 (U.S. Bureau of the Census 2000b). However, generations of exploitation and neglect have had a deleterious effect on the cultures, lifestyles, and well-being of Native Americans. Expelled from their native lands and resettled on prisonlike reservations where they were prohibited from practicing native religions and other displays of Indian culture, Native Americans have experienced great difficulty in sustaining and preserving their ethnic identities. Although attempts to force acculturation to Anglo-European practices through a variety of intrusive measures (for example, schools and forced relocation to urban areas) have succeeded in reducing the range and diversity of Native American cultural practices, important differences in their lifestyles and family practices persist. Because the degree of diversity within Native American populations is exceptional and the range of marriage and family practices very broad, the review of such families in Part IV of this volume is necessarily selective and restricted to a relatively few cultural types.

The final section of the text, Part V, is devoted to a more general examination of minority families and social change, highlighting the main points and conclusions about such families presented in the preceding chapters and the manner in which these families are coping with social and economic changes currently under way in American society.

REFERENCES

Baca Zinn, Maxine, and D. Stanley Eitzen. 1993. *Diversity in Families.* New York: Harper and Row.

Banton, Michael. 1974. "1960: A Turning Point in the Study of Race Relations." *Daedalus* 103(2):31–44.

Blauner, Robert. 1972. *Racial Oppression in America.* New York: Harper and Row.

Bonacich, Edna. 1973. "A Theory of Middleman Minorities." *American Sociological Review* 38:583–594.

Early, Frances. 1983. "The French-Canadian Family Economy and Standard-of-Living in Lowell, Massachusetts, 1870." In *The American Family in Social Historical Perspective,* edited by Michael Gordon, 482–503. New York: St. Martin's Press.

Farley, R., and Walter Allen. 1987. *The Color Line and the Quality of Life: The Problem of the Twentieth Century.* New York: Russell Sage Foundation.

Glazer, Nathan. 1983. *Ethnic Dilemmas 1964–1982.* Cambridge, MA: Harvard University Press.

Glazer, Nathan, and Daniel P. Moynihan (eds.). 1970. *Beyond the Melting Pot.* Cambridge, MA: MIT Press.

————1975. *Ethnicity: Theory and Experience.* Cambridge, MA: Harvard University Press.

Glenn, Evelyn, N. 1987. "Racial-Ethnic Women's Labor: The Intersection of Race, Gender and Class Oppression." In *Hidden Aspects of Women's Work,* edited by C. Bose, R. Feldberg, and N. Sokoloff, 46–73. New York: Praeger.

Goldsea: Asian American Demographics. 2000. *Asian Immigration Declines.* (Internet: gold-sea.com/AAD/immigration.html).

Gordon, Milton. 1964. *Assimilation in American Life.* New York: Oxford University Press.

————. 1975. "Toward a General Theory of Racial and Ethnic Group Relations." In *Ethnicity: Theory and Experience,* edited by N. Glazer and D. P. Moynihan, 84–110. Cambridge, MA: Harvard University Press.

Harrison, A., F. Serafica, and H. P. McAdoo. 1984. "Ethnic Families of Color." In *Review of Child Development Research,* edited by R. D. Parke, 329–367. Chicago: University of Chicago Press.

Heckman, F. 1983. "Toward the Development of a Typology of Minorities." In *Minorities: Community and Identity,* edited by C. Fried, 9–24. New York: Springer-Verlag.

Heer, David. 1961. "The Marital Status of Second-Generation Americans." *American Sociological Review* 26:233–241.

Jiobu, Robert. 1988. *Ethnicity and Assimilation.* Albany, NY: SUNY Press.

Kessler-Harris, A., and V. Yans-McLaughlin. 1978. "European Immigrant Groups." In *Essays and Data on American Ethnic Groups,* edited by T. Sowell, 107–137. Washington, DC: Urban Institute.

Lieberson, Stanley. 1980. *A Piece of the Pie: Black and White Immigrants since 1880.* Berkeley, CA: University of California Press.

Lieberson, Stanley, and Mary Waters. 1988. *From Many Strands: Ethnic and Racial Groups in Contemporary America.* New York: Russell Sage Foundation.

Maldonado, Lionel, and Joan Moore (eds.). 1985. *Urban Ethnicity in the United States: New Immigrants and Old Minorities.* Newbury Park, CA: Sage.

Model, Suzanne. 1988. "The Economic Progress of European and East-Asian Americans." In *Annual Review of Sociology,* Vol. 14, edited by W. R. Scott and J. Blake, 363–380. Palo Alto, CA: Annual Reviews.

Moore, Joan. 1973. "Colonialism: The Case of the Mexican-Americans." In *Introduction to Chicano Studies,* edited by L. I. Duran and R. Bernard. New York: Macmillan.

————. 1981. "Minorities in the American Class System." *Daedalus* 110:275–299.

Nee, Victor, and Herbert Wong. 1985. "Asian-American Socioeconomic Achievement: The Strength of the Family Bond." *Sociological Perspectives* 28:281–306.

Newman, William. 1973. *American Pluralism: A Study of Minority Groups and Social Theory.* New York: Harper and Row.

Olzar, Susan. 1989. "Labor Unrest, Immigration, and Ethnic Conflict in Urban America, 1880–1914." *American Journal of Sociology* 94(6):1303–1333.

Omni, Michael, and Howard Winant. 1986. *Racial Formation in the U.S.: From the 1960s to the 1980s.* New York: Routledge and Kegan.

Park, Robert. 1950. *Race and Culture.* Glencoe, IL: Free Press.

Petersen, William. 1971. *Japanese Americans: Oppression and Success.* New York: Random House.

————. 1980. "Concepts of Ethnicity." In *Harvard Encyclopedia of American Ethnic Groups,* edited by S. Thernstrom, 234–242. Cambridge, MA: Harvard University Press.

Schermerhorn, R. A. 1970. *Comparative Ethnic Relations.* New York: Random House.

Simpson, George, and J. M. Yinger. 1985. *Racial and Cultural Minorities.* New York: Plenum.

Sowell, Thomas. 1981. *Ethnic America: A History.* New York: Basic Books.

Steinberg, Stephen. 1989. *The Ethnic Myth: Race, Ethnicity, and Class in America,* Boston: Beacon Press.

Takaki, Ronald. 1987. *From Different Shores: Perspectives on Race and Ethnicity in America.* New York: Oxford University Press.

Taylor, Ronald L. 1979. "Black Ethnicity and the Persistence of Ethnogenesis." *American Journal of Sociology* 84:1401–1423.

Thernstrom, Stephen. 1982. "Ethnic Groups in American History." In *Ethnic Relations in America,* edited by L. Liebman, 3–26. Englewood Cliffs, NJ: Prentice-Hall.

U.S. Bureau of the Census. 1996. *Statistical Abstract of the United States: 1996.* Washington, DC: U.S. Government Printing Office.

————. 2000a. May 1999 *Current Population Survey.* Washington, DC: U.S. Government Printing Office.

————. 2000b. *Statistical Abstract of the United States: 1999.* Washington, DC: U.S. Government Printing Office.

van den Berghe, P. 1970. *Race and Ethnicity.* New York: Basic Books.

————. 1978. *Race and Racism: A Comparative Perspective.* New York: Wiley.

Wagley, Charles, and Marvin Harris. 1956. *Minorities in the New World.* New York: Columbia University Press.

Wax, Murray. 1971. *Indian Americans: Unity and Diversity.* Englewood Cliffs, NJ: Prentice-Hall.

Wilkinson, Doris Y. 1987. "Ethnicity." In *Handbook of Marriage and the Family,* edited by M. Sussman and S. Steinmetz, 183–210. New York: Plenum.

Yinger, Milton. 1976. "Ethnicity in Complex Societies." In *The Uses of Controversy in Sociology,* edited by O. Larson and L. Coser, 197–216. New York: Free Press.

PART I

African American Families in the United States

With a population of 33.9 million in 1996 and 35.4 million in 2000, African Americans are the largest and most visible minority group in the United States (U.S. Bureau of the Census 2000). Although less diverse in composition than other racial ethnic groups considered in this volume, the African American population is characterized by a variety of subgroups, cultures, and nationalities, as indicated by the sizable numbers of Haitian, Jamaican, Trinidadian, and other West Indian, African, and Latin American peoples among its ranks. In fact, as the 1990 census revealed, nearly 20 percent of the increase in the African American population between 1980 and 1990 was due to immigration from the West Indies, Latin America, and African countries, representing an estimated 1.3 million people, or 4 percent of the total African American population. Between 1980 and 1997, immigration accounted for 16 percent of the growth in the black population in the United States (U.S. Bureau of the Census 1998). Regional location, urbanization, and socioeconomic status are other sources of diversity within the African American community. As noted in the Introduction, a history of servitude, followed by a prolonged period of legal discrimination, enforced segregation, and exclusion, has profoundly affected the institutional properties, integrity, and functioning of African American families; and recent structural shifts in the economy and associated trends are creating new disparities in the structure and quality of family life between blacks and whites in the United States.

In his chapter on African American families,[1] Ronald L. Taylor discusses how the study of such families has evolved through successive theoretical perspectives—from the pejorative tradition reflected in E. Franklin Frazier's classic study of black family life and its transformation under various historical conditions to the "cultural variant" perspective of the contemporary period in which black families are perceived as different but legitimate functional forms, together with findings from recent historical research that underscore the relevance of the historical experiences of African Americans, to an understanding of contemporary patterns of black family life. In addition, selected trends in marriage and divorce, family structure, the living arrangements of children and youth, and interracial marriage, among others, are examined, and the implications of these trends for the future of African Americans are assessed.

Robert E. Millette examines how West Indian families have sought to cope with the cultural conflicts between the "companion" type family form in the United States, with its emphasis on affection and consensus, and the more paternalistic family forms that prevail in the Caribbean to which the West Indian families have been accustomed. Following a discussion of the structure of households and families in the Caribbean and the value orientations embraced by many West Indian immigrants to the United States, Millette identifies three patterns of socialization that characterize efforts of these immigrants to become acculturated to the African American community and the wider society. He terms these modes of adaptation as "maintainers," "social strivers," and "social isolates." Each is characterized by the degree of acceptance or rejection of American norms and values as they relate to the form and functioning of West Indian families. Millette concludes that West Indian families that are isolated from the West Indian community and have relinquished traditional familial behaviors and roles (i.e., the "social isolates"), experience less family conflict than other West Indian families.

In his discussion of Haitian immigrant families in New York City, Michel S. Laguerre utilizes the microeconomic theory of the business firm to delineate many of the features of household organization and linkages between kin-related households both in the United States and in Haiti. Noting the key role of the family household in facilitating the immigration of family members from the half-island republic to the United States, he argues that the Haitian household functions much like a multiproduct corporation, operating on the basis of short- and long-tern planning, revenue, and profit maximization, competition, investment in both human and physical capital, and sometimes aggressive takeovers and mergers. Moreover, like any ordinary firm, the family household may develop subsidiaries at home and abroad in order to expand its basis of operation, exploit a foreign market, and ensure its survival. This is the rationale for Laguerre's study of the Haitian immigrant family household in New York City as a subsidiary household of the headquarters household in Haiti.

Although Laguerre does not say so, his headquarters-subsidiary approach to the study of family household organization among Haitian immigrants may have general utility for the study of the family dynamics of other West Indian immigrants as well.

ENDNOTE

1. Throughout this volume, the terms *African American* and *black* are used interchangeably.

REFERENCES

U.S. Bureau of the Census 1998. The official Statistics: Population Profile of the United States, Special Reports. Washington, DC: U.S. Government Printing Office.
————. 2000. Current Population Survey, March 2000. Washington DC: U.S. Government Printing Office.

CHAPTER 1

Black American Families

Ronald L. Taylor

> The contempt we have been taught to entertain for the blacks makes us fancy many things that are founded neither in reason nor experience.
>
> Alexander Hamilton

Misconceptions about the nature and quality of family life among black Americans are pervasive and deeply entrenched in American popular thought. Although black families have received far less systematic study than white families, they are the subject of even more sweeping generalizations. Even though greater conceptual, methodological, and analytical sophistication is more evident in studies of black American families undertaken during the past several decades, pejorative characterizations of these families still predominate in the social science literature (Farley and Allen 1987; Taylor and others 1990).

The study of black families, like the study of American families in general, has evolved through successive theoretical formulations. Using white family structure and processes as the norm, the earliest studies of black families characterized them as impoverished versions of white families in which the experiences of slavery, economic deprivation, and racial discrimination had induced pathogenic and dysfunctional features (Billingsley 1968; Young 1970). The classic statement of this perspective is found in the work of E. Franklin Frazier, whose study, *The Negro Family in the United States* (1939), was the first comprehensive analysis of black family life and its transformation under various historical conditions—slavery, emancipation, and urbanization (Edwards 1968).

Frazier argued that slavery destroyed African familial structures and cultures and gave rise to a host of dysfunctional family features that continued to undermine the stability and well-being of black families well into the twentieth century. Foremost among these features was the emergence of the black "matriarchal," or maternal, family system. According to Frazier, the matriarchal unit was a product of slavery and the conditions of rural Southern life, which weakened the economic position of black men and their authority in the family. Moreover, this family form was inherently unstable and productive of pathological outcomes within the family unit, including high rates of poverty, illegitimacy, crime, delinquency, and other problems associated with the socialization of black children. Noting the two traditions of black family life that developed as adaptations to slavery, emancipation, and migration to Northern urban areas, Frazier concluded that the female-headed family had become a common tradition among large segments of lower-class black migrants to the North during the early twentieth century. The two-parent male-headed household represented a second tradition among a small minority of blacks who enjoyed some measure of freedom during slavery, had independent artisan skills, and owned property.

Frazier saw an inextricable connection between economic resources and black family structure and concluded that as the economic position of blacks, particularly black men, improved, their conformity to normative family patterns would increase. However, his important insight regarding the link between family structure and economic resources was obscured by the inordinate emphasis that he placed on the instability and "self-perpetuating pathologies" of lower-class black families, an emphasis that powerfully contributed to the pejorative tradition of scholarship in this area (Valentine 1968).

During the 1960s, Frazier's characterization of black family life gained wide currency with the publication of Daniel Moynihan's *The Negro Family: The Case for National Action* (1965), in which weaknesses in black family structure were identified as a major source of social problems in black communities. The "Moynihan Report," as it came to be called, attributed high rates of welfare dependency, out-of-wedlock births, educational failure, drug addiction, and other problems to the "unnatural" dominance of women in the family:

> At the heart of the deterioration of the fabric of Negro society is the deterioration of the Negro family. It is the fundamental source of weakness of the Negro community at the present time. The white family has achieved a high degree of stability and is maintaining that stability. By contrast, the family structure of lower-class Negroes is highly unstable, and in many urban centers is approaching complete breakdown. (Moynihan 1965:5)

Relying heavily on the historical work of Frazier and Stanley Elkins (1963), Moynihan traced the alleged "tangle of pathology" that characterized contemporary urban black families to the experience of slavery and three hundred years of racial oppression, which, he concluded, had caused "deep-seated structural distortions" in the family and community life of black Americans.

Although the "Moynihan Report" was largely a restatement of what had become conventional academic wisdom on black families during the 1960s, his generalized indictment of all black families ignited a firestorm of criticism and debate, and it inspired a wealth of new research and writings on the nature and quality of black family life in America (Rainwater and Yancey 1967; Staples and Mirande 1980). In fact, the 1970s saw the beginning of the most prolific period for research on black families, with more than fifty books and some five hundred articles published during that decade alone, representing a fivefold increase over the literature produced in all of the years since the publication of W. E. B. DuBois's pioneering study of black family life in 1909 (Farley and Allen 1987; Staples and Mirande 1980). Although some of this work was polemical and defensively apologetic, much of it sought to replace ideology with research and to provide alternative perspectives for interpreting observed differences in characteristics of black and white families (Allen 1978; Heiss 1975; Hill 1972).

Billingsley (1968) and other critics (for example, Scanzoni 1971; Staples 1971) of the pathology approach to family life called attention to the tendency in the literature to ignore majority family patterns among black Americans and the emphasis on findings derived from studies of low-income and typically problem-ridden families. These studies are generalized and accepted as descriptive of the family life of all black families, with the result that popular but erroneous images of such families are nourished and perpetuated. In his examination of the research literature of the 1960s, Billingsley (1968) concluded that when the vast majority of black families were considered, evidence refuted the characterization of black family life as unstable, welfare dependent, and matriarchal. Indeed, despite a history of racial oppression and material deprivation, black families, he noted, exhibited a remarkable resilience and "adaptive capacity" to survive relatively intact under a variety of adverse environmental conditions. In his view and in the view of a growing number of scholars in the late 1960s and early 1970s, observed differences between black and white families were largely the result of differences in socioeconomic position and of differential access to economic resources (Hill 1972; Scanzoni 1971; Williams and Stockton 1973).

Thus the 1970s witnessed not only an expansion of the quality and quantity of research on black families but also a shift away from a social pathology perspective to one emphasizing the resilience and adaptiveness of black families under a variety of social and economic conditions. The new emphasis reflected what Allen (1978) has referred to as the "cultural variant" perspective, which treats black families as different but legitimate functional forms. From this perspective, "black and white family differences [are] taken as given, without the presumption of one family form as normative and the other as deviant" (Farley and Allen 1987:162). In accounting for racial differences in family patterns, some scholars emphasize poverty and other socioeconomic factors as key to explaining such differences (Billingsley 1968; Jewell 1988; Scanzoni 1971); other writers stress elements of the West African cultural heritage, together with distinctive experiences, values, and behavioral modes of adaptation developed in this country, as major determinants (Nobles 1978; Young 1970). Still others (Sudarkasa 1988) point to evidence supporting both interpretations and argue for a more comprehensive approach.

Although scholars continue to debate the origin and extent of racial differences in family life, the "cultural variant" model and other revisionist perspectives that emerged in recent decades provide a much-needed corrective to the ethnocentric and historically pejorative tradition of scholarship in this area by highlighting the limitations of conventional perspectives, calling attention to the diversity, strengths, and assets of black families, and illuminating many of the cultural features distinctive to black family organization (Staples and Mirande 1980; Taylor 1991). Although empirical evidence in support of revisionist interpretations of black family life is still limited, findings from recent historical research have shed new light on the relationship of changing historical circumstances to characteristics of black family organization—from the experience of slavery and postemancipation through the transition to northern urban communities—and underscore the relevance of historical experiences to contemporary patterns of family life.

BLACK FAMILY LIFE IN HISTORICAL PERSPECTIVE

The thesis, long dominant in the historical and social science literature, that slavery decimated black culture and created the foundation for unstable, female-dominated households whose legacy is evident in contemporary family life has been rendered obsolete by the recent pioneering historical research of Blassingame (1972), Furstenberg and others (1975), and Gutman (1975; 1976), among others. These works document how black families created and sustained a rich cultural and family life despite the harsh and abusive nature of slavery. In his examination of more than two centuries of slave letters, autobiographies, plantation records, and other materials, Blassingame (1972) meticulously documented the nature of community, family organization, and culture among American slaves. He concluded that slavery was not "an all-powerful, monolithic institution which strip[ped] the slave of any meaningful and distinctive culture, family life, religion or manhood." (p. vii). To the contrary, the relative freedom from white control that slaves enjoyed in their quarters enabled them to create and sustain a rather complex social organization that incorporated "norms of conduct, defined roles and behavioral patterns" and provided for the traditional functions of group solidarity, defense, mutual assistance, and family organization, including child-rearing practices. Although the family had no legal standing in slavery and was frequently broken, Blassingame notes its major role as a source of survival for slaves and a mechanism of social control for slaveholders, many of whom encouraged "monogamous mating arrangements" as insurance against runaways and rebellion. In fashioning familial and community organization, slaves drew upon the many remnants of their African heritage, merging those elements with American forms to create a distinctive culture, features of which persist in the contemporary social organization of black family life and community.

In a similar vein, Genovese's analysis of plantation records and slave testimony (1974/1981) led him to conclude that despite severe constraints on the ability to enact and sustain normative family roles and functions, "slaves created impressive norms of family, including as much of a nuclear family norm as conditions permitted and . . . entered the postwar social system with a remarkably stable base" (1974:452). He attributes this stability to the extraordinary resourcefulness and commitment of slaves to marriage relations and to a "paternalistic compromise" or bargain between masters and slaves that recognized certain reciprocal obligations and rights, including recognition of slaves' marital and family ties. According to Genovese, only the most dehumanized slaveholders failed to recognize such ties: "Masters not only saw the bonds between husbands and wives, parents and children, they saw the bonds between nieces and nephews and aunts and uncles and especially between brothers and sisters" (1974:455). He argues that although slavery often undermined the role of black men as husbands and fathers, their function as role models for their children and providers for their families was considerably greater than was generally supposed. Many took an active role in child-rearing and socialization and supplemented the meager family diets provided by slaveholders by fishing and trapping animals. Even so, the tenuous position of male slaves as husbands and fathers and the more visible and nontraditional roles assumed by female slaves gave rise to legends of matriarchy and the emasculated man, but Genovese argues that the relationship between slave men and women came closer to approximating gender equality than was possible for white families.

By far the single most important recent historical work that has forced major revisions in previous scholarship on black family life during slavery is Herbert Gutman's landmark book, *The Black Family in Slavery and Freedom* (1976). Inspired by the controversy surrounding the "Moynihan Report" and its thesis that black family disorganization was a legacy of slavery, Gutman made ingenious use of quantifiable data derived from plantation birth registers and marriage applications to re-create family and kinship structures among blacks, both during slavery and after emancipation. In addition, he marshaled compelling evidence to explain how blacks developed an autonomous and complex culture that enabled them to cope with the harshness of enslavement, the massive relocation from relatively small economic units in the upper South to vast plantations in the lower South between 1790 and 1860, the experience of legal freedom in the rural and urban South, and the transition to Northern urban communities prior to 1930.

Gutman reasoned that if enslavement produced the widespread development of fatherless matrifocal families among blacks sufficiently strong to be passed on from a generation born to slavery to a generation of black Americans residing in contemporary urban ghettos, as was claimed by conventional wisdom, then such a condition should have been more common among urban blacks closer in time to slavery—that is, among blacks in 1850 and 1860—than among urban blacks in 1950 and 1960. Through careful examination of census data, marriage licenses, and personal documents for the period after 1860, he found that stable, two-parent households predominated during slavery and after emancipation and that families headed by black women at the turn of the century were hardly more prevalent than among comparable white families. Gutman thus concluded:

> At all moments in time between 1860 and 1925—that is, from an adult generation born in slavery to an adult generation about to be devastated by the Great Depression of the 1930s . . . the typical Afro-American family was lower class in status and headed by two parents. That was so in the urban and rural South in 1880 and 1900 and in New York City in 1905 and 1925. The two-parent household was not limited to better advantaged Afro-Americans . . . It was just as common among farm laborers, sharecroppers, tenants, and Northern and Southern urban unskilled laborers and service workers. It accompanied the Southern blacks in the great migration to the North that has so reshaped the United States in the twentieth century. (p. 456)

For Gutman, the key to understanding the durability of black families during and after slavery lies in the distinctive African American culture that evolved from the cumulative slave experience and provided a defense against some of the more destructive and dehumanizing aspects of that system. Among the more enduring and important aspects of that culture has been the enlarged kinship network and certain domestic arrangements that, during slavery, formed the core of evolving black communities and the collective sense of interdependence.

Other research provides additional support for the conclusion that the two-parent household was the norm among slaves and their descendants. In their study of the family composition of blacks, native-born whites, and immigrants to Phila-delphia for the period 1850 to 1880, Furstenberg and others (1975) discovered from their analysis of census data that most black families, like those of other ethnic groups, were headed by two parents (75 percent of blacks versus 73 percent for native whites). Moreover, they found that ex-slaves were less likely than their Northern-born counterparts to reside in households headed by couples, leading these researchers to conclude that a combination of economic and urban factors, together with the extremely high mortality rate among black men, accounted for the observed increases in female-headed households in that city over time. Pleck (1973) Reports similar results from her study of black family structure in late–nineteenth-century Boston, noting that the couple-headed household "prevailed among all occupational levels and among families of both urban and rural origins" (p. 153) during that period. In short, as these and other studies show, although female-headed households were common among blacks during and following slav-ery, such households were by no means typical. In fact, as late as the 1960s, three-fourths of black households were headed by couples (Degler 1980; Jaynes and Williams 1989; Moynihan 1965). This was generally the case in the rural South as well as in Northern urban areas.

The finding that black nuclear families and kin-related households remained in-tact and survived the experience of slavery, Reconstruction, the Great Depression, and the transition to Northern urban communities points to the importance of considering more contemporary developments and factors in explaining the signif-icant changes in black family life that have occurred since the 1960s.

CONTEMPORARY BLACK FAMILY PATTERNS

The past four decades have seen significant changes in the structure and stability of American families. These changes include declining rates of marriage and higher rates of divorce, a reduction in fertility rates, an increase in female-headed households, higher proportions of births to unmarried mothers, a higher percent-age of children living in single-parent households, and a larger percentage of chil-dren living in poverty (Farley and Allen 1987; Jaynes and Williams 1989). Although these demographic trends have been similar for both blacks and whites, their im-pact on black families has been more substantial, resulting in greater differentia-tion from white families and increasingly dissimilar marital and family experiences for these groups (Staples 1988; Wilson 1987).

SELECTED PATTERNS AND TRENDS

Since 1960, the number of black households has increased at nearly twice the rate of white families—93 percent versus 55 percent. In 1998, black households numbered 12.5 millions, compared with 86 million white households. Of these households, 59.5 million white and 8.4 million black were classified as family households by the U.S. Bureau of the Census (2000b), which defines a *household* as the person or persons occupying a housing unit, whereas a *family* is defined as consisting of two or more persons who live in the same household and are related by birth, marriage, or adoption. Thus family households are households maintained by individuals who share their residence with one or more relatives, whereas nonfamily households are maintained by individuals with no relatives in the housing unit. In 1998, 67.4 percent of blacks and 69 percent of whites lived in families. In 1990, 71 percent of blacks and 70 percent of whites lived in families. (U.S. Bureau of the Census 2000b). However, nonfamily households have been increasing at a faster rate than family households among blacks because of delayed marriages among young adults, which postpone the formation of married-couple households; higher rates of marital disruption (that is, divorce and separation), resulting in the creation of two separate households; and sharp increases in the number of unmarried couples cohabiting outside of marriage (Glick 1988).

Family households vary by type and composition. The U.S. Bureau of the Census categorizes families into three types: married-couple or husband-wife families, single female–headed families, and single male–headed families. Family composition refers to whether the household is *nuclear,* that is, contains parents and children only, or *extended,* that is, nuclear plus other relatives.

To take account of the diversity in types and composition of black family structure, Billingsley (1968) added to these conventional categories *augmented* (that is, nuclear plus nonrelated persons) families, and modified the definition of nuclear family to include *incipient* (that is, a married couple without children), *simple* (a couple with children), and *attenuated* (a single parent with children) families. However, these conceptual and analytical distinctions ignore an important characteristic of black families—their "extendedness" (Farley and Allen 1987). Blacks are significantly more likely than whites to live in extended households that "transcend and link several different households, each containing a separate (or seemingly so) family" (Farley and Allen 1987:168). In 1991, for example, 22 percent of black households were extended, in contrast to 10 percent of white households. The greater proportion of extended households among blacks has been linked to the extended family tradition of West African cultures (Nobles 1978; Sudarkasa 1988) and to the economic marginality of many black families, which has encouraged sharing and exchanging resources, services, and emotional support among family units spread across a number of households (Cherlin 1981; Stack 1974).

Like most families in the United States, the majority of black families are maintained by a married couple or by a single parent with children. In 1992, 80 percent of black families and 90 percent of all families regardless of race were of one or the other of these types (Glick 1997). Of the remainder of black families not of these types, the majority consist of grandparents and their grandchildren or of sisters and brothers and other relatives.

Although married-couple families are the most common type of family structure among black Americans, the proportion of such families has continued to decline since the 1940s. Between 1940 and 1971, the proportion of black husband-wife families declined by 10 percent (from 77 to 67 percent). By 1998, the proportion of such families fell precipitously to 47 percent (U.S. Bureau of the Census 2000b). Although the proportion of husband-wife families also declined among whites, the decrease was less dramatic (from 88 percent in 1971 to 81 percent in 1998). During the same period, the percentage of black families headed by women also increased dramatically, from 19 percent in 1940 to 46 percent in 1991. This proportion has remained fairly consistent throughout the 1990s—black female-headed households constituted 46 percent in 1995 and 47 percent in 1998 (U.S. Bureau of the Census 2000b). This shift in the distribution of black families by type is associated with a number of complex, interrelated social and economic developments, including sharp increases in separation and divorce rates, male joblessness, and fertility rates among young unmarried women (Jaynes and Williams 1989; Wilson and Neckerman 1986).

Marriage and Divorce

A significant trend with respect to marriage during the past two decades has been the tendency among young black adults to postpone marriage to a later date than that of persons of other races. This trend reversed the traditional pattern of blacks' marrying at younger ages than whites and has contributed importantly to changes in the distribution of black families by type. In 1960, 56 percent of black men and 36 percent of black women aged 20 to 24 were never married; in 1980, the corresponding figures had increased to 79 percent for men and 69 percent for women in this age cohort. By 1989, 85 percent of all 20 to 24-year-old black men and 78 percent of all black women in this age group had never been married. By 1998, the numbers had increased even more—91.9 percent of black men and 85 percent of black women aged 20 to 24 had never been married. The pattern and percentages are slightly different for whites. In 1989, 76 percent of white men and 60 percent of white women aged 20 to 24 had never been married. By 1998, the percentages of never-married whites had risen to 82 percent of men and 67 percent of women (U.S. Bureau of the Census 1998b).

The substantial increase in the proportion of never-married young black adults is explained in part by such factors as continuing high rates of unemployment, especially among young men, college attendance, military service, and an extended period of cohabitation prior to legally consummating marriage (Blackwell 1991; Glick 1988). An unbalanced gender ratio is also seen as an important contributing factor to declining marriage rates among blacks. In their examination of gender ratios, Guttentag and Secord (1983) concluded that the ratio of men to women was unusually low among blacks. In fact, few populations in the United States had gender ratios as low as those of black Americans. Whereas the ratio of white men to women has remained relatively close to 100 in the prime marriage categories of 20 to 49, the ratio for black men to women has been lower. During the 1980s, the 20 to 24 age group had 97 men for every 100 women; this ratio fell to 96 by ages 30 to 34, and to 94 by ages 45 to 49. Because black women outnumbered black men in each of the age categories 20 to 49, the resulting "marriage squeeze" put black women at a significant disadvantage in the marriage market, causing an unusually large proportion of them to remain unmarried (Farley and Allen 1987). However, Glick (1997) observed a reversal of the marriage squeeze among blacks in the age categories 18 to 27 during the past decade: in 1995, there were 102 black men for every 100 black women in this age range. He concludes that "[w]hereas the earlier marriage squeeze made it difficult for Black women to marry, the future marriage squeeze will make it harder for Black men" (Glick 1997:126).

Black men and women are not only marrying at later ages (if at all) but are spending fewer years in their first marriages and are slower to remarry. Since 1960, a sharp decline has occurred in the years that black women spend with their first husbands and a corresponding rise in the interval of separation and divorce between the first and second marriage (Espenshade 1985; Farley 1984).

On the basis of data from the National Fertility Surveys of 1965 and 1970, twice as many black couples as white couples (10 percent versus 5 percent) who reached their fifth wedding anniversary ended their marriage before their tenth anniversary (Thornton 1978), and about half of black and a quarter of white marriages were dissolved within the first fifteen years of marriage (McCarthy 1978). Given the shortage of black men in each of the age categories from 20 to 49, it is not surprising that the proportion of divorced women who remarry is lower among black than among white women. Thus, on the basis of marriage, divorce, and remarriage rates for the period 1975 to 1980, black women could expect to spend only 16 years of their 73-year life span with a spouse, whereas white women spend 33 years of their 77-year life span with a husband—a difference of 17 years (Farley 1984; Jaynes and Williams 1989).

Sharp increases in marital disruption (defined as separation or divorce) and low remarriage rates have resulted in a significant decline in the percentage of black adults who are currently married and living in husband-wife families with their spouses (Table 1). In 1988, for example, 68 percent of all black men ever married (aged 15 and over) were living with their wives; by 1998, the percentage had dropped to 36 percent. In 1988, 11 percent of black men ever married were separated from their wives, 15 percent were divorced, and 6 percent were widowed. In 1998, 5 percent of black males were married and living separate from their wives, 9 percent were divorced, and 3 percent were widowed. The pattern for black women is different. About half of ever-married black women (aged 15 and over) were living with their husbands in 1988. Of the remainder, 19 percent were widowed, 15 percent were married with spouse absent, and 16 percent were divorced (U.S. Bureau of the Census 1989a). By 1998, the percentage of black women who were married and living with their spouse had dropped to 29 percent; 12 percent were divorced, and 10 percent were widowed (U.S. Bureau of the Census 1999). These data belie the common but erroneous perception that the majority of black men are divorced or separated from their spouses and absent from the home. The percentage of black women who are widowed also underscores the significant contribution of this factor to the percentage of black families headed by women.

TABLE 1. Marital Status of Ever-Married Black Persons 15 Years and Over by Sex, 1998

MARITAL STATUS	MALE (%)	FEMALE (%)
Never married	46.0	41.5
Married, spouse parent	36.2	28.9
Married, spouse absent	5.2	7.4
Separated	(3.6)	(5.9)
Other	(1.6)	(1.5)
Widowed	3.4	10.0
Divorced	9.2	12.2
TOTAL	100.0	100.0

Source: U.S. Bureau of the Census, Current Population Reports, Series P-20 "Marital Status and Living Arrangements: March 1998." (update)

Interracial Marriage

Not until 1960 were national data on the number of interracial marriages in the United States provided by the Census. In that year, some 29 states maintained legal restrictions against such marriages. In 1967, the Supreme Court struck down as unconstitutional a Virginia law prohibiting marriages between persons of different races and declared such prohibitions in all other states unconstitutional.

Since 1960, black-white interracial married couples have increased sixfold, but the number of such unions remains relatively small. Between 1960 and 1970, black-white marriages increased from 0.44 percent to 0.70 percent of all marriages in the United States (Blackwell 1977). Of the 310,000 interracial married couples reported in 1970, 65,000, or 21 percent, were classified as black-white married couples. By 1980, the number of such marriages had climbed to 167,000, and by 1998, to 330,000 (Joint Center for Political and Economic Studies 1999). Despite the phenomenal rise in interracial unions, black-white marriages in the United States are still an infrequent occurrence. In 1980, interracial married couples represented about 3 percent of all married black couples, and three-fourth of those marriages involved a black husband and a white wife (Glick 1988). By 1990, this pattern declined to 71 percent. Although the number of black women who marry interracially has also grown since 1970, the increase has been less dramatic. Of the 65,000 black-white married couples in 1970, 24,000 (37 percent) involved a black wife and a white husband. By 1990, the number more than doubled to 61,000, or 29 percent of the total number of black-white marriages, and in 1998, the number spiked to 120,000, or 36 percent of such marriages (U.S. Bureau of the Census 1996). As a percentage of all married couples, black-white marriages more than tripled between 1960 and 1998; however, whereas such marriages represented 34 percent of all interracial marriages in 1960, they represented 25 percent of all interracial marriages in 1998 (U.S. Bureau of the Census 1998a).

Research designed to explain the observed difference in the incidence of interracial marriage by gender has failed to establish clear relationships. Neither social class nor educational factors provide consistent results. For example, although highly educated black men are more likely to marry interracially, this tendency is less true for highly educated black women or white men. With regard to the greater frequency of marriage between a black man and a white woman, Blackwell (1991:119–120) suggests that one explanation may be that many black men are "seduced by the highly publicized 'somatic norm image' that accentuates the desirability of Nordic features, especially lightness of skin. Some black men find the white female more attractive and are drawn to the 'once-forbidden' or aganathamous partner." For such men, a white partner may serve to enhance their ego and sense of status. Many white men, however, may avoid marriage with a black partner because of the social disapproval, stigma, or perceived impediment to upward mobility that such unions might bring. On the other hand, Collins (1988) hypothesizes that distinctive patterns of socialization in black communities that encourage women to be independent and less subservient to men may explain the lower rate of intermarriage for black women and the tendency of black men to seek marriage partners outside of their racial group.

Whatever the explanation, interracial marriages appear to be less successful than intragroup marriages. Analyzing 1970 census data for first marriages initiated during the 1950s and still intact in 1970, Heer (1974) found that although 78 percent of black-white couples were still living together, 63 percent of the couples with a black husband–white wife were still intact and 47 percent of the couples with a white husband–black wife had a continuing marriage. Although the proportions were slightly smaller. Glick's (1988) analysis of 1980 census data revealed the same pattern. These and other data (such as Monahan 1970) suggest that, on the whole, interracial marriages are only moderately less successful than intraracial marriages. When the general social disapprobation that interracial couples frequently encounter is considered, such marriages are remarkably resilient.

Fertility and Family Size

The average size of all American families in 1991 was 3.18—3.12 persons for white families and 3.51 for black families (U.S. Bureau of the Census 1992). Although the average size of American families stayed the same from 1991 to 1997, white families went from 3.12 persons in 1991 to 3.02 persons in 1998. Black families also went from 3.51 in 1991 to 3.42 in 1998 (U.S. Bureau of the Census 1998c). Thus, black families are larger than white families and are more likely than other families to have young children among their members. In 1998, 58 percent of black families included children under 18 years of age, compared with 50 percent of all families (U.S. Bureau of the Census 1999). In addition to children, black families are more likely to include other relatives and unrelated individuals than are white families.

The greater proportion of black families with children reflects the higher fertility rates of black women. Historically, the fertility rates of black women have exceeded those of white women. As far back as the period following the Civil War, black families averaged 1.2 children more than white families (Farley and Allen 1987). And as recently as 1939, black women averaged 2.9 births during their lifetime, and white women 2.2 births. Although the childbearing rates of black women have fallen sharply since the 1960s, they remain above the rates for white women. In 1984, the total fertility rate—that is, the number of children a woman would bear in her lifetime if the rates of a given year remained fixed—was 2.2 for black and 1.7 for white women, a difference of 0.5 children. This rate represents a decline from 1960, when rates were 4.5 for black and 3.5 for white women, a difference of one child, and indicates convergence in fertility rates for the two racial groups.

Urbanization, rising levels of educational attainment, increasing acceptance and use of contraception, and abortion are major contributing factors to declining rates of childbearing among black women in recent decades (Farley and Allen 1987; Tucker and Mitchell-Kernan 1995; Wilson and Neckerman 1986). The increasing urbanization of the black population and higher levels of educational attainment have paralleled declines in birth rates among black women. Between 1940 and 1980, for example, the proportion of black women of childbearing age declined from 42 to 14 percent, and the median educational attainment of young black women rose from less than 7 years of schooling to more than 12 years during that period. In their analysis of data from the 1980 census, Farley and Allen (1987) found that both region of birth and region of current residence influenced rates of fertility for black but not for white women. Black women born and living in the South had higher fertility rates than black women born and living in other regions. The presence of a sizable rural population in the South is assumed to explain the higher fertility rates of black women in that region. As with other groups, the relationship between educational attainment and fertility is strong for black Americans. Black women with a college degree or more education have half as many children as black women who failed to complete high school (Reid 1982).

Family planning, whether in the form of contraception or abortion, has also been strongly embraced by the majority of black women. In 1965, 23 percent of black married women were not using some form of birth control; by 1982, this percentage had declined to only 14 percent (Farley and Allen 1987). The percentage of black married women who obtain abortions exceeds the percentage of married white women who do. In 1980, 35 percent of all nonwhite women (most of whom are black) obtained abortions, while only 24 percent of white women terminated their pregnancies with abortions (Farley and Allen 1987). A major change over the past few years has been the distribution of abortions between white and nonwhite populations (all women, married and unmarried). In 1990, only 35 percent of abortions were performed on nonwhite women, but by 1996, that percentage had risen to 41 percent, indicating that more nonwhite women are using abortion as a potential option to having children.

Although the difference in fertility rates between black and white married women aged 25 and over virtually disappeared during the past three decades, childbearing among younger and unmarried black women has steadily increased over this period. For example, between 1940 and 1960, approximately 18 percent of black infants and 2 percent of white infants were born to unmarried women. By the mid-1980s, almost six out of ten black infants and one in eight white infants were born to unmarried women (National Center for Health Statistics 1986). In 1997, 69 percent of all births to black women were to unmarried women—up from

68 percent in 1990. Also in 1997, 22.5 percent of all births to black women were to teenage mothers, down from 23.1 percent in 1990. By contrast, in 1997, 26 percent of all births to white women were to unmarried women, and 11.3 percent were to teenage mothers (U.S. Bureau of the Census 2000b). In short, out-of-wedlock births now comprise a greater proportion of total births to black women than they did in the past and are an important contributor to the rise in the proportion of female-headed families in black communities during the past three decades (Wilson and Neckerman 1986).

Female-Headed Households

The proportion of female-headed households has always been higher for blacks than for whites, but this racial discrepancy has grown larger in recent decades. Since the 1960s, the proportion of adult women who head their own families has risen for both blacks and whites, but the increase has been larger for black women.

The proportion of all female-headed households has increased steadily since the mid-1900s, although much more quickly for minority families than for white families. In 1960, 22 percent of black families were female-headed. By 1991, the percentage had risen to 46 percent, but has remained fairly consistent since then, constituting 46 percent in 1995 and 47 percent in 1998. By contrast, in 1980, 12 percent of white households were headed by women; in 1990, it was 13 percent, and in 1998, it was 14 percent (U.S. bureau of the Census 2000b). For families with children under 18, in 1998, 57 percent of black family groups were headed by women, while 21 percent of white family groups were headed by women. This is not a great rise for black women, who headed 49 percent of families with children in 1980, but it is a big rise for white women, who headed only 15 percent of families with children in 1980 (U.S. Bureau of the Census 2000b). The category "female-headed" includes women of various marital statuses—that is, never married; married, spouse absent, widowed; and divorced. Female heads of families differ significantly by race on these dimensions. In 1998, 48 percent of black female family householders were classified as never married, compared with 22 percent of white female heads. Also in 1998, 23 percent of black female heads were divorced, 16 percent were married with the spouse absent, and 13 percent were widowed. In contrast, in 1998, 42 percent of white female heads were divorced, 15 percent were married with the spouse absent, and 21 percent were widowed (U.S. Bureau of the Census 2000b). Whereas widowhood accounted for nearly a quarter (21 percent) of female-headed households among whites, it accounted for 15 percent of black female–headed households.

Thus, for adult black women aged 25 to 44, increases in both the percentage of never-married women and disrupted marriages (that is, separation and divorce) are important contributors to the rise in female-headed households; for white women of the same age group, marital dissolution or divorce is the single most important factor (Jaynes and Williams 1989). Moreover, changes in the living arrangements of women who give birth out of wedlock or experience marital disruption have also played a significant role in the rise of female-headed households among both blacks and whites. In the past, women who experienced separation, divorce, or a child out of wedlock were more likely to move in with their parents or other relatives, creating subfamilies and thereby avoiding the classification of female-headed. However, in recent decades more and more of these women have established their own households. Between 1960 and 1990, for example, the proportion of divorced or separated black women who headed families rose from 40 percent to 44 percent; among whites the proportion increased from 35 to 59 percent during this period. By 1998, the proportion of black women had fallen to 36 percent but had increased to 63 percent for white women (U.S. Bureau of the Census 1999).

A growing proportion of female-headed households consists of unmarried teenage mothers with small children. Although overall fertility rates among black and white teenage mothers have declined sharply in recent years, out-of-wedlock childbearing among women under 20 years of age has increased. For example, births to black women aged 15 to 17 fell from 73 per 1,000 in 1980 to 62 per 1,000 in 1997; for black women aged 18 to 19, the birth rate fell from 135 per 1,000 to 131 during this period. Among white teenagers aged 15 to 17, the change was from 26 births per 1,000 in 1980 to 27 per 1,000 in 1997; and from 73 per 1,000 to 77 per 1,000 for teens 18 to 19 during this period. On the other hand, the proportion of children born out of wedlock to teenagers rose from 77 per 1,000 black women in 1960 to 107 in 1989; among whites, the comparable change was from 7 per 1,000 in 1960 to 28 in 1989. In 1995, over 60 percent of all births to teens occurred outside of marriage—nearly three times the rate of the early 1960s (U.S. Bureau of the Census 1998a).

A number of factors account for the persistent racial difference in fertility and births outside of marriage by young women. From their analysis of racial differences in nonmarital fertility rates in 1980, Cutright and Smith (1988) concluded that such differences are due to racial differences (1) in sexual activity; (2) in contraception; (3) in abortion (both spontaneous and induced); and (4) between the races in the proportion of premarital pregnancies that are legitimized by marriage before the child's birth. Because a greater proportion of black teenage women are sexually active (National Center for Health Statistics 2001), they are at greater risk of conceiving than white teenage women. In addition, black teenage women engage in sexual activity at an earlier age. For example, in 1995, 2 percent of white teenage females were sexually experienced (i.e., had had sexual intercourse at least once) before the age of 13, compared with 6 percent of black females; by age 17, nearly half of white females (45 percent) and nearly two-thirds of black females (63 percent) had become sexually experienced. Moreover, sexually active black teenage women (and men) are less likely to use contraception at first sexual intercourse than white teenagers (National Center for Health Statistics 2001). For example, in 1988, 32 percent of black and 17 percent of white female teenagers reported that they never used contraceptives. However, by 1995, the percentage of black and white female teenagers aged 15 to 19 who used no contraceptive method was identical at 27 percent (National Center for Health Statistics 2001). Until recently, black teenage women were also less likely than their white counterparts to choose abortion, thereby contributing to the higher out-of-wedlock birthrates for black teenage women. For example, in 1980, there were 85 abortions per 1,000 births to white teenager women, in contrast to 65 abortions per 1,000 births to black teenagers. Finally, white teenage women were significantly more likely to legitimize a child before birth through marriage than were black teenagers (Cutright and Smith 1988). However, by 1996, abortion rates among both black and white teenagers were reversed and had decreased dramatically to 22.6 for white women and 62.9 per 100 for black women (Alan Guttmacher Institute 1999).

As a result of these trends, the number of black women under 35 who were heads of families constituted a larger proportion of single mothers by the mid-1980s than they had in past decades. For example, whereas only 26 percent of black women under age 35 were family heads in 1950, the proportion grew to 43 percent in 1983. However, the proportion dropped to 19 percent by 1998 (U.S. Bureau of the Census 2000a Table 80). The proportion of white female family heads under 35 also increased during the period, from 12 percent in 1950 to 29 percent in 1983, and fell slightly to 28 percent in 1998 (U.S. Bureau of the Census 1979, 1984, 2000a; Wilson and Neckerman 1986).

In sum, growth in the proportion of black female-headed households is largely a function of several recent developments. Higher rates of divorce and marital separation, lower remarriage rates for black women, and increases in the number of unmarried teenage mothers forming their own households have combined to increase the proportion of black female single-parent families. The rise in single-parent families has serious social and economic consequences for the family living arrangements of black children and adults. As shown in the next section, black female-headed families with children under 18 years have increased significantly during the past two decades, and these families constitute a growing proportion of the population living in poverty.

LIVING ARRANGEMENTS OF CHILDREN AND YOUTH

One of the most significant developments of the last two decades has been the rapidly declining proportion of black children under 18 years of age who live in a family in which both parents are present. Although the proportion of all children living with both parents has declined during the past two decades, this trend has affected black children and youth to a much greater extent than their white counterparts. In 1965, 70 percent of black children under 18 years of age lived with both parents. By 1990, the proportion had fallen to 38 percent; and in 1998, it was 36 percent. In both 1990 and 1998, more black children lived with their mothers only (51 percent) than with both parents (38 percent and 36 percent respectively). Within the white population, eight in ten children under 18 lived with both parents in 1990, and 74 percent in 1998. The percentage of white children living with their mothers increased only from 16 percent in 1990 to 18 percent in 1998 (U.S. Bureau of the Census 1998b, 2000b).

The growing number of black families headed by women has had a substantial impact on the well-being of black children and youth because female-headed households experience much higher rates of poverty and deprivation than other families. The number of poor black children under 18 years of age in female-headed households rose from 1.5 million in 1959 to 3.3 million in 1982. By 1987, 60 percent of black children residing with their mother lived in poverty, in contrast to 14 percent of black children living with both parents. By 1998, these percentages had declined to 48 and 49 respectively. Among whites, 39 percent of children in female-headed households lived in poverty in 1987, and only 7 percent residing with both parents lived below the poverty line. In 1998, these percentages had declined to 21 percent and 5 percent, respectively (U.S. Bureau of the Census 2000a). Thus, female-headed families are at a significant disadvantage economically compared with families headed by couples, regardless of race. The median income of black female-headed households in 1994 was $14,650 compared with $40,432 for two-parent black households in which both spouses worked. Among whites, the corresponding figures were $22,605 for female-headed households, versus $45,555 for couple-headed families in which wives worked (U.S. Bureau of the Census 1996). In recognition of the overrepresentation of female-headed households among the nation's poor, irrespective of race, the term *feminization of poverty* has been used to highlight the gender-based inequities and economic condition of a growing proportion of women and children (Bane 1986; Ross and Sawhill 1975).

As a number of studies have shown, black female–headed households with children are not only more likely to be in poverty but are also more likely than other families to be persistently poor (Duncan 1984; Hill 1981). According to research by Bane and Ellwood (1983a, 1983b), the average child who becomes poor when the family changes from male-headed to female-headed experiences poverty lasting nearly twelve years. But the average black child can expect to experience poverty lasting almost two decades. Hence, a considerable number of black youth can expect to face their first years of adult life in poverty (Taylor 1991).

Black and white children differ sharply in their living arrangements and level of economic well-being. Whereas nearly four out of five white children under 18 reside with both parents, the majority of black children live in mother-only households. Moreover, half as many white children as black are likely to spend some time in a mother-only or single-parent household (Bumpass 1984; Jaynes and Williams 1989).

The positive relationship between family structure and family income is key to understanding changes in other measures of well-being among black children during the past two decades because family structure and poverty are shown to have adverse effects on educational attainment (Parelius and Parelius 1978) and employment opportunities (Freeman 1978) and to be positively associated with delinquency and crime (Freeman and Holzer 1985). It is important to bear in mind, however, that the disadvantages for children often associated with one-parent or female-headed households are obliterated in high-income single-parent families, both black and white, indicating that family structure per se is not critical to the economic well-being of family members but rather that economic opportunity is (Aschenbrenner 1978).

How well black children succeed in overcoming the disadvantages associated with single-parent households depends greatly on the nature or features of the kinship network available to them. Networks of kin often play a vital role in sustaining what otherwise might be fragmented families by providing economic and emotional support as well as assisting with child care and other household duties. Research has shown that black single-parent families often consist of a number of kin spread over several households, who share and exchange resources, services, and responsibilities for children born in and out of wedlock (Cherlin 1981; Stack 1974). Mothers of black teenage parents, for example, are shown to take an active role in the parenting of grandchildren (Brooks-Gunn and Furstenberg 1986; Wilson 1989), and as Taylor and others (1990:998) point out, the support that "adolescent mothers receive from their extended family generally and their own mothers in particular has a positive impact on their educational and economic achievement and parenting skills and their children's development." Thus, when the black female-headed household is seen in the context of the larger kinship system, one can appreciate how the network of relatives often serves to "buffer economic adversity and complement aspects of family functioning lacking in mother-only families" (Hatchett 1991:101).

FAMILY STRUCTURE AND FAMILY DYNAMICS

Although black families are typically stereotyped as matriarchal, the more common pattern of authority in these families is equalitarian, characterized by complementarity and flexibility in family roles (Billingsley 1968; Blackwell 1991; McAdoo 1978; Scanzoni 1977). In fact, egalitarian modes of family functioning are common even among low-income black families, in which one would expect, on the basis of the normative pattern of white families, the more traditional patriarchal authority structure.

Past assessments of black family structure have cited such modes of family functioning as evidence of pathology or structural weakness because they were contrary to the gender-role division of labor in majority families. Such was the view of Moynihan in his analysis of black family patterns in the 1960s. He wrote,

> There is, presumably, no special reason why a society in which males are dominant in family relationships is to be preferred to a matriarchal arrangement. However, it is clearly a disadvantage for a minority group to be operating on one principle, while the great majority of the population, and the one with the most advantages to begin with, is operating on another. Ours is a society which presumes male leadership in private and public affairs. The arrangements of society facilitate such leadership and reward it. A subculture, such as that of the Negro American, in which this is not the pattern, is placed at a distinct disadvantage. (1965:29)

With the rise of the women's movement, coupled with changing gender-role preferences and behavior among women and men in the general population, egalitarian modes of family functioning among blacks are now being considered in a different and more positive light (Hatchett 1991; Scott-Jones and Nelson-LeGall 1986). For example, in assessing the implications for white families of the broadening of work and marriage experiences of women, Scanzoni (1977:339) concludes that "the long-term trend for whites is likely to be convergence with the gender-role egalitarianism of blacks."

Egalitarianism in black family functioning is a legacy of slavery, in which the traditional gender division of labor was largely ignored by slaveholders, and black men and women were "equal in the sense that neither sex wielded economic power over the other" (Jones 1985:14). As the historian Blassingame has noted, the experience of slavery "led to the creation of America's first democratic family in the (slave) quarters, where men and women shared authority and responsibility" (1972:178). As a result of historical experience and economic conditions, traditional gender distinctions in the homemaker and provider roles have been less rigid in black families than in white (Beckett and Smith 1981). Because black women have historically been involved in the paid labor force in much larger proportions than white women and because the difference in earnings between men and women has been less significant for blacks than for whites, Scott-Jones and Nelson-LeGall (1986) argue that "blacks have not experienced as strong an economic basis for the subordination of women, either in marital roles or in the preparation of girls for schooling, jobs, and careers" (p. 95).

Findings from the National Survey of Black Americans (Jackson 1991) provide further empirical documentation for the view that black men and women are relatively egalitarian in their attitudes about gender roles and power in the family. In her analysis of these data, based on a national household sample of 2,107 black Americans, Hatchett (1991) found strong support for an equalitarian division of family responsibilities and tasks among respondents in the survey:

> More than 88% of women and men agreed . . . that men and women should share in child care and household tasks and more than 98% agreed that blacks should spend more time raising their children. Three out of every four black Americans also feel that both men and women should have jobs to support the family. In addition to these egalitarian views of familial roles, the majority of our respondents did not feel that having a job took away from a woman's relationship with her husband or children. (p. 90)

For men, support for an egalitarian division of labor within the family did not differ by education or socioeconomic level, but education was related to attitudes toward the sharing of family responsibilities and roles among women. That is, college-educated women were more likely than women with less education to support flexibility and interchangeability of family roles and tasks. With the exception of attitudes toward motherhood, for which a large majority of both genders subscribed to a more traditional or conservative view (that is, that motherhood is the most fulfilling role for women), Hatchett found strong support for liberal gender-role norms among black Americans.

Egalitarian attitudes toward familial roles among black Americans are reflected in their child-rearing attitudes and practices (Taylor 1991). In her analysis of gender-role socialization in black families, Lewis (1975) found few patterned differences in parental attitudes toward male and female roles. Age and relative birth order were found to be more important determinants of differential treatment and behavioral expectations for children than was gender. Lewis's observations are consistent with findings from a number of other studies (Ladner 1971; Rainwater

1974; Young 1970). Schutz (1977) found no evidence of rigid gender-role socialization during infancy and early childhood among the low-income families he studied in St. Louis, and he observed that gender-role socialization for men occurred largely outside the home and under the tutelage of peers. The relative absence of emphasis on differential gender socialization during early childhood has been attributed to elements of African American culture that tend to synthesize rather than dichotomize traditional behavioral traits by gender (Boykin and Toms 1985; Lewis 1975).

Through their early socialization practices, black parents seek to inculcate in both boys and girls similar traits of assertiveness, independence, and self-confidence (Lewis 1975). However, as children grow older, socialization practices are adapted to reflect "more closely the structure of expectations and opportunities provided for black men and women by the dominant society" (Lewis 1975:237)—that is, geared to the structural conditions that constrain familial role options for black men and women in society. However, as Franklin (1984) points out, such shifts in emphasis and expectations can often inculcate in black men and women components of gender-role definitions that are noncomplementary or incompatible, creating a potential source of conflict in their marital relationships. For many black men, the male gender-role becomes extremely complex and problematic:

> Its complexity arises from Black males being socialized to adopt an androgynous sex-role and simultaneously being expected to perform according to the white masculine sex-role paradigm in certain instances. An additional factor which makes the . . . male sex-role difficult for Black males to fulfill in a functional manner (as far as the larger society is concerned) is that Black males are only permitted to exhibit certain "masculine" traits of their androgynous sex-role within the Black subculture. (Franklin 1984:60)

According to Franklin, black women experience a similar dilemma. In the course of their socialization, two different and contradictory messages are often received:

> One message states, "Because you will be a Black woman, it is imperative that you learn to take care of yourself because it is hard to find a Black man who will take care of you." A second message frequently received by young Black females that conflicts with the first message is "your ultimate achievement will occur when you have snared a Black man who will take care of you." (Franklin 1986:109)

Such contradictory expectations and mixed messages, Franklin contends, often lead to incompatible role enactments by black men and women and frequent conflict in their relationships.

Despite greater acceptance of role flexibility and power-sharing in black families, conflict around these issues figures prominently in black marital instability. In their study of marital instability in the first marriages of both black and white couples, Hatchett and others (cited in Hatchett 1991) found young black couples at odds over current gender roles in the family: For black husbands, concern over their ability to function in the provider role was found to be an important source of instability in their marriages. Moreover, black marriages were more likely to be unstable.

> . . . if black men felt their wives had equal power in the family, and if black wives felt there was not enough role sharing in regard to family tasks and responsibilities . . . Most black women appear to feel that keeping the arrangement as it is (i.e., egalitarian) is not only desirable but a necessity. A large number of black men, in the other hand, feel that assuming the long-denied traditional gender roles of whites is part of the general struggle to achieve racial equality. (Hatchett 1991:103)

Changes under way in the attitudes and definitions of familial roles among young black couples are undoubtedly tied to social and economic trends in the larger society, where such forces are altering the structure and internal dynamics of many American families.

BLACK FAMILIES AND SOCIAL CHANGE

The past four decades have brought profound changes in the family lives of black Americans, including unprecedented increases in female-headed households, marital disruptions, out-of-wedlock births, and the percentage of children living in poverty. As a result, black families have become less "conventional" (as defined by the societal norms of monogamous, nuclear households) and more diverse in their composition and structure than white families (Jaynes and Williams 1989; Jewell 1988; Taylor 2000). Although a variety of factors have been invoked to explain the growing differences by race in family organization and processes, the most salient explanations include changes in the economic status of black men and women, the scarcity of men as marriage partners, growth in family assistance benefits, and changing attitudes and values in marriage.

Male joblessness has been identified as a major underlying factor in changing patterns of marriage and family life among black Americans. Wilson and his colleagues at the University of Chicago (1986; 1987) have established relationships between black male unemployment and (1) high divorce rates, (2) low remarriage rates, and (3) the high proportion of children being born to unmarried women. Although black men have historically participated in the labor force at higher levels than white men, their employment rates have been declining since the 1940s and fell sharply among men aged 24 and younger during the 1960s. By 1985, 46 percent of black men between the ages of 16 and 62 were not in the labor force. However, by 1999, the percentage had fallen to 32 percent (Joint Center for Political and Economic Studies 1999). Such high rates of unemployment are shown to be related to marital instability—that is, divorce and separation—and the incidence of female-headed households (Ross and Sawhill 1975; Sawhill and others 1975). Moreover, as Wilson and Neckerman (1986) and Wilson (1996) have shown, sharp declines in employment among black men and women aged 16 to 24 in recent years have paralleled changes in marriage rates in this age category and suggest that the inability of black men to support a family has made marriage less attractive to young men and women.

In addition to the role of male joblessness in changing patterns of marriage and family life among blacks, some researchers have emphasized the growing economic independence of women as an important contributing factor. Thus, Farley and Bianchi (1991) argue:

> As economic opportunities for women expand, more of them assume breadwinner roles, and they are increasingly able to maintain an adequate life-style apart from a husband. In some circumstances, they may have the resources to bear and raise children without engaging in the traditional exchange of domestic service for economic security. The financial independence of women decreases the "economic utility" of being married and may lead young women to delay their nuptials while also encouraging women to end marriages they find unsatisfactory. (pp. 10–11)

Citing increases in educational attainment and labor force participation, as well as significant improvements in the occupational distribution of employed women, Farley and Bianchi observe that over the past two decades, the earnings of black women rose faster than the earnings of black men and that black women are "catching up" with black men more rapidly than white women are "catching up" with white men. Hence, they hypothesize that the increased economic independence of black women, as measured by their earnings or income, together with the high rates of joblessness among black men, may have reduced the incentive of many unmarried women to marry and discouraged formerly married women from remarrying. Although the evidence is indirect, trends in the earnings of black men and women are generally consistent with the growing racial difference in marriage patterns.

Changes in black family structure are also hypothesized to result from a shortage of black men as suitable marriage partners. For example, Wilson and Neckerman (1986) contend that unbalanced gender ratios resulting from disproportional black male mortality and incarceration rates, in concert with high levels of male joblessness, have created a limited pool of "marriageable" men for black women. Research by Farley and Bianchi (1991) and other findings (Jaynes and Williams 1989) are consistent with this hypothesis. Marital availability ratios (Goldman and others 1984), which take into account such factors as the income, educational attainment, and incarceration rates among men vis-à-vis women in various age ranges, have been calculated for blacks using data based on marriage patterns in 1980. The results indicate

> . . . that unmarried women above age 22 are in marriage pools that contain relatively few men. For unmarried women at age 25, for example, there were 931 men per 1,000 women. After age 28, the availability ratios for black women fall sharply, and at these ages, there is a substantial shortage of men; for example, for unmarried black women at age 34, the ratio is 642 men per 1,000 women. (Jaynes and Williams 1989:539)

Comparing these data with the availability ratios for whites, black women are clearly faced with a much tighter marriage market than white women. In 1985, for example, the gender ratio for young unmarried persons was 102 for whites and only 85 for blacks (Farley and Bianchi 1991:13). In general, these and other data (for example, Wilson 1987) support the hypothesis that male availability is an important factor in explaining racial differences in marital and family status.

Some investigators hypothesize that greater access by poor families to federal and state transfer payments, together with increases in benefit levels and the creation of such programs as Medicaid and food stamps during the 1960s and early 1970s, is mainly responsible for the rise in marital dissolution, female-headed households, and other changes in black family structure in recent decades (Gilder 1981; Murray 1984). According to this hypothesis, the availability of welfare benefits has allowed premaritally pregnant women to forgo marriage and to bear and keep their children, has encouraged unhappy married parents to break up, and has enabled young unmarried mothers to form separate households rather than share a household with their parents. Thus, the growth of liberal welfare policies, it is argued, has led to higher rates of out-of-wedlock births, divorce, and female-headed households.

A number of studies have sought to assess the impact of welfare benefits on the structure and stability of families. These studies have yielded inconclusive, largely negative results. In assessing the effects of public assistance on out-of-wedlock births, a number of studies have compared illegitimacy rates or ratios across states with varying welfare benefit levels. Overall, such studies have found no relationship between the level of welfare benefits and births to unmarried women, or more precisely, have not found that the availability of welfare benefits leads women to bear more children (Ellwood and Bane 1984; Ellwood and Sumners 1986). In fact, the percentage of black children living in female-headed households increased sharply during the 1970s, while benefit levels and the number of households receiving such benefits declined (Wilson and Neckerman 1986).

Studies focusing on the relationship between welfare and marital dissolution report mixed results. A few studies have found welfare to have a modest effect on separation and divorce among low-income families, whereas other studies report no effect. Early reports from the income-maintenance experiments conducted in Denver and Seattle claimed that a guaranteed income to families at or near the poverty line resulted in increased rates of marriage breakups (Bishop 1980; Groenveld and others 1980). However, subsequent analyses of data from these and other experimental sites concluded that the income maintenance program had no significant effect on marital stability (Cain and Wissoker 1987–1988). Summarizing the research findings in this area, Jaynes and Williams (1989) conclude that "collectively, the evidence is that family assistance benefits play a small part in divorce decisions" (p. 531).

Whereas research indicates that family assistance has no effect on the incidence of out-of-wedlock births and only a small effect on separation and divorce rates, its effect on the living arrangements of single mothers is found to be substantial. Research by Ellwood and Bane (1984) indicates that the availability of welfare assistance apparently encourages single mothers to form their own households rather than share a residence with their parents. Moreover, the welfare benefits may also discourage unmarried pregnant women from obtaining an abortion and may reduce the likelihood that a mother remarries rapidly following the dissolution of her previous marriage (Hutchens 1979).

Overall, except for its significant effect on the living arrangements of single mothers, family assistance is shown to have little systematic impact on family structure (Duncan and others 1988). Hence, as Ellwood and Bane have concluded, "Welfare simply does not appear to be the underlying cause of the dramatic changes in family structure of the past few decades" (1984:8).

Some observers speculate that changed attitudes toward conjugal living and the institution of marriage among blacks may partly account for observed changes in family structure and living arrangements during the past few decades. Because several studies (Ladner 1971; Melton and Thomas 1976) have found that black men and women tend to value the instrumental characteristics (that is, the ability to provide financial security) of potential mates more than their white counterparts, the worsening economic prospects of black men in recent decades may have had the effect of diminishing the value of marriage as an institution.

Although this hypothesis has yet to be tested, the National Survey of Black Americans (NSBA) provides some documentation of black attitudes toward and values in marriage. The results of the NSBA survey with respect to marriage and conjugal living are reported by Hatchett (1991). When asked to evaluate a number of reasons for living with a person of the opposite sex in terms of their importance to them, 69 percent of the respondents in the survey thought that conjugal living was very important for raising children and for companionship (67 percent). Moreover, 61 percent of the respondents thought that conjugal living was important for a good love life, and 48 percent mentioned financial security as important. However, women were more likely to mention financial security as an important reason for living with a person of the opposite sex, whereas men were more likely to emphasize the socioemotional aspects (for example, companionship and good love life) of marriage. Such attitudes were influenced by education. As their level of education increased, men were less likely to emphasize the socioemotional dimensions of conjugal living, whereas women with a high school education or less and those with four years of college or more emphasized the socioemotional dimension more than black women with some education beyond high school.

With respect to attitudes toward the institution of marriage, results from the NSBA survey reveal that, despite the high incidence of divorce and separation, marriage remains a strong value for a majority of black Americans. In responding to the statement that "there are so few good marriages these days that I don't know if I want to be married," 40 percent agreed with the statement, whereas 50 percent disagreed. Moreover, married and never-married respondents, both men and women, were more likely to reject negative evaluations of marriage than individuals who had been married but were divorced or separated.

Although, according to these data, marriage is still a strong value among large numbers of black Americans, Hatchett concludes that "the reasons for getting married among blacks appear to predispose many to never marrying, or to separation or divorce if they do marry" (1991:102). This tendency is so, she argues, because of the different emphases that black men and women place on instrumental and socioemotional values in marriage. For women, it is financial security; for men, love, companionship, and children:

> Herein lies the contradiction or lack of fit between values and opportunity that have generated . . . adaptations in (black) family formation . . . The size of the pool of "marriage-able men," given black women's criteria, has decreased dramatically in the past 30 years or so . . . The cumulative effects of racial stratification in this country, as well as the current restructuring of the economic sector, have resulted in large numbers of jobless, low paid, and incarcerated black men. Although black women with higher education place less emphasis on marrying for financial security than those with less education, the pool of employed black men with similar education is much less than that for other black women. All in all, the future looks bleak for black women finding marriage partners, if the economic marginality of black men does not decrease. (Hatchett 1991:102–103)

Each of the explanations just examined plays an important role in the observed changes in black family organizational patterns of the past few decades, although the contribution of family assistance benefits to such changes appears to have been grossly overstated in popular accounts, whereas the role of black male joblessness has been largely neglected (Staples 1988; Wilson and Neckerman 1986). In a succinct statement of the relationship between black family instability and male joblessness, Scanzoni (1971:309) observes:

> The inescapable conclusion . . . is that the black family in America, as much as the white family, is shaped by its relationship to the economic opportunity structure. This relationship is mediated primarily via the occupation of the male-head-of-household. Where he is not present, as is often the case in the lower-class, this has certain negative consequences for the family. And where he is present, the degree of his integration with the opportunity system influences most, if not all, aspects of husband-wife and parent-child interactions.

The key to understanding changing black family patterns is the changing relationship of such families to the economic and social institutions of the larger society. In large measure, black-white differences in family organization and process reflect differential access to the economic resources, benefits, and rewards of American society. Thus, if the prospects for black family formation and stability are to improve, the myriad economic and social forces that obstruct the access of many black Americans to the opportunity structure must be eliminated.

REFERENCES

Alan Guttmacher Institute. 1999. *Why Is Teenage Pregnancy Declining? The Roles of Abstinence, Sexual Activity and Contraceptive Use.* New York: Alan Guttmacher Institute.

Allen, Walter. 1978. "The Search for Applicable Theories of Black Family Life." *Journal of Marriage and the Family* 40:117–129.

Aschenbrenner, J. 1978. "Continuities and Variations in Black Family Structure." In *The Extended Family in Black Societies,* edited by D. Shimkin, E. M. Shimkin, and D. Frate, 181–200. The Hague: Mouton.

Bane, Mary Jo. 1986. "Household Composition and Poverty." In *Fighting Poverty: What Works and What Doesn't,* edited by S. Danziger and D. Weinberg, 209–231. Cambridge, MA: Harvard University Press.

Bane, M., and D. Ellwood. 1983a. "The Dynamics of Dependence: The Routes to Self-Sufficiency." Report supported by the U.S. Department of Health and Human Services Grant. John F. Kennedy School of Government, Harvard University. Mimeo.

———. 1983b. *Slipping into and out of Poverty: The Dynamics of Spells.* Working Paper 1199. Cambridge, MA: National Bureau of Economic Research.

Beckett, Joyce, and Audrey Smith. 1981. "Work and Family Roles: Egalitarian Marriage in Black and White Families." *Social Service Review* 55:314–326.

Billingsley, Andrew. 1968. *Black Families in White America.* Englewood Cliffs, NJ: Prentice-Hall.

Bishop, John. 1980. "Jobs, Cash Transfers, and Marital Instability: A Review and Synthesis of the Evidence." *Journal of Human Resources* 15:301–334.

Blackwell, Henry. 1991. *The Black Community: Diversity and Unity.* New York: Harper-Collins.

Blackwell, James. 1977. "Social and Legal Dimensions of Interracial Liaisons." In *The Black Male in America,* edited by Doris Wilkinson and Ronald Taylor, 219–243. Chicago: Nelson-Hall.

Blassingame, J. 1972. *The Slave Community.* New York: Oxford.

Boykin, A. W., and F. D. Toms. 1985. "Black Child Socialization: A Conceptual Framework." In *Black Children,* edited by H. P. McAdoo and J. L. McAdoo 33–54. Beverly Hills, CA: Sage.

Brooks-Gunn, J., and Frank Furstenberg. 1986. "The Children of Adolescent Mothers: Physical, Academic, and Psychological Outcomes." *Developmental Review* 6:224–251.

Bumpass, Larry. 1984. "Children and Marital Disruption: A Replication and Update." *Demography* 21:71–81.

Cain, Glenn, and Douglas Wissoker. 1987–1988. "Do Income Maintenance Programs Break Up Marriages? A Reevaluation of SIME-DIME." *Focus* 10(4):1–15.

Cherlin, A. 1981. *Marriage, Divorce, Remarriage.* Cambridge, MA: Harvard University Press.

Collins, R. 1988. *Sociology of Marriage and the Family.* Chicago: Nelson-Hall.

Cutright, Philips, and Herbert Smith. 1988. "Intermediate Determinants of Racial Differences in 1980 U.S. Normal Fertility Rates." *Family Planning Perspectives* 20(2):119–123.

Degler, Carl. 1980. *At Odds: Women and the Family in America from the Revolution to the Present.* New York: Oxford University Press.

Duncan, Greg. 1984. *Years of Poverty, Years of Plenty.* Ann Arbor: Survey Research Center, Institute for Social Research, University of Michigan.

Duncan, Greg, Martha Hill, and Saul Hoffman. 1988. "Welfare Dependency Within and Across Generations." *Science* 239:467–471.

Edwards, G. Franklin. 1968. *E. Franklin Frazier on Race Relations.* Chicago University of Chicago Press.

Elkins, Stanley. 1963. *Slavery.* Chicago: University of Chicago Press.

Ellwood, D., and M. Bane. 1984. "The Impact of AFDC on Family Structure and Living Arrangements." Report prepared for the U.S. Department of Health and Human Services. John F. Kennedy School of Government, Harvard University. Mimeo.

Ellwood, D., and L. Sumners. 1986. "Poverty in America: Is Welfare the Answer or the Problem?" In *Fighting Poverty: What Works and What Doesn't,* edited by S. Danziger and D. Weinberg, 78–105. Cambridge, MA: Harvard University Press.

Espenshade, Thomas. 1985. "Marriage Trends in America: Estimates, Implications, and Underlying Causes." *Population and Development Review* 11(2):193–245.

Farley, Reynolds. 1984. *Blacks and Whites: Narrowing the Gap.* Cambridge, MA: Harvard University Press.

Farley, Reynolds, and Walter Allen. 1987. *The Color Line and the Quality of Life in America.* New York: Oxford University Press.

Farley, Reynolds, and S. Bianchi. 1991. "The Growing Racial Differences in Marriage and Family Patterns." In *The Black Family,* edited by R. Staples, 5–22. Belmont, CA: Wadsworth.

Franklin, Clyde. 1984. *The Changing Definition of Masculinity.* New York: Plenum.

———. 1986. "Black Male–Black Female Conflict: Individually Caused and Culturally Nurtured." In *The Black Family,* 3rd ed., edited by R. Staples, 106–113. Belmont, CA: Wadsworth.

Frazier, E. Franklin. 1939. *The Negro Family in the United States.* Chicago: University of Chicago Press.

Freeman, Richard. 1978. "Black Economic Progress Since 1964." *The Public Interest* 52:52–68.

Freeman, Richard, and N. Holzer. 1985. "Young Blacks and Jobs—What We Now Know." *The Public Interest* 78:18–31.

Furstenberg, F., T. Hershberg, and J. Modell. 1975. "The Origins of the Female-Headed Black Family: The Impact of the Urban Experience." *Journal of Interdisciplinary History* 6:211–233.

Genovese, Eugene. 1965. *The Political Economy of Slavery.* New York: Vintage Books.

———. 1974/1981. *Roll Jordan Roll: The World Slaves Made.* New York: Pantheon.

Gilder, George. 1981. *Wealth and Poverty.* New York: Basic Books.

Glick, Paul. 1997. "Demographic Pictures of African American Families." In *Black Families,* edited by H. McAdoo, 118–138. Beverly Hills, CA: Sage.

Goldman, N., C. Westoff, and C. Hammerslough. 1984. "Demography of the Marriage Market in the United States." *Population Index* 50(1):5–25.

Groenveld, L., N. Brandon Tuma, and M. Hannan. 1980. "The Effects of Negative Income Tax Programs on Marital Dissolution." *Journal of Human Resources,* 15:654–674.

Gutman, Herbert. 1975. "Persistent Myths about the Afro-American Family." *Journal of Interdisciplinary History* 6:181–210.

———. 1976. *The Black Family in Slavery and Freedom, 1750–1925.* New York: Pantheon.

Guttentag, M., and P. F. Secord. 1983. *Too Many Women.* Beverly Hills, CA: Sage.

Hatchett, Shirley. 1991. "Women and Men." In *Life in Black America,* edited by J. Jackson, 84–104. Newbury Park, CA: Sage.

Heer, David. 1974. "The Prevalence of Black-White Marriage in the United States, 1960 and 1970." *Journal of Marriage and the Family* 36:246–258.

Heiss, Jerold. 1975. *The Case of the Black Family.* New York: Columbia University Press.

Hill, Martha. 1981. "Some Dynamic Aspects of Poverty." In *Five Thousand American Families: Patterns of Economic Progress,* Vol. 9, edited by M. S. Hill, D. Hill, and J. Morgan. Ann Arbor: Institute for Social Research, University of Michigan.

Hill, Robert. 1972. *The Strength of Black Families.* New York: Emerson Hall.

Hutchens, Robert. 1979. "Welfare, Remarriage, and the Marital Search." *American Economic Review* 69(3):369–379.

Jackson, James (ed.). 1991. *Life in Black America.* Newbury, CA: Sage.

Jaynes, Gerald, and Robin Williams (eds.). 1989. *A Common Destiny: Blacks and American Society.* Washington, DC: National Academy Press.

Jewell, K. Sue. 1988. *Survival of the Black Family.* New York: Praeger.

Joint Center for Political and Economic Studies. 1999. *Family and Household Structure: Fact Sheets Living Arrangement of Children/Trends in Poverty/Employment and Unemployment.* Washington, DC. JCPES Website. July.

Jonés, J. 1985. *Labor of Love, Labor of Sorrow: Black Women, Work, and the Family from Slavery to the Present.* New York: Basis Books.

Ladner, Joyce. 1971. *Tomorrow's Tomorrow: The Black Woman.* Garden City, NY: Doubleday.

Lewis, Diane. 1975. "The Black Family: Socialization and Sex Roles." *Phylon* 36:221–237.

McAdoo, H. P. 1978. "Factors Related to Stability in Upwardly Mobile Black Families." *Journal of Marriage and the Family* 40(4):761–776.

McCarthy, James. 1978. "A Comparison of the Probability of the Dissolution of First and Second Marriages. *Demography* 15:345–359.

Melton, W., and D. L. Thomas. 1976. "Instrumental and Expressive Values in Mate Selection of Black and White College Students." *Journal of Marriage and the Family* 38(3):509–517.

Monahan, Thomas. 1970. "Are Interracial Marriages Really Less Stable?" *Social Forces* 48:464–469.

Moynihan, Daniel. 1965. *The Negro Family: The Case for National Action.* Washington, DC: U.S. Government Printing Office.

Murray, Charles. 1984. *Losing Ground: American Social Policy, 1950–1980.* New York: Basic Books.

National Center for Health Statistics, 1986. *Monthly Vital Statistics Report,* Vol. 35, no. 4, supplement. Washington, DC: U.S. Department of Health and Human Services.

———. 2001. *Sexual Activity and Contraceptive Practices Among Teenagers in the United States, 1988 and 1995.* Vital Health Statistics 23 (21). Washington, DC: U.S. Department of Health and Human Services.

Nobles, Wade. 1978. "Toward an Empirical and Theoretical Framework for Defining Black Families." *Journal of Marriage and the Family* 40:679–688.

Parelius, A., and J. Parelius. 1978. *The Sociology of Education.* Englewood Cliffs, NJ: Prentice-Hall.

Pleck, Elizabeth. 1973. "The Two-Parent Household: Black Family Structure in Late Nineteenth-Century Boston." In *The American Family in Social-Historical Perspective,* edited by M. Gordon, 152–178. New York: St. Martin's Press.

Rainwater, Lee. 1974. *Behind Ghetto Walls: Black Family Life in a Federal Slum.* Chicago: Aldine.

Rainwater, Lee, and William Yancey (eds.). 1967. *The Moynihan Report and the Politics of Controversy.* Cambridge, MA: MIT Press.

Reid, John. 1982. *Black America in the 1980s.* Population Bulletin, Vol. 37. Washington, DC: Population Reference Bureau.

Ross, Heather, and Isabel Sawhill. 1975. *Time of Transition: The Growth of Families Headed by Women.* Washington, DC: Urban Institute.

Sawhill, Isabel, G. Peabody, C. Jones, and S. Caldwell. 1975. *Income Transfer and Family Structure.* Washington, DC: Urban Institute.

Scanzoni, John. 1971. *The Black Family in Modern Society.* Boston: Allyn and Bacon.

———. 1977. *The Black Family in Modern Society: Patterns of Stability and Security.* Chicago: University of Chicago Press.

Schutz, David. 1977. *Coming Up Black: Patterns of Ghetto Socialization.* Englewood Cliffs, NJ: Prentice-Hall.

Scott-Jones, D., and Sharon Nelson-LeGall. 1986. "Defining Black Families: Past and Present." In *Redefining Social Problems,* edited by E. Seidman and J. Rappaport, 83–100. New York: Plenum.

Stack, Carol. 1974. *All Our Kin.* New York: Harper.

Staples, Robert. 1971. "Toward a Sociology of the Black Family: A Decade of Theory and Research." *Journal of Marriage and the Family* 33:19–38.

———. 1988. "The Black American Family." In *Ethnic Families in America,* edited by C. Mindel, R. Habenstein, and R. Wright, 303–324. New York: Elsevier.

Staples, Robert, and Alfredo Mirande. 1980. "Racial and Cultural Variations Among American Families: A Decennial Review of the Literature on Minority Families." *Journal of Marriage and the Family* 42(4):157–173.

Sudarkasa, Niara. 1988. "Interpreting the African Heritage in Afro-American Family Organization." In *Black Families,* edited by H. P. McAdoo, 27–43. Newbury Park, CA: Sage.

Taylor, Robert, Linda Chatters, M. Tucker, and E. Lewis. 1990. "Developments in Research on Black Families: A Decade Review." *Journal of Marriage and the Family* 52:993–1014.

Taylor, Ronald L. 1991. "Childrearing in African-American Families." In *Child Welfare: An Africentric Perspective,* edited by J. Everett, S. Chipungu, and B. Leashore, 119–155. Princeton, NJ: Rutgers University Press.

———. 2000. "Diversity Within African American Families." In *Handbook of Family Diversity,* edited by D. H. Demo, K. Allen, and M. Fine, 232–251. New York: Oxford University Press.

Thornton, Arland. 1978. "Marital Instability Differentials and Interactions: Insights from Multivariate Contingency Table Analysis." *Sociology and Social Research* 62(4):572–595.

Tucker, M. Belinda, and Claudia Mitchell-Kernan (eds.). 1995. *The Decline in Marriage Among African Americans.* New York: Russell Sage Foundation.

U.S. Bureau of the Census. 1979. *Household and Family Characteristics: March 1978.* Current Population Reports, Series P-20, No. 340. Washington, DC: U.S. Government Printing Office.

———. 1983. *Census of the Population, 1980.* Washington, DC: U.S. Government Printing Office.

———. 1984. *Household and Family Characteristics: March 1983.* Current Population Reports, Series P-20, No. 388. Washington, DC: U.S. Government Printing Office.

———. 1985. *Characteristics of the Population below the Poverty Level.* Current Population Reports, Series P-60, No. 149. Washington, DC: U.S. Government Printing Office.

———. 1989a. *Marital Status and Living Arrangements: March 1988.* Current Population Reports, Series P-20, No. 433. Washington, DC: U.S. Government Printing Office.

———. 1989b. *Statistical Abstract of the United States: 1989.* Washington, DC: U.S. Government Printing Office.

———. 1990. *Marital Status and Living Arrangements: March 1989.* Current Population Reports, Series P-20, No. 445. Washington, DC: U.S. Government Printing Office.

———. 1992. *Marriage, Divorce, and Remarriage in the 1990's.* Current Population Reports, Series P-23-180. Washington, DC: U.S. Government Printing Office.

———. 1996. *Statistical Abstract of the United States: 1996.* Washington, DC: U.S. Government Printing Office.

———. 1998a. *The Official Statistics: Population Profile of the United States.* Special Reports P 23-194. Washington, DC: U.S. Government Printing Office.

———. 1998b. *Marital Status and Living Arrangements: March 1998.* Current Population Reports. Washington, DC: U.S. Government Printing Office.

———. 1998c. *Household and Family Characteristics: March 1998.* Current Population Reports. Washington, DC: U.S. Government Printing Office.

———. 1999. *Statistical Abstract of the United States: 1999.* Washington, DC: U.S. Government Printing Office.

———. 2000a. *Current Population Surveys: March 2000.* Washington, DC: U.S. Government Printing Office.

———. 2000b. Current Population Survey, March 1999. Washington, DC: U.S. Government Printing Office.

Valentine, Charles. 1968. *Culture and Poverty*. Chicago: University of Chicago Press.

Williams, J. Allen, and Robert Stockton. 1973. "Black Family Structures and Functions: An Empirical Examination of Some Suggestions Made by Billingley." *Journal of Marriage and the Family* 35:39–49.

Wilson, Melvin. 1989. "Child Development in the Context of the Black Extended Family." *American Psychologist* 44:380–385.

Wilson, William J. 1987. *The Truly Disadvantaged*. Chicago: University of Chicago Press.

Wilson, William J., and Kathryn Neckerman. 1986. "Poverty and Family Structure: The Widening Gap between Evidence and Public Policy Issues." In *Fighting Poverty: What Works and What Doesn't*, edited by S. Danziger and D. Weinberg, 232–259. Cambridge, MA: Harvard University Press.

———. 1996. *When Work Disappears: The World of the New Urban Poor*. New York: Alfred A. Knopf.

Young, V. H. 1970. "Family and Childhood in a Southern Negro Community." *American Anthropologist* 72:269–288.

Zelnik, Melvin, and John Kantner. 1980. "Sexual Activity, Contraceptive Use and Pregnancy among Metropolitan-Area Teenagers, 1971–1979. "*Family Planning Perspectives* 12:230–237.

CHAPTER 2

West Indian Families in the United States

Robert E. Millette

INTRODUCTION

In the West Indies the main function of the family is reproduction. As in Africa, marriage in the Caribbean is an alliance between two families or bodies of kin.[1] In America, on the other hand, "modern marriage is called upon to fulfill new functions of friendship and emotional support, partly as a result of mobility and isolation of the couple and partly in response to new cultural expectations stimulated by the changing status of women and other trends."[2] With the emphasis on happiness and self-actualization, American couples seek mates who will be good companions and for whom they feel affection.

The purpose of this chapter is to examine how West Indian families are coping with the culture conflict of the Old and the New World ways of behavior. More specifically, we will examine how the Maintainers, the Social Isolates, and the Social Strivers[3] are "managing" the companionship type of family with its emphasis on affection and consensus.[4]

DATA COLLECTED

The bulk of the data for this article was collected during the summer of 1986. A questionnaire consisting of open- and closed-ended questions was mailed to five hundred West Indians in the New York, New Jersey, Pennsylvania, Washington, D.C., and Delaware areas. The sample was randomly selected from a mailing list of thirteen thousand West Indians. Additionally, library data were gathered from the Research Institute for the Study of Man (New York), Brooklyn Public Library, Lincoln University Library (Special Collections), and Florida International University, and from structured and unstructured interviews with 25 divorced West Indian families.

WEST INDIAN MIGRATION

West Indian immigration to the United States dates back to the mid-nineteenth century. Between 1820 and 1970, Charles reports that about 1 million (roughly 2 percent) of the legal immigrants to the United States came from the English-speaking Caribbean.[5] By 1974, some 16 percent of the 394,861 immigrants in the United States were West Indians. The U.S. Immigration reports (1959–1973) show that in this immigrant group, women outnumber men and that the group is composed largely of professional, clerical, managerial, sales, craftspeople, operatives, and laborers. The percentage of professionals has decreased since 1967. The 1965 U.S. Immigration and Nationality Act has been responsible for a large influx of household workers. Thousands of West Indians have used domestic work as a means of getting permanent residence (a green card). Therefore, West Indian women from the lower and middle and as well as from the upper strata of their societies are found working as domestic servants in metropolitan New York and New Jersey.

Data from the Immigration and Naturalization Service indicate that migrants from the English-speaking Caribbean tend to migrate in family groups less frequently than do most other migrants. Dominguez reports, "Of a total of 384,685 immigrants admitted to the United States between 1967 and 1973, there were 277,444 (59.1 percent) who were classified as housewives, children or other individuals with no reported occupation."[6] An examination of the 1970 census data shows that Caribbean families have been able to improve their economic position in the United States. The median income for these families (excluding Cubans and Puerto Ricans) was $8,296. Palmer notes that although this median income was substantially greater than that of black American families, it was below the $9,327 for all American families.[7]

This apparent economic success has not resulted in social and political acceptance by the larger society. Most West Indians, regardless of economical, educational, or political achievements, are viewed by both black and white Americans as something of an oddity. In order to deal with the inequalities that confront them and to forge a new way of life, the majority of West Indians reject the American stratification system. These individuals have been labeled *Maintainers*[8] and comprise the first group examined in this chapter.

A second group, the *Social Isolates,* feel that their compatriots refuse to acknowledge their success because of their compatriot's knowledge of their past. More specifically, the Social Isolates' claim for social recognition among their community is rejected. Therefore, they seek out American friends, especially those who share similar culture, experiences, and rejection.

The *Social Strivers,* a third group, accept the American stratification system. However, unlike the Maintainers and the Social Isolates, they engage in both American and West Indian activities.

Within the context of these constructs, the impact of migration, social change, and technology on West Indian families in the United States is examined. To facilitate understanding of the foregoing, a brief review of the literature and an examination of the conditions and structure of West Indian families before they migrated to the United States is offered.

HOUSEHOLD AND FAMILY

The research literature on the West Indian family structure is, at best, sketchy. The first comprehensive study was conducted by Herskovits, and the main focus of his work was to examine the persistence of Africanism in the New World. "They were not studies of Caribbean family structure, but of family forms among the descendants of Africans, and the relation of those forms to the general structural features of African societies."[9] Herskovits and Du Bois looked to Africa and the institution of slavery for explanations of an Afro-American social organization.[10]

Frazier, on the other hand, did not view American blacks as displaced Africans. Instead, he regarded them as Americans trying to forge a new way of life in a society that is hostile, discriminatory, and oppressive. He said that deviations from normal American patterns of behavior were due to the hostile climate that blacks are confronted with in the South.[11] Myrdal puts it more strongly when he said that "in practically all its divergencies, American Negro culture is not something independent of general American culture. It is a distorted development, or a pathological condition, of the general American culture."[12] Frazier also documents the fact that American blacks had rebuilt a stable family structure along the lines of paternalism.[13]

A close examination of the Caribbean family structure uncovers the existence of paternalism as well as certain aspects of African residues. Therefore, these two approaches became attractive to both American and Caribbean social scientists. Most of these earlier researchers aligned with either Frazier's or Herskovits's approach. Henriques accepts Frazier's thesis that the economic and social conditions of slavery precluded development of stable nuclear families. He said that the high incidence of conjugal turnover, illegitimacy, and maternal households was due primarily to the economically and socially depressed condition of the West Indian family.[14] In the 1950s, social scientists concentrated their research on explaining the high illegitimacy rates, extraresidential mating, matrifocal arrangements, and casual mating.[15]

The earlier approaches were limited in scope because they failed to explore the relationships between consensual and legal cohabitation. Matthews (1953) said that the nonlegal union came about as a result of slavery and the plantation system. Such relationships, which might appear to be disorganized, are the free choices of the people. The decisions of most West Indian men and women to enter into nonlegal relationships must be examined within the social context in which they are made. Marriage is connected with the attainment of a certain socioeconomic standing, a demonstration of ambition and social adulthood. It is also considered by the majority of West Indians as the ideal.

This chapter is not intended to continue the Frazier and Herskovits debate, since such an approach would obscure examination of the elements and relations that give West Indian families their particular qualities and form.[16] Rather, the intent is to capture the world that West Indians have constructed to cope with slavery, the plantation system, and the social and domestic forms of socialization that existed in the Caribbean. A companion task is examination and analysis of how West Indian families in North America are coping with migration, technology, discrimination, prejudice, and the loss of social status and personhood in the United States.

SOCIAL ARRANGEMENTS

In the Caribbean, the man is the major wage earner and the final authority in all major decisions. As the breadwinner and authority figure, he is expected to provide adequately for his family's physical, social, economical, and psychological needs. Smith concludes that "a man with any pride cannot see his wife and children inadequately housed or fed, nor can he allow others to take advantage of them without taking the offender to court."[17] For a man to feel that he is unable to support his family is intolerable, since familial support is the basis for the respect and authority that is afforded him. Smith was partly correct when he said,

> In the lowest status group the only basis for male authority in the household unit is the husband/father's contribution to the economic foundation of the group, and further that where there is both insecurity in jobs where males are concerned and opportunities for women to engage in money-making activities, including farming, there is likely to develop a situation where men's roles are structurally marginal in the complex of domestic relations.[18]

These economic considerations, although very important, are not the only determinants of male authority. The Caribbean social structure says that the man must be the authority figure in his household and in society. The larger society frowns on women who are assertive. West Indian men, therefore, do everything in their power to maintain their manhood. Because of the social stigma attached to a man's being a "mama's boy," women date and marry men who are strong, dependable, and willing to take on the responsibilities of being the head of the household.[19]

In the Caribbean, headship corresponds with the ownership of the house. The household head is the person whom the community as well as the household members regard as head of the domestic unit. It sometimes happens that the woman who is the dominant member of a household is not formally recognized as the head. "Headship is formal leadership and entails formal responsibility . . ."[20] The head of the household among West Indian folk (a) owns the house and land;

(b) decides who may visit or stay in the household; and (c) has the prominent role of the household group. In a study of Grenville, a small town on the eastern coast of Grenada, Smith found that "few married males are not heads of their own homes . . . and that women with absent spouses tend to assert headship of their own homes."[21]

Moses supports the claim by Smith and others that "economic contributions from women need not result in higher status, especially if existing cultural traditions define their activities as less prestigious than those of men."[22] For most elite, middle-class, lower-class, and elite working-class families, the husband is considered the head of the household and the ultimate authority figure. The man continues to be the head of the household even though he is away from the island for several years.

SEXUAL EXCLUSIVITY

Caribbean men who control their wives' and mistresses' sexual activities are accorded higher status by the society. Men who are unable to have their women to themselves are viewed as weak and are therefore ranked lower. It is socially acceptable, however, for men to have legal wives and several mistresses. Smith reports that there is also a well-marked pattern of extramarital mating on the part of high status males. Along with the middle-class emphasis upon respectable patterns of behavior that differentiate them from the lower classes, there is an old and pervasive pattern of sexual license for men . . . "The Europeans set the pattern of mating outside marriage by their willingness to take black or colored mistresses . . .[23]

Girls and women, on the other hand, are expected to be "pure," whereas boys and men "sow their wild oats."[24] Open instances of infidelity among Caribbean women are quite low. A woman who is unfaithful to her husband or common law husband runs the risk of losing his support and of breaking up her relations with her children.[25]

The society laughs at men who are upwardly mobile and are unable to hold onto their women. Men whose wives or mistresses have extramarital affairs are labeled "soffee." A soffee is a man who is unable to satisfy his woman sexually. And to be labeled sexually weak could mean a loss of social, political, and economical status. Therefore, the insistence of West Indian men on sexual exclusivity of the woman has much more to do with the maintenance of status than with morality.

West Indian men use violence, or the threat of violence, to prevent their wives, keepers, or mistresses from extramarital sexual affairs. They also withhold economic support, use blackmail (the loss of jobs, the loss of upper-class contacts, the loss of promotion), and the threat of removing the children's names from their wills to prevent their wives or keepers from engaging in extramarital affairs.

The social status that is attached to marriage keeps West Indian women in their place. Married women tolerate the double standards so that they can be seen in the eyes of the larger society as "good women." Good women are those who accept the authority of their husbands (legal or extralegal), are responsible parents, take care of their family's domestic needs (cook, clean, sew, wash, iron), and do not "run around with every Tom, Dick, and Harry." The "good woman" label also applies to extralegal relationships. For example, women who are "faithful concubines," "keepers,"[26] "Christian families," or "companionate unions"[27] are also expected to obey their husbands and to take care of the domestic needs of their husbands and children. Women in nonlegal relationships want to be labeled good women, since "good women" are the ones whom most men will eventually marry. Marriage "is indeed valued as the appropriate status for mature and independent couples of middle or senior years . . ." Thus, in the West Indian communities marriage has dual meanings, as a condition of personal status and as the most esteemed form of mating.[28] Furthermore, marriage grants full adult status to the individuals who are marrying, as well as complete emancipation from parental control.[29]

In America, the man is no longer the major wage earner. The societal and religious restrictions that maintain leadership, authority, and sexual exclusivity, and obedience have been redefined in America. This redefinition of the situation means that West Indian families have to adjust to the changes that are occurring in the larger society. Accordingly, the rest of this chapter will discuss the changes that have occurred.

Our research indicates that the West Indian families are experiencing severe marital and interpersonal problems in the following areas:

(a) The double standards as they relate to extramarital affairs, domestic arrangements, financial responsibility, sex, and in-law meddling. However, most family problems are kept secret.
(b) Infidelity, which heads the list of complaints among Caribbean women. Seventy-five percent of the respondents (N = 55) told us that their husband's relationship with his mistress has become public knowledge.
(c) Complaints from several male respondents about their wives' or other women's questioning their manhood. "We have always had a wife and a mistress on the side," one man told us, and "For my wife to now insist that I cannot have an outside woman is a direct attack on my manhood. I am the man and therefore should be free to do as I please."[30]
(d) The fact that the women who complained the most were better educated, upwardly mobile urban dwellers. Women who attended church regularly told us that they are constantly praying for their husbands, who are living in sin. This rationalization of wanting to help their husbands has helped to maintain marital stability and the continuance of the double standard.

THE IMPACT OF MIGRATION

Sociologists such as Burgess and Locke,[31] Edwards,[32] Frazier,[33] and Ogburn and Nimkoff[34] have agreed that industrialization destroys traditional family structure. The city affords comparative freedom from the religious restraints imposed by the churches, freedom from neighborhood organizations, freedom from gossip, and freedom from the mores and folkways of the Caribbean. However, this new freedom creates a sense of normlessness. And since tradition and sentiment no longer

furnish the guide for living, the West Indians were forced to make their own variations of conduct and thereby develop rational attitudes toward their new environment. More specifically, Burgess and Locke[35] and Merton[36] suggest that a group
will form new norms in a normless situation and that these new norms will be for-
mulated around predominant values. Since the predominant value in America is
equality between men and women,[37] we can expect that equality would become an
important factor for Caribbean-American families. Women are now openly seeking
equality in sexual freedom, decision making, ownership of property, and the running of the household. Furthermore, they are demanding that their husbands assist with cooking, cleaning, caring for children, and other household chores.

The effect of migration has had tremendous effects, as can be seen in the distinct socialization patterns of West Indian families. These patterns have been conceptualized as those of Maintainers, Social Isolates, and Social Strivers. The rest of
this chapter will explore how each of these groups are coping or failing to cope
with the changes that are occurring.

THE MAINTAINERS

The Maintainers are West Indians who do not reject the West Indian stratification
system, values, norms, and beliefs:

> There is a strict hierarchical structure among members of this group. Membership
> is based not on personal achievement in America but on a careful evaluation of one's
> past, old friendship ties, family name, skin color, and social class . . . The ex-businessman,
> ex-schoolmaster, ex-minister of government, the ex-lawyer or the ex-chief of police usu-
> ally provide the leadership for this clique. The ideologies that hold the Maintainers to-
> gether are reverence for the past, a total rejection of the American stratification system,
> and the quest to maintain the old society in the new world . . .[38]

The Maintainers also feel that "a man must hold on to his West Indian values. A re-
spondent told us that 'in this country, the man has to be tough. We cannot let
those damn women dominate us. You give them an inch and they want a mile.
What would my friends in Grenada say if they hear that my wife is dominating me?
I will not allow any woman to tell me how to run my house.'"[39] This strict reverence
for the past is causing serious marital problems.

Change in this group, for both men and women, is very slow. Because of the
clique system that has emerged, the Maintainers are able to retain the majority of
their culture. Unlike Shibutani and Kwan[40] and Park,[41] we did not find that industrial cities are the "graveyards to traditions." However, there is some loosening of
social, religious, cultural, and communal values. As a result of the reduced influence of the community, the anonymity that the larger society provides, and the
quest for equality, both men and women are experimenting with marital structures
and forms that were immoral, degrading, and downright ridiculous in the West Indies. For example, extramarital sex and extramarital dating have increased among
this group. The fear of punishment of social and communal threats as an instru-

ment of controlling extramarital sex no longer work. The majority of the women interviewed told us that wife-beating would not be tolerated in the United States. Mrs. W. S. said that she is not afraid of her husband. "He tried to beat me once. I immediately got on the telephone and called the cops. Since this incident, he realized that I was not joking. Few women will tolerate wife beatings. New York, thank God, has taught us."

The definition of what constitutes a "good husband" has also changed. The respondents told us that they want their husbands to possess the following qualities:

(a) Ability to take care of their family
(b) Ability to be affectionate
(c) Ability to head a family that provides companionship, happiness, freedom, and self-actualization

Kamarovsky observes that "modern marriage is called upon to fulfill new functions of friendship and emotional support, partly as a result of mobility and isolation of the couple and partly in response to new cultural expectations stimulated by the changing status of women and other trends."[42]

Sex and sexual activities are seldom discussed by the Maintainers. For example, 68 percent of the women told us that their husbands reprimanded them when they tried to discuss sex. Any attempts on the part of these women to enjoy the sexual act were forbidden. The church in medieval England, as well as in the Caribbean, taught that sexual desires were evil and that passionate love was to be condemned. "Even between husband and wife such impulses were regarded as sinful . . . hence the use of contraceptives was obviously evil, because they could have no other purpose than to facilitate the enjoyment of sex without helping to perpetuate the species . . ."[43]

With the emphasis on equality, self-actualization, and freedom, the majority of these women told us that they no longer view sex as only a reproductive act. Such concepts as "satisfaction," "fun," "enjoyment," "pleasure," and "sensation" were used by these women to describe what they expect to get from the sexual act. "This expectation put a new binder on husbands and created new complexities when the woman did not find the satisfaction to which she now felt entitled in the bonds of a proper monogamous marriage."[44] About 25 percent of women in Maintainer families have engaged or are engaging in extramarital relationships. These relationships have not, in many instances, led to a large rate of divorce or separation, since most of the husbands are unaware of their wives' outside activities. However, in instances in which the outside relationships became known to husbands, they separated from or divorced their wives.

The double standard concerning sexual exclusivity continues among the Maintainers. The men are determined to maintain the same levels of authority and control that they had in the Caribbean. They told us that they will not "give up their manhood." Many claim that they would divorce their spouse rather than be humiliated by her. Men continue to demand that their wives be "loyal, obedient, and accept their responsibilities as housewives, mothers, entertainers, and nurses." More specifically, they expect their wives to see them as the boss—the sole authority figure. Of the men that we interviewed, 95 percent said that they were engaged in at least 1 outside sexual relationship; 10 percent were involved in as many as 10 to 15. Blackwell's observation that urbanization permitted experimentation with social relationships between the sexes is salient here.[45] In spite of their extramarital relationships, the women interviewed continue to see themselves as "good women." Their husbands, on the other hand, are refusing, in the face of changing values, norms, and roles, to change or alter their definition of the situation. When asked to rate their relationship, 35 percent of the women and 30 percent of the men said that they were very satisfied; 45 percent of the women and 37 percent of the men said that they were satisfied. The women who said that they were dissatisfied told us that they are "giving their husband time to change . . . time to realize that he cannot run the family as he did in the Caribbean." Only 5 percent of the men that we interviewed (the Maintainers) said that they have considered divorcing their wives. Divorce and, to a lesser extent, separation are partly controlled by the West Indian community. Family considerations in America, as well as in the Caribbean, the fear of family rejection, and the influence of earlier religious, cultural, and social socialization are responsible for the low divorce rate among West Indian families, especially among the Maintainers. For example, the techniques for socialization of boys in the Maintainer family continue to saddle many of them with irrational and damaging anxieties about their ability to implement the male role. These boys are finding out that many of the things that they observe and learn from their fathers are not acceptable in the larger American society.

THE SOCIAL ISOLATES

The Social Isolates are successful educationally and professionally. However, their successes are not always recognized and regarded by other West Indians. This lack of recognition causes them to withdraw mentally and sometimes physically from the West Indian community. The Social Isolates socialize with individuals who see them as successful individuals and who are not overly interested in their past. Their new friends are usually black Americans from the Deep South—Alabama, Mississippi, North and South Carolina, Virginia, and Louisiana.[46]

Social isolation is used by the Social Isolates to cover up for their inability to compete with the Strivers, who are recognized by the majority of their compatriots as West Indian leaders. The refusal of the West Indian community to accept and recognize the Social Isolates for their achievements in America is due to the rigid stratification system that exists in the Caribbean. Family name, geographical location, skin color, and kinship ties continue to be important indicators for assigning social status.[47] The Social Isolates are constantly reminded of their past lower-class status through jokes, direct confrontation, and others' refusal to accept them as equals. Unlike the Maintainers, the Social Isolates try to forget their past. As a result, they are better socially adjusted to deal with the problems of the larger society.

Of the three family types, the Social Isolates are best able to deal with the marital changes with which they have been confronted. Unlike the Maintainers, the men are more involved in the day-to-day running of the family and in the division of labor.

The Social Isolates are experiencing fewer marital conflicts in the areas of sexual exclusivity, authority, and child-rearing. In great contrast to the Maintainers, only 5 percent of the Social Isolate families were very dissatisfied with their relationships. Both men and women in this family type said that their lives were centered around having a good family. An interviewee told us, "My countrymen have refused to accept me, America has discriminated against me, my family envies my profession and economic successes . . . my wife, however, respects and admires me and my children give me all the encouragement and support that I need to succeed as a contractor . . . it's only fair that I return the support and love that I receive from them."[48] Such sentiment is widespread among the Social Isolates. Their families become the one thing that gives them, both men and women, a sense of self-worth. Family relationships, therefore, are carefully guarded and cherished.

This group registered the lowest percentage of extramarital sex. Respect, admiration, fear of jeopardizing the relationship, and concern for what the community would say were given as reasons why these individuals do not engage in outside relationships. Headship and authority were areas in which the Social Isolates experienced less conflict than the Maintainers and Strivers. In this family, the man is considered the head of the household. However, we found that decision making is a shared process. This supports the findings by McAdoo that black American fathers are moving toward an egalitarian relationship in the decision making and power relationship in the home.[49]

THE STRIVERS

The Strivers accept the American stratification system. Unlike the Maintainers, they engage in both American and West Indian activities.[50] And like the Social Isolates, they were members of the Caribbean middle, lower, and upper classes. In America, they are the college-educated, the laborers, the plumbers, the professionals, and the community leaders. The distinguishing characteristic of the Strivers is their quest for success and leadership.

In the Caribbean, the Strivers were usually teachers, bankers, civil servants, policemen, politicians, small farmers, and small businessmen. Even though they were successful in their respective countries, they were generally locked into dead-end positions. The Strivers' dreams of attending college or university, getting a management position, or becoming an investor are realized in America. The Strivers view America as their opportunity for achieving higher status and social honor. Needless to say, they fully accept the American dream and certain aspects of the American culture.

The Strivers are progressive and liberal in areas such as education, politics, employment, and economics, but quite conservative in their views of the family and child-rearing. This refusal to change and to accept the new definitions of the situation, as they relate to Caribbean families, is causing severe marital strains for both husbands and wives. Most male Strivers insist on maintaining the old West Indian family structure in the new society. They, like the Maintainers, are determined that their wives remain submissive, loyal, obedient, and dependent. The Strivers continue to see themselves as the sole wage earners and the authority figures. Any departure from "the traditional marital contract" is viewed as a direct attack on their manhood.

The women in this group are upwardly mobile and are quick to point out that "the old West Indian way of life has no place in America." They insist that the American family structure, which stresses equality for everyone, is superior to the authoritarian structures that were common-place in the Caribbean. After approximately one year in the United States, they seek equality in the following areas: (a) decision making, (b) household chores (e.g., housecleaning, cooking, and taking care of the children), (c) freedom to do what they please, and (d) exclusive sex rights over their men.

This finding indicates that the new societal and marital scripts have changed. Women are now demanding equality, freedom, self-actualization, self-respect, and the ability to do as they please socially, economically, and sexually. They are no longer prepared to accept the familial system that they were accustomed to in the Caribbean. Additionally, these women are looking for relationships that are exciting, fulfilling, and romantic.

Both West Indian men and women have described their American counterparts as sexually excitable, aggressive, loving, romantic, and caring. Both groups told us that they will "venture out" if their spouses are unable to satisfy their sexual desires. The maintenance of the Striver family is no longer governed by the regularity of the man's employment. Several of the women believe that they would be better off by themselves. Whether this belief is true or imagined, these women felt that they are capable of attracting mates that are more compatible and upwardly mobile. Male Strivers have similar feelings and expectations.[51] Scott seems to have captured this situation well when she said that "as work, and husbands, moved out of the home, women were destined to become discontented and eventually to work out a new pattern of usefulness for themselves."

For the Strivers, economic and political successes resulted in serious familial problems. Like the Sicilians in Gabaccia's study referred to in the following quote, the Strivers claimed that New York destroyed the family: "Mobility influenced the ways in which immigrants pursued their social ideals, freed in so many other ways from the restraints imposed by Sicilian agrotowns. Anxieties about privacy and the compensatory myth of male dominance gradually disappeared as immigrants built new social networks in New York."[52]

CONCLUSION

The three family structures discussed in this chapter are all influenced by the norms and values of the American society. The family structure of the Social Isolate is the one least influenced by migration. Both men and women in this group are committed to developing relationships that are beneficial to the entire family. The willingness of Striver women to accept their husbands as the heads of the households and the willingness of the men to treat their wives as equal partners are mainly responsible for the marital stability of this family structure. The refusal of the Maintainers to accept the new definition of the situation is causing severe marital strains. Even though changes are slow in the Maintainer family, women are, nevertheless, questioning the authority of their husbands, insisting that they do not engage in extramarital affairs, and demanding a say in the running of the family.

The Striver family is experiencing the most conflict. Both husbands and wives place great emphasis on self-actualization, success, happiness, and freedom. The traditional marital contract that maintained marital stability in the Caribbean is not applicable in America. Like the Maintainers, the Strivers continue to experiment with extramarital sex. However, the men, in both groups, see their wives' infidelity as a direct attack on their manhood.

West Indian migration to America has resulted in normlessness and a redefinition of the traditional marital contract, at least as it was defined and practiced in the Caribbean. The Strivers, Maintainers, and Social Isolates are presently developing new norms to cope with the changes that they are experiencing. The data presented throughout this paper indicate that West Indian men are more reluctant than West Indian women to accept the new definition of the situation. Their refusal to assimilate and internalize the American value system of equality, freedom, and justice for all is causing and will continue to cause marital problems for the Strivers, Maintainers, and Social Isolates.

The Social Isolates have accepted assimilation and have internalized many of the norms and values of the larger society. They have, like the Cubans, "adjusted well to the United States as a host country—according to indices of social organization, family stability, upward mobility, dependency . . ."[53] We should point out that our conclusions are based on a pilot study. We will study this family type further to determine whether they "repress or displace hostile feelings"[54] in order to present a sense of marital stability. We agree with Simmel, as quoted by Coser, that

> . . . it is necessary for one to probe beneath behavioral manifestations in order to disclose the full extent of social reality . . . the lack of conflict in a relationship cannot be taken to indicate that the relationship is stable and secure or that it is free from potential disruptive strains. We must concern ourselves with latent as well as manifest elements within a relationship if its full meaning is to be disclosed analytically.[55]

ENDNOTES

1. A. R. Radcliffe-Brown, "African Kinship," in A. R. Radcliffe-Brown and D. Forde, eds., *African Systems of Kinship and Marriage* (London: Oxford U. Press, 1950).
2. M. Kamarovsky, *Blue Collar Marriage* (New York: Random House, 1967).
3. R. E. Millette, *New Grenada in Brooklyn, Social Stratification and Adaptation Among First Generation Immigrants* (New York: Associated Faculty Press, 1987/in press).
4. E. W. Burgess and H. J. Locke, *The Family: From Institution to Companionship* (New York: American Books, 1953).
5. H. J. Charles, "Patterns of West Indian Emigration, 1880–1970," mimeographed paper presented at the Atlantic History and Culture Seminar, Johns Hopkins University.

6. V. R. Dominiquez, *From Neighbor to Stranger: The Dilemma of Caribbean People in the United States,* Antilles Research Program, Yale University, 1975, p. 14.
7. R. Palmer, "Migration from the Caribbean to the States: The Economic Status of the Immigrants," in R. S. Bryce-Laporte and D. M. Mortimer, eds., *Caribbean Immigration to the United States* (Washington, DC: Research Institute on Immigration. Smithsonian Institute, 1976).
8. Millette (1987/in press).
9. R. T. Smith, "Culture and Social Structure in the Caribbean: Some Recent Work on Family and Kinship Studies," in M. M. Horowitz, ed., *Peoples and Cultures of the Caribbean* (New York: Natural History Press, 1971).
10. M. J. Herskovits, *The Myth of the Negro Past* (Boston: Beacon, 1958); W. E. B. Du Bois, *The Negro American Family* (New York: New American Library, 1969).
11. E. F. Frazier, *The Negro Family in the United States* (Chicago: University of Chicago Press, 1966).
12. Gunnar Myrdal, *An American Dilemma: The Negro Problem in Modern Democracy* (New York: Harper and Row, 1944), p. 28.
13. Frazier (1966).
14. F. Henriques, "West Indian Family Organization," in L. Comitas and D. Lowenthal, eds., *Work and Family Life: West Indian Perspective* (New York: Anchor, 1973).
15. R. T. Smith, "The Family in the Caribbean," in V. Rubin, ed., *Caribbean Studies: A Symposium,* Jamaica Institute of Social and Economic Research, University of the West Indies, 1957.
16. Comitas and Lowenthal (1973).
17. R. T. Smith, *The Negro Family in British Guiana: Family Structure and Social Status in the Villages* (New York: Humanities Press, 1965).
18. Ibid.
19. Millette (1987/in press).
20. M. G. Smith, *West Indian Family Structure* (Seattle: University of Washington Press, 1962), p. 16.
21. Ibid.
22. Y. T. Moses, "Female Status and Male Dominance in the West Indian Community," in C. Steady, ed., *The Black Woman Cross Culturally* (Cambridge, MA: Schenkman Publishing Company, 1981).
23. Smith (1971).
24. S. A. Queen and J. B. Adams, *The Family in Various Cultures* (New York: J. B. Lippincott Company, 1952).
25. Smith (1965).
26. Henriques (1973).
27. T. S. Simey, *Welfare and Planning in the West Indies* (London: Oxford University Press, 1946).
28. E. Clarke, "Variations in Jamaican Domestic Patterns," in Comitas and Lowenthal (1973).
29. Cohen, Y. A.
30. Interview with Mr. H. S., July 1986.
31. Burgess and Locke (1953).
32. J. H. Edwards, ed., *The Family and Change* (New York: Alfred A. Knopf, 1960).
33. Frazier (Chicago, 1966).
34. W. F. Ogburn and M. F. Nimkoff, *Technology and the Changing Family* (Boston: Houghton Mifflin, 1955).
35. Burgess and Locke (1953).
36. R. Merton, *Social Theory and Social Structure* (Glencoe, IL: Free Press, 1957).

37. See Robin M. Williams, *American Society, A Social Interpretation,* 2nd Edition (New York: Alfred A. Knopf, 1960), pp. 409–417.
38. Millette (1987/in press).
39. Ibid.
40. T. Shibutani and K. M. Kwan, *Ethnic Stratification: A Comparative Approach* (London: Macmillan, 1965).
41. R. E. Park, "Racial Assimilation in Secondary Groups," in *Race and Culture: Essays in the Sociology of Contemporary Man* (London: Free Press, 1950).
42. Kamarovsky (1967).
43. Queen and Adams (1952).
44. A. F. Scott, *The Southern Lady: From Pedestal to Politics 1830–1930* (Chicago: University of Chicago Press, 1970).
45. J. E. Blakwell, *The Black Community: Diversity and Unity* (New York: Dodd, Mead and Company, 1975).
46. Millette (1987/in press).
47. Ibid.
48. Ibid.
49. J. L. McAdoo, "Involvement of Fathers in the Socialization of Black Children," in H. P. McAdoo, ed., *Black Families* (Beverly Hills, CA: Sage, 1981).
50. Millette (1987/in press).
51. Scott (1970).
52. D. R. Gabaccia, *From Sicily to Elizabeth Street: Housing and Social Change Among Italian Immigrants, 1880–1930* (New York: State University of New York Press, 1984).
53. Dominiquez (1975)
54. L. Coser, *The Functions of Social Conflict* (New York: Free Press, 1956).
55. Ibid.

CHAPTER 3

Headquarters and Subsidiaries: Haitian Immigrant Family Households in New York City

Michel S. Laguerre

Although Haitians have been coming to the United States sporadically, it has been only in the past 30 years—since the beginning of the administration of President François Duvalier in 1957—that large numbers of immigrants from the half-island republic have established themselves in such cities as Miami, New York, Boston, Los Angeles, Chicago, and Washington, D.C.[1] The 1980 census provides a breakdown in terms of age and gender of the Haitian immigrant population, but these data are approximate rather than exact numbers (Table 1). The offshoot communities that Haitian immigrants have developed, with large networks of family relationships, are very much connected to each other via flow of mutual financial aid, periodic visits, and telephone communications. The family household is seen to play a key role in the articulation of the interactions between communities of various kin-related households both in the United States and in Haiti.

The study of immigrant families has generated a good deal of interest and research. Some of it focuses on the adaptation process of immigrants in terms of their socialization into the mainstream culture and values of the host society and their participation in the formal and informal sectors of the economy (Bonacich and Modell 1980; Borjas 1986). Other observers have emphasized the network of relationships that immigrants have established to sustain themselves (Anderson 1974). As a result of previous research, we are now better equipped to understand the functioning of family enterprises among ethnic communities (Light 1972); the differential adaptation of both parents and children; the participation of the family in voluntary organizations; and the ethnic, class, gender, and generational factors associated with the involvement of immigrants in the political economy of urban America (Portes and Bach 1985). Many of the features encountered in the adaptational process of immigrants are not peculiar to any particular ethnic or racial group but seem to be found across the board. One of the strategic features—the process of subsidiarization and headquarterization of the immigrant family household—that has not yet

TABLE 1. Gender and Age of Immigrants by Country of Birth: Haiti

	TOTAL	MALE	FEMALE
Both genders	92,395	44,901	47,494
0 to 14 years	7,664	3,993	3,671
15 to 44 years	64,372	31,965	32,407
45 to 64 years	16,607	7,878	8,729
65 years and over	3,752	1,065	2,687

Source: U.S. Census 1980, Bureau of the Census, Washington, DC, U.S. Department of Commerce.

been conceptualized, operationalized, and analyzed constitutes the main focus of this chapter.

One of the best ways to understand the organization of the Haitian immigrant family household in New York City is through the application of the microeconomic theory of the firm. That is, it is possible to argue that the Haitian immigrant family household functions like a firm and may consist of a headquarters household linked to one or more subsidiary households or of one or more subsidiary households linked to a headquarters household. The relationship of the headquarters household to the subsidiary household, the headquarterization of the subsidiary, the subsidiarization of the headquarters, the development of new subsidiaries, and the mergers that may ensue are the loci of the dynamics of the system that we propose to examine in this chapter.

It is contended that family households behave like firms and are, in fact, multiproduct firms (Laguerre 1990; Reid 1934). The family household, like any ordinary firm, is a corporation that functions on the basis of short- and long-term planning, revenue and profit maximization, cost minimization, competition, investment in both human and physical capital, and sometimes aggressive takeovers (such as divorce and remarriage) and mergers.[2] Moreover, like any firm, the family household may also develop subsidiaries at home and abroad, in order to expand its basis of operation, exploit a foreign market, and ensure its survival. This is the rationale for the study of the Haitian immigrant family household in New York City as a subsidiary household in the process of becoming a headquarters.

It should be noted at the outset that the Haitian immigrant population is diverse not only in terms of its settlement patterns and geographical locations but also in terms of socioeconomic characteristics. These offshoot communities are not homogeneous but are stratified along class lines. The 1980 census provides a glimpse of the hierarchy of incomes earned by Haitian immigrant family households (see Table 2).

PHASES OF HAITIAN MASS IMMIGRATION INTO THE UNITED STATES

Economic disparities among Haitian American households can be traced to the history of Haitian immigration into the United States, which can be divided into three phases. The first phase included roughly the years 1957 to 1964. François

TABLE 2.   Haitian Immigrants in the United States: 1979

	W REGION	S REGION	NC REGION	NE REGION
Households	188	5,865	543	12,587
Less than $5,000	52	1,647	50	2,036
$5,000 to 7,499	17	939	44	1,433
$7,500 to 9,999	28	687	20	1,619
$10,000 to 14,999	27	1,159	73	2,565
$15,000 to 19,999	30	667	115	2,225
$20,000 to 24,999	—	316	57	1,264
$25,000 to 34,999	28	307	89	923
$35,000 to 49,999	—	84	78	388
$50,000 or more	6	49	17	134
Median	$9,732	$8,761	$18,306	$12,116
Mean	$13,495	$10,923	$22,254	$13,932
Families	126	4,527	473	10,596
Median Income	$11,000	$9,172	$18,867	$12,867
Mean Income	$16,114	$11,453	$23,118	$14,491

Source: U.S. Census 1980, Bureau of the Census, Washington, DC, U.S. Department of Commerce.

Duvalier became president in 1957, and in 1964 he named himself president-for-life. Many opposition politicians and professionals left the half-island republic during that period. Well-educated and in some cases well-off by Haitian standards, these members of the elite sincerely believed that the Duvalier government would soon collapse and that they would therefore be able to return to Port-au-Prince to reunite with their families and resume business as usual. Many of them were able to attend professional schools or to find jobs because they were here legally.

The second phase of Haitian immigration into the United States began after the inauguration of "Papa Doc" as president-for-life with the escalation of violence by the civilian militia known as "tonton macoutes." The elite politicos were then in a rush to send for their families, and middle-class Haitians who were hoping for a swift change in the political environment were also leaving en masse, in most cases with tourist visas. That middle-class emigration reached its peak between 1965 and 1971.

The third phase began with the transfer of power from "Papa Doc" to his son, Jean Claude "Baby Doc" Duvalier. It is characterized by the mass migration of lower-class Haitians, both urban dwellers and peasants. The development of light manufacturing industries in the early 1970s attracted a sizable number of would-be workers to Port-au-Prince, which positioned them one step closer to either New York or Miami. With the continued support by the U.S. government of the president-for-life, many poor Haitians felt that their deferred dream could be realized only by migrating to the United States. Unlike the first two phases, which can be characterized as a legal and an "airplane migration" (many became illegal aliens because they overstayed the duration of their visas), the third phase was mostly an illegal and a "sailboat migration" directed toward Miami (or Florida in general) as the preferred port of entry.

The headquarters-subsidiary relations affect differently the different social classes in the Haitian American community. Upper-class or elite families depend less on either the subsidiary or the headquarters because each side is more likely to be self-sustaining financially. Because they migrated legally, they did not risk much that could affect the rest of the family in terms of losing money because of status as illegal aliens.

Middle-class immigrants have been involved in bringing members of their families to the United States and have been successful in doing so. Because of their education, skills, and contacts among fellow expatriates, middle-class individuals in subsidiary households have been able, through various means, to acquire legal status in this country, allowing them to carve an economic niche for themselves. The headquarters-subsidiary model that follows is based on this social class category more than on the others.

Although among poor Haitians, the headquarters household depends more on the overseas subsidiary household than do the other categories, the subsidiary households have been less successful in their ability to bring the rest of their families to the United States. This lack of success may be explained in part because of the forms of migration (sailboat migration) that they are forced to use, the inability of many of them to achieve legal status once they are in the country, and the difficulties of the majority in securing well-paying jobs.

THE SENDING FAMILY HOUSEHOLD AS A HEADQUARTERS-FIRM

One may not be able to understand the adaptation of the first-generation immigrant family household in New York City if one does not pay attention to its structural link to the sending family household in Haiti and also to the household management factor. The subsidiary household in New York is the result of a process that began at the headquarters household in Haiti. The motivation for creating the New York household and the rules that govern the relations between these two entities must be sought in the sending family household. It is difficult to make sense of the economic behavior of the subsidiary household without some understanding of the nature of its links to the headquarters household in Haiti. That relational aspect constitutes a key factor influencing the appropriation of the domestic budget and other decisions that the subsidiary household is called upon to make in order to ensure its own survival and success.

When it is proposed that the sending family household behaves like a firm, and this is the case for all of the subsidiary households as well, we mean to indicate that households are economic corporations that strive to achieve the maximum security for their members, that they create appropriate managerial skills, and that they develop subsidiaries to prevent or minimize the possibility of group bankruptcy.

The sending family household is willing to make sacrifices to let younger members of the family migrate to New York to establish subsidiary households there.

The headquarters household on the island collects funds to help pay the passage, takes over the duties performed by the departing member, reminds the individual of his or her responsibilities vis-à-vis the remaining members, and continues to send him or her money if the household can afford it until the migrant is able to find a job. All of this activity constitutes a major strain on the resources of the headquarters household, but such ventures are seen as investments in human capital for the future because the immigrant is expected to send remittances once he or she finds a job in New York City.

It is important to stress that a sizable fraction of the capital that the headquarters household needs to maintain itself is invested in the departing members. The success of the enterprise, that is, to be able to establish a subsidiary household in New York City, has a positive return for the headquarters, but its total or partial failure (that is, inability to get the precious U.S. visa or to find employment) may also be detrimental to the sending family.

For the sending family, migration is the long-term goal to maintain its economic stability. However, the decision to migrate is based on its assessment of the situation in terms of (1) the risk factors, (2) capital accumulation to secure the papers and plane tickets, (3) investment in human capital, and (4) planning strategy and prospects.

As in the case of the everyday operation of any firm, the sending family takes calculated risks to ensure its long-term survival. Moreover, as in any risk-taking situation, the actor does not have complete control over all of the relevant variables. In any case, great care is taken to ensure the success of the operation in terms of the selection of the member of the family to migrate, the time of the year, the selection of the proper travel agent, and the preparation and collection of the necessary papers. These strategies are developed in order to reduce the probability of a negative outcome.

The accumulation of capital to defray the travel expenses of the immigrant is achieved through the participation and contributions of all the working members of the family. Sometimes property is sold and money borrowed from friends to accomplish this goal. These considerations explain why much planning is undertaken in advance to identify the best strategies to ensure a positive result.

The chief concept that must be stressed is that the headquarters household sees migration as a way of establishing a subsidiary household abroad. This perception has come about for two reasons. First, the economic situation on the island has become bleaker with each passing year, and the government does not provide economic assistance to the unemployed or the aged. Second, a secure basis of economic support in New York goes a long way toward protecting the headquarters against any unforeseen economic adversity. Thus, the establishment of a subsidiary household is undertaken for the purpose of investing in the future of both the headquarters and the subsidiary, alleviating the load of the headquarters, and exploiting a foreign economic environment where market conditions are more favorable and reliable than conditions at home. This perception, which is part of the intellectual outlook that the subsidiary inherits from the headquarters, shapes the way in which the subsidiary household is managed.

THE IMMIGRANT FAMILY HOUSEHOLD AS A SUBSIDIARY FIRM

Like the headquarters household, the subsidiary household is a multiproduct firm. It establishes and manages itself by taking into consideration the economic conditions of the headquarters household, the external market conditions of its adopted country, and its long-range strategy for success. The immigrant establishes a subsidiary household in order to accomplish the following goals: to (1) strengthen its economic base, (2) help other members of the sending family household to migrate, (3) send remittances to the headquarters household, (4) provide incoming family members a base of operation so that they can establish their own subsidiary households, and (5) develop itself in the future as a headquarters household.

The immigrant accomplishes the first goal by acquiring permanent resident status and a job. If he or she decides to get married, the selection of the mate is undertaken in the context of the criteria just mentioned and his or her willingness to participate in this grand economic scheme. The couple may take an apartment with the expectation of getting a house later. The house or apartment is used as a way station for incoming members of the family.

The strategy of helping other members to migrate is used principally to ease the burden of the headquarters and to meet the moral obligations of the subsidiary. The migration of members from the headquarters helps to decrease over time the amount of money the subsidiary needs to send back home.

The subsidiary is expected to and does send remittances back to the headquarters household. The size of the remittances depends on the kind of work the immigrant is able to find, the obligations of the subsidiary in terms of living expenses and other overhead costs, and the employment conditions of the headquarters. Remittances cover two types of expenses: the regular amount that the immigrant sends periodically and any lump sum that may be requested to cover specific expenses, such as buying a plane ticket.

By the time the immigrant establishes the subsidiary household abroad, the headquarters has gone through a contraction process, and with the migration of more members, the size and the frequency of the remittances decrease. This process may continue until the old headquarters is merged with the subsidiary, which by then may have reached headquarters status.

In studying the adaptation of the immigrant family, it is important not simply to look at its links with the headquarters household on the island but also to analyze the household management system. Key questions concerning the operation of the household as a firm can be answered by focusing on the budget.

Household management cannot be seen solely as an internal domestic issue, for it depends also on the interaction of the household with the society at large and the management of other dependent households. Household management is based on the same principles that inform the management of any successful firm, that is, budgetary planning and discipline in relation to projections, revenues, profits, and costs.

Fluctuation in the local economy that affects employment prospects may put limitations on the household economy and its management. Household management is affected by external market conditions in general and the labor market in particular. This is the case for the breadwinner who cannot find work for a while, so that the income on which the household depends is temporarily curtailed. A structural readjustment program must be implemented to deal effectively with the crisis and to prevent bankruptcy.

The management of the headquarters household may also have its impact on the subsidiary household in two different ways. First, it affects directly the management and the financial basis of operation of the subsidiary household. For example, when the members of the headquarters household are employed, the subsidiary household is not expected to send money. But in time of unemployment, the economy of the subsidiary household must be stretched to help others. Sometimes the subsidiary must work two jobs in order to be able to help the headquarters. Second, the phase that the headquarters household may be in also affects the economy of the subsidiary. For example, retirement may alter the household economy of the subsidiary as it is called upon to provide additional money to others.

One aspect of household economy that sheds light on the adaptation process is the budget and the way it is managed. One cardinal point is that the total revenue of the household cannot be used to cover immediate household expenses, and the immigrant household does not have complete control over the expenses of dependent households. Part of the revenue is used to cover expenses incurred by the headquarters household and other dependent households.

This double aspect of the subsidiary budget shows the constraints under which the subsidiary household is forced to operate. It functions with a budget smaller than the total revenue of the household. It has little control over the percentage of money sent back home because that final amount depends on negotiations over the amount requested. The amount requested also depends on a series of factors that the headquarters cannot control, such as, for example, unemployment. Routine remittances can be factored into the subsidiary household budget because they are recurrent expenses; however, nonbudgeted requests cannot always be fulfilled without placing severe constraints on the domestic budget.

Expenses incurred by the headquarters can become a critical problem of management for the subsidiary when they are incidental. For example, supplementary funds may be requested because someone is ill or some other unpredictable expense has arisen. Fluctuation in the economy of the sending family because of negative economic trends directly affects the subsidiary household. When things go awry in the headquarters household, the subsidiary is asked to intervene monetarily.

Part of the revenue of the subsidiary may be used to defray expenses incurred by incoming members of the family. Those who migrate to New York live free in the subsidiary household until they are able to find employment and move out. The subsidiary may be able to forecast a budget to pay for these additional expenses incurred by family members. However, it becomes more difficult to adjust the household budget when friends and acquaintances are sent by the headquarters to stay for a while in the subsidiary household. In interviews conducted by the writer in 1977 in preparation for the book *American Odyssey: Haitians in New York City* (Laguerre 1984), and during the summer of 1990 with Haitian immigrants living in

New York City and in the San Francisco Bay Area (Laguerre 1995), it was revealed that sometimes neighbors or friends of the headquarters family are given the addresses and phone numbers of the subsidiary so that they can find a place to stay until they are able to find a job. If in need, they usually request help from the subsidiary or live there as self-invited guests or guests of the headquarters.

Part of the budget of the subsidiary may be set aside to cover the expenses of the members of the headquarters when they reach old age. They may at that time either remain on the island or migrate to New York to produce a merger. These extra expenses must be picked up by the subsidiary because of the absence of a welfare system in Haiti. Furthermore, the dependence of the headquarters on the subsidiary comes about after the period of resettlement. If the subsidiary fails to sustain itself abroad, the migrant may return home and merge with the headquarters household. This possibility may happen especially in the early phase of the settlement process if the migrant is unable to secure permanent resident status or some other legal status that makes him or her eligible for employment.

THE MODEL

The preceding analysis linking the headquarters household in Haiti to the subsidiary household in New York City allows us now to identify the parameters of the model that help explain the functioning of the first-generation Haitian immigrant family household. For clarification, we focus on one typical case, that of a couple with two children. This representative example sheds much light on the Haitian family experience in the United States in general and in New York City in particular. The model takes into consideration the developmental cycle of both the headquarters and the subsidiary household, the relational structure between them, and the impact of one on the organization of the other. It also provides us with clues for understanding the nature of the differences between the first- and second–generation immigrant family households. However, this last point forms the basis for a separate investigation of the organization of the second-generation immigrant family household and therefore is not dealt with in detail in this chapter. The model with its generative and transformative properties is delineated in six phases.

Phase 1

The first phase locates the departure of the migrant in the history of the headquarters household (Figure 1). In this instance, the headquarters household comprises the husband, wife, son, and daughter. The history of the headquarters household reveals that the migration of a member (in this case, the son) to New York City occurred at the end of the "stability phase" of the household, that is, the period after the birth of the last child and before the departure of any children from the household. The "stability phase" is usually preceded by two other phases. It is worthwhile to identify the phases here, as they help us to understand the relations between household composition and migration. For Peron and Lapierre-Adamcyk (1986), the developmental cycle of the household goes through five different phases:

Headquarters Household
(Haiti)

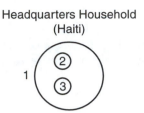

FIGURE 1 Phase 1. 1 = couple (in Haiti); 2 = son; 3 = daughter

The pre-reproduction phase goes from the formation of the household up to the birth of the first child. The expansion phase comprises the period between the birth of the first and last child. The stability phase occurs after the birth of the last child when all the children are still living with their parents. The contraction phase begins with the departure of the first child and ends with that of the last child. The post-reproduction phase is the period during which the couple live together until the dissolution of the household. (p. 358)

One would not normally expect the migration of the children to occur during the first two phases because they are simply too young. There are two important reasons why migration of the daughter or the son or both would occur during the contraction phase of the headquarters household. One reason is that the person is likely to be at least a young adult capable of taking care of himself or herself abroad; and second, if the family member decides to migrate, it is more often than not to seek employment or to attend a university or post–secondary school training center abroad.

Phase 2

The second phase begins with the establishment of a subsidiary household in New York City (Figure 2). This also coincides with the prereproduction phase of the subsidiary household. The creation of a subsidiary household means four different things. One is that it may reduce in the long term the financial burden of the headquarters if the migrant-to-be was not working while living there. It may otherwise also increase, at least in the short term, the financial burden of the headquarters if the family member was contributing to the household economy but is unable to do

FIGURE 2 Phase 2. 1 = couple (in Haiti); 2 = son; 3 = daughter; → = dependent relations

Headquarters (Haiti)

Subsidiary (New York)

so during the early phase of his or her resettlement. This is a period of adjustment and hesitation during which the subsidiary household may not be able to help the headquarters. Once it is settled, it is in a better position to help.

Two, the establishment of the subsidiary household in New York is, for the head-quarters in Haiti, an investment in the human capital for the future. The subsidiary serves as a shield of protection against economic adversity for the headquarters.

Three, the existence of the subsidiary household in New York makes possible the migration of another member (in this case, the daughter) of the headquarters household. Her adaptation in the new country tends to be less traumatic and severe than that of the son because a member of the family is waiting to welcome her to the city.

Four, the success of the subsidiary household (that is, creating a nuclear family, finding an apartment and a good job) indicates that the merger of the headquarters with the subsidiary may already be in the making and that it will be done overseas, that is, in New York.

Phase 3

The third phase focuses on the migration of another member (the daughter) of the headquarters household (Figure 3). This migration may be done in one step, directly from the headquarters household in Haiti to the subsidiary household in New York. It can also be done in two steps, as in this case. The daughter, instead of migrating to New York, got married and established a subsidiary household on the island. Three households are then interacting—the headquarters, the subsidiary at home, and the subsidiary abroad. The establishment of a subsidiary at home may

FIGURE 3   Phase 3. 1 = couple (in Haiti); 2 = son; 3 = daughter and family;
→ = dependent relations

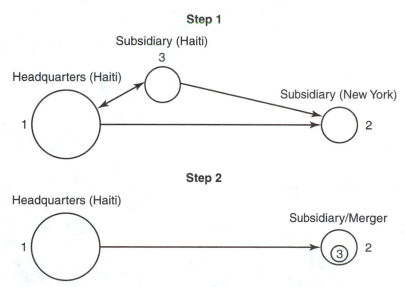

either alleviate or increase the financial burden of the subsidiary abroad. To the extent that the new subsidiary can take care of itself and help the headquarters financially, the subsidiary abroad does not have to worry much about them. The subsidiary at home may become an extra burden if it cannot support itself.

The establishment of a subsidiary at home may delay, but not eliminate, the possibility for other members of the headquarters household to migrate. In this instance, the second step is migration of the married daughter to New York, which creates a merger in the overseas subsidiary.

Phase 4

The fourth phase comprises three different processes: the subsidiarization of the headquarters, the headquarterization of the first subsidiary, and the establishment of a second subsidiary abroad (Figure 4). During this phase, the headquarters loses its central position because it does not control the financial operation and is transformed into a subsidiary dependent on immigrant households abroad. By the same token, the first subsidiary becomes the headquarters because of its central position with regard to the first headquarters and the second subsidiary. The second subsidiary goes through a process of reassembling itself through the migration of the husband and a child who were left behind. The phase of family expansion may resume for the second subsidiary.

Phase 5

This phase coincides with the period of merger, the decomposition of the first headquarters, and the complete headquarterization of the first subsidiary (Figure 5). Merger with the first subsidiary was accomplished with the migration of the old

FIGURE 4   Phase 4. 1 = couple (in Haiti); 2 = son and family; 3 = daughter and family; 4 = son of son; 5 = daughter of son; → = dependent relations; ↔ = interdependent relations

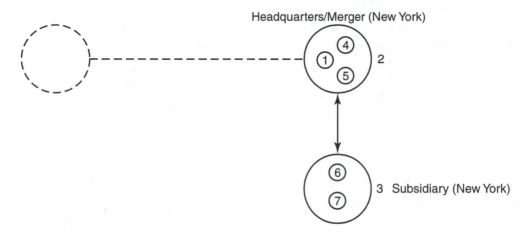

Headquarters/Merger (New York)

FIGURE 5   Phase 5. 1 = couple (parents); 2 = son and family; 3 = daughter and family; 4 = son of son; 5 = daughter of son; 6 = son of daughter; 7 = daughter of daughter; ----- = dissolution of household; ↔ = interdependent relations

parents to New York. Three rules seem to govern the identification of a subsidiary as the new headquarters of the extended family. One is the living presence of the parents from the old headquarters household. The second is financial stability and leadership provided to the network of households. The third is seniority—that is, the first or oldest household of this extended family that was established in New York. However, the content of the relations between the first subsidiary and the old headquarters is not the same as between the first and second subsidiary. The latter are not parent-children relations but rather brother-sister relations. Moreover, financially speaking, one household does not totally depend on another; the relations are more symmetrical.

Phase 6

This last phase coincides with the establishment of the second-generation subsidiary households (Figure 6). In this example, all of the first-generation households have become headquarters vis-à-vis the subsidiary households established by the children. The second-generation subsidiaries do not operate on the same rules as the first-generation ones. The main difference between them is that whereas the first rely on "kin insurance," the second rely on "market insurance." The political economy, not the family, has changed the kinship rules. The writer agrees with Becker (1981:242) when he notes that

> . . . family insurance through gifts and loans to members in distress [is] less necessary in modern societies. Individuals can "self-insure" by borrowing in the capital market during bad times or by saving during good times. Moreover, market insurance based on the experience of thousands of families provides more effective protection against fire, death, old age, ill-health and other hazards than any single family can.

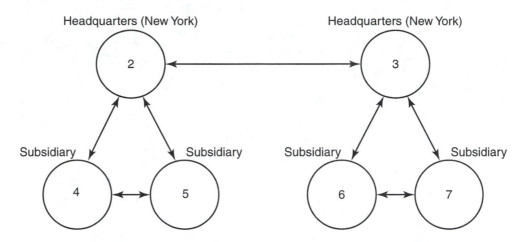

FIGURE 6   Phase 6. 2 and 3 = first-generation immigrant couples; 4, 5, 6, and 7 = second-generation immigrant couples; ↔ = interdependent relations

In other words, the first-generation headquarters household does not depend financially on the second-generation subsidiary household in the new context.

CONCLUSION

This method of analysis, which consists of placing in perspective the headquarters household in relation to the subsidiary household, avoids the tendency to focus only on the latter without seeing its symmetrical and asymmetrical relationships to other households in the network. The adaptation of the immigrant household depends in large measure on its interaction with the headquarters. The phases that the immigrant household goes through are in some cases structurally linked to phases in other households and the economic conditions under which the headquarters household operates. In fact, sometimes they are even produced by these external households. Although otherwise affected by the values and norms of the host society, the economic behavior of Haitian immigrants continues to be influenced by their commitment to help members of the family whom they left behind. Indeed, to a certain extent, the subsidiary households that they establish in the United States function much like "welfare agencies" vis-à-vis the headquarters households on the island.

The headquarters-subsidiary approach to the study of the immigrant household that we propose indicates that the subsidiary household is localized both in space ("overseas") and in time (in the process of becoming a headquarters). It is positioned between the institution (headquarters) from which it emerges and the institution (second-generation subsidiary) created by the children of the immigrants. The relation of the subsidiary to the headquarters is one of financial dependence. This pattern seems largely to evaporate in the relation of the first-generation subsidiary to the second-generation subsidiary. In terms of the management of its finances, the second-generation subsidiary resembles more the average mainstream American family than the first-generation subsidiary does.

This analysis reveals a series of mechanisms that help us to understand the way in which Haitian immigrant households organize their budgets. It explains how and why the budget is split to cover expenses incurred by other households and how the subsidiary household is involved in helping the old headquarters financially, in creating mergers, and in helping to establish other overseas subsidiaries.

According to the model, a distinction must be made between the first- and second-generation immigrant families. With regard to first-generation families, a series of observations have been made that may have policy implications:

1. The total revenue of the household cannot be considered to be available to cover immediate household expenses. A portion of it is returned to the home island or is used to defray expenses incurred by visiting friends and relatives.
2. This observation implies that some of the families who are not considered poor in official statistics may be poor in reality.
3. The official statistics on income do not adequately reflect the nature of the economic conditions of first-generation immigrant families. They reflect the total income, not the income that is available to sustain the household after remittances are extracted from it.
4. The ensuing consequence is that some poor families are shut off from governmental help because they are believed on the basis of their income to make enough money to take care of themselves.
5. The first-generation subsidiary household continues to serve as a "welfare agency" even after a merger with the old headquarters has been accomplished. Until the old parents become eligible for welfare or other assistance, their expenses must be paid by the subsidiary household. Resources that the subsidiary household could accumulate to free itself of poverty or to save for retirement are used instead to care for aging parents.
6. First-generation immigrants should be distinguished from the second-generation and native ethnic minority communities for the purpose of understanding their mode of operation and their needs. They are in many ways different communities, even if they are of the same ethnic background. Unlike the second generation, the first may have obligations to relatives who still reside in the home country.

ENDNOTES

1. I am grateful to Ronald Taylor for his helpful comments on an earlier draft of this chapter.
2. For a theoretical and empirical elaboration on the urban family household as a multi-product firm and immigrant households as overseas subsidiaries, see Laguerre 1990, pp. 50–76 and 141–157. The organization of the Haitian family is further analyzed in Laguerre 1978a and 1978b.

REFERENCES

Anderson, Grace M. 1974. *Networks of Contacts: The Portuguese of Toronto.* Waterloo, Ontario: Wilfrid Laurier University Publications.

Becker, Gary. 1981. *A Treatise on the Family.* Cambridge, MA: Harvard University Press.

Bonacich, Edna, and John Modell. 1980. *The Economic Basis of Ethnic Solidarity: Small Business in the Japanese American Community.* Berkeley: University of California Press.

Borjas, George J. 1986. *The Self-Employment Experience of Immigrants.* Cambridge. MA: National Bureau of Economic Research (NBER Working Paper Series no. 1942).

Laguerre, Michel S. 1978a. "Ticouloute and His Kinfolk: The Study of a Haitian Extended Family." In *The Extended Family in Black Societies,* edited by D. B. Shimkin and others, 407–445. The Hague: Mouton.

———. 1978b. "The Impact of Migration on Haitian Family and Household Composition." In *Family and Kinship in Middle America and the Caribbean,* edited by R. Romer and A. Marks, 446–481. Leiden: Department of Caribbean Studies, Royal Institute of Linguistics and Anthropology.

———. 1984. *American Odyssey: Haitians in New York City.* Ithaca, NY: Cornell University Press.

———. 1990. *Urban Poverty in the Caribbean.* New York: St. Martin's Press.

———. 1995. "Haitians in New York City." In *Encyclopedia of New York City,* edited by K. T. Jackson. New Haven: Yale University Press.

Light, Ivan H. 1972. *Ethnic Enterprise in America: Business and Welfare among Chinese, Japanese and Blacks.* Berkeley: University of California Press.

Peron, Yves, and Evelyne Lapierre-Adamcyk. 1986. "Le Cycle de la Vie Familiale Comme Cadre d'Analyse de la Statistique des Familles." *Les Familles Aujourd'hui,* 2:357–364.

Portes, Alejandro, and Robert L. Bach. 1985. *Latin Journey: Cuban and Mexican Immigrants in the United States.* Berkeley: University of California Press.

Reid, Margaret G. 1934. *Economics of Household Production.* New York: Wiley.

PART II

Hispanic American Families in the United States

The term *Hispanic* is an umbrella label used to refer to a highly diverse population, composed of individuals who share ancestral ties to Spain or the Latin American countries. The Spanish-origin population in the United States has increased dramatically during the past two decades. As recently as 1950, fewer than 4 million residents on the mainland of the United States were counted as Hispanic by the census, representing less than 3 percent of the total population. The number increased to 14.6 million in 1980 and to 22.3 million in 1990, and rose by nearly 50 percent to 32.8 million in 2000, accounting for 12 percent of the total U.S. population. Of the nearly 33 million Hispanics in 2000, 66 percent were of Mexican ancestry, 9 percent were Puerto Rican, and 4 percent were Cuban. The remaining 21 percent included sizable numbers of Dominicans, Salvadorians, Colombians, and other Central and South Americans, each group with its own distinct history, characteristics, and pattern of adaptation in the United States.

Because of the diversity of national origins, distinct immigration histories, and the absence of a firm sense of collective identity among the segments of this population, some analysts have questioned the use of the term *Hispanic* as an appropriate ethnic label in referring to the Spanish-origin population in the United States. They argue that the "Hispanic" population is a group in formation, rather than a consolidated minority, whose boundaries and self-definition are in a state of flux. Nevertheless, the term remains useful in referring collectively to this diverse population, provided that its multiple origin is recognized.

Focusing on Mexican-origin families in the United States, Maxine Baca Zinn and Angela Y. H. Pok examine patterns of adaptation and continuity among those families in the Southwest, where they have been subjected to ongoing patterns of institutional discrimination that, while fostering the development of unique Mexican cultural and ethnic characteristics, have also created serious problems for the quality of family life in that region. Following a historical overview of Mexican family life in the Southwest and a brief discussion of contemporary patterns and trends, Zinn and Pok turn to a critical examination of family structure and dynamics, giving particular attention to familism and the gender-specific division of labor as characteristic features of Mexican American family life. They conclude by discussing how Mexican American families are affected by social and economic changes in the larger society.

In his chapter on Puerto Rican families on the mainland of the United States, Hector Carrasquillo draws attention to the bicultural context of Puerto Rican family life, that is, how the family patterns and household organization of this group are influenced by the ease with which mainland and island Puerto Rican cultures interact and how such interactions over time have contributed to the emergence of a syncretic culture in both places. Comparing the "traditional" Puerto Rican family with contemporary family forms, Carrasquillo notes the bicultural accommodation that has occurred in family norms as recent migrants blend selected aspects of traditional Puerto Rican family values with North American Anglo values better to reflect the dual orientation of the members of mainland Puerto Rican culture. He concludes with an assessment of the impact of structural changes in the wider society on the functioning of Puerto Rican families and the long-term implications of these changes.

Lisandro Pérez chronicles the evolution of the Cuban American community in the United States, beginning in the 1830s and culminating in 1980 when the notorious Mariel boatlift took place. As he shows, the majority of persons of Cuban origin in the United States have been reluctant migrants, impelled by the forces of political change in Cuba and arriving with the expectation of returning. Nor has their presence in the United States been "typical" of the immigrant experience in this country. The special circumstances of their migration produced atypical family characteristics, particularly among Cubans arriving during the past three decades, which include a predominance of women and the middle-aged and elderly and persons of relatively high professional status and incomes. One of the most distinctive features of the Cuban family in the United States is the widespread existence of the three-generation family, which Pérez identifies as an important source of the relative affluence of Cuban American families and the mechanism that facilitates the upward mobility of its members.

CHAPTER 4

Tradition and Transition in Mexican-Origin Families

Maxine Baca Zinn and Angela Y. H. Pok

The phenomenal growth of the Latino population in the United States is a frequent media topic. Magazines and newspapers feature daily stories of the social transformations wrought by large-scale immigration from Latin countries. Latinos are now tied with African Americans as the largest minority, soon destined to surpass the black population. Despite such recent attention, the family patterns of this minority group are often misunderstood. Common stereotypes treat Latino families as cultural artifacts. They are thought to be traditional and close-knit, and to weather adversity better than families of other racial-ethnic backgrounds. Such myths only obscure the reality of family life among people of Mexican origin.

This chapter examines Mexican-heritage families from several different vantage points. After a brief glance at the general characteristics of the Mexican-origin population, the chapter presents a historical overview of family life in the Southwest. This is followed by a look at how social science perspectives on Mexican-heritage families have changed over time. It considers current economic and demographic upheavals in society and their effects on Mexican-origin families. The chapter then examines contemporary family patterns and trends, and concludes with a critical examination of family dynamics.

Two fundamental themes guide this inquiry of Mexican-origin families. These families are constructed by powerful social, economic, and political forces in the larger society. At the same time, they are settings in which different family members adapt in a variety of ways to changing social conditions. These themes set the foundation for understanding how and why Mexican families in the United States will continue to change in the next decade. Contrary to the thinking that viewed minority family patterns as a cause of their subordination in American society, this chapter underscores the adaptational qualities of Mexican-origin families.

Often the larger society lumps various Latino groups together under the hybrid label *Hispanic*. This practice can obscure important differences between Hispanic groups. The category *Hispanic* was created by federal statisticians to provide data on people of Mexican, Cuban, Puerto Rican, and other Hispanic origins in the United States. Many prefer the term *Latino* or use it interchangeably with *Hispanic*. Although these terms are useful for charting broad demographic changes in society, they have little value as an ethnic group category. When used as panethnic terms, *Hispanic* and *Latino* conceal variation in the family characteristics of Latino groups (for a review of the widespread family diversity among Latino groups, see Baca Zinn and Wells 2000).

Since it first attempted to gather information on Hispanics in the 1960 Census, the U.S. Bureau of the Census has modified its method of identifying the Hispanic population with each decennial census. Consequently, intercensus comparisons are somewhat uncertain. For most data-collection activities, including the census, self-identification is used to identify Hispanics. In the 1990 census, information was collected on five "racial" groups—White, Black, Asian, Pacific Islanders, and American Indians—and two "ethnicities"—Hispanic and non-Hispanic. In that census, more than 40 percent of Hispanics identified their race as "other." The census bureau counted these Hispanics as "White." The 2000 census changed racial and ethnic classification by allowing people to select more than one race and as either Hispanic or non-Hispanic (Pollard and O'Hare 1999:8).

Hispanics, according to the U.S. Census guidelines, are an ethnic group, not a racial group. Despite this official government designation, Hispanics *are* racialized in the United States. This is the Hispanic population paradox: Hispanics are classified as an ethnic category, yet "Hispanic" encompasses heterogeneous ethnic groups. At the same time, although Hispanics are not *officially* defined as a race, they are *socially* defined in racial terms. In other words, Hispanics are treated as a racial group, and many identify themselves as belonging to a distinctive racial category.

In reality, there is no such thing as biological race. Instead, the characteristics that distinguish racial categories are socially defined. Whereas past racial classification in the United States was based on a black white dichotomy, the social definition of race has changed over time. Groups previously defined as members of specific ethnic backgrounds such as Japanese Americans and Mexican Americans have been racialized as Asians and Hispanics. New patterns of immigration and the power relations that accompany them are changing our social definitions of race. The social construction of the categories "Hispanic/Latino" as a racial group is what is important. Social relations with Latinos are institutionalized. People identified and labeled Hispanics are treated differently—that is, as a distinctive racial group. As a social category, Latinos experience distinctive treatment in virtually all areas of social life. In the aggregate, Latinos fall well behind non-Hispanic whites on most indicators of status and well-being. They face obstacles to entering the economic mainstream of society. They have lower levels of educational completion, lower incomes, lower standards of living, and lower life expectancy. These inequalities reflect ongoing patterns of institutional discrimination that create serious problems for families. Like blacks, Asians, and Native Americans, Latinos are defined in racial terms. They are viewed as different from and inferior to whites. Nevertheless, as noted earlier, the Latino label masks extraordinary diversity.

In this chapter, we disaggregate the family characteristics of Mexican-origin families from those of other Latino groups. The terms *Mexican-origin, Mexican-heritage,* and for simplicity, *Mexican,* include those who have been in the United States for several generations as well as the immigrant population. Both native-borns (Mexican Americans or Chicanos) and immigrants are subordinated by the wider society. And although they share many features, Mexican-origin families are multiracial, multicultural, and multilingual. They are marked by differences of nativity, citizenship status, region, religion, class, gender, and sexual orientation.

Several characteristics distinguish Mexicans from other minorities in the United States (see Table 1). First, they make up the largest segment of the diverse groups that comprise the Latino population. In 2000, they numbered 21.7 million, accounting for 66.1 percent of Hispanics in the United States and making Mexican-origin Hispanics more than seven times the estimated number of 2.95 million Puerto Ricans (U.S. Bureau of the Census 2001). Second, the Mexican-origin population continues to receive migrants in waves that have made America a "permanently unfinished" society (Portes and Rumbaut 1996). Mexicans have been at the forefront of newcomers making their way into the United States. Although immigration from Mexico is not a new phenomenon, it has changed in important ways. Originally it was a rural flow. Today, it has become mostly urban, with 88 percent of the new arrivals going to metropolitan areas (U.S. Immigration and Naturalization Service 1998). In addition, the flow of Mexican immigration is formed overwhelmingly by urban workers, farm laborers, and their families (70 percent). Only 6 percent of the new arrivals are professionals (Portes and Rumbaut 1996:40–41). In some areas, large-scale immigration is changing the proportion of Mexicans born in the United States and those who are immigrants. For example, in 1960, immigrants were a rarity among Mexicans in California when 82 percent of all Mexicans were born in the United States. Today, 61 percent of all Mexicans are born in the United States, whereas 37 percent of Mexicans are foreign-born (U.S. Bureau of the Census 1998b).

By 2000, the concentration of immigrants was so high that it formed a virtually new population with family characteristics that differ from those of the native-born Mexican or "Chicano" brethren. Although immigration has become a major social trend, little attention has been given to key aspects of family life among U.S.-born and foreign-born, to Mexican immigrants and second generation Mexican families (Romo 1986; Portes and Rumbaut 2001; Suárez-Orozco and Suárez-Orozco 1995). Along with continued immigration, the Mexican population will continue to grow disproportionately because of high birthrates and a young age structure. Women of Mexican origin have the highest fertility levels of any Hispanic group and higher fertility levels than non-Hispanic whites. Taken together, these distinguishing characteristics of Mexican-origin families present compelling challenges to students of the family.

MEXICAN FAMILY HISTORY IN THE SOUTHWEST

Families of Mexican descent have been incorporated into the United States both by conquest and by migration (the following is based primarily on Baca Zinn and Eitzen forthcoming). In 1848, at the end of the Mexican War, the United States

TABLE 1. Population Characteristics by Race and Ethnic Groups, 1998

	Median Household Income	Families below Poverty Level (in percentages)	Poverty Rate for Children under 18 (in percentages)	Female Head of Household (in percentages)	High School Graduate (in percentages)	Labor Force Participation (in percentages)	Unemployment Rate (in percentages)
All U.S.	$38,885	10.0	26.5	15.0	82.8	67.1	4.5
White	$40,912	8.4	10.6	14.0	83.7	67.3	3.9
African American	$25,351	23.6	37.0	46.7	76.0	65.6	8.9
Asian American	$46,637	10.2	18.0	11.7	85.0	68.5	4.6
Hispanic	$28,330	24.7	34.4	23.2	56.1	67.9	7.2
Mexican	**$27,088**	**25.8**	**35.4**	**20.0**	**49.7**	**68.8**	**7.3**
Puerto Rican	$23,729	31.5	43.5	37.7	63.9	60.0	8.3
Cuban	$37,537	15.6	16.4	15.1	70.3	61.3	6.0
Central/South American	$32,030	18.4	26.6	23.2	64.0	72.9	6.1
Other Hispanic	$30,130	25.0	31.6	34.0	71.1	65.3	7.8

Sources: U.S. Bureau of the Census. 1999. Statistical Abstract of the United States: 1999, 119th ed. Washington, DC. Washington, DC: U.S. Government Printing Office. Tables 51, 52, 55, 73, 263, 649, 651, 760, and 761.
U.S. Bureau of the Census. 2000f. Statistical Abstract of the United States: 2000, 120th ed. Washington, DC: U.S. Government Printing Office. Table 737.
U.S. Bureau of the Census. 2000a–e. Current Population Reports: P20-527, P20-530, P20-534, P20-209, and P60-210. Washington, DC: U.S. Government Printing Office.

acquired a large section of Mexico, which is now the Southwestern United States. With the signing of the Treaty of Guadalupe Hidalgo, as many as 100,000 Mexicans living in that region became residents of U.S. territory. The American takeover disrupted traditional family life through land displacement of the indigenous people, new laws, and new labor systems.

The military conquest was accompanied by the beginnings of industrial development and by the growth of agriculture, ranching, railroads, and mining in the region. Rapid economic growth in that region resulted in a labor shortage. U.S. businesses recruited Mexican workers to migrate north for work at low wages in railroad construction and agriculture (Portes and Rumbaut 1996).

Prior to the American takeover and the beginnings of industrial development, Mexicanos, whether natives of northern Mexico or immigrants from southern Mexico, were people of Mexican heritage, largely peasants, whose lives had been defined by a feudal economy and daily struggle on the land for economic survival. This pastoral life was disrupted. With the coming of the railroads and the damming of rivers for irrigation, Mexicans were denied most of the advantages that went to ruling-class Anglos. They no longer owned the land; now they were the source of cheap labor, an exploited group at the bottom of the social and economic ladder.

Mexican immigration to the United States increased substantially in the early twentieth century, although immigration from Mexico had been growing since the late 1880s. But Mexican workers who migrated north for work in the late nineteenth century and late in the first half of the twentieth century often did not settle down permanently:

> The prevailing "ebb and flow" or "revolving door" pattern of labor migration was calibrated by seasonal labor demands, economic recessions, and mass deportations. Although some employers encouraged the immigration of Mexican women and entire families in order to stabilize and expand the available, exploitable work force, many other employers, assisted at times by government-sponsored "bracero programs," recruited only men for elastic, temporary labor supply, a reserve army of labor that could be discarded when redundant. Employers did not absolutely command the movement of Mexican workers, but employers' needs constructed a particular structure of opportunities that shaped migration. (Hondagneu-Sotelo 1995:177)

Migratory labor made families highly susceptible to disruption. Historian Richard Griswold del Castillo (1984) provides a powerful historical example of family arrangements among Mexican Americans in Southwestern cities during the latter half of the nineteenth century, concluding that a large proportion of households (38 percent) were female-headed, even though extended, two-parent families remained the "ideal type." Although migratory labor systems clearly restricted family life, Mexican families were flexible, pluralistic, and adaptive in surviving the rigors of economic marginality and frontier life. Disruptions and reformulations in family structure were commonplace, but family networks were durable (Griswold del Castillo 1984; Vega 1995:5).

Cities in the American Southwest served as focal points for reconstituting the Mexican family constellations and for the construction of new families north of the border. Extended family networks were crucial in dealing with migration and in reinforcing Mexican customs and values (Sanchez 1990:252).

Mexican familism (a strong orientation and obligation to the family) took several forms and served many purposes. The family consisted of a network of relatives, including grandparents, aunts, uncles, married sisters and brothers and their children, and also *compadres* (coparents) and *padrinos* (godparents) with whom Chicanos actively maintained bonds (Ramirez and Arce 1980:9). The *compadrazgo* system of godparents established connections between families and in this way enlarged family ties. "Godparents were required for the celebration of major religious occasions in a person's life: baptism, confirmation, first communion, and marriage." At these times, godparents "entered into special religious, social, and economic relationships with the godchild as well as with the parents of the child." They acted as coparents, "providing discipline and emotional and financial support when needed." As *compadres* they were expected to become the closest friend of the parents and members of the extended family (Griswold del Castillo 1984:40–44).

Family roles in the nineteenth century were strongly gendered. Women did domestic work and cared for children within the home while men did productive work outside the household. Exceptions to this pattern could be found in rural areas, where women tended gardens or looked after domestic animals (Barrera 1979). This division began to break down as more and more women entered the paid labor force, stimulated by the dire economic situations that affected so many Chicano families after 1870. Albert Camarillo has described how traditional patterns of employment and family responsibilities were altered in Santa Barbara, California:

> The most dramatic change was the entrance of the Chicana and her children as important wage earners who contributed to the family's economic survival. As male heads of household faced persistent unemployment, their migrations to secure seasonal work in the other areas of the country or region became more frequent. In these instances the Chicana assumed the triple responsibilities of head of household, mother, and wage earner. No longer able to subsist solely on the income of the husband, the Chicana and her children were forced to enter the unskilled labor market of Anglo Santa Barbara. The work they performed involved domestic services and agriculture-related employment. (Camarillo 1979:91)

During the 1800s, Chicanas were incorporated into the agricultural labor market as entire families entered the pattern of seasonal and migratory fieldwork. Initially, Chicanas and their children were employed as almond pickers and shellers and olive harvesters. During the almond and olive harvests, men were usually engaged in seasonal migratory work. During some seasons, however, especially the early summer, the entire family migrated from the city to pick fruit. Chicano family labor had become essential for the profits of growers. Families often left their homes in Santa Barbara for several weeks, camping out in the fields where they worked (Camarillo 1979:93).

Large-scale immigration from Mexico greatly expanded the Mexican/Chicano presence in the Southwest. Migrating in a chainlike pattern, Mexican family units were reconstructed in the United States. This process provided an increase in the supply of cheap Chicano labor, which was "placed" in the labor force according to gender. Men were incorporated into the segmented labor market in agriculture, ranching, mining, and railroads, and as common laborers in urban industrial occupations. Women were incorporated into the segmented labor market in domestic work, canning and packinghouses, the textile industry, and agriculture (Camarillo 1979:221). The gender system of work prevailed throughout the Southwest. In El Paso, Texas, for example, Mario Garcia (1981) found that from 1890 through 1920, women worked mainly as servants and laundresses, as garment workers, and as cooks and dishwashers.

Race and gender placed Mexican-heritage women in subordinate work outside the home. In addition, a distinctive system of Mexican patriarchy controlled the private-sphere activities of women. As both daughters and wives, Mexican women were instructed to be obedient and submissive to both their parents and their husbands. Domesticity and motherhood were primary virtues. Whether or not they labored outside the home, they were subject to a gender division of labor in which their primary task was to care for their husbands and children and to accept subordination as a natural condition. The "private" patriarchy meshed neatly with the patriarchy of the Southwest economy. Wage-earning mothers and daughters were responsible for domestic duties. The work women did outside the home was considered less important than that of men, and their wages only supplemented those of men. Despite these conditions, the wage labor of Mexican-heritage women contributed greatly to family adjustment in a colonized setting (Garcia 1980).

Besides their roles as workers, wives, and mothers, women in particular guarded Mexican cultural traditions within the family—not consciously, but as a matter of practice (Garcia 1980:128). Certain customs practiced during the 1920s by Mexican immigrant families throughout the Southwest promoted Mexican tradition. These customs included folklore, songs and ballads, birthday celebrations, saints' days, baptisms, weddings, and funerals in the traditional Mexican style. Through the family, Mexican culture was nurtured.

Immigration to the United States during the nineteenth and early twentieth century served to replenish both the Mexican population and their cultural traditions in the areas of settlement. The large presence of poor immigrant families in Southwestern cities gave rise to studies portraying Mexican family life as a social problem for American society.

This thinking was rooted in the development of family studies as a new field. Family studies emerged out of a deep fundamental belief in the need to study and ameliorate social problems (Thomas and Wilcox 1987:27). During the 1920s and 1930s, the social-problems approach to family life led to studies of Mexican immigrants that highlighted (1) their foreign patterns and habits, (2) the moral quality of family relationships, and (3) the prospects for their Americanization. A prominent sociologist of the time, Emory Bogardus, observed that fathers had primitive attitudes concerning large numbers of children and that mothers had fatalistic attitudes, viewing children as gifts from God. These primitive family relationships were seen as natural representations of the lower-class culture (Bogardus 1934:25).

Social reforms of the times favored the enforced modernization of the Mexican immigrant family:

> Teachers of Americanization, directors, settlement workers, and visiting nurses, should make the most of the opportunity they have in bringing to the Mexican the right attitude toward his family . . . The Americanization of the women is as important as that of the men. They are harder to reach, but are more easily educated. They can realize in a moment that they are getting the best end of the bargain by the change in the relationships between men and women which takes place under the new American order. "Go after the women" should become a slogan among Americanization workers, for after all, the greatest good is to be obtained by starting the home of right . . . The man's moral qualities may be doubtful, but at least the womenfolk and the children are undefiled. (White 1971:33–35)

Social reformers, social workers, and sociologists of the early twentieth century assumed that Mexicans and other minorities should and would eventually become acculturated and take on the family characteristics of middle-class white Americans. This was to become a guiding theme in the study of Mexican-origin families.

OLD AND NEW PERSPECTIVES

In examining Mexican-heritage families, we can distinguish between a *cultural approach,* which treats minority families as cultural artifacts, and a *structural diversity approach,* which views all families in society as shaped through their interaction with social structures (Baca Zinn and Eitzen 2002). The difference between these two approaches lies in whether Mexican culture or structural and contextual conditions are the primary units of analysis. The cultural approach views Mexican-origin families as special cultural cases that are different from a standard family form. It emphasizes family patterns passed down from generation to generation, such as close-knit family forms, male dominance, and other traditionally "Mexican" ways of relating within families. In the past, such patterns were viewed as cultural exceptions to the rule of standard family development. The reasoning was that traditional "cultural baggage" created serious problems for Mexican families.

In the past two decades, scholars have replaced this cultural deficit model of Mexican-heritage families. New approaches have found that alternative family patterns do not reflect deviance, deficiency, or disorganization. Instead of representing outmoded cultural forms handed down from generation to generation, Mexican family lifestyles often reflect adaptive responses to social and economic conditions. What were once labeled culturally deficient family patterns are now viewed as family strategies and solutions to constraints imposed by social structures in the larger society. A structural diversity approach explores the close connections between the internal dynamics of family life and the structural forces that shape *all* families in society, albeit in different ways. The very forces that organize society as a whole create different contexts for family living and different group-based family patterns through their unequal distribution of social resources and opportunities. Instead of being an intrinsic property of Mexicans themselves, their family forms are shaped by the adaptations of family members to the social situations and contexts in which they are socially located (Baca Zinn and Eitzen 2002).

GLOBAL REORGANIZATION AND FAMILY UPHEAVALS

During the last quarter of the twentieth century, profound social transformations swept the United States and fundamentally redefined family life. Among the best-documented family changes are family composition, the participation of women in the workforce, patterns of marriage and divorce, and the proportion of households headed by women. These trends reflect social changes that are more far-reaching and occurring faster than at any other time in history. They are global in scope and are produced by economic and demographic transformations that are redefining families throughout the world. Mexican-origin families are not exempt. They have been bombarded by global reorganization that includes (a) the structural transformation of the U.S. economy and (b) immigration and the new demands for immigrant labor. These social upheavals have extraordinary consequences for Mexican-origin families and the individuals within them.

Economic Restructuring

Four factors are at work in economic restructuring: new technologies based primarily on the computer chip, global economic interdependence, capital flight, and the domination of the information and service sectors over basic manufacturing industries (Baca Zinn and Eitzen 2001). Together, these factors have redesigned jobs, reorganized cities and regions, and exacerbated inequalities. They have affected the lives of people in all social categories, families, and communities, and will continue to do so for the foreseeable future. However, the magnitude of economic restructuring is different throughout society. The disproportionate effects of economic and industrial change are most visible in three trends: (1) structural unemployment, (2) the changing distribution and organization of jobs, and (3) the low-income generating capacity of jobs. Each of these three trends has significant consequences for Mexican-origin families in that they create a socioeconomic context in which family life is constructed and maintained.

Families are affected when their resources are reduced, when they face economic and social marginalization, and when family members are threatened by unemployment or are actually laid off. The economic deprivation that they face forces them to adjust in ways that other poor families do: having single-parent families, relying on kin networks, sharing housing costs, and having multiple wage-earners among family members.

As a firmly established blue-collar workforce, Mexicans have tended to work in economic sectors most vulnerable to cyclical unemployment and in some manufacturing industries that are threatened with decline. Mexican-origin workers have been hard hit by plant closings created by the exodus from the West and Southwest for cheaper locales. Although most of the Mexican-origin population lives in areas with booming economies, they do not always profit from regional growth. Many of the growth industries that employ Mexicans pay poorly and have weak unions. Thus, although growth does create jobs, many of these are in service and low-wage manufacturing. Few in the population have enough training for high-wage jobs in the new industries (Moore 1989).

The restructuring of the U.S. economy has reshaped economic opportunities for Mexicans (Ortiz 1996). The shift away from manufacturing to services has meant that new jobs offer low wages and poor working conditions. New immigrants who are vulnerable to exploitation by employers generally fill these jobs.

The impact on Mexicans of economic restructuring has been and will remain uneven. Where plant closings and factory layoffs have been studied among Mexican-origin workers, predictable family stresses and disruptions have been documented (Castro-Selipe et al. 1987). In other cases, industrial restructuring has been found to generate employment. Many Mexican-origin women have found their work opportunities expanded in electronics and apparel factories. Such work not only often creates new forms of race and gender exploitation but also offers only marginal income. However, it also allows many Mexican women to keep their families afloat when their husbands have lost their jobs because of economic reorganization (Zavella 1984). Changes in industrial employment affect women and men differently, and these patterns have staggering effects on family life.

As industrial restructuring reorganizes work, women in all social categories are drawn into the labor force. Mexican women are no exception. Of the 66 million women in the civilian labor force in 2000, 6.35 million (9.6 percent) were of Hispanic origin. Of this 6.35 million, 60 percent were of Mexican origin (U.S. Bureau of the Census 2001). This represents an important departure from the earlier patterns. Mexican-origin women have historically had among the lowest rates of labor force participation. This increase in women's employment has created far-reaching changes in family life, but it has not stabilized Mexican families nor diminished the impact of poverty. Like women in the larger society, Mexican women have experienced both rising levels of employment and higher poverty rates that are associated with the growth of female-headed households. Although Mexican-origin people have the highest proportion of married-couple families, they are not immune to the feminization of poverty. Poor female-headed households with or without the support of extended kin mean problems for mothers and their children.

The Mexican-origin population has been affected by changes in the larger economy that polarized the occupational structure into "good" jobs and "bad" jobs. Few in the Mexican-origin population have enough training for high-wage jobs. They are dropping further behind in education and training just when jobs require more technical knowledge and higher levels of education. This trend is one of the most crucial barriers to the well-being of Mexican families. Mexicans (along with other Latino ethnic groups) have the highest rates of school dropouts in the country. Undereducated people suffer in the employment world, and their families pay a high price.

Immigration in the Current Era

Another transformation that is changing society and families is massive immigration. The United States is currently experiencing its second major wave of immigration. Between 1991 and 1998, a record number of 7.6 million immigrants were admitted for permanent residence in the United States (U.S. Immigration and Naturalization Service 1998). One million immigrants are being added to the U.S. population annually.

Two features of the current immigrant population make it different from previous waves of migration into the United States. First, immigrants arrive not from Northern Europe but from the Third World, especially Asia and Latin America. Almost 80 percent of today's immigrants hail from Asia, Mexico, the Caribbean, Central America, and South America (U.S. Immigration and Naturalization Service 1999). Second, women and children make up a large share of today's immigrants. In 1998, 53.5 percent of all immigrants admitted to the United States were female (U.S. Immigration and Naturalization Service 1998). Immigrant children and U.S.-born children of immigrants are the fastest-growing segments of the U.S. child population. For example, in 1997, 20 percent of the child population were either immigrant children or U.S.-born children of immigrants (Portes and Rumbaut 2001).

Today, Mexicans lead in both legal and undocumented immigration. In 1998, 20 percent of all immigrants legally admitted to the United States were from Mexico, more than the four next-largest groups combined (U.S. Immigration and Naturalization Service 1999). In contrast, between 1901 and 1910, migrants from Mexico comprised less than one percent of the U.S. immigrant population. Mexican immigration reflects broader immigration trends. Over half (57 percent) of legally admitted immigrants from Mexico are female, whereas 35 percent are 19 years old or younger (U.S. Immigration and Naturalization Service 1998).

Among legally admitted Mexican immigrants, 57 percent live in the West (U.S. Bureau of the Census 2001). The majority reside in California, Texas, and Illinois, in the following metropolitan areas: Los Angeles–Long Beach, Riverside–San Bernardino, and Chicago (U.S. Immigration and Naturalization Service 1998). Although it is difficult to track undocumented immigration, it has been estimated that, in 1998, 2.7 million of the 5 million undocumented immigrants came from Mexico (U.S. Bureau of the Census 1999).

Today's immigrants face a new set of problems, which are a result of global reorganization, discussed before, including the structural transformation of the U.S. economy and the demands for immigrant labor. Because Mexicans comprise a large proportion of today's immigrant population, Mexican immigrant families are especially affected by these changes.

How are Mexican families involved in immigration? Under the provisions of the Immigration Act of 1990, gaining immigrant status generally requires a sponsor, who may be a U.S. citizen, a legal resident, a U.S. employer, or in the case of refugees, the U.S. government. Of those options, the most common route to immigration involves a close family member. The majority, 55 percent, are immediate relatives of U.S. citizens (U.S. Immigration and Naturalization Service 1999). Thus, immigration to the United States is largely a family affair.

Adaptation is a central dynamic in immigrant family life. Although immigrant families have always been fluid and flexible, today's immigration is adding new forms to U.S. family arrangements. The immigration laws, which favor migrants with family connections, have a snowball effect that enhances the potential for further migration (chain migration), both legal and extralegal (the following is based primarily on Baca Zinn and Eitzen forthcoming). Such chaining processes often lead to dense ethnic concentrations in cities where extended families are closely networked:

> Such spatial concentration of kin and kith serve to provide newcomers with manifold sources of moral, social cultural, and economic support that are unavailable to immigrants who are more dispersed and help to explain the gravitational pull exerted by places where family and friends of immigrants are concentrated. (Rumbaut 1997:7)

Family connections make immigration possible, and they help migrants cope with life in a new social setting. At the same time, immigration is transforming families and households in fundamental ways.

Exceptions to the family-oriented immigration often occur. For example, many young, typically manual workers, leave their families behind for months at a time while they work in the United States. These *transnational families* find their family ties stretched across national boundaries, thereby causing extraordinary emotional, financial, and physical stress for family members (Chavez 1992:119).

Even motherhood can be stretched across national boundaries. *Transnational motherhood* is an arrangement whereby Mexican immigrant women work in the United States while their children live in Mexico (Hondagneu-Sotelo and Avila 1997). This arrangement is difficult for parents and children, but it is sometimes the only choice if workers are to take advantage of better wages in the United States. Transnational mothering is closely linked with the globalization of economies that create new demands for immigrant labor (Chang 2000; Hondagneu-Sotelo 2001).

In other circumstances, undocumented immigrants may have families in the United States. This situation occurs by having their spouse join them or by marrying U.S. citizens or legal residents. The children of these unions, if born in the United States, are U.S. citizens. This arrangement leads to the unusual situation of families that consist of a mix of legal statuses. Chavez (1992) calls these families *binational*, since they consist of both undocumented immigrants and U.S. citizens or legal residents.

Recent feminist scholarship has inspired some fundamental changes in migration studies. Early migration scholarship often ignored women, making it seem as if only men migrated. Today's scholarship examines how immigration and gender relations are reshaping family dynamics. Several important studies have examined the relationship between immigration and gender. In her study of undocumented Mexican immigrants, Hondagneu-Sotelo demonstrated that gender shapes migration and that the migration process itself reduces traditional patriarchal relations:

> As traditional family patriarchy weakens, immigrant women assume more active public and social roles, and these activities ultimately advance their families' integration in the

United States . . . in the aggregate, these activities anchor family settlement. Women advance settlement for their families, and in the process, they consolidate their own new-found status in the family. (Hondagneu-Sotelo 1994:149)

Like gender relations, generational relations are a new topic in migration research. Immigration is often shaped by children's needs and involvement. For example, Thorne and her colleagues found that parents' decisions to bring children to the United States from Mexico were based on the following considerations: possession of money to pay for the journey; needs and circumstances of family members here and at home; expressed desires of the children themselves; and parents' views of what is safe, appropriate, or good for children of different ages and genders. Mexican immigrant children not only participate in housework activities but also use acquired skills to negotiate for family members in various social contexts. They may use their knowledge of English to translate for parents and other adults (Thorne et al. forthcoming). Family dynamics are transformed as ideas about adult power and authority, as well as children's autonomy and status, change.

SELECTED PATTERNS AND TRENDS

Evidence that accumulated over the past two decades reveals that Mexican-origin families are undergoing many of the transitions facing U.S. families in general, yet important differences exist. The continuing influx of immigrants from Mexico combines with systems of class and racial inequality to produce hardships not faced by mainstream families.

Several characteristics of the Mexican-origin population create severe disadvantages for family living. Mexicans in this country lag behind the white population on most measures of socioeconomic status. This situation is not surprising because many are immigrants, and immigrants typically have low status. Making generalizations about Mexican-origin families is particularly complex because it involves assessing two distinct groups—the native-born and the foreign-born. On most indicators of well-being, native-born Mexicans are better off than their foreign-born counterparts (O'Hare 1989). Although native-born Mexicans are better off in general, some rather startling findings have emerged from recent research on the family patterns of immigrants to Los Angeles. Hayes-Bautista (1989) discovered that immigrants arrive in the United States with strong families but that they do not sustain "positive" family characteristics over time and generation. Studying census data on Mexican immigrant families, this sociologist discovered high rates of family formation, low welfare dependency, and high labor-force participation. In successive generations, these characteristics appear to become weakened.

Low-status occupations and high unemployment have especially serious consequences for family life because they translate into low incomes and high poverty rates. Median family income for Mexican-origin families in 2000 was $30,400, compared with the non-Hispanic median income of $51,206 (U.S. Bureau of the Census 2001). Whereas the median family income for Mexicans is below that of non-Hispanics, per-person income is actually lower because Mexican-origin people tend to have large families.

In 1999, 21.2 percent of Mexican-origin families had incomes below the poverty threshold, compared with only 5.5 percent of non-Hispanic families (U.S. Bureau of the Census 2001). This is the case despite the fact that a large proportion of poor Mexican families have members in the workforce.

Marriage and Divorce

Marriage is very much the norm for Mexicans. Compared with other Hispanics and non-Hispanics, Mexicans (both women and men) are more likely to be married. Despite their overall precarious economic existence, they are more "pro-nuptial" than other disadvantaged groups. Family demographers describe the inconsistent pattern of Mexican American nuptiality as follow: First-marriage rates among Mexican Americans are similar to those among Anglos despite economic circumstances that closely resemble African Americans (Oropesa, Lichter, and Anderson 1994). Their age at first marriage is also somewhat lower than that for both other Hispanics and non-Hispanics. Marriage patterns have often led to conjectures that Hispanics in general and Mexicans in particular have more stable families than others. The evidence does not support this assumption. Vega reports that

> Bean and Tienda's review of 1980 census data found negligible variations in rates of marital disruption between non-Hispanic Whites, Mexican Americans and Cuban Americans, but Puerto Rican rates that are much higher than those of the other groups. Although other investigators . . . had reported lower divorce rates for Mexican Americans, Bean and Tienda point out that when separation is included in marital disruption, such differences disappear. (Vega 1990:1016)

Fertility and Family Size

As noted earlier, an important characteristic of Mexican-origin families is their large size. Average household size for Hispanics in 1998 was 3.92 compared with 3.02 for non-Hispanic whites (U.S. Bureau of the Census 1998a). Among Hispanic subgroups, Mexican families had the highest proportions of families with five or more members. For example, in 2000, 33 percent of Mexican families, compared with 12.1 percent of non-Hispanic families, had five or more members (U.S. Bureau of the Census 2001).

Although steadily declining, the high rates of childbearing among Mexican-origin women are evident in all age categories and levels of education. The persistently high birthrate among Mexican women has been variously interpreted in terms of religion, class, and culture. With reference to religion, the question is whether Mexicans as a group overwhelmingly self-identify as "Catholic" and support the national pattern of Catholics being less supportive of contraceptives and more positive about large families. The second explanation has emphasized the generally low socioeconomic status of Mexicans in the United States, explaining that their low income and lack of education make fertility control difficult for them. The third interpretation focuses on a cultural explanation to account for high fertility; that is, their values are assumed to be different from those of others in terms of family size. Contrasting evidence can be found for each explanation (Andrade 1980). New evidence shows that increasing proportions of Mexican women approve of and/or use birth control when it is available (Moore and Pachon 1985:105).

Type of Family

The large increase in the number of families headed by women is one of the most important social developments of the past decade. A small but growing proportion of Mexican-origin families are headed by women. Still, female-headed households are less prevalent among Mexicans (21 percent in 2000, compared with 23.4 percent among Hispanics in general) and slightly more prevalent than among non-Hispanics (17 percent) (U.S. Bureau of the Census 2001). A clear relationship exists between household composition and economic well-being. Female-headed households are especially vulnerable. In 1999, 38.4 percent of Mexican-origin families maintained by women were below the poverty threshold (U.S. Bureau of the Census 2001).

FAMILY STRUCTURE AND FAMILY DYNAMICS

Traits commonly associated with Mexican-origin families in the United States are (1) familism, an assortment of beliefs and behaviors associated with family solidarity and kinship networks, and (2) a gender-specific division of labor.

Familism

For decades, familism has been considered to be a defining feature of the Mexican-origin population. Presumably, family is one of the strongest areas of life, more important for Mexicans than for Anglos. This characteristic pertains not only to the nuclear family but also to a wider circle of kin—the extended family that includes aunts, uncles, grandparents, cousins, in-laws, and even *compadres*.

In contrast to the prevailing view that familism is primarily a Mexican cultural preference handed down through the generations, studies show that Mexican kinship patterns are socially constructed. In other words, familism is shaped by structural and contextual factors. Mexican-origin familism has different components, it serves varied purposes, and it takes multiple forms.

Familism contains four key components. The first component, *demographic familism,* refers to macrocharacteristics of Chicano families, such as family size, whereas the second component, *structural familism,* measures the incidence of multigenerational or extended households. The third component, *normative familism,* taps the value that Mexican-heritage people place on family unity and solidarity. The fourth, *behavioral familism,* refers to the level of interaction between family and kin networks (Ramirez and Arce 1980).

Compadrazgo is another feature of familism among Chicanos and Mexicans. It refers to two sets of relationships with "fictive kin": (1) "*padrinos y ahijados,*" or godparents and children, and (2) parents and godparents who become "*compadres,*" or coparents. The *compadrazgo* system of godparents enlarges family ties by creating connections between families. According to Griswold del Castillo, "Godparents were required for the celebration of major religious occasions in a person's life: baptism, first communion and marriage." At these times, godparents "entered into special religious, social and economic relationships with the godchild as well as the parents of the child." They acted as coparents, "providing discipline and emotional and financial support when needed." As *compadres,* they were expected to become the closest friend of the parents and members of the extended family (Griswold del Castillo 1984:40–44).

Familism serves varied purposes. Studies spanning the past three decades have found that kinship networks often compensate for resources withheld by the larger society. In poor Mexican-origin communities, family extension is a system for coping with socioeconomic marginality (Alvirez and Bean 1976; Angel and Tienda 1982; Hoppe and Heller 1975; Keefe 1984; Lamphere et al. 1993; Mindel 1980; Uttal 1999; Velez-Ibanez 1996). Yet, kinship networks are not maintained for socioeconomic reasons alone. They operate as systems of cultural, emotional, and mental support (Keefe 1984; Mindel 1980; Ramirez 1980). Familism among Mexican-heritage adults has been associated with high levels of education and income (Griffith and Villaviciencio 1985), and among adolescents as a form of social capital linked with academic success (Valenzuela and Dornbusch 1994).

Kinship networks have long been used in the migration of Mexicans to the United States (Chavez 1992; Hondagneu-Sotelo 1994; Macklin 1996; Portes and Bach 1985; Samora and Lamana 1967; Wells 1976). As discussed earlier, Mexican immigrants create a process of chain migration, using kin to find housing and employment, and to be a buffer against the upheavals associated with migration. Among immigrants, extended kinship is a classic social adaptation as transnational families are stretched across space, time, and national borders.

Kinship networks among Mexican-origin people are varied depending on distinctive social conditions such as immigrant versus nonimmigrant status and generational status. Comparing Mexican immigrants with Mexican Americans, Glick (1999) found differences in the types of extended family households formed by each group. Mexican immigrants were more likely than Mexican Americans to share living arrangements with relatives from within the same generation, but they are much less likely to live with relatives from multiple generations. At the same time, the simple description of "immigrant" versus "native" patterns does not adequately characterize the pattern of exchange. Rather, Glick found a life course dimension to exchanges with extended kin:

> Mexican Americans, who are more likely to live in extended family households consisting of multiple generations, engage in economic exchanges from older adults to younger adults. Mexican immigrants, who are more likely to live with relatives at similar stages of the life course are more likely to exchange resources with these kin in other households as well. (Glick 1999:745)

As with other racial-ethnic groups including African Americans and Asian Americans, Mexican-origin people with higher socioeconomic standing retain by choice strong patterns of kin interaction. Although a cultural perspective would predict that familism fades in successive generations, Velez-Ibañez (1996) found high elaborated second- and third-generation extended family networks actively maintained through frequent visiting, ritual celebrations, and the exchange of goods and services.

Gender, Power, and Family Activity

No assumption is more deeply ingrained in scholarly and popular thinking about Mexican-origin families than that of male dominance. *Machismo,* the Mexican masculinity cult, has long been thought to be responsible for many of the family and socialization patterns that create problems for Mexicans. The term *machismo* has gained popular usage in American society, referring to exaggerated masculinity, physical prowess, and male chauvinism. In the social science literature about Mexicans and Chicanos, machismo is the primary concept used to explain family structure and inadequate personality development. It is based on the assumption that exaggerated masculinity represents a compensation for cultural inferiority (Baca Zinn 1982:2). Early research on Mexican families in the United States focused on the "macho-dominated" authoritarian Mexican American family in which the male demands complete deference, respect, and obedience from his wife and children.

From today's vantage point, these early studies "sound like ludicrous stereotypes-projections of the scholars' individual racism rather than valid indicators of the culture and its people" (Segura and Pierce 1993). Although such stereotypical writings about overcompensating men and submissive women have given way to more balanced empirical works on gender, questions about male domination continue to be important. Although themes of patriarchy remain, the nature of male dominance is different from that described in earlier studies.

A wave of revisionist work on marital power conducted in the 1970s and 1980s found that wives and husbands share in family activities and decision making (Baca Zinn 1980; Cromwell and Cromwell 1978; Grebler et al. 1970; Hawkes and Taylor 1975; Ybarra 1982). These studies refute the stereotype of macho-dominated Mexican-origin families, but they do not dispute that gender is still a major determinant of family activities. Marital role relationships in Mexican-origin families are neither male-dominated nor egalitarian, but, like families in general, they reveal a range of patterns between these opposing models.

Certain social conditions appear to be associated with greater equality for wives. The most striking is wives' employment. Again, there are parallels between historical and current patterns. Richard Griswold del Castillo (1979), in his historical work on the Los Angeles barrio from 1850 through 1890, found that increased female involvement outside the family altered the role of women in the household as well as relations between women and men. Contemporary studies have suggested that Mexican women's employment patterns, like those of women around the world, provide them with resources and autonomy that alter the balance of family power (Baca Zinn 1982; Coltrane and Valdez 1993; Pesquera 1993; Williams 1990; Ybarra 1982; Zavella 1987). But women's employment, by itself, does not eradicate male dominance. This is one of the main lessons of Zavella's (1987) study of

Chicana cannery workers in California's Santa Clara Valley. Women's cannery work was circumscribed by the inequalities of class, race, and gender. As seasonal, part-time workers, the women gained some leverage in the home, thereby creating temporary shifts in their day-to-day family lives, but this leverage did not alter the balance of power.

Fernandez-Kelly and Garcia's (1990) comparative study of women's work and family patterns among Cuban Americans and Mexican American's found strikingly different configurations of power. Immigrant Mexican women in Los Angeles found themselves in a process of proletarianization, where their labor was required for family survival, whereas many Cuban women left the labor force when short-term goals of improving living standards were attained.

Other conditions associated with varying patterns in the division of domestic labor are women's and men's occupational statuses and relative economic contributions to their families. Studies by Pesquera (1993), Coltrane and Valdez (1993), and Coltrane (1996) found a general "inside/outside" dichotomy (wives doing most housework, husbands doing outside work and sharing some child care), but women in middle-class jobs received more "help" from their husbands than did women with lower earnings.

Recent works on Mexican-origin families have sought to bring *men* more fully into view (Coltrane 2001). In an important study of Mexican immigrant men, Hondagneu-Sotelo and Messner (1994) discussed the diminution of patriarchy that comes with settling in the United States. They showed that the key to gender equality in immigrant families is women's and men's position in the larger society. Mexican immigrant men's status is low, because of racism, economic marginality, and possible undocumented status. Meanwhile, as immigrant women move into wage labor, they develop autonomy and economic skills. These conditions combine to erode patriarchal authority.

WHAT WE LEARN FROM MEXICAN-ORIGIN FAMILIES

These are truly extraordinary times for family study. Accelerated social changes that are affecting families in all racial categories are creating widespread variation in "the American family." The growing diversity of family life offers the potential to sharpen, as never before, our understanding of how families are related to the larger social world. In this renewed concern for how families respond to and absorb external changes, Mexican-origin families can be a vital thread in the overall family revisioning effort. They are both similar to and different from families in other racial groups. Similarities stem from social changes that are reshaping all families, whereas differences emerge from the varied social locations of Mexican-origin families.

Mexican-origin families can teach us much about the interplay between families and society—about how people with severely constrained options and choices nevertheless forge family lives that are suited to their needs and social settings. In the twenty-first century, new demographic realities and their accompanying social divisions pose great challenges to family scholars and society at large. The future of the

United States as a postindustrial democracy may well depend on improving the status of its diverse racial groups and their families.

REFERENCES

Alvirez, David, and Frank D. Bean. 1976. "The Mexican-American Family." In *Ethnic Families in America,* edited by C. H. Mindel and R. W. Habenstein, 271–292. New York: Elsevier.

Andrade, Sally. 1980. "Family Planning Practices of Mexican Americans." In *Twice a Minority, Mexican American Women in the United States,* edited by M. Melville. St. Louis: CV Mosby.

Angel, Ronald, and Marta Tienda. 1982. "Determinants of Extended Household Structure: Cultural Pattern or Economic Need?" *American Journal of Sociology* 87:1260–1383.

Aponte, Robert. 1991. "Urban Hispanic Poverty: Disaggregations and Explanations." Unpublished paper.

Baca Zinn, Maxine. 1980. "Employment and Education of Mexican-American Women: The Interplay of Modernity and Ethnicity in Eight Families." *Harvard Educational Review* 50:47–62.

———. 1982. "Chicano Men and Masculinity." *The Journal of Ethnic Studies* 10:29–44.

Baca Zinn, Maxine, and D. Stanley Eitzen. 2001. "Economic Restructuring and Systems of Inequality at Century's End." In *Race, Class, and Gender: An Anthology,* edited by M. L. Anderson and P. H. Collins, 229–233. Belmont, CA: Wadsworth.

———. Forthcoming. *Diversity in Families,* 6th edition. Boston: Allyn and Bacon.

Baca Zinn, Maxine, and Barbara Wells. 2000. "Diversity Within Latino Families: New Lessons for Family Social Science." In *Handbook of Family Diversity,* edited by D. H. Demo, K. R. Allen, and M. A. Fine, 252–273. New York: Oxford University Press.

Barrera, Mario. 1979. *Race and Class in the Southwest.* Notre Dame, IN: University of Notre Dame Press.

Bogardus, Emory. 1934. *The Mexican in the United States.* Los Angeles: University of Southern California Press.

Camarillo, Albert. 1979. *Chicanos in a Changing Society: From Mexican Pueblos to American Barrios in Santa Barbara and Southern California, 1884–1930.* Cambridge, MA: Harvard University Press.

Castro-Selipe, G., Gloria Romero, and Richard Cerventes. 1987. "Long-term Stress Among Latino Women After a Plant Closing." *Sociology and Social Research* 71(2):85–87.

Chang, Grace. 2000. *Disposable Domestics.* Cambridge, MA: South End Press.

Chavez, Leo R. 1992. *Shadowed Lives: Undocumented Immigrants in American Society.* New York: Harcourt Brace College Publishers.

Coltrane, Scott. 1996. *Family Man.* New York: Oxford University Press.

———. 2001. "Stability and Change in Chicano Men's Family Lives." In *Men's Lives,* 5th ed., edited by M. S. Kimmel and M. A. Messner, 451–466. Boston: Allyn and Bacon.

Coltrane, Scott, and E. O. Valdez. 1993. "Reluctant Compliance: Work-family Role Allocation in Dual Earner Chicano Families." In *Men, Work, and Family,* edited by J. Hood, 151–175. Newbury Park, CA: Sage.

Cromwell, Vicky L., and Donald E. Cromwell. 1978. "Perceived Dominance in Decision Making and Conflict Resolution among Anglo, Black and Chicano Couples." *Journal of Marriage and the Family* 40: 749–759.

Fernandez-Kelly, Patricia, and Anna Garcia. 1990. "Power Surrendered and Power Restored: The Politics of Home and Work among Hispanic Women in Southern California and Southern Florida." In *Women and Politics in America,* edited by L. Tilly and P. Gurin, 130–149. New York: Russell Sage Foundation.

Garcia, Mario T. 1980. "La Familia: The Mexican Immigrant Family, 1900–1930." In *Work, Family, Sex Roles, Language,* edited by M. Barrera, A. Camarillo, and F. Hernandez, 117–140. Berkeley: Quinto Sol International.

———. 1981. *Desert Immigrants, the Mexicans of El Paso, 1890–1920.* New Haven: Yale University Press.

Glick, Jennifer E. 1999. "Economic Support From and To Extended Kin: A Comparison of Mexican Americans and Mexican Immigrants." *International Migration Review* 33 (Fall):745–765.

Grebler, L., Joan W. Moore, and Ralph C. Guzman. 1970. *The Mexican American People: The Nation's Second Minority.* New York: Free Press.

Griffith, J., and S. Villavicienco. 1985. "Relationships Among Culturation, Sociodemographic Characteristics, and Social Support in Mexican American Adults." *Hispanic Journal of Behavioral Science* 7:75–92.

Griswold del Castillo, Richard. 1979. *The Los Angeles Barrio, 1850–1890: A Social History.* Berkeley: University of California Press.

———. 1984. *La Familia.* Notre Dame, IN: University of Notre Dame Press.

Hawkes, Glenn R., and Minna Taylor. 1975. "Power Structure in Mexican and Mexican-American Families." *Journal of Marriage and the Family* 37:807–811.

Hayes-Bautista, David. 1989. "Latino Adolescents, Families, Work, and the Economy: Building upon Strength or Creating a Weakness?" Paper prepared for the Carnegie Commission on Adolescent Development, Washington, DC.

Hondagneu-Sotelo, Pierrette. 1994. *Gendered Transitions: Mexican Experiences of Immigration.* Berkeley: University of California Press.

———. 1995. "Women and Children First: New Directions in Anti-Immigrant Politics. *Socialist Review* 25(1):169–190.

———. 2001. *Doméstica.* Berkeley: University of California Press.

Hondagneu-Sotelo, Pierrette, and Ernestine Avila. 1997. "'I'm Here, But I'm There': The Meanings of Latina Transnational Motherhood." *Gender & Society* 11(October):548–571.

Hondagneu-Sotelo, Pierrette, and Michael A. Messner. 1994. "Gender Displays and Men's Power: The 'New Man' and the Mexican Immigrant Man." In *Theorizing Masculinities,* edited by H. Brod and M. Kaufman, 200–218. Newbury Park, CA: Sage.

Hoppe, Sue Kier, and Peter Heller. 1975. "Alienation, Familism, and the Utilization of Health Services by Mexican-Americans." *Journal of Health and Social Behavior* 16:304–314.

Keefe, S. 1984. "Deal and Ideal Extended Familism Among Mexican Americans and Anglo Americans: On the Meaning of 'Close' Family Ties." *Human Organization* 43:65–70.

Lamphere, Louise, Patricia Zavella, and Felipe Gonzales. 1993. *Sunbelt Working Mothers: Reconciling Family and Factory.* Ithaca, NY: Cornell University Press.

Macklin, Barbara June. 1976. *Structural Stability and Culture Change in a Mexican American Community.* New York: Arno Press.

Massey, Douglas, Rafael Alarcon, Jorge Durand, and Umberto Gonzales. 1987. *Return to Aztlan.* Berkeley: University of California Press.

Mindel, Charles H. 1980. "Extended Familism among Urban Mexican Americans, Anglos, and Blacks." *Hispanic Journal of Behavioral Sciences* 2:21–34.

Moore, Joan W. 1989. "Is There a Hispanic Underclass?" *Social Science Quarterly* 70:265–284.

Moore, Joan W., and Harry Pachon. 1985. *Hispanics in the United States.* Englewood Cliffs, NJ: Prentice-Hall.

O'Hare, William P. 1989. "Assimilation and Socioeconomic Advancement of Hispanics in the U.S." Population Reference Bureau Staff Working Papers.

Oropesa, R. S., Daniel T. Lichter, and Robert N. Anderson. 1994. "Marriage Markets and the Paradox of Mexican American Nuptuality." *Journal of Marriage and the Family* 56(November):889–907.

Ortiz, Vilma. 1996. "The Mexican-origin Population: Permanent Working Class or Emerging Middle Class?" In *Ethnic Los Angeles,* edited by R. Waldinger and M. Bozorgmehr, 247–277. New York: Russell Sage Foundation.

Pesquera, Beatríz M. 1993. "In the Beginning He Wouldn't Lift Even a Spoon: The Division of Household Labor." In *Building with Our Hands,* edited by A. de la Torre and B. M. Pesquera, 181–198. Berkeley: University of California Press.

Pollard, Kelvin M., and William P. O'Hare. 1999. "America's Racial and Ethnic Minorities." *Population Bulletin* 54(September):entire issue.

Portes, Alejandro, and Robert L. Bach. 1985. *Latin Journey.* Berkeley: University of California Press.

Portes, Alejandro, and Rubén G. Rumbaut. 1996. *Immigrant America: A Portrait,* 2nd ed. Berkeley: University of California Press.

———. 2001. *Legacies: The Story of the Immigrant Second Generation.* Berkeley: University of California Press.

Ramirez, Oscar. 1980. "Extended Family Support and Mental Health Status Among Mexicans in Detroit." *Micro, Onda, LaRed, Monthly Newsletter of the National Chicano Research Network:*2.

Ramirez, Oscar, and Carlos Arce. 1980. "The Contemporary Chicano Family: An Empirically Based Review." In *Explorations in Chicano Psychology,* edited by A. Baron, Jr. New York: Praeger.

Romo, Harriet. 1986. "Chicano, Transitional and Undocumented Mexican Families: Perceptions of the Schooling of Their Children." In *Mexican Immigrants and Mexican Americans,* edited by H. L. Browning and R. O. De La Garza, 175–193. Austin, TX: CMAS Publications.

Rumbaut, Rubén G. 1997. "Ties That Bind: Immigration and Immigrant Families in the United States." In *Immigration and the Family,* edited by Alan Booth, Ann C. Crouter, and Nancy Landale, 3–46. Mahway, NJ: Lawrence Erlbaum Associates.

Samora, Julian, and Richard Lamana. 1967. *Mexican-Americans in a Midwest Metropolis.—A Study of East Chicago.* UCLA Study Project Advance Report.

Sanchez, George J. 1990. "Go After the Women: Americanization and the Mexican Immigrant Women, 1915–1929." In *Unequal Sisters: A Multicultural Reader in U.S. Women's History,* edited by E. C. DuBois and V. L. Ruiz, 250–263. New York: Routledge.

Segura, Denise A., and Jennifer L. Pierce. 1993. "Chicana/o Family Structure and Gender Personality: Chodorow, Familism, and Psychoanalytic Sociology Revisited." *Signs* 19:62–91.

Suárez-Orozco, Carola, and Marcelo Suárez-Orozco. 1995. *Transformations: Immigration, Family Life, and Achievement Motivation.* Stanford: Stanford University Press.

Thomas, Darwin L., and Jean Edmondson Wilcox. 1987. "The Rise of Family Theory." In *Handbook of Marriage and the Family,* edited by M. B. Sussman and S. S. Steinmetz. New York: Plenum.

Thorne, Barrie, Marjorie Faulstich Orellana, Wan shun Eva Lam, and Anna Chee. Forthcoming. "Raising Children, and Growing Up, Across National Borders: Comparative Perspectives on Age, Gender, a Migration." In *Gender and U.S. Immigration: Contemporary Trends,* edited by P. Hondagneu-Sotelo. Berkeley: University of California Press.

U.S. Bureau of the Census. 1998a. "Household and Family Characteristics: March 1998 (Update)." Current Population Reports, P20-515. October 1998. Washington, DC: U.S. Government Printing Office.

————. 1998b. "The Hispanic Population in the United States: March 1997 (Update)." *Current Population Reports,* P20-511. July 1998. Washington, DC: U.S. Government Printing Office.

————. 1999. *Statistical Abstract of the United States: 1999,* 119th ed. Washington, DC: U.S. Government Printing Office.

————. 2000a. "Money Income in the United States: 1999." *Current Population Reports,* P60-209. September 2000. Washington DC: U.S. Government Printing Office.

————. 2000b. "Poverty in the United States: 1999." *Current Population Reports,* P60-210. September 2000. Washington, DC: U.S. Government Printing Office.

————. 2000c. "The Black Population in the United States: Population Characteristics, March 1999." Current Population Reports, P20-530. September 2000. Washington, DC: U.S. Government Printing Office.

————. 2000d. "The Asian Pacific Islander Population in the United States: Population Characteristics, March 1999." *Current Population Reports,* P20-534. September 2000. Washington, DC: U.S. Government Printing Office.

————. 2000e. "The Hispanic Population in the United States: Population Characteristics, March 1999." *Current Population Reports,* P20-527. February 2000. Washington, DC: U.S. Government Printing Office.

————. 2000f. *Statistical Abstract of the United States: 2000,* 120th ed. Washington, DC: U.S. Government Printing Office.

————. 2001. "The Hispanic Population in the United States, March 2000." *Current Population Reports,* P20-535. March 2001. Washington, DC: U.S. Government Printing Office.

U.S. Immigration and Naturalization Service (INS). 1998. *1998 Statistical Yearbook of the Immigration and Naturalization Service.* Washington, DC: U.S. Government Printing Office.

————. 1999. *Legal Immigration, Fiscal Year 1998.* Annual Report, No. 2, July 1999. Washington, DC: U.S. Government Printing Office.

Uttal, Lynet. 1999. "Using Kin for Child Care: Embedment in the Socioeconomic Networks of Extended Families. *Journal of Marriage and the Family,* Vol. 61, No. 4 (November): 845–857.

Valenzuela, A., and S. Dornbusch. 1994. "Familism and Social Capital in the Academic Achievement of Mexican Origin and Anglo Adolescents." *Social Science Quarterly* 75:18–36.

Vega, William A. 1990. "Hispanic Families in the 1980s: A Decade of Research." *Journal of Marriage and the Family* 52:1015–1024.

————. 1995. "The Study of Latino Families: A Point of Departure." In *Understanding Latino Families,* edited by Ruth E. Zambrana, 1–17. Thousand Oaks, CA: Sage Publications.

Velez-Ibañez, Carlos G. 1996. *Border Visions: Mexican Cultures of the Southwest United States.* Tucson: University of Arizona Press.

Wells, M. J. 1976. "Emigrants from the Migrant Stream: Environment and Incentive in Relocation." *Aztlan: International Journal of Chicano Studies Research* 7:267–290.

White, Alfred. 1971. "The Apperceptive Mass of Foreigners as Applied to Americanization: The Mexican Group." M.A. Thesis: University of Southern California. Reprinted by R and E Research Associates.

Williams, Norma. 1990. *The Mexican American Family: Tradition and Change.* Dix Hills, NY: General Hall.

Ybarra, Lea. 1982. "When Wives Work: The Impact on the Chicano Family." *Journal of Marriage and the Family* 44:169–178.

Zavella, Patricia. 1984. "The Impact of Sun Belt Industrialization on Chicanas." *Frontiers* 8:21–27.

————. 1987. *Women's Work and Chicano Families.* Ithaca: Cornell University Press.

CHAPTER 5

The Puerto Rican Family

Hector Carrasquillo

The migration of Puerto Ricans to the mainland United States is perhaps one of the most unique movements in the long history of American immigration. Because of the development of relatively inexpensive air transportation, the proximity of the island to the mainland, and the political status of Puerto Rico as a Commonwealth of the United States whose people maintain American citizenship, emigrants to the United States have been able to maintain close relationships with the island and its culture (Gurak and Rogler 1980). Moreover, the return migration from America to Puerto Rico, particularly since the 1970s, has been much more prevalent than was the case with previous immigrant groups (Vázquez Calzada 1978).

These specific Puerto Rican factors, combined with the growth of Hispanic influence on American life in general, have provided Puerto Rican communities in the United States with a rather different character than that of previous ethnic migrations. Whereas previous immigrants have become assimilated to American culture fairly quickly—adopting its overall values while keeping their distinctive culture for "special occasions" and the periphery of life—Puerto Ricans have established a much stronger bicultural framework for their lives. This is reflected in the development of characteristic language patterns, with a creative syncretism of English and Spanish becoming the norm, and in new social relationships that fit neither established mainstream Puerto Rican patterns nor traditional mainland culture.

This syncretic culture is made especially complex in that the island culture of Puerto Rico also has been undergoing significant change in recent years. Most particularly, the pattern of immigration and return migration has had a significant effect in both places. For example, San Juan has become a relevant point of reference for many in New York, and New York is a major center of Puerto Rican culture, even for those who live on the island. Because of the ease with which the mainland and island Puerto Rican cultures interact, a vital new culture, taking aspects of both, has emerged in both places, particularly in urban areas of the island.

Changes under way in Puerto Rico and on the mainland inevitably affect family patterns and other features of Puerto Rican life in both places, although the impact of these changes on family organization has yet to be adequately investigated in context. This chapter reviews the literature on Puerto Rican families residing on the mainland of the United States. Because this area of study is in a state of flux and has yet to receive the systematic attention that it deserves, what is presented here makes no claim to being definitive. Rather, what follows is a portrait or snapshot of a Hispanic population, many of whose familial characteristics are in a state of flux. We begin with a look at the structure of the "traditional" Puerto Rican family, then examine contemporary family patterns, and conclude with a discussion of the implications of some recent developments for the future of Puerto Rican family life in the United States.

THE TRADITIONAL PUERTO RICAN FAMILY

It must be immediately acknowledged that to write of the "traditional" Puerto Rican family is to engage in a deep oversimplification. Even when the island culture was relatively uninfluenced by migration, many variations in family form could be found in accordance with a family's social status, wealth, geographical location, race, or age-cohort group (Sánchez-Ayéndez 1988). However, certain general characteristics that are important for understanding the development of the Puerto Rican family in the United States can, if considered with caution because of generalizations, be mentioned and used as a basis for comparison with the Puerto Rican family as it exists within the mainland community of the United States.

The structure of the "traditional" Puerto Rican family was that of the modified extended family. This is not to suggest that the nuclear family is not a functioning unit; in fact, the nuclear core functions as "the fundamental unit in family living" (Padilla 1958:169), particularly in urban areas. However, individual family members are intertwined with a kinship group that is both larger than that typical in mainstream North American culture and also characterized by a greater number of contacts. Although the extended family arrangement has been greatly modified in recent years, it remains an important part of most Puerto Rican lives. Thus, Padilla (1958) notes that even among migrant families, genealogies and family stories remain in families for several generations, and distant relatives are viewed with concerned interest. Geographically, the extended family members ideally live very close to each other, often in the same household (Blatt 1979).

Thus, whereas American culture is oriented toward an emphasis on the individual as the basic unit of society—although formal and informal support systems certainly do exist—Puerto Rican culture sees the survival and happiness of the individual as consequent upon his or her embeddedness within the larger family. The individual by himself or herself is seen as relatively weak and as having inadequate emotional and practical resources for solving the problems that life presents (Bastida 1979). Moreover, even identity is conferred upon a person not so much as an individual but as a member of the family unit. It is within that unit that social obligations and resources are centered. This is to say that Puerto Rican culture has a familistic orientation. Fitzpatrick (1971) writes as follows:

> The world to a Latin consists of a pattern of intimate personal relationships, and the basic relationships are those of his family. His confidence, his sense of security and identity are perceived in his relationship to others who are his family. (p. 73)

Moreover, the extended family provides a primary source of emotional and material support for its members (Stycos 1952). To an extent, this tendency indicates that the family is set in opposition to the rest of the social world (Stycos 1955). Whereas relationships with family members are quite close, there may be a pattern of keeping a greater social distance from those who are not within the boundaries of the family unit. Such people may, in fact, be mistrusted (Mintz 1966; Wells 1972). Thus, it can be said that Puerto Rican culture accepts the social value of familism, which can be defined as a way of life that "emphasizes the almost sacred bonds between relatives, the compelling obligations toward relatives, the duty to help and express concern for them" (Rogler and Cooney 1984:74).

However, as noted later, this relationship is modified by a relative looseness in defining the boundaries of the kin network, and as long as someone is accepted within the network—whether or not actual blood relationships exist—he or she is treated in the same manner as are family members.

This kinship extends vertically through generations as well as horizontally beyond immediate nuclear family members. Most important of these intergenerational relationships are with grandparents. Puerto Rican grandparents generally play a much greater role in child-rearing than is typical in American families, although in no sense should this situation be considered to suggest that the grandparent, as patriarch or matriarch, has the final decision on such matters or is completely integrated into the nuclear family (Tumin and Feldman 1971). Rather, the grandparent plays a critical role as a provider of services such as baby-sitting and as a giver of advice to the less experienced parents. Moreover, the obligations are mutual: the sons and daughters are expected to provide financial, emotional, and social support for their aged parents and in many cases to provide housing for them. Thus, the grandparent's role is much more vital in the traditional Puerto Rican family than it is in the American family.

The extended family also reaches beyond the bounds of strict kinship relationship (Padilla 1987). Particularly important is the godparent (*compadrazgo*) relationship, which is instituted within the Catholic Church. In the traditional Puerto Rican family, however, as in many traditional Latin and Mediterranean Catholic cultures, the godparent relationship implies more than the honorific or spiritual relationship that exists formally within Catholic religion. The individuals within the *compadrazgo* relationship are expected to feel deep affection for each other and also to provide assistance and financial aid when the need arises (Fitzpatrick 1971). Such persons thus, despite the absence of blood relationships, might be seen as forming a part of the extended family.

Less formal but also very important in the traditional Puerto Rican family is the practice of informally adopting children as *hijos de crianza* (Sánchez-Ayéndez 1984). Although such adoption can at times be mainly an expression of affection, when biological parents die or other crises disrupt the family's stability, this form of adoption may involve actual assumption of the parental role, even in the absence of formal legal adoption. Within such a context, the informally adopted child has a relationship with his or her fictive parent that follows closely the obligations and rights of an actual parent-child relationship.

Thus, whereas in mainstream North American culture, distinct boundaries exist between nuclear and extended families and between the kinship group and those not related, these boundaries are neither strictly nor identically drawn in the traditional Puerto Rican family. This quality is partially the result of the personalist orientation of Puerto Rican culture: Rather than emphasizing abstract faceless relationships and social encounters, only those relationships that have a close personal dimension of face-to-face contact are considered to be truly real.

These differences also extend to status relationships within the family. Among the most profound differences is the great respect that is accorded members of older generations. In mainstream American culture, the elderly are often excluded as irrelevant "old-timers" or otherwise given a degraded social status. Traditional Puerto Rican culture, on the other hand, adopts the central value of *respeto,* or respect. Such respect is due to every human being, but it is especially expressed in the deference that should be given to those who are older. This deference is not an earned one based upon the accomplishments of a lifetime but simply accrues to the elderly person on the basis of his or her generational status. Even where great informal affection is involved, as in a parental or grandparental relationship, in some situations the informal displays of affection must be replaced by a more formal and deferential display of respect toward the elder.

Gender norms are also very different from the North American ideal of a relatively homogeneous egalitarianism. In the traditional Puerto Rican family, gender roles are distinctly defined. That is, there is a clear distinction between *trabajo de hombre* and *trabajo de mujer* (Rogler and Cooney 1984). Moreover, the roles connected with men are accorded a higher formal status than those connected with women (Landy 1959; Safa 1974). This gender differentiation is further embedded within the differing cultural ideals of male *machismo* and female *marianismo.*

Machismo is a cultural value that attributes to men a natural sexual aggressiveness and a strong sense of competitiveness with regard to other men. The man must prove himself and his virility, in part through fathering many children (Brameld 1959). Within this culture, extramarital affairs are considered a positive sign of masculinity for men (Tumin and Feldman 1971). Moreover, men ritually establish an authority that is—theoretically—total within the family (Stycos 1955). This authority is backed by expectations that he will provide for and protect the family (Mussen and Beytagh 1969). However, more egalitarian structures do emerge in families of college-educated men and women (Tumin and Feldman 1971).

The hierarchical family structure often establishes a degree of distance between the father and the other family members; a study by Hill and associates, cited by Blatt (1979), found that 87 percent of Puerto Rican fathers expressed a preference for being respected rather than loved. Unlike women, men's lives are not centered exclusively on the family and household. They are expected to maintain relations with men outside the family and generally have an externalist orientation (Blatt 1979).

For women in the traditional family pattern, the home is the center of existence and the place where she fulfills the major obligations of her social role: household keeping and child-rearing (Landy 1959; Safa 1974). In opposition to the adventures demanded of men by the *machismo* norm, the *marianismo* (Stevens 1973) norm demands that women model themselves after the chaste life of the Virgin Mary, although a positive value is placed on high fertility (Blatt 1979). Although they are not, of course, expected to abstain from sexual relations with their husbands, they ideally are supposed to establish something analogous to the purity of the Virgin and, like the model, establish fulfillment through the family rather than through personal endeavors. Thus, she has primary responsibility for most household and child-rearing functions, although in rural areas of Puerto Rico the man tends to assume responsibility for purchasing food (Blatt 1979).

Children were also closely associated with the home and in rural areas were expected to remain close to the mother at all times. They tend to take an active role in helping the family by doing chores from an early age (Blatt 1979).

Thus, the picture provided by the traditional Puerto Rican family is that of a strongly patriarchical social group in which gender and generational roles are strongly differentiated and defined. The family is the central institution in this society, and through it individuals gain their identity.

THE CONTEMPORARY PUERTO RICAN FAMILY IN THE UNITED STATES

One might expect that this traditional family structure would have quickly been disrupted upon immigration into the United States. The traditional agricultural roots upon which the traditional modes of life were established had little relevance to the situation in the urban centers of mainland America into which Puerto Ricans have tended to settle. Language and culture separate the traditional Puerto Rican lifestyle from that prevalent on the mainland. Moreover, on the mainland they are faced with a culture that values the individual highly, that has adopted highly egalitarian family norms, and that uses a high level of strongly formalized social relationships. If the Puerto Rican immigrant were to assimilate into the mainland culture, he or she would, it seems, have to give up the values that have been dominant on the island.

As was noted before, however, such assimilation has not taken place in any thorough manner. Living within urban barrios and facing discrimination, Puerto Ricans have often had little positive contact with the dominant culture and thus have been able to avoid total assimilation. Moreover, the close contact that Puerto Ricans have retained with the island culture has further allowed them to maintain their own culture. Although most have been denied entry into the mainstream, the barrio has provided an important alternative environment in which to maintain or forge personal and social identify (Padilla 1987), and this has had a strong effect in limiting the level of integration of Puerto Ricans into the mainstream of American society. As Padilla (1987:70) notes,

> Puerto Rican migrants had little inclination to learn anything but the most rudimentary American ways, for they had little interest in settling permanently in America.

Finally, during this period, the mainland culture has tended to place less emphasis on the necessity of assimilation than during previous periods of immigration. Although some disagree with the purposes of these programs, bilingual school programs and Puerto Rican studies departments in institutions of higher education have allowed for the development of a mainland Puerto Rican identity that is not entirely assimilated into that of North American Anglo society. Thus, there have been strong counterbalancing forces against the full dissolution of traditional Puerto Rican family value systems even within the mainland. The extended family and the informal social networks of the barrio have provided a means of resisting the dominant culture or of compensating for the rejection of Puerto Ricans by that culture. Several writers have indicated that the value of familism retains at least some of its force within the mainland context (Fitzpatrick 1971; Padilla 1958).

On the other hand, the social and economic environment even of the Puerto Rican barrio is sufficiently different from that of the agrarian environment of the Puerto Rican village—or even the environment of urban Puerto Rico—that some change might be expected. The Puerto Rican migrant might not assimilate into his or her new country, but on some level would have to accommodate to it. Thus, what occurred was neither the maintenance of traditional Puerto Rican values nor the adoption of North American Anglo values but, rather, the development of a bicultural society that creatively merged English and Spanish into a "Spanglish" that expresses the dual orientation of the members of mainland Puerto Rican culture (Szapocznik and Kurtines 1979). It is therefore unlikely that the North American Puerto Rican family would fully accept the traditional family norms described before.

The nature of this bicultural accommodation is the central research issue facing the study of the contemporary Puerto Rican family. In many ways, this is a unique adaptation to American life, but it also may represent a pattern of immigration that is more characteristic of the highly pluralist age that has resulted from modern transportation and communications. As immigrants become more able to keep in touch with their old world while living in the new and are able to make periodic visits back to the old world, the line between the old and the new becomes blurred, and the type of accommodation needed is more likely to become bicultural.

These issues are particularly important with regard to the question of generational progression. Whereas members of the first generation grew up within the island culture, members of the second generation are acculturated within the mainland environment, even if their childhood included periodic trips back to Puerto Rico. An important factor is likely to be contact with the school system of the dominant culture. A typical immigrant pattern finds the second generation assimilating more thoroughly and quickly into the new environment, often acting as an agent of change for the members of the older generation.

Within the context of the immigrant family, this process often leads to high levels of generational conflict, with the younger generation seeking to adopt the values and behavior patterns of the new land and the older generation resisting those values and patterns. In some cases, the expertise that the child obtains in the ways of the new land can lead to a curious form of role reversal as the son or daughter takes on the task of educating the parent, much of whose experience is no longer relevant in the new social environment. Such role reversals can lead to cognitive dissonance and to considerable anxiety. An important issue is how this typical pattern relates to the bicultural situation of Puerto Ricans.

Rogler and others (1982) examined subjective ethnic identity in terms of language, age of emigration, education, and neighborhood composition, and found that the generational pattern is not entirely absent from Puerto Rican parents and children. Children tend to feel less exclusively Puerto Rican than their parents, and the level of Puerto Rican identification varies inversely with education (at least up to high school graduation) and directly with age at emigration. That is, those who have been exposed more to North American culture, or perhaps, in the case of education, who have greater opportunity in that culture, are less likely to identify themselves primarily as Puerto Rican. This research, however, also demonstrates that even children who grow up on the mainland establish bicultural identities. The authors write,

> Although the children's Puerto Rican ethnic identity is significantly less than that of their parents, the pattern of children's responses suggests movement to biculturalism as opposed to complete assimilation. Only 45 percent of the children consider themselves to be exclusively Puerto Rican; the remaining children consider themselves to be part Puerto Rican and part American. Not even one of the Puerto Rican children considers himself or herself to be exclusively American. Children also tend to use both English and Spanish in speaking to family, friends and neighbors as opposed to English only. The children with a good knowledge of English did not abandon Spanish and reported their knowledge of Spanish to be better than average. In terms of attitudinal preferences, the children's responses are closer to "no preference" than to preference for American culture. (p. 212)

This is quite different from the situation of earlier immigrant groups, in which the second generation sought to establish a strong American identity, leaving later generations to seek to reconnect with their ethnic roots. Moreover, 80 percent of the child generation studies by these authors expressed a desire that their children retain their Puerto Rican identity (Rogler and Cooney 1984).

Some evidence indicates that the level of ethnic identify within the Puerto Rican family has increased rather than decreased as Puerto Ricans have become established on the mainland. Examining rates of intermarriage with non–Puerto Ricans for the years 1949 to 1959—that is, the years of the first great influx of Puerto Ricans to North America—Fitzpatrick (1971) found that rates were comparable to those of earlier ethnic groups who had entered American society. This movement away from the family—which, as was noted before, is the center of identity in traditional Puerto Rican culture—could be seen as strong evidence of assimilation into American life. Examining the data for 1975, however, Rogler and Cooney (1984) found that only 29.5 percent of Puerto Ricans married outside their ethnic group. This finding was significantly lower than for any other Hispanic group in New York, despite the greater number of second-generation Puerto Ricans. This, the author note, may be due to the larger community available to Puerto Ricans than to other groups, but in any event it indicates a persistent commitment to the Puerto Rican community in marriage decisions among second-generation New York residents.

Although the examination of ethnic identity is indicative of biculturalism and perhaps a willingness to maintain what is relevant from the culture of the old society, such ideological commitment may not always be expressed in actual behavior. Often, members of an ethnic group need to maintain strongly symbolic connections with the traditional social structure even when they have moved away from the neighborhood that contained the life and values of that culture. For example, Orsi (1985) examined the social functions of an Italian religious feast in Spanish Harlem and found that one such function was the establishment of a symbolic bond between the generations that had little actual reality. Such persons were "men and women of severed memories: they remembered a time and a place they no longer even remotely inhabited" (p. 153). That this may be relevant to Puerto Rican culture is indicated by Rogler and Cooney's (1984) finding that although later generations were retaining a Puerto Rican ethnic identity, they were also moving away from or modifying many of the values of traditional Puerto Rican culture.

Thus, it is necessary not only to examine the ethnic identification made by members of the generations but also to look at the way family life is actually conducted between generations. Within the context of Puerto Rican families, this involves the interrelated questions of female gender roles and the extent to which the family has become more egalitarian, as would be the case if it accommodated to the American ideal of family structure. Similarly, a movement away from the extended and toward a more exclusive focus on the nuclear family would indicate an accommodation with American patterns of family life.

There is some indication that both on the island and in the United States the greater educational and occupational opportunities that are open to women in the nontraditional world have affected the power structure within family systems. As early as 1968, Weller found that island Puerto Rican women who were employed had more power than those who were not employed. Rogler and Procidano (1986) also found a movement toward a more modern egalitarian family. Rogler and Cooney (1984) found that whereas older women tended to identify the linear family as the main locus of satisfaction and concern, the younger women tended to identify with the spousal family for the same concerns, and Leavitt (1974) found that such women wanted a greater degree of mutual participation than might be found in the traditional family system.

The work of Cooney and associates (1982) provides some evidence that second-generation Puerto Ricans living in the United States have to some extent adopted a modern model of the family. Whereas men tend to have more power than women, they also tend to have higher socioeconomic achievements, indicating that resources have become the source of power. The authors interpret this finding to indicate that in America, the Puerto Rican family is in transition toward a more egalitarian arrangement. Moreover, a significantly greater percentage of members of the child generation studied by Rogler and Cooney (1984) shared household tasks—although even among the child generation only one third of the children reported sharing such tasks—and leisure time activities, seemingly indicating a loosening of the role distinctions between the genders. These authors further indicate that immigrant families differ from the island family model by a greater sharing of decision-making. Moreover, this change of attitude was characteristic of both men and women. This seems to indicate that the mainland Puerto Rican culture is much less dominated by the man than was the traditional culture of the island.

The relationship between the family and the outer world seems to be shifting along with the family's internal structure as the process of adapting to life in America progresses. Cooney and associates (1981) found that the younger generation of women expressed less of a familistic orientation than the older generation. This indicates that these younger women are less willing to retain the family as their primary area of activity and emotional affiliation. This study also documents a lessening of a pro-fertility norm, indicating an important change from the traditional values, although one that the authors note is also characteristic of contemporary island society. The loss of some dimensions of familistic values may also be demonstrated in the loss of the deferential acts connected with the value system of *respeto* on the mainland (Colleran 1984; Sánchez-Ayéndez 1984).

One aspect of this change involves a movement away from wholly familistic values. Thus, Rogler and Cooney (1984) found that whereas about one half of the parental generation believed that one should not move away from proximity to one's parents to obtain a better position, 70 percent of the second generation disagreed with this view. This finding indicates that the familistic value has been at least somewhat compromised by the more individualistic value system characteristic of the United States and the nontraditional world in general.

These changes, in general, are not limited to the mainland. As early as 1959 Brameld found that the long absences of migrant fathers tended to reduce the patriarchical orientation of island families; after fending for themselves while their husbands were on the mainland, Puerto Rican women and children were not able or did not want to return to the old family power structure.

On the other hand, Puerto Ricans living on the mainland still retain elements of the extended family. For example, among Puerto Ricans living in New York City, there is at least weekly intergenerational visiting in 77 percent of all cases, indicating that at least elements of the modified extended family pattern of the traditional model have been retained (Rogler and Cooney 1984). Moreover, such contacts had instrumental value, with members of both the parent and the child generations depending upon informal family relationships for help more than upon nonrelated peers or social agencies. The authors found that refraining from helping a relative in need is a source of guilt. This indicates that the personalistic value system has been retained, despite the other modifications that have occurred in the Puerto Rican family and Puerto Rican culture. This dependence upon the family exists even among those who are most educated.

More radical than the shift toward egalitarian family models, however, is the great increase in female-headed, matrifocal families in mainland Puerto Rican communities. Such families necessarily violate the norms of the traditional male and female roles and might be expected to raise considerable problems of social and psychological adjustment for those who continue to accept those norms. On the other hand, such patterns of family life have been found to be positive adjustments to the social conditions among some groups of the poor, both in the United States and in the Caribbean. Although such households exist, particularly among the poor, in Puerto Rico toward the latter part of the family life cycle (Safa 1974), significant numbers of families on the mainland have a single female–headed structure from the family's beginning or adopt this structure early in the family's history.

Several authors have argued against a positive interpretation of the trends. Peltro and associates (1982), for example, studying a Puerto Rican community in Hartford, Connecticut, found a significant correlation between female-headed families and unemployment. Mizio (1974) found that the increase in marital instability was in fact due to an inability to live up to the norms rather than to changing norms; because the Puerto Rican man is often unable to fulfill his normatively defined role as provider for the household, the temptation is great to act out the *machismo* norm in nontraditional ways that are unconstrained by traditional responsibilities. This tendency may in turn lead to conflict with women, who are not receiving the economic support traditionally provided by the men. This interpretation finds that an attempt to apply some of the traditional values to a new social ecology increases conflict and leads to further erosion of the culture.

Thus, the acculturation of the Puerto Rican family to its new situation in urban communities on the mainland is still in flux. Although the extended family structures continue to play an important role in providing informal support in difficult circumstances, the Puerto Rican family—the central institution of traditional Puerto Rican society—is changing and, particularly among the most poor, becoming more unstable. The reasons why this change—which is seemingly so inimical to the value system of the culture—is taking place are currently not well understood. It is quite possible that one factor involves the structure of the welfare system, which makes it difficult for a woman who is living with husband and children to get benefits. Under such circumstances, familial disintegration may—ironically—be a prerequisite to the survival of the family members. If the husband is unable to provide adequately for the family and if the family would be economically better off without his presence, his absence becomes more likely.

The traditional patriarchal value system and the inability of many Puerto Rican men to live up to the demands of this system on the mainland may provide a psychological dynamic that contributes to family instability. If the culture requires that a man provide security for his wife and children and that he represent them to the wider world, he is likely to feel strong self-doubt and anxiety when he is unable to fulfill these expectations. Under such circumstances, withdrawal from psychological identification with the family unit may be a means by which the man comes to reconcile his need to live up to the ideal of *machismo* with his inability to obtain a job with an adequate salary and his inability to protect his family from the problems of a harsh socioeconomic environment. He may emphasize the aspects of *machismo* that take him outside the family—the valorization of extramarital sexual conquests and maintaining a distance from what are perceived as "woman's affairs"—while downplaying the responsibilities of the traditional male role as provider and protector.

A similar dynamic among blacks has been identified by Liebow (1967) in a classic account of street-corner life among black men. Liebow's research indicated that the marital instability characteristic of the men he studied did not stem from their rejection of the traditional husband role as much as from a sense of inadequacy that derived from their self-perceived inability to fulfill that role. Rather than face what they considered to be their own failure as men, they adopted a stance that made it impossible to sustain long-standing relationships. Given the very strong traditional view of marriage that is encouraged in Puerto Rican society, one might expect that such a pattern would also develop in that society. This is a major issue that demands more attention by students of the Puerto Rican family.

CONCLUSION

Placed in a difficult circumstance of poverty and cultural alienation, the Puerto Rican family has had to adapt to radically new conditions, and it inevitably has changed as emigrants have struggled to survive and live satisfying lives after leaving their homeland. These struggles are continuing, and it can be expected that change will continue to occur in the coming years. Puerto Ricans, both on the mainland and in Puerto Rico, have had to adapt traditional social norms, including those involving the family, to changed circumstances. Still, the old tradition retains its influence. Although the Puerto Rican family has come to conform to some extent to the dominant modern model of the family, its greater emphasis on familistic—albeit modified familistic—values distinguishes it from the mainstream North American family. Thus, as in other areas of life and culture, the Puerto Rican family has established a value system and modes of behavior that encompass elements of both cultures.

It must be noted, however, that the Puerto Rican mainland culture has not been established once and for all. As the Puerto Rican middle class continues to grow and as the march of generations proceeds, one can expect to see continuing change. It is difficult to predict exactly how such change will occur. The study of the Puerto Rican family thus can be expected to remain an important area of investigation as its development is traced over time.

REFERENCES

Bastida, E. 1979. "Family Integration and Adjustment to Aging among Hispanic American Elderly." Unpublished doctoral dissertation, University of Kansas.

Blatt, Irwin B. 1979. *A Study of Culture Change in Modern Puerto Rico,* Palo Alto, CA: R & R Research Associates.

Brameld, T. 1959. *Remaking of a Culture.* New York: Harper.

Colleran, K. 1984. "Acculturation in Puerto Rican Families in New York City." *Research Bulletin,* Hispanic Research Center, Fordham University 7:2–7.

Committee on the Post Office and Civil Service, United States Commerce. 1986. *Selected Demographic Characteristics of the United States Hispanic Population and of Hispanic Subgroups.* Washington, DC: U.S. Government Printing Office.

Cooney, R. S., R. M. Hurrel, and V. Ortiz. 1982. "Decision Making in Intergenerational Puerto Rican Families." *Journal of Marriage and the Family* 44:621–631.

Cooney, R. S., L. H. Rogler, and E. Schroder. 1981. "Puerto Rican Fertility: An Examination of Social Characteristics, Assimilation, and Minority Status Variables." *Social Forces* 59:1094–1113.

Fitzpatrick, J. 1971. *Puerto Rican Americans: The Meaning of Migration to the Mainland.* Englewood Cliffs, NJ: Prentice-Hall.

Fitzpatrick, J., and D. T. Gurak. 1979. *Hispanic Intermarriage in New York City: 1975.* New York: Fordham University, Hispanic Research Center.

Fitzpatrick, J., and J. P. Fitzpatrick. 1982. "Intermarriage among Hispanic Ethnic Groups in New York City." *American Journal of Sociology* 87:921–934.

Gurak, D. T., and L. H. Rogler. 1980. "Hispanic Settlement in New York: Work, Settlement and Adjustment." *Research Bulletin,* Hispanic Research Center, Fordham University 3:5–8.

Landy, D. 1959. *Tropical Childhood.* Chapel Hill: University of North Carolina Press.

Leavitt, R. R. 1974. *The Puerto Ricans: Cultural Change and Language Deviance.* Tucson: University of Arizona Press.

Liebow, Elliot. 1967. *Tally's Corner.* Boston: Little, Brown.

Mintz, S. W. 1966. "Puerto Rico: An Essay in the Definition of a National Culture." In *Selected Background Papers.* San Juan: Puerto Rico Commission on the Status of Puerto Rico.

Mizio, E. 1974. "Impact of External Systems on the Puerto Rican Family." *Social Casework* 55:76–83.

Mussen, P., and L. Beytagh. 1969. "Industrialization, Child Rearing Practices and Children's Personality." *The Journal of Genetic Psychology* 115:195–216.

Orsi, R. A. 1985. *The Madonna of 115th Street.* New Haven: Yale University Press.

Padilla, E. 1958. *Up from Puerto Rico.* New York: Columbia University Press.

Padilla, F. M. 1987. *Puerto Rican Chicago.* Notre Dame, IN: University of Notre Dame Press.

Peltro, P. J., M. Roman, and N. Liriano. 1982. "Family Structures in an Urban Puerto Rican Community." *Urban Anthropology* 11:39–57.

Rogler, L. H., and R. S. Cooney. 1984. *Puerto Rican Families in New York: Intergenerational Processes.* Maplewood, NJ: Waterfront Press.

Rogler, L. H., R. S., Cooney, and V. Ortiz. 1982. "Intergenerational Change in Ethnic Identity in the Puerto Rican Family." *International Migration Review* 14:193–213.

Rogler, L. H., and M. E. Procidano. 1986. "The Effect of Social Networks on Marital Roles: A Test of the Bott Hypothesis in an Intergenerational Context." *Journal of Marriage and the Family* 48:693–701.

Safa, H. I. 1974. *The Urban Poor of Puerto Rico.* New York: Holt, Rinehart and Winston.

Sánchez-Ayéndez, M. 1984. "Puerto Rican Elderly Women: Aging in an Ethnic Minority Group in the United States." Unpublished Doctoral Dissertation, University of Massachusetts at Amherst.

———. 1988. "Puerto Ricans in the United States." In *Ethnic Families in America,* edited by C. Mintel, R. Habenstein, and R. Wright. New York: Elsevier.

Stevens, E. P. 1973. "Marianismo: The Other Face of Machismo in Latin America." In *Female and Male in Latin America,* edited by A. Pescatello. Pittsburgh: University of Pittsburgh Press.

Stycos. J. M. 1952. "Family and Fertility in Puerto Rico." *American Sociological Review* 17:572–580.

————. 1955. *Family and Fertility in Puerto Rico.* New York: Columbia University Press.

Szapocznik, J., and W. Kurtines, 1979. "Acculturation, Biculturalism, and Adjustment among Urban Americans." In *Acculturation: Theory, Models and Some New Findings,* edited by A. M. Padilla. Boulder, CO: Westview Press.

Tumin, M. M., and A. S. Feldman. 1971. *Social Class and Social Change in Puerto Rico,* 2nd ed. Indianapolis: Bobbs-Merrill.

U.S. Bureau of the Census. 1990. Current Population Reports, Series P-20, No. 444, *The Hispanic Population in the United States: March, 1989.* Washington, DC: U.S. Government Printing Office.

Vázquez Calzada, J. L. 1978. *La Población de Puerto Rico y su Trayectoria Histórica.* San Juan: Escuela de Salud Pública, Universidad de Puerto Rico.

Weller, R. H. 1968. "The Employment of Wives, Dominance and Fertility." *Journal of Marriage and the Family* 30:437–442.

Wells, H. 1972. *La Modernización de Puerto Rico.* Rio Piedras, Puerto Rico: Editorial Universitaria.

CHAPTER 6

Cuban American Families

Lisandro Pérez

An estimated 1,035,000 persons of Cuban origin or descent live in the United States (U.S. Bureau of the Census 1988). Most of that population was born in Cuba, arriving in the United States after 1959, the year that a process of revolutionary change was initiated in the island. Profound in its scope and pervasiveness, that revolution prompted a massive exodus that has resulted in the creation during the past three decades of the third-largest single nationality group among U.S. Hispanics.

The exiles from revolutionary Cuba do not, however, constitute the first community of Cubans established in the United States. Migration from the island to this country has a long history, an understandable phenomenon given the proximity of the two nations and their interlocking histories.

THE CUBAN FAMILY IN THE EARLY COMMUNITIES

Starting in the 1830s, Cuban nationalism was taking shape, and so was a sense of rebellion against Spanish colonial authority.[1] One consequence of that process was the start of the first politically motivated migrations from Cuba to the United States. The destination was usually New York, although New Orleans also emerged as an important community, especially during the 1840s and 1850s.

Aside from their political activism, little is known about those first Cuban communities in the United States. In comparison with later waves, their numbers were relatively small. The New York Cuban community probably did not exceed 3,000 persons at midcentury (Pérez 1985a:25). Its most prominent members formed part of the intellectual elite of the island, who found themselves persecuted in Cuba by an increasingly repressive Spanish colonial government. Many probably arrived without their families and, as with most political exiles, intended to return to the island at the first opportunity.

The outbreak in 1868 of a long and bloody insurrection against Spanish authority in the island dramatically increased the number of Cubans migrating to the United States. Among the exiles were prominent cigar manufacturers, who found it difficult to maintain production in the midst of the turmoil.

Relocating to Key West, New York, and later to Ybor City, on the outskirts of Tampa, Florida, the manufacturers established factories that attracted cigar workers from the island. Ybor City, named after the cigar manufacturer who established it in 1886, became a Cuban "company town" centered entirely on the production of cigars. It quickly became the largest Cuban community in the United States and remained so until its decline in the 1930s (Pérez 1983:20).

The Cuban family in the Florida cigar-making communities of Ybor City and Key West was heavily influenced by the peculiar conditions of migration from Cuba. The skills of cigar-making were learned by men, and although certain types of employment were reserved for women, the Florida cigar factories attracted primarily men from the island. According to the figures from the U.S. censuses taken from 1900 to 1930, the gender ratio (number of men for every 100 women) of the Cuban-born population of the United States never dropped below 120. Furthermore, immigration statistics for each year from 1911 to 1932 show that 70 to 80 percent of all Cuban men entering the United States during those years were single.

A contributing factor to the high proportion of single men in the Cuban cigar-making communities was the temporary nature of much of the migration. Given the proximity to Cuba and the absence of immigration restrictions, many cigar workers were literally migrant laborers, crossing and recrossing the Florida Strait. Single men can be expected to predominate in such temporary migration streams.

Most of the chronicles of Key West and Ybor City, however, seem to indicate that despite the presence of a large transitory male population, the core of the community was composed of families who lived there continuously for generations. Apparently, it remained into the twentieth century a fairly traditional family system. The insular "company town" structure of Ybor City and the constant contact with the nearby homeland retarded considerably the process of acculturation. Traditional patterns brought from Cuba tended to persist.

There is evidence, for example, that many households contained extended and multigenerational families. In addition, one of the themes consistently found in accounts of the community is the importance of the double standard of morality. Its manifestations were the strict parental supervision of the courtship behavior of unmarried women and the differences between genders in adherence to norms regarding marital fidelity (Federal Writers' Project 1939:305, 344).

The double standard of morality formed part of a strong patriarchal tradition that Cuban immigrants brought with them from the island's colonial society.[2] It was a tradition that was reflected in, and protected by, the Spanish Civil Code, which was in effect in Cuba even after the end of Spanish colonial rule in 1898 (Pérez 1980:238).

The Code had two outstanding interrelated features with respect to family matters: the placing of private property rights in the hands of men and the absolute authority granted to the head of the family. The husband, for example, was designated the head and administrator of the community property and was given broad discretionary powers to manage and dispose of the property without the consent of the wife. The woman had "domain" over her half but could not commit or donate that property in any way without the approval of the husband. The Spanish Code also gave the father sole *patria potestas* over the children, but the mother could exercise it only in his absence (Camus 1924:38–39).

The Civil Code also specified that although adultery was a legitimate cause for divorce, it was not to be applied equally to both genders: "The adultery of the wife in any case, and of the husband when it results in a public scandal, or the neglect of the wife." (Betancourt 1934:93)

There were complicated provisions regarding legitimacy, all intended to make clear distinctions between "legitimate," "illegitimate," and "natural" children. One provision even guaranteed the right of a husband or his legitimate heirs to take legal action against the claims of legitimacy made by an offspring born during the 300 days following the dissolution or legal separation of the marriage. The long and elaborate clauses that regulated inheritance included the restriction that a widow could not remarry during the 301 days following the death of her husband (Camus 1924:31).

The Spanish Civil Code gave legal support to the patriarchal social and economic system that predominated in colonial Cuba. It was the system that Cuban migrants to the Florida cigar-making communities brought with them.

By the 1930s, the Cuban communities in Key West and Ybor City were declining. The compelling economic and political factors that had led to their establishment decades earlier were no longer present. The center of the Cuban cigar-making industry shifted back to Havana, and many of the cigar-makers returned there from Florida (Pérez 1986a).

THE CUBAN REVOLUTION OF 1959 AND CUBAN MIGRATION TO THE UNITED STATES

In 1959, a process was initiated that in a few years would totally alter Cuba's social, economic, and political institutions. The government that rose to power in that year rapidly transformed a dependent capitalist economic system, closely intertwined with the United States, into a centrally planned system presumably guided by Marxist-Leninist principles, in conflict with the United States and in close alliance with and dependence on the Soviet Union.[3]

Such a radical transformation and its consequences for the daily lives of the entire population prompted an unprecedented exodus from the island to the United States. Never before in the long history of Cuban migration to the United States had the flow of persons attained the levels reached in the three decades that followed 1959.

The size of that postrevolutionary migration has fluctuated greatly, primarily in response to the availability of the means to leave Cuba. Three major waves occurred during three distinct time periods: (1) 1959 to 1962, when regular commercial air traffic moved between the United States and Cuba; (2) 1965 to 1973, the years during which an airlift, or "freedom flights," operated between Cuba and Miami; and (3) nine months in 1980, when the notorious Mariel boatlift took place (Pérez 1986b: 129–131). In all, it is estimated that more than one million persons have left the island, representing one tenth of the total Cuban population.

Emigration from socialist Cuba has traditionally been viewed as a class phenomenon, one that has been described as a successive "peeling-off," starting at the top, of the layers of the prerevolutionary class structure (Pérez 1984:17). Although this socioeconomic selectivity has frequently been overstated, it is evident that during the first wave, in the early 1960s, Cuba's upper socioeconomic sectors, those most likely to be alienated by the elimination of a capitalist system and the severing of ties with the United States, were overrepresented in the exodus (Fagen and others 1968:19).

Furthermore, the Cuba of 1959 was not the Cuba of the nineteenth century that the migrants to Ybor City and Key West had left. Largely because of the influence of the United States, Cuba underwent a rapid modernization process during the first half of the twentieth century. Urbanization occurred at a rapid pace, fertility and mortality dropped sharply, per capita income was relatively high, and consumer goods from the United States were widely available (Díaz-Briquets 1983; Díaz-Briquets and Pérez 1981; International Bank for Reconstruction and Development 1951:35–42; Marrero 1987). Neolocality was the norm, and a transition was underway from the stereotypical patriarchal marriage to one based more on egalitarianism and companionship (Aguirre 1981:400). These indicators of modernization were not equally evident throughout the social class system, but it was precisely the most modernized sector of prerevolutionary Cuban society that participated massively in the postrevolutionary exodus.

The modernization of twentieth-century Cuba was manifested in the family-related legislation enacted, which significantly altered and liberalized the old Spanish Civil Code. A 1930 law, for example, added "mutual consent" to the list of valid grounds for divorce and permitted the granting of divorces simply upon the request of both parties (República de Cuba 1939:2189–2193).

The 1940 Constitution (section 1, title 5) included a clause that reaffirmed a married woman's full civil status, recognizing her right to exercise freely "commerce, industry, profession or occupation without marital license or authorization," as well as to dispose freely of the fruits of her labor. The Constitution also abolished "all classifications based upon the nature of filiation" (República de Cuba 1963:14–15).

A 1950 law introduced the following reforms: (1) *patria potestas* was to be exercised jointly by the father and the mother; (2) spouses were designated joint administrators of the community property, and one could not dispose of the property without the consent of the other; and (3) in a broad and sweeping clause, the law abrogated any existing provisions that in any way diminished equality between men and women (República de Cuba 1950:27553–27554).

These progressive family statutes reflected a society that by midcentury had reached a level of modernization at the vanguard of most of Latin America. The more privileged and modernized segments of that society formed the catalyst and the core of the postrevolutionary exodus to the United States. This is a phenomenon that cannot be emphasized enough in any attempt to understand the Cuban family in the United States and the ways in which it is fairly unique among immigrant families and Hispanic families in this country.

CHARACTERISTICS OF CUBANS AND CUBAN FAMILIES IN THE UNITED STATES

Data from the Decennial Censuses and the Current Population Surveys conducted by the U.S. Bureau of the Census have yielded a fairly clear profile of the sociodemographic characteristics of the Cuban population of this country and of the composition of the family unit.[4] That profile is presented in this section, and the most significant indicators are summarized in Table 1.

Place of Residence

Overwhelmingly, Cubans in the United States are urbanites; about 98 percent live in urban areas. More importantly, they are increasingly concentrating in one metropolitan area: Greater Miami. In the 1980s, about 55 percent of all U.S. Cubans lived in southern Florida, whereas a decade earlier only about 40 percent lived there. Two other fairly large concentrations of Cubans are found in Greater New York and Los Angeles.

One reason for the concentration in Miami has been the creation there of the best example in the United States of a true ethnic enclave. Established primarily by the Cuban exiles of the first wave, it is a community characterized by high levels of entrepreneurship. Miami's Hispanics have a much higher per capita rate of busi-

TABLE 1.   Selected Family-related Characteristics of the Cuban, Mexican, Puerto Rican, and Total U.S. Populations

CHARACTERISTICS	CUBAN	MEXICAN	PUERTO RICAN	TOTAL U.S.
Percent of all women 15 years of age and over divorced	9.3	6.5	9.0	7.3
Percent of all persons under 18 living with two parents	78.1	74.8	50.9	76.7
Percent of all families headed by women, no husband present	14.9	16.4	35.3	14.3
Number of mother-child subfamilies per 1,000 families	10.0	24.8	17.5	13.3
Percent of all persons 65 and over who are "other relatives" of the head of the household	30.7	16.7	20.2	8.9
Percent of all persons 65 and over who live in group quarters, including inmates of institutions	1.3	3.5	2.8	5.9

Source: U.S. Bureau of the Census (1983b:167).

ness ownership than any other Hispanic community in the United States. Business ownership, in a wide variety of sales and services—including professional services—has made it possible for Cubans to create an institutionally complete ethnic community in which the immigrant can live out the entirely of his or her life.[5]

Such a unique ethnic enclave has a number of important implications for the Cuban community in the United States. It has served as a magnet, drawing Cubans from throughout the country as well as the recent arrivals from the island. The enclave has special consequences for the processes of acculturation and assimilation as well as for interethnic relations; it provides the new immigrant with employment opportunities within a familiar culture and language, and it is linked with high rates of female labor participation, as discussed later.

Age and Gender Composition

As was true with the Cuban communities of Ybor City and Key West, immigrant populations tend to be young and composed primarily of men. Not so with the exodus from socialist Cuba, which has included an unusually high proportion of middle-aged and elderly persons. Prior to the Mariel boatlift of 1980—in which men predominated—women outnumbered men in the migration stream from Cuba.

The median age of U.S. Cubans is 39 years (compared with 32 for the total U.S. population). Whereas about 37 percent of the U.S. population was 40 years of age and over in 1988, the corresponding percentage among Cubans was 49. Focusing exclusively on those 65 and over, the percentage for the population of U.S. Cubans in those ages was nearly 13. In the United States as a whole, 12 percent were over 65.

The 1980 U.S. Census, taken prior to the Mariel boatlift, showed a gender ratio (number of men for every 100 women) of 90.8, much lower than the ratio for the total U.S. population (94.5). The figure for the Mexican-origin population was 103.4. Recent figures show that the Mariel boatlift has had the effect of balancing somewhat the ratio for Cubans.

These age and gender characteristics are understandable only in the context of the conditions of Cuban emigration. The Cuban government has prohibited (except during the boatlift) the emigration of men of military age. That restriction had a particular impact on the age and gender composition of the migrants arriving between 1965 and 1973 through the airlift. It caused an extraordinarily low gender ratio (82.3) among those who were between 25 and 40 years of age in 1980. This shortage of male immigrants has had obvious implications for the possibilities for Cuban women to marry within the ethnic group, a special problem during the 1970s, when that cohort was in the prime marital ages.

The high proportions of elderly and middle-aged persons among U.S. Cubans are also rooted in the conditions of migration. During the 1960s, young families, with household heads in their late 20s and early 30s, predominated in the exodus. These are the middle-aged Cubans of the 1980s. The elderly were probably the age group most alienated by the sweeping changes introduced by the Cuban revolution. Because this age group was largely a dependent population, the Cuban government facilitated its departure, especially during the airlift (Queralt 1983:51).

The proportions of the elderly and the middle-aged are also boosted by the relatively small proportion of children. Only 16 percent of the Cuban population of the United States in 1988 was under 16 years of age (compared with 24 percent in the total U.S. population). The explanation for this finding, of course, is a low birth rate.

Fertility

The 1980 U.S. Census showed that in every maternal age category, the number of children born to Cuban women is extraordinarily low in comparison with all other Hispanic groups in the United States. Furthermore, the level of reproduction of Cuban women is not only below that of all U.S. women, but even below the levels of white women living in U.S. metropolitan areas.

This very low level of fertility is of great importance in understanding the composition of the Cuban household in the United States. It is the reason why, on average, Cuban families are smaller than other families in the United States and much smaller than other Hispanic families.

In explaining this low birthrate among Cuban women, it is important to keep in mind the earlier discussion regarding the levels of modernization Cuba had reached by the 1950s and the fact that the Cuban exodus drew disproportionately from the most modernized sectors of that society. Cuba's birthrate continues to be one of the lowest of this hemisphere.

An additional factor contributing to the low birthrate among Cubans is the importance placed on upward mobility in the United States and the high rates of labor force participation among Cuban women. Both factors are examined later.

Marital Status and Intermarriage

Reflecting a population in which middle-aged and elderly persons predominate, the marital status of U.S. Cubans shows relatively high proportions of married, divorced, and widowed persons, with a correspondingly low percentage of persons who have never been married.

A high proportion of divorced persons is especially evident among women, as shown in the first row of Table 1. Although this circumstance may well be the result of a high divorce rate, it may also reflect the relative disadvantage that a divorced Cuban woman faces if she wishes to remarry within the group, given the numerical abundance—noted earlier—of women in the cohort that is now roughly between the ages of 35 and 50. The usual gap between the genders in the percentage who are divorced is especially pronounced among Cubans.

The imbalance between the genders in certain age groups may also have had an impact on the incidence of intermarriage. Some studies have shown that Cubans, in comparison with other Hispanic groups in the United States, are most likely to marry outside their particular group (Boswell and Curtis 1983:183; Fitzpatrick and Gurak 1979:25).

Although high rates of intermarriage are frequently accepted as indicators of a rapid rate of assimilation, it may well be that in the case of Cuban women, intermarriage—especially in the 1970s—was a response to an unfavorable "marriage market" within their ethnic group due to the lopsided gender ratio.

Household Composition

The Cuban population of the United States exhibits a unique sociodemographic profile, shaped by an unusual set of circumstances. It is therefore not surprising that it shows a family structure substantially different from that of many other ethnic families. The data from the U.S. Bureau of the Census on household composition illustrate those differences.

The data in Table 1 present a fairly clear picture of the Cuban family in the United States. Solely for comparative purposes, the figures on Mexicans and Puerto Ricans living in the United States are presented, as well as data on the total U.S. population.

It is interesting that among Cubans, the high proportion of divorced women does not translate itself into family characteristics usually associated with a high divorce rate. Compared with the other groups in Table 1, Cubans have (1) the highest proportion of children under 18 living with both parents; (2) a fairly low percentage of families headed by women with no husband present; and (3) the lowest incidence of mother-child subfamilies (that is, mother and child residing within a larger family).

One interpretation for this combination of features is that the divorced Cuban woman returns to her parents' household but, because of the low level of fertility, she is not likely to be accompanied by children. A hypothesis consistent with those figures is that childless couples are much more likely to divorce than couples with children. Given the low level of fertility, the divorce rate could be maintained at fairly high levels even if it is being inhibited by the presence of children.

One of the most distinctive features of the Cuban family in the United States is the relatively widespread existence of the three-generation family. The last two lines in Table 1 verify this phenomenon. Compared with the other groups in the table, the Cuban elderly are much more likely to be classified as "other relatives" of the head of the household. "Other relatives" are those who are neither the spouse nor the children of the head of the household. For persons 65 and over, it is reasonable to assume that these are the parents or parents-in-law of the head. Of all the populations shown in the table, the Cuban elderly are least likely to be heads of households and much more likely to live with their children. They are also less likely, as the figures in Table 1 demonstrate, to live in "group quarters," which include nursing homes.

Clearly, a relatively large number of Cuban elderly are residing in household arrangements that are not typical for the rest of the elderly in the United States. This phenomenon can be traced primarily to cultural norms and values regarding the care of the elderly. Many Cubans believe it is disgraceful to have a widowed parent living alone or in a nursing home. Furthermore, because most of the Cuban elderly arrived in this country past their working ages, they were in an especially vulnerable situation in adjusting to life in this country, both economically and culturally. It would have been difficult to face that adjustment as heads of house-holds.

One result of the importance of the three-generation family among U.S. Cubans is that the Cuban community thus far has not created the need for facilities to house and care for the dependent elderly, at least not to the degree that we would expect in a population with so many older persons. This situation is likely to start changing rapidly, however. As noted previously, a very large proportion of Cubans in the United States are between the ages of 40 and 60. Those in the relatively large middle-aged cohort are the middle generation of the three-generation family. In the next few years they will begin swelling the ranks of the elderly. By century's end, Cubans over 65 will nearly double in number. It is not clear whether they and their children, most of whom were born in the United States, will adhere to the val-ues that have thus far reinforced the maintenance of the three-generation family.

The aging of the Cuban population of the United States will also accelerate the process, noted earlier, toward greater concentration of Cubans in South Florida. That large middle-aged group also composed the bulk of the resettlements away from Miami implemented by the U.S. government during the 1960s and early 1970s. It can be reasonably expected that of those who have not already returned to Miami, many will do so when they retire.

THE FAMILY AND THE CUBAN SUCCESS STORY

Cubans in the United States are frequently regarded as an immigrant group that has achieved tremendous economic success. Although the Cuban "success story" is largely a stereotype that oversimplifies the complexities and diversity of the eco-nomic adjustment of Cuban immigrants, it does have some basis in the data avail-able from the U.S. Bureau of the Census.

Consistently, Cubans have exhibited economic characteristics that reflect a more prosperous population than other U.S. minority and immigrant groups. For literally every measure of family income, Cubans evidence levels superior to those of the rest of the Spanish-origin population, levels that are only slightly below the corresponding measure for the total U.S. population. In other words, a greater gap exists between the general Spanish-origin population and Cubans than between Cubans and the total U.S. population. This pattern is true for median family in-come as well as the proportion living below the poverty level.

The relative economic success of U.S. Cubans cannot be fully understood with-out taking into consideration the economic organization of the Cuban family, an organization that facilitates upward social mobility. Data on individual—not fam-ily—income suggest that the Cubans' comparatively high family income is largely not the result of high individual income. This point can be examined further with data on family income according to the number of workers in the family (Table 2). Focusing, for example, on families with just one worker, one finds that the median income of Cuban families is not much higher than for the total Spanish-origin population, and it is substantially below the income of all U.S. families, a very dif-ferent situation than is observed with data on family income. In other words, when

TABLE 2. Median Family Income by Number of Workers in Family: Cuban,
           Spanish-Origin, and Total U.S. Populations, 1979

	CUBAN	TOTAL SPANISH-ORIGIN	TOTAL U.S.
No workers	$4,440	$4,349	$7,791
One worker	$12,629	$11,153	$16,181
Two workers	$20,732	$18,570	$23,058
Three or more workers	$28,620	$26,394	$31,880

Source: U.S. Bureau of the Census (1983b:167).

we control for number of workers in the family, the difference between the median income of Cuban and U.S. families widens, and the level of the former draws much closer to the median family income of all Hispanics.

In Table 3, the key to the Cubans' relatively high family income levels is apparent: they, quite simply, have proportionately more workers per family than both the Hispanic and the U.S. populations. This feature is especially apparent among families with three or more workers. Comparatively few Cuban families have just one worker. Consistent with this observation is the finding, also derived from the 1980 U.S. Census, that among persons 16 years of age and above, the Cuban-origin population has higher rates of labor force participation than other Hispanics and the U.S. population in general (U.S. Bureau of the Census 1983b:167).

The relatively large number of workers per family and the higher rates of labor force participation among Cubans can be traced primarily to the levels of female employment. Compared with other Hispanic women and with the female population of the United States (16 and over), Cuban women are more likely to be in the labor force, as clearly shown by the figures in Table 4. Not only are Cuban women more likely to be working, but they are also more likely to be working full-time year-round. Furthermore, the substantial gap between the labor force participation rates of Cuban women and the other two populations remains unaltered when one focuses on married women with husband present and on married women with husband present and young children.

The last row in Table 4 is an extraordinary set of figures that demonstrates the economic importance of the high rates of labor force participation of young Cuban mothers. The median income of married-couple families with children

TABLE 3. Percent Distribution according to Number of Workers in Family: Cuban,
           Spanish-Origin, and U.S. Families, 1979

	CUBAN	TOTAL SPANISH-ORIGIN	TOTAL U.S.
All families	100.0	100.0	100.0
No workers	10.4	12.6	12.8
One worker	28.5	35.0	33.0
Two workers	42.5	38.5	41.7
Three or more workers	18.6	13.9	12.5

Source: U.S. Bureau of the Census (1983b:167).

TABLE 4. Selected Labor Force and Income Characteristics of the Cuban, Spanish-Origin, and Total U.S. Populations, 1979

	CUBAN	TOTAL SPANISH-ORIGIN	TOTAL U.S.
Percent of all women 16 and over in the labor force	55.4	49.3	49.9
Of all women 16 and over in the labor force, percent employed full-time year-round	47.1	37.4	40.1
Percent in labor force of all married women 16 and over with husband present	58.9	48.3	49.2
Percent in labor force of all married women 16 and over with husband present and own children under 6 years of age	50.5	43.0	43.9
Median income of married-couple families with own children under 6 years of age	$20,334	$15,219	$19,630

Source: U.S. Bureau of the Census (1983b:167).

under 6 years of age is actually higher among Cubans than it is in the total U.S. population.

The high incidence of labor force participation among Cuban women in the United States should not be interpreted as an indication of widespread egalitarianism in gender-role definitions. Although there has probably been a trend toward modernization of the relationship between the genders in Cuban households in the United States, research has shown that in the Cuban community, high rates of female labor force participation coexist with fairly traditional gender-role orientations. Female employment is still viewed largely as purely instrumental in assisting and furthering the family's economic status (Ferree 1979:44–45; Prieto 1987:85). This view is consistent with the findings of Ortiz and Cooney (1984) that gender-role attitudes are not important in explaining the labor force behavior of Hispanic women.

Two factors, previously analyzed, facilitate the high rates of labor force participation among Cuban women: low fertility and the three-generation family. Low levels of reproduction facilitate female employment and upward social mobility. The elderly members of the household contribute to the economic welfare of the family. Their most obvious contribution is to serve as caretakers for their grandchildren, thereby facilitating the employment of their daughter or daughter-in-law.

The Cuban elderly also help to further the household's economic position through direct contributions of the family's income. Aside from the possibility of income through gainful employment, financial contributions may derive from Social Security or public assistance income. Although, as Queralt (1983:55–56) notes, the income that elderly Cubans receive from those sources is relatively limited (recent immigrants are not likely, for example, to draw heavily from Social Security), the fact that a high proportion of those elderly persons live with their children means that the funds that they do receive from those sources contribute to raising the income of the three-generation household in which they reside.

Although the three-generation family among Cubans is undoubtedly a product of the group's norms and values, the practice is reinforced and maintained by its economic functionality, providing a mechanism for the contribution of the elderly to the family's socioeconomic status and mobility.

Further evidence that the Cuban family is structured to facilitate social mobility is provided by one additional result of the 1980 U.S. Census: Cubans under 35 years of age exhibit rates of school enrollment that are superior to the enrollment figures for the total U.S. and Spanish-origin populations (U.S. Bureau of the Census 1983b:163). This process occurs despite the fact, mentioned earlier, that the Cuban family has, compared with those other populations, a significantly higher number of workers. In terms of school enrollment, it should also be added that, consistent with the high rates of female labor force participation, Cuban children 3 and 4 years of age exhibit far higher rates of school enrollment than preschoolers in the other two populations (U.S. Bureau of the Census 1983b:163).

Cubans can be said, then, to have a "family work ethic." As such, the Cuban "success story," at least at the individual level, has been overstated. The key to the economic achievements of Cuban immigrants lies in the apparently high degree of economic cooperation within the family. It is a family whose principal economic characteristics are tailored to facilitate upward mobility: a relatively large number of workers, high rates of female employment, the presence of an elderly generation that contributes directly and indirectly to the household's economic welfare, low fertility, and high levels of school enrollment.

MARITAL INSTABILITY

The high proportion of divorced women among U.S. Cubans, noted earlier, merits closer attention. As noted before, that high proportion may be, in part, the result of the low rate of remarriage among Cuban women due to an unfavorable marriage market created by the numerical imbalance between the genders.

Marriages among U.S. Cubans, however, may be subject to particular pressures that lead to higher rates of marital conflict and dissolution. One such pressure originates precisely in the success orientation and family work ethic that have resulted in high rates of female labor force participation. It is likely that definitions of the male role have not totally adjusted to the realities of female employment so as to permit greater sharing of household tasks. Consequently, Cuban women have the double burden of employment and domestic responsibilities (Yanez 1986:11A). This situation, of course, is not unique to Cubans. But it is likely that, compared with the norms in the dominant society, the male role has remained somewhat more traditional among Cubans, whereas the expectations of the performance of women in domestic tasks has remained fairly high. This arrangement, of course, creates a structural condition conducive to marital conflict.

Another factor that places pressures on the marriages of U.S. Cubans has been the process of adjustment to a new society. Although this pressure is typical among immigrants, Cubans are immigrants who felt compelled to leave their homeland. As reluctant immigrants, they have experienced special problems in their psychosocial adjustment to the new country. Given the traditional socioeconomic selectivity of the exodus, many likely experienced drastic downward mobility in the migration process. Thus, they may have redefined marital relations, creating stress in the relationship.

ACCULTURATION, THE NEW GENERATION, AND SOCIAL CHANGE

Many signs indicate that U.S. Cubans retain the culture of their home country to a high degree. Rogg and Cooney (1980:49), for example, found that although some acculturation has taken place, the bulk of their respondents could still be categorized as "mostly Cuban" on a scale of cultural assimilation. They also found that a majority were "below average" in their ability to speak English, a finding supported by a later survey that found that most Cubans use only Spanish at home and in many of their daily activities (Díaz 1980:48–50).

In Dade County, Florida, where Cubans account for a majority of the foreign-born population, 43 percent of its residents were found by the 1980 U.S. Census to speak a language other than English at home. Of those who speak a foreign language at home, one-third indicated that they speak English "not well or not at all" (U.S. Bureau of the Census 1983b:163).

Retention of the language and cultural patterns of the country of origin is not surprising. The overwhelming majority of U.S. Cubans are immigrants, with an overrepresentation of the middle-aged and elderly. The bulk of the population arrived in this country only within the past three decades. In relative terms, it is a fairly recent immigrant group.

The creation of an institutionally complete enclave in Miami has retarded the processes of acculturation and assimilation because the enclave serves to insulate the immigrant from the dominant culture. Another factor, especially important in the early stages of the exodus, is the perception that many U.S. Cubans have of themselves as reluctant migrants, compelled to leave their country, but with the expectation of returning and consequently with little desire or motivation to assimilate into this society.

It is also important to remember that there have been periodic waves of massive arrivals from Cuba, the largest and most recent of which was the Mariel boatlift. The new arrivals are fresh from the culture of origin, and they renew and reinforce that culture within the immigrant community.

Despite these strong forces favoring cultural retention, the Cuban community in the United States is not likely to be an exception to the usual intergenerational shift toward greater acculturation and assimilation. English is the principal language among Cubans who have lived all or most of their lives in the United States. Szapocznik and others (1978) found sharp intergenerational differences among U.S. Cubans in the level of acculturation, with early adolescents demonstrating the highest scores of all age groups in measures of behavioral acculturation. Furthermore, males evidence greater acculturation than females. An exaggerated acculturational gap is a major source of intergenerational conflicts. Alienation between parents and children is usually found in Cuban families with interactional problems (Kurtines and Miranda 1980:181–182; Szapocznik and others 1978:42–44).

An important focus of intergenerational tensions is the conflicting value orientation with respect to dependence and independence (Bernal 1982:197). Cuban culture foments the continued dependence of children on their parents, even in the teenage years and beyond. Children, however, are more likely to have internalized the norms of independence commonly found in U.S. society.

One adaptation that reduces intergenerational tension is "biculturality," by which each generation adjusts to the other generation's cultural preferences. In the words of Szapocznik and Hernandez (1988:168), "parents learn how to remain loyal to their ethnic background while becoming skilled in interacting with their youngsters' Americanized values and behaviors, and vice versa."

Acculturation is evident in the changes in paternal supervision over the courtship behavior of unmarried women. In the early years of the Cuban exodus, in the 1960s, many of the norms brought from Cuba requiring strict supervision were clearly being followed. The use of chaperons, such as the mother, grandmother, or a younger sibling of the woman, was widespread. In time, this practice gave way to the "double date," by which a measure of supervision acceptable to the woman's parents was presumably provided by another couple.

At present, it is probably safe to say that the "single date" predominates, although substantial supervision and concern over the premarital behavior of young women continue. It is likely that, compared with the norm in American society, Cuban women probably start dating at a somewhat later age. To a large extent, the double standard of morality is still very evident among Cubans in the United States.

CONCLUSION

The Cuban presence in the United States has never been "typical" of the U.S. immigrant experience. The cigar-makers of Ybor City and the exiles from socialist Cuba were reluctant migrants, impelled by the forces of political change and arriving with the expectation of returning.

The special context of their migration produced atypical family characteristics, especially among Cubans arriving during the past three decades. A predominance of women and the middle-aged and elderly, low fertility, and relatively high income are not traits generally found among immigrants.

Much is still not known about the Cuban family, especially its children. Those born in the United States of Cuban parents are thus far an enigma. Their rates of acculturation and assimilation into U.S. society are difficult to predict in the absence of any comprehensive and representative study. The extent of intergenerational changes within the Cuban community is a crucial question in assessing not only the direction of the Cuban family in the United States but also the future of the metropolitan area in which most Cubans live: Greater Miami. The new Miami Cubans are already making their presence felt in the city, and it is evident that the future of Miami will be, in large measure, shaped by them.

ENDNOTES

1. For a comprehensive treatment of the rise of nationalism in the nineteenth century and its manifestations in the Cuban communities in the United States, see Poyo (1989).
2. An excellent analysis of the importance of class and color on the marriage and family norms of colonial Cuba can be found in Martínez-Alier (1974). For an ethnographic approach to the sexual politics of pre-Castro Cuba, especially the double standard of morality, see Mulhare (1969).
3. An extensive literature exists on the process of revolutionary change in Cuba and its consequences. For two of the most comprehensive analyses, see Domínguez (1978) and Mesa-Lago (1981).
4. Most of the data in the next two sections were compiled from U.S. Bureau of the Census (1983a, 1983b). Figures of a more recent date than the 1980 decennial census were derived from the Bureau's latest Current Population Report on the Spanish-Origin Population of the United States (U.S. Bureau of the Census 1988). The data from the Bureau are for persons who identified themselves as being of "Cuban origin or descent." For a more detailed and extensive treatment of the analysis presented in the next two sections, see Pérez (1985b, 1986c).
5. The enclave in Miami—its dynamics and implications—has occupied the attention of most researchers on the Cuban community in the United States in recent years (Portes and Bach 1985; Wilson and Martin 1982; Wilson and Portes 1980).

REFERENCES

Aguirre, Benigno E. 1981. "The Marital Stability of Cubans in the United States." *Ethnicity* 8:387–405.

Bernal, Guillermo. 1982. "Cuban Families." In *Ethnicity and Family Therapy,* edited by Monica McGoldrick, John Pearce, and Joseph Giordano, 187–207. New York: The Guilford Press.

Betancourt, Angel C. 1934. *Código Civil.* La Habana: Rambla, Bouza y Cía.

Boswell, Thomas D., and James R. Curtis. 1983. *The Cuban-American Experience: Culture Images and Perspectives.* Totowa, NJ: Rowman and Allanheld.

Camus, E. F. 1924. *Código Civil Español Explicado.* La Habana: Imprenta Arroyo, Fernández y Cía.

Díaz, Guarioné M. (ed.). 1980. *Evaluation and Identification of Policy Issues in the Cuban Community.* Miami: Cuban National Planning Council.

Díaz-Briquets, Sergio. 1983. *The Health Revolution in Cuba.* Austin: University of Texas Press.

Díaz-Briquets, Sergio, and Lisandro Pérez. 1981. "Cuba: The Demography of Revolution." *Population Reference Bureau Bulletin Series* 36:1–41.

Domínguez, Jorge I. 1978. *Cuba: Order and Revolution.* Cambridge, MA: Belknap Press.

Fagen, Richard R., Richard A. Brody, and Thomas J. O'Leary. 1968. *Cubans in Exile: Disaffection and the Revolution* Stanford: Stanford University Press.

Federal Writers' Project. 1939. "Ybor City." Unpublished.

Ferree, Myra Marx. 1979. "Employment without Liberation: Cuban Women in the United States." *Social Science Quarterly* 60:35–50.

Fitzpatrick, Joseph P., and Douglas T. Gurak. 1979. *Hispanic Intermarriage in New York City.* New York: Fordham University Hispanic Research Center.

International Bank for Reconstruction and Development. 1951. *Report on Cuba.* Washington, DC: International Bank for Reconstruction and Development.

Kurtines, William M., and Luke Miranda. 1980. "Differences in Self and Family Role Perception among Acculturating Cuban-American College Students: Implications for the Etiology of Family Disruption among Migrant Groups." *International Journal of Intercultural Relations* 4:167–184.

Marrero, Leví. 1987. *Cuba en la Década de 1950: Un País en Desarrollo.* Puerto Rico: Ediciones Capiro.

Martínez-Alier, Verena. 1974. *Marriage, Class, and Colour in Nineteenth Century Cuba.* London: Cambridge University Press.

Mesa-Lago, Carmelo. 1981. *The Economy of Socialist Cuba: A Two-Decade Appraisal.* Albuquerque: University of New Mexico Press.

Mulhare, Mirta de la Torre. 1969. "Sexual Ideology in Pre-Castro Cuba: A Cultural Analysis." Ph.D. dissertation, University of Pittsburgh.

Ortiz, Vilma, and Rosemary Santana Cooney. 1984. "Sex-Role Attitudes and Labor Force Participation among Young Hispanic Females and Non-Hispanic White Females." *Social Science Quarterly* 65:392–400.

Pérez, Lisandro. 1980. "The Family in Cuba." In *The Family in Latin America,* edited by M. S. Das and C. J. Jesser, 235–269. New Delhi: Vikas Publishing House.

———. 1983. "The Rise and Decline of the Cuban Community in Ybor City, Florida, 1886–1930." Paper presented at the meetings of the Latin American Studies Association, September 29–October 1, Mexico City.

———. 1984. In *Cubans in the United States,* edited by Miren Uriarte-Gastón and Jorge Cañas Martínez, 12–21. Boston: Center for the Study of the Cuban Community.

———. 1985a. "The Cuban Community of New York in the Nineteenth Century." Paper presented at the meetings of the Latin American Studies Association, April 17–20, Albuquerque, New Mexico.

———. 1985b. "The Cuban Population of the United States: The Results of the 1980 U.S. Census of Population." *Cuban Studies/Estudios Cubanos* 15:1–18.

———. 1986a. "A Case of Return Migration to the Caribbean: Cuban Cigarworkers and the Decline of the Florida Cigar Industry, 1911–1930." Paper presented at the meetings of the Caribbean Studies Association, May 28–31, Caracas, Venezuela.

———. 1986b. "Cubans in the United States." *The Annals of the American Academy of Political and Social Science* 487:126–137.

———. 1986c. "Immigrant Economic Adjustment and Family Organization: The Cuban Success Story Reexamined." *International Migration Review* 20:4–20.

Portes, Alejandro, and Robert L. Bach. 1985. *Latin Journey: Cuban and Mexican Immigrants in the United States.* Berkeley: University of California Press.

Poyo, Gerald R. 1989. *With All, and for the Good of All: The Emergence of Popular Nationalism in the Cuban Communities of the United States, 1848–1898.* Durham, NC: Duke University Press.

Prieto, Yolanda. 1987. "Cuban Women in the U.S. Labor Force: Perspectives on the Nature of Change." *Cuban Studies/Estudios Cubanos* 17:73–91.

Queralt, Magaly. 1983. "The Elderly of Cuban Origin: Characteristics and Problems." In *Aging in Minority Groups,* edited by R. L. McNeely and J. N. Colen, 50–65. Beverly Hills: Sage.

República de Cuba. 1939. *Gaceta Oficial* 28:2189–2193.

————. 1950. *Gaceta Oficial* 48:27553–27554.

————. 1963. *Constitución.* Reprint. Miami: Judicatura Cubana Democrática.

Rogg, Eleanor Meyer, and Rosemary Santana Cooney. 1980. *Adaptation and Adjustment of Cubans: West New York, New Jersey.* New York: Fordham University Hispanic Research Center.

Szapocznik, Jose, and Roberto Hernandez. 1988. "The Cuban American Family." In *Ethnic Families in America,* 3rd ed., edited by C. H. Mindel, R. W. Habenstein, and R. Wright, Jr., 160–172. New York: Elsevier.

Szapocznik, Jose, Mercedes A. Scopetta, and Wayne Tillman. 1978. "What Changes, What Remains the Same, and What Affects Acculturative Change in Cuban Immigrant Families." In *Cuban Americans: Acculturation, Adjustment and the Family,* edited by J. Szapocznik and M. C. Herrera, 35–19. Washington, DC: National Coalition of Hispanic Mental Health and Human Services Organizations.

U.S. Bureau of the Census. 1983a. *1980 Census of Population, General Population Characteristics, United States Summary.* Washington, DC: U.S. Government Printing Office.

————. 1983b. *1980 Census of Population, General Social and Economic Characteristics, United States Summary.* Washington, DC: U.S. Government Printing Office.

————. 1988. *The Hispanic Population in the United States: March 1988 (Advance Report).* Washington, DC: U.S. Government Printing Office.

Wilson, Kenneth L., and W. Allen Martin. 1982. "Ethnic Enclaves: A Comparison of the Cuban and Black Economies of Miami." *American Journal of Sociology* 88:135–160.

Wilson, Kenneth L., and Alejandro Portes. 1980. "Immigrant Enclaves: An Analysis of the Labor Market Experiences of Cubans in Miami." *American Journal of Sociology* 86:295–319.

Yanez, Luisa. 1986. "Study Shows Changes in Cuban Women in U.S." *The Miami News,* March 11:11A.

PART III

Asian American Families in the United States

The 1990 census identified more than thirty subgroups of the Asian population in the United States, with the Chinese, Filipino, Japanese, Asian Indian, Korean, and Vietnamese representing more than 90 percent of the total. With the passage of the 1965 Immigration Act, the Asian population increased dramatically, from 1.4 million in 1970 to 3.5 million in 1980. By 1990, the number had grown to 7.2 million, and by 1999, to 10.9 million, representing 4 percent of the total population and making Asian Americans the fasting-growing and the third largest minority group after African Americans and Latinos. As a group, Asian Americans vary widely in their characteristics, according to their cultural origins, language, and recency of immigration. Because of their longer tenure in the United States, Chinese and Japanese Americans tend to be more generationally diverse and less culturally distinct in some of their characteristics than Asian American groups who have entered the United States in more recent decades. Whereas less than 30 percent of the Japanese population was foreign-born in 1980, the proportion of foreign-born among Filipinos, Koreans, and Vietnamese was 65, 82, and 91 percent, respectively. Overall, nearly 40 percent of Asian Americans in the six major groups counted in the 1990 census reported immigrating to the United States since 1970. Such high proportions of recent immigrants among Asian Americans carry significant implications for family organization, community stability, and integration among Asian American populations and for their economic progress in American society.

In their examination of Chinese American families, Evelyn Nakano Glenn and Stacey G. H. Yap begin by challenging the tendency in the social science literature to focus on the cultural resources of Chinese Americans in explaining various features of their family and community life. They focus instead on those legal and administrative practices and institutional structures in the United States that have constrained family formation among Chinese Americans and on the efforts on their part to mobilize various resources to ensure their survival on a daily basis and intergenerationally. Accordingly, they analyze the nature of family formation among Chinese Americans during three distinct periods, each characterized by a different set of institutional and political conditions that inspired specific strategies for carrying on production and reproduction of the family. The effect of these earlier experiences on contemporary features of Chinese American family life is also assessed, as is the impact of recent demographic, political, and social trends.

An approach similar to that taken by Glenn and Yap is used by Dana Y. Takagi in her chapter on Japanese American families. She too notes the inadequacies of culture-based explanations in accounting for some of the more important features of Japanese American family life and takes instead a critical perspective that emphasizes the role of such historical factors as changing immigration policies, institutional discrimination, and the transformation of gender and kin systems in shaping Japanese American family experiences. Toward this end, she focuses on two broad historical periods that mark Japanese American family experiences and encompass three kinship-defined generations of Japanese Americans: the Issei (first-generation), the Nisei (second-generation), and the Sansei (third-generation). In each period, the organization of the family is shown to have been shaped by historical forces external to the family and its members. She concludes with a discussion of current family patterns among Japanese Americans.

In her chapter on the latest Asian population to enter the United States in significant numbers, Nazli Kibria reviews the major trends of Vietnamese American family life and considers how settlement in the United States has affected Vietnamese family patterns. Reviewing the demographic characteristics of this group, she notes its low median age (21.5 years in 1980), the preponderance of adult men among recent arrivals, and the implications of these characteristics for current trends in marriage, divorce, and childbearing among the Vietnamese. The complex composition of Vietnamese households and the efforts to reconstruct extended family structures that were disrupted by the resettlement process in the United States are also discussed. Among the more significant developments in the Vietnamese community identified by Kibria are the increasing influence of the young in determining the cultural norms and standards of community life and the erosion of core familial values as a consequence of the speedy absorption by Vietnamese children of American values and beliefs.

Focusing mainly on Korean immigrant families in the United States, Pyong Gap Min examines how structural conditions (i.e., the economy and the community context) and Korean's traditional family ideology mutually influence each other and shape family dynamics and relationships. He shows that immigration to the United States has led to a phenomenal increase in the number of Korean women in the labor market but that their greater economic role has been less effective in enhancing their marital power and status in the family than that of American wives in general. The large proportion of Korean women working as unpaid workers in the family business, together with their concentration in small business firms, which isolates them from the equalizing influences of the larger society, are cited by Min as major factors accounting for the persistence of traditional gender role ideology among Korean immigrants. Among other significant changes in the family characteristics of Korean immigrants noted by Min are smaller families and households, as well as higher divorce rates and marital discord, all of which appear to be associated with the greater involvement of Korean women in the labor force. He concludes that Korean American family characteristics will become similar to those of white families as second generation adults compose a larger share of Korean families in the United States.

In her chapter on Asian Indian families, Bandana Purkayastha emphasizes the interaction of large-scale social structures and cultural expectations in influencing family life among Indo-Americans in the United States over the past three decades. Because of the highly restrictive immigration policy toward immigrants from Asia prior to 1965, the number of Asian Indians in this country remained relatively small and insignificant. However, the past three decades have seen a dramatic increase in the number of Asian Indians in the United States. In contrast to their counterparts who arrived prior to 1965, the majority of recent immigrants are well-educated professionals who have managed to avoid much of the hostility and discrimination experienced by those who entered during earlier periods. Purkayastha focuses on three overlapping aspects of Indo-American family life—creating ideal families, evolving parental roles, and the relationship between immigrant parents and their children—to highlight the complex dynamics of family life.

CHAPTER 7

Chinese American Families

Evelyn Nakano Glenn with Stacey G. H. Yap

Today, when the academic achievements of Asian American "whiz kids" are widely touted in the popular media, it is easy to forget that for much of their history, Chinese Americans were among the most vilified minorities in the United States. In the late nineteenth and early twentieth centuries, Chinese immigrants were depicted as backward, immoral, filthy, rat-eating, opium-crazed heathens (Dower 1986; Miller 1969; Saxton 1971). They constituted a "yellow peril," an unassimilable horde whose willingness to work long hours for low pay threatened the livelihood of white working men.

Public attitudes took a 180-degree turn in the post–civil rights era, as Chinese Americans, along with the Japanese and other Asian Americans, came to be proclaimed a "model minority." It was asserted that through sheer hard work, they had overcome racism and poverty to reach educational and income levels exceeding even those of European Americans. Seeking an explanation for the extraordinary "success" story, observers turned to the family and cultural values. Strong family ties, discipline and close control over children, and emphasis on collective solidarity over individual interest, made for children who were motivated, well behaved, and obedient in school (Sollenberger 1968; Tsai 1986:162). Many of these characteristics could be traced to traditional Chinese culture, in particular to Confucianism, with its emphasis on filial piety, respect for elders, and reverence for tradition.

The praise heaped on the Chinese American family, although seemingly beneficent, has less benign implications. It tends to gloss over the long history of legal and political assaults on Chinese American family life: laws and policies that restricted immigration, economic activity, residence, political participation, and legal rights. It also shifts attention away from the economic and social difficulties that many immigrant families experience today, some of which are a legacy of past policies. The elevation of the Chinese American family also serves to deny the needs of other minority groups who are deemed less worthy. Thus, the supposed fortitude of Chinese American families is contrasted to the alleged "family disorganization" of blacks and Hispanics. The case of the Chinese, along with other Asian American groups, seems to support the argument that some groups have cultural resources that enable them to resist the demoralizing effects of poverty and discrimination. By implication, the lack of success of other groups can be attributed in some measure to weaknesses in their cultures. The Chinese family is held out as an object lesson to other minority groups that if they only emulated the Chinese, they too could pull themselves up by their bootstraps.

Social science treatments of the Chinese American family have shared the tendency to focus on supposedly unique aspects of Chinese American family structure and to rely on cultural explanations. In contrast to the weight given to economic and political constraints shaping black and Hispanic family life, social science research on Chinese families has interpreted characteristics of Chinese American families as expressions of traditional Chinese values and practices. This approach has grown out of the dominant assimilationist school of race relations. The assimilation model focuses on the initial cultural and social differences of the immigrant groups and attempts to trace the process of assimilation over time. In the case of family, studies have typically begun by examining traditional Chinese family patterns, then discussing how these patterns are expressed in a new setting and undergo gradual change through acculturation (for example, Haynor and Reynolds 1937; Hsu 1971; Kung 1962; Weiss 1974). The features identified as typical of Chinese American families and as evidence of cultural continuity are (1) stability, indicated by low rates of divorce and illegitimacy; (2) close ties between generations, shown in low rates of adolescent rebellion and delinquency; (3) economic self-sufficiency, demonstrated by avoidance of welfare and a propensity toward involvement in family businesses; (4) conservatism, expressed by retention of Chinese language and customs in the home (Glenn 1983); and (5) female subordination, shown in close controls over women and wives' responsibility for domestic work.

Each of these characteristics can be interpreted in terms of specific aspects of Chinese culture. For example, familism—the valuing of family over the individual—is credited for the rarity of divorce. Similarly, the principles of Confucianism, filial piety, respect for elders, and reverence for tradition are cited as the philosophical bases for absence of adolescent rebellion and retention of Chinese language and customs in the home. The family-based agricultural system is seen as the precedent for immigrants' involvement in family enterprise. Patrilineal inheritance, patrilocal residence, and ancestor worship are seen as elevating the status of men and devaluing that of women. Changes in the patterns over time are seen as evidence of acculturation. Thus, for example, changes in husband-wife relations are expected to become more egalitarian as Chinese Americans adopt dominant culture (that is, "American") norms.

A close examination of the history of Chinese American family life and of the dynamics within contemporary families, however, reveals the inadequacy of the cultural assimilationist model. The cultural approach emphasizes the uniqueness and homogeneity of Chinese American families. In actuality we find considerable diversity among classes and subgroups and variation in family structures in different historical periods. Further, we find evidence of similarities between Chinese American families and those of other oppressed minorities, groups subjected to similar constraints. Although the assimilation model emphasizes continuity and gradual, linear change, we find dramatic shifts in family organization correlated with alteration in external constraints.

The perspective that we adopt in this chapter starts at a different point, not with Chinese culture but with conditions Chinese Americans have confronted in the United States; of special note are legal and administrative practices governing immigration, labor market structures restricting economic mobility, and laws limiting political rights. Our focus is on the dialectic between institutional structures that constrain family formation and the efforts of individuals and households to carry out the production and reproduction needed to maintain themselves both on a daily basis and intergenerationally. Within this schema, culture is not an autonomous determinant, but a resource that individuals and households actively shape and mobilize for survival. In short, we recognize the interaction of social structure, culture, and human agency.

In line with recent Third World, feminist, and Marxist critiques of family sociology (see Glenn 1987), we challenge the view of the family as a bounded private sphere separate from "nonfamily." Indeed, it is precisely the interaction between larger political economic forces and family dynamics that needs to be understood. Also in line with these critiques, we reject the view of family as a monolithic entity with unitary interests. Although the family is bound together by economic interdependence and survival needs, it is also divided along gender and generational lines. The interests of husbands and wives, children and parents, are not the same; family members do not make equal contributions or gain equal benefits. Therefore, conflicts arise over division of labor and distribution of resources. Different family forms have different patterns of gender and generational relations. Looking at the Chinese American family in this way leads us to recognize areas of continuities and discontinuities with experiences of other oppressed racial groups.

HISTORICAL BACKGROUND

The lives of Chinese Americans have been shaped by their presence in the United States as labor migrants. In the second half of the nineteenth century, capitalists who controlled the economies of the Far West needed a vast labor force to build the region's infrastructure (Cheng and Bonacich 1984). The Chinese were the first and largest stream of Asian labor recruited to perform the arduous work of extracting wealth from the mines, reclaiming agricultural land, building the transcontinental railroad, and performing domestic services for the largely male white population (Saxton 1971). The U.S. presence as a colonial power in China made it a logical source of labor. Economic chaos, partly engendered by colonial incursions, had displaced a significant portion of southern peasantry from the usual means of livelihood, leaving them free to migrate (Ling 1912). As an imperial power, the United States could impose special conditions to ensure a cheap and easily controlled workforce.

Imposition of special restrictions was spurred by, and ultimately justified in terms of, racist ideology. Antipathy to the Chinese preceded their arrival, as Western missionaries, diplomats, and traders in the nineteenth century had spread the image of the Chinese as depraved heathens, capable of viciousness, treachery, and cruelty (Miller 1969). Western colonial contacts with Africa and Asia led to further elaboration of these images and the development of scientific racism, theories of the biological inferiority of colored peoples. The Chinese, along with other Asians and Africans, were considered savages, primitive and childlike. At the same time, China's vast size and population gave rise to fear. The "yellow peril" became the embodiment of these fears as the image of hordes of Chinese overrunning the white race became known throughout the western world (Dower 1986).

The Chinese were to be allowed entry strictly to provide labor, not to become permanent settlers. They were treated as individual units of labor without regard to any family ties. Only prime age male workers were allowed entry, and they were not allowed to bring dependents. The labor market in California was stratified into separate tiers to prevent the Chinese from competing for better jobs with native whites. The Chinese were confined to jobs considered too dirty, dangerous, or demeaning for whites and were paid on a separate and lower wage scale. In addition, California and other western states imposed special head taxes and prohibited them from carrying on certain types of businesses. The Chinese were put in a special legal category. They could not become naturalized citizens—a right denied until 1943—and were denied most civil rights, including the right to testify in court against whites. In 1879 the new California constitution denied suffrage to "all natives of China, idiots, and insane persons" (Dower 1986:154).

The exploitability of the Chinese meant that they could be used to keep wages low. They were thus seen as a threat to white workers, who excluded them from their unions and agitated for their exclusion from the United States. In the 1870s, following completion of the railroad and an economic recession, the Chinese were driven out of mining camps, rural areas, and small towns and forced to congregate in urban Chinatowns. Finally in 1882, spurred by mounting pressure from nativist organizations and working men's groups, Congress passed the Chinese Exclusion Act, which prohibited immigration of Chinese of the "laboring class." The Chinese became the first group denied entry on purely racial grounds. The effect of these restrictions was to keep Chinese men in the status of alien guests, restricted to a few occupations, contained in urban ghettos, and denied normal family life for nearly 100 years.

These circumstances provide an alternative explanation of the features previously described as originating in Chinese culture: (1) low divorce rates may result when spouses are forced to stay together because of the lack of economic options outside of family enterprises; (2) low delinquency rates may reflect the paucity of adolescents in the population before 1950; (3) avoidance of welfare is necessitated by the illegal status of many immigrants and the lack of access to sources outside the community; (4) retention of Chinese language and custom is a logical outcome of ghettoization and denial of permanent membership in American society.

That the Chinese population did not die out altogether despite the obstacles is a testimony to their ingenuity and determination. How they managed to survive and what kinds of families they forged is the subject of the next sections.

We can identify three distinct historical periods demarcated by shifts in legal and political conditions. In each period we find one or more distinct family formations that represent specific strategies for carrying on production and reproduction under prevailing institutional constraints.

1850 to 1920: The Split-Household Family

During the first 70 years of Chinese presence in the United States, from 1850 to 1920, one can hardly talk about family life among the immigrants. As Table 1 shows, the population was overwhelmingly composed of adult men with very few women and children. Between 1860 and 1910, the gender ratio fluctuated between 13 and 27 men for every woman (see Table 1). In 1900, the Chinese population consisted of less than 4 percent children 14 and under, compared with 37.4 percent of the U.S. population of whites of native parentage.

The first 30 years, from 1850 to 1882, was a period of relatively open immigration. An estimated 300,000 Chinese left Guangdong Province to work in California and the West. The vast majority were male laborers, about half of whom left wives behind (Coolidge 1909). Many were too poor to pay for their own passage and came on the credit ticket system, which obligated them to work for a term of 7 years to pay off the transport. These "birds of passage" intended to return after accumulating enough to acquire land and retire; in the meantime, they sent remittances to support relatives. At least two-thirds succeeded in returning, so that the population of Chinese never exceeded 110,000.

A small segment of the immigrants were merchants who were allowed to bring wives or concubines and children. Thus the few Chinese families in the United States were of the wealthier merchant class. We know little about what went on in the households, because outsiders rarely penetrated their walls. Women had bound feet and seldom ventured abroad (Haynor and Reynolds 1937). An observer of New York's Chinese quarters noted, ". . . especially is the wife thus carefully excluded from view, except to those of her own sex; and if she has occasion to visit another woman every precaution must be taken to avoid observation. Usually a closed carriage is employed to convey her, even though the distance be less than a block away." Another writer described the living quarters of merchants in San Francisco as modest: "Married people indulge in a little more room than the bachelor of the same class, but the furniture even of the merchant's family home is of the simplest, and more limited than at the store establishment save an extra plant or so. Indeed the wife is kept so secluded that all show may be dispensed with" (quoted in Lyman 1968:325).

At the other end of the scale of "respectability" was the only other sizable group of Chinese women, prostitutes (Goldman 1981; Hirata 1979). Most of these were "indentured" or "enslaved" women who had been lured, bought from impoverished parents, or kidnapped by Chinese procurers working for the tongs that controlled the trade. Once transported to the United States, the women were sold,

TABLE 1. Chinese Population in the United States, by Gender, Gender Ratio, Percentage Foreign-Born, and Percentage under Age 15, 1860–1980

YEAR	TOTAL	MALE	FEMALE	MALE:FEMALE RATIO	PERCENTAGE FOREIGN-BORN	PERCENTAGE AGED 14 OR UNDER
1860	34,933	33,149	1,784	18.58		
1870	63,199	58,633	4,566	12.84	99.8	
1880	105,465	100,686	4,779	21.06	99.0	
1890	107,475	103,607	3,868	26.79	99.3	
1900	89,863	85,341	4,522	18.87	90.7	3.4
1910	71,531	66,856	4,675	14.30	79.3	[a]
1920	61,639	53,891	7,748	6.96	69.9	12.0
1930	74,954	59,802	15,152	3.95	58.8	20.4
1940	77,504	57,389	20,115	2.85	48.1	21.2
1950	117,140	76,725	40,415	1.90	47.0	23.3
1960	236,084	135,430	100,654	1.35	39.5	33.0
1970	431,583	226,733	204,850	1.11	46.9	26.6
1980	812,178	410,936	401,242	1.02	63.3	21.1

[a]*Figures for California, Oregon, and Washington—which together has a somewhat lower male:female ratio (11.33) than the United States as a whole—show 7.0 per-cent of the Chinese population to be under age 15 in those states.*

Source: U.S. Censuses, 1872, 1883, 1895, 1902, 1913, 1922, 1933, 1943, 1953, 1963, 1973, and 1988. List of specific tales available upon request.

139

forced to sign long-term contracts, and held in bondage in brothels in the Chinese quarters of San Francisco and other Western cities and in Western mining camps. According to Pascoe (1990), the severe shortage of women subjected them to severe exploitation but also presented them with some opportunities. Escaping from prostitution was difficult, because the tongs and individual pimps who reaped enormous profits from their exploitation relentlessly tracked down runaway women. Women who were unable to escape rarely lived out the 4- or 5-year terms of their contracts. Fortunate women were rescued by a lover or a missionary group or were redeemed by a wealthy client. Because of the shortage of women, they had a good chance of becoming respectable wives. Pascoe (1990) found records showing that the Presbyterian Mission House in San Francisco arranged for several hundred marriages for rescued prostitutes in the peak years of operation between 1874 and 1928. The largest group of husbands came from the stratum of small merchants, just below the Chinatown elite, who came to form the "middle class" in Chinatown.

It seems likely that many Chinese laborers in America eventually would have sent for wives, as overseas Chinese did in Singapore and Hawaii (Glick 1980; Purcell 1965). Or they might have married native women, as their compatriots in the Philippines and Peru did (Hunt and Walker 1974; Wong 1978). Both these possibilities were precluded for Chinese men in the United States. An antimiscegenation statute in California forbade marriages between Chinese and other races, and in 1870 the Page Law, designed to curb the Chinese prostitution trade, was passed. The application process for Chinese women was made difficult and arduous, and female applicants were subjected to repeated questioning and badgering. Its effect, according to Pfeffer (1986), was to discourage and bar laborers' wives, resulting in a decline in the proportion of women among the immigrant population. Whereas the male population increased by 42,000, the female population grew by a mere 213 between 1870 and 1880. Passage of the Chinese Exclusion Act of 1882 cut off any possibility of wives of laborers entering.[1] Renewals of the act in 1892 and 1902 further restricted entry and return. Finally, all immigration from Asia was cut off by the 1924 Immigration Act. By that time the various restrictions had had their desired effect. The population of Chinese had dwindled from a high of 107,000 in 1890 to 61,000 by 1920. Chinese men left in this country confronted a stark choice. They could return to China to face the same economic hardships that drove them to migrate in the first place, or they could remain, condemned to eternal bachelorhood or to permanent separation from wives and children.

A small loophole remained: relatives of U.S. citizens—Chinese born in the United States—were allowed entry. This group was small, but the 1906 earthquake and fire that destroyed most municipal records in San Francisco expanded the number of those who could make the claim without its being disprovable. After that event, Chinese residents could claim American birth, visit China, report the birth of a son, and thereby create an entry slot. Years later the slot could be used by a relative, or the papers could be sold to a young man wanting to immigrate. In such cases the "paper son" assumed the name and identity of the alleged son. These slots enabled many families to adopt sojourning as a long-term economic strategy. Successive generations of men were sent abroad as paper sons to work and remit money to support the kin group. In some Guangdong villages, remittances from overseas workers constituted the main source of income. It has been estimated that between 1937 and 1940 alone, overseas Chinese in the United States, Southeast Asia, and other overseas locations remitted $2 billion.

This sojourning strategy gave rise to a distinct family formation, the *split-household family* (Glenn 1983). In this arrangement, production or income earning was separated from the main household and carried out by a member living abroad, while reproduction—that is, maintaining the family home, socializing children, caring for the elderly and infirm, maintaining family graves, and the like—was the responsibility of wives and other relatives in the home village. The family as an interdependent economic unit thus spanned two continents. This arrangement allowed maximum exploitation of the male worker. His labor could be bought cheaply because the cost of reproduction was borne by the labor of wives and other relatives in the home village.

Gender and Generational Relations.

The split household is perhaps the ultimate form of gender segregation, with husbands and wives leading completely separate lives. Men abroad lived in "bachelor" societies (Nee and Nee 1973). Employed as laborers or engaged in small business, they resided in rented rooms or shared quarters with other men. Lacking actual kin ties, they constructed fictive "families," district, dialect, and clan associations, the latter based on descent from a mythical ancestor (Lyman 1986). These associations provided security, sociability, and mutual aid. As is common in predominantly male communities, many sojourners found outlets in opium, gambling, and prostitutes. The irregular legal status of "paper sons" made them especially vulnerable to exploitation; fearful of exposure, they were forced to work long hours in shops, restaurants, and factories for low pay and to remain obedient to the associations that provided aid. Those frugal or lucky enough to save passage money returned periodically to China to visit and father more children. Others, either through ill fortune or personal problems such as gambling, never accumulated passage money and had to stay on year after year.

For women left behind, it was a period of massive social change and political upheavals, and they struggled to keep the family together against daunting odds. The ideal was for wives to reside with the husbands' kin group; the in-laws were responsible for safeguarding their chastity and keeping them under the ultimate control of their husbands. Yet a Chinese American sociologist who lived in villages inhabited chiefly by women, children, and older folks left behind by sojourners in the 1930s and 1970s reported that wives had a great deal of power and independence: "They had to make the daily decisions affecting the life of the family, and they learned how to handle money and deal with people outside the home. Naturally these women became extremely self-reliant" (Sung 1987:175).

Maxine Hong Kingston's stories of three women in her family illustrate the diverse fates of women left behind by husbands. The first, about a young unnamed aunt who became pregnant by another man, suggests that the community imposed heavy penalties on women who "strayed," even if she were the victim of rape. Another aunt was abandoned by her husband, who married another woman in America and never visited or sent for her, despite repeated pleas. Unlike some husbands who "disappeared," he at least continued to send remittances. Her own mother exercised considerable initiative during her father's absence. She attended a traditional Chinese medical college and became a village doctor to support herself and three children. Her father, a small laundry owner, sent for her after nearly 20 years abroad; the couple established a new family with several more children. Kingston's mother's story and Sung's observations remind us that assumptions about Chinese women's complete lack of self-determination need to be questioned. Many women displayed considerable resourcefulness to ensure their own and their children's survival.

Generational relations were inevitably affected by parental separation. The life story of Lao T-ai-t'ai, a Han woman who lived from 1867 to 1938, suggests that for Chinese women the uterine family—based on ties between mother, children, and grandchildren—rather than the patriarchal family was the emotional center of life (Pruitt 1967; see also Wolf 1972). With fathers gone, these ties became even more central; Sung (1987:175) reported, "Female influence in childbearing was dominant. The children were surrounded by their mothers, aunts, grandmothers, and perhaps grandfathers returned from abroad." The mother-child tie, especially with the eldest son, normally an important source of leverage in the extended kin household, was further strengthened. In contrast, the father-child tie was weakened by prolonged absence. Because many years passed between visits, children were spaced far apart, and the father was often middle-aged or elderly when the youngest child was born. The age difference increased the formality and distance of the relationship.

1920 to 1965: The Small Producer Family

Despite obstacles to family formation, we start to see the growth of families in urban Chinatowns in the 1910s. The increase of women and children in the population reflects this growth. Between 1910 and 1930, the ratio of men to women fell from about 14:1 to 4:1, and the percent of children (14 and under) rose from 3.4 percent in 1900 to 20.4 percent by 1930 (Table 1). Most of these early families were formed by small entrepreneurs, former laborers who had managed to accumulate sufficient capital to start a small laundry or shop, often in partnership with other men. They could then register as merchants and send for wives. Aside from sentimental reasons—a desire for companionship and affection—small entrepreneurs had sound economic motives for wanting families in America because women and children were a source of free labor. The intensive exploitation of family labor gave hand laundries and grocery stores the margin needed to make a profit.

The number of families took an even more dramatic leap in the 1930s, 1940s, and 1950s because of changes in immigration regulations. The 1924 immigration law was modified in 1930 to permit wives of merchants and women married to American citizens before 1924 to immigrate (Chinn and others 1969), and in recognition of its alliance with China in World War II, the U.S. government repealed the Chinese Exclusion Act in 1943 and created a token quota of 105 entrants a year. More openings were created by two other changes: the "Bride's Act" of 1946, which permitted entry to wives and children of permanent residents (as well as citizens), and the Immigration Act of 1953, which gave preferential entry to relatives of citizens. The vast majority of those who entered under these two acts were women. They fell into two general categories: wives who had been separated from sojourning husbands, sometimes for decades, and brides of servicemen, citizens, and residents who had visited China and had a "hasty" marriage arranged (Lee 1956; for a novelistic treatment, see Chu 1979).

During this period, roughly 1920 to 1960, the typical immigrant and first-generation family operated as a unit of production, with husband, wife, and children engaged in work in the family business—a laundry, restaurant, or small store. Members worked long hours for no wages. For convenience or lack of means, living quarters were often located above or behind the shop. Thus family and work life were fused. Production and reproduction were integrated and carried on simultaneously. Responsibilities for both were allocated along gender and generational lines. A woman who grew up in a family laundry in the 1930s and 1940s noted that the family's work day started at 7 A.M. and ended at midnight 6 days a week. Although the laundry was sent out for washing, it was dried, sprinkled, starched, and ironed in the back room. Tasks were assigned by age and gender. Father did the difficult hand ironing of shirts, while mother operated the collar and cuff press, younger children folded laundry and made up parcels, and older children ironed handkerchiefs and underwear. At the same time, mothers supervised their children's homework, related folk stories and legends, and prepared meals. Fathers admonished children and chatted with relatives. Older children entertained and supervised younger children (for popular accounts see Kingston 1976; Lowe 1943; Wong 1950).

Gender and Generational Relations.   The small producer family was in many ways a continuation of the peasant family in China and similar to agrarian families engaged in family production around the world (see Young and Wilmott 1973). In sharp contrast to the complete separation of men and women in the split household, husband and wife were constantly together as partners. Husband and wife were mutually interdependent in that he needed her as much as she needed him. Another circumstance contributing to relative egalitarianism was the absence of in-laws. This freed wives from subordination to their husbands' parents. Many of the informants who grew up in a small producer family recalled their mothers as the disciplinarians and dominant figures in the household (Glenn 1983).

The interdependence did not mean that husband-wife relations were necessarily harmonious. Women who had rejoined their husbands or who were "hasty brides" suffered many adjustment problems. Many were appalled by the squalor of their living quarters and dismayed by having to work as hard as or harder than they had in China (Yung 1986:43). They often suffered from isolation because they spoke little English and had no friends or relatives for support and sympathy. This isolation often put them at a disadvantage in relation to husbands, who had resided in the United States for years. Long separation made even long-time mates strangers to each other. Brides who came over after arranged marriages scarcely knew their husbands. Relations were sometimes strained by age disparity. In many cases, men in their forties, who had worked in the United States for years before returning, married women in their teens or twenties.

Working long hours in cramped, damp, or overheated conditions took its toll on the health of family members, a burden felt especially by women, who were primarily responsible for the welfare of children. Tuberculosis and other diseases were rampant in Chinatown (Lee and others 1969). Although men typically worked hard, wives worked longer hours, first up to fix the morning meal and last to bed after cleaning up and preparing for the next day.

Despite the stresses, most marriages remained intact. The low divorce rate may reflect lack of choice. Spouses could not survive on their own, and there was no place for divorced women in the community. Some women believed that their only recourse was suicide. Sung (1967) found that the suicide rate among Chinese in San Francisco was four times that of the city as a whole and that victims were predominantly women.

Close parental control of children was fostered by living and working conditions. There was constant interaction, with parents speaking to children in Chinese and supervising them.[2] Language and cultural tradition were transmitted through this daily interaction. With so many individuals working in close quarters for extended periods of time, conflict had to be kept to a minimum. Discipline and cooperation were stressed, and self-expression was curbed. Children were expected to obey parents; older brothers and sisters helped discipline younger siblings, who were expected to defer to older siblings.

A circumstance limiting parental authority was the family's location in an "alien" culture. Arriving as adults, they rarely acquired more than a rudimentary knowledge of English. Children, once they reached school age, rapidly learned to speak and write English. They became cultural mediators and agents for the family. Children of 8 or 9 years accompanied their parents to the bank, read documents, translated notices in stores, and negotiated with customers. They could exercise considerable discretion in deciding what information to relay to their parents (see Tan 1989). Thus the normal pattern of dependence was reversed.

Among families in which the father was abroad for many years before sending for wife and children, the dominance of the mother-child tie often continued after reunification. Initially the father seemed a virtual stranger to the children, so mother continued to play the central role in child-rearing, education, and discipline. Although Sung calls this pattern matriarchal, it is probably more accurate to call it matrifocal (cf. Stack 1974). Women did not have economic power or authority, but they were the emotional centers of the household. Women were the keepers of family tradition, keeping track of ancestors' anniversaries, passing on family stories, and organizing activities for New Year's and other festival days. If we recall the importance of the uterine family to Chinese women, we see matrifocality not as a departure from the past but as an adaptation of established relationships.[3]

1965 to the Present: Diverse Chinese American Families

The 1950s and 1960s were a period of growing heterogeneity among Chinese Americans along class and generational lines. Although there have always been class divisions, particularly between the merchants who controlled the large businesses in Chinatown and workers employed in those businesses, a number of factors contributed to ethnic solidarity. Almost all immigrants prior the 1940s came from a few villages in Guangdong Province and thus shared a common language and culture. Despite many internal conflicts, forced ghettoization and the hostility of the outside world made for a degree of defensive cohesiveness. Most Chinatown residents depended in one way or another on the tourist trade and had a common interest in keeping down open conflict (Light and Wong 1975). The tightly organized community, made up of clan and other voluntary organizations and headed by the Chinese Consolidated Benevolent Association, integrated men of different social classes (Kuo 1982). Vertical ties were strengthened at the expense of horizontal ties between men in a similar class position. In addition, color barriers prevented Chinese from entering white-collar occupations and the skilled crafts. Even those with educational and technical credentials were often forced into small businesses or other forms of self-employment, like their less educated compatriots. Ethnicity often took precedence over class in determining one's economic niche.

This situation changed during and after World War II, as color barriers began to fall in the professions. Opportunities expanded further as a result of the civil rights movement in the 1960s, and sizable numbers of Chinese Americans were able to enter occupations consistent with their education and training. Increased social mobility of this educated segment created a class division between better-educated professionals and business owners (middle class) and less educated manual workers and petty entrepreneurs (working class).

A second factor contributing to diversity was the entry of several different cohorts of immigrants after 1943. These new immigrants were much more varied in background than earlier immigrants. True, those who entered under the 1943 and 1946 Bride's Act and under the family reunification provisions of the 1953 act came from the same regions and class backgrounds as the earlier immigrants. However, a significant cohort of young professionals and students also came in the 1940s and 1950s to study at American universities. Thousands were stranded by the revolution and were allowed to stay on as refugees.[4] Others migrated for economic reasons, entering as students and applying for a change to permanent resident status once they arrived.

The biggest change in immigration took place with passage of the Immigration Act of 1965, which scrapped the national-origin quotas and made family reunification and the filling of needed occupations the chief criteria for entry. Each country was given a 20,000-person annual limit, but spouses, parents, and children were exempt from the quota. Under these provisions, between 20,000 and 30,000 Chinese have entered every year, primarily from Hong Kong (see Wong 1986). These post-1965 immigrants range from working-class families who arrived with little except what they carried to those with substantial assets who were seeking a secure place to invest their capital.

Linked to both occupational mobility and new immigration is increased residential dispersion. Some observers differentiate between suburban and Chinatown-based Chinese families. This distinction correlates with generation, class, and recency of immigration. Working-class immigrants often settle initially in or near urban Chinatowns to get acclimated; they can get by speaking only Chinese and can find ready-made contacts to get jobs. After establishing themselves, they may move out into other areas of the city or to the suburbs, often to areas already settled by Chinese, forming satellite Chinatowns. More affluent immigrants often go immediately to locations outside Chinatown and can afford to purchase a home. Professionals, whether immigrants or American-born, are more likely to live in predominantly white suburbs. These choices have implications for whether Chinese culture and identity are maintained in the next generation.

These divisions have given rise to numerous subtypes of families, of which four are fairly sizable.

Old Immigrant Families. These are an aging segment of the small producer families, formerly split households who are now united and residing together in the United States. The fathers immigrated before 1965, starting out as sojourners, but were able to send for family members under the war bride, refugee, or family reunification laws mentioned earlier. They often started as laborers but now own a business. These families are Chinatown connected, coming from the same areas around Canton as the late-nineteenth-century founders of Chinatown and speaking the same Toysan dialect. Wong (1985) describes the old immigrant family as traditional in outlook, retaining Chinese notions of a gender and an age hierarchy of authority, filial piety, and collectivity. Although only recently formed as a family group, their roots in the United States often go back a century or more. In families in which sojourning was a long-term family strategy, several generations of men in the same family immigrated and passed on a family business from generation to generation. In one family history recounted to Glenn by a 21-year-old college student, the great-grandfather arrived as a paper son in the 1890s, worked for 20 years, and sent for his son, the student's grandfather. Grandfather helped great-grandfather run a small business. Great-grandfather later returned to China, leaving grandfather to carry on the business and forward remittances. In the 1940s, grandfather sent for father. Up to that point, none of the wives had left China; then, in the late 1950s, father returned to China and brought back his wife to the United States. Finally, after nearly 70 years, the first birth of a child on American soil took place. The student was only a first-generation American even though four generations of her family had been in the United States.

Professional Immigrant Families. These consist of an older segment, who arrived as students in the 1940s and 1950s, and a younger segment, who entered after the Immigration Act of 1965. The lowering of discriminatory barriers mentioned earlier speeded the integration of professional immigrants. These immigrants differed not only in education, but also in linguistic and regional background from earlier immigrants. They came from urban backgrounds, were educated in Hong Kong, mainland China, or Taiwan, and are Mandarin-speaking, in contrast to the Cantonese-origin, Toysanese-speaking resident Chinese population. These differences increased the social gulf between scholar-professionals and Chinatown-based Chinese.

The scholar-professional immigrants live in white middle-class neighborhoods in the city or in white suburbs and are employed in mainstream institutions. Although their work and neighborhood contacts are primarily with European Americans, they may socialize with other Chinese of similar backgrounds. A survey of Chinese professionals in California found that 70 percent of the respondents spent either an equal amount of time with Chinese and non-Chinese or more time with non-Chinese.

Wong (1985) describes this group as considerably westernized even before immigrating; having come from major cities, they had adopted Western clothing, recreation, eating, and living habits. Clausen and Bermingham (1982) found that a high percentage of professional immigrants in California had grown up in homes where members spoke Western languages, principally English, and that they themselves had been guests in Western homes and had part of their education in Western-style schools. Some are Christian converts, who are especially likely to subscribe to Western cultural practices, such as free marriage and the primacy of the husband-wife tie.

Households are generally nuclear in form. However, some professional immigrants have taken advantage of the opening up of relations between the United States and China to sponsor parents' immigration. Thus some extended families have been reconstituted. Wives usually also have college or postgraduate degrees, and many are employed in professional, managerial, and administrative support occupations and may also manage their own investments. Our impression from interviewing Chinese professional women for a study of high-tech industries is that when both husband and wife are professionals, they have a sense of economic partnership between them and therefore relative equality. Parents are concerned about their children's education, and they have the resources to provide them the experiences they need to succeed, from music lessons to summer jobs in business. A professional immigrant woman employed as a high-level manager in a high-tech firm told Glenn that she and her husband bought a small resort in the mountains and put their teen-aged sons in charge to give them the opportunity to run a business.

Because of the sojourning strategy adopted by Chinese in response to racist immigration policies, the growth of *American-born Chinese families* was retarded. Despite their continuous presence in the United States, the Chinese American population remained largely "foreign-born" for almost 100 years. Most immigrant groups shift over time to English as a first language and lose traditional cultural practices. The Chinese were often viewed as unassimilable because they retained their language and customs decade after decade. What was not apparent to many people is that the resident population was constantly being replaced by new immigrants. Thus it was not until 1940 that the majority of Chinese were American-born; by 1960, more than 60 percent of the Chinese in this country were born here. It seemed that the Chinese were at long last becoming assimilated. The huge influx of immigrants after 1965 dramatically changed the balance once again, and by 1980, 63.3 percent of the Chinese population were foreign-born. Thus American-born families, although a sizable segment, have once again become the minority. Because of the many different cohorts of immigration, American-born Chinese are quite heterogeneous, ranging from fourth- or fifth-generation descendants of nineteenth-century pioneers to fifth-generation children of postwar immigrants. This segment tends to be college educated, and with the fall of discriminatory barriers, they can find white-collar jobs outside the ethnic enclave. In 1980, fully 38.8 percent of all American-born men 15 and over were employed as professionals and managers and another 29.7 percent as technical, sales, and administrative support employees (U.S. Bureau of the Census 1988).

Many were born in Chinatown, but they aspire to better living conditions outside Chinatown. This move represents a shift in economic orientation from immigrant parents. Immigrants were concerned with minimizing current spending in order to save money to invest in business or real estate, to send children to China for education, or to save for the future. They were willing to put up with cramped and substandard housing to save on rent. American-born Chinese are less willing to sacrifice present comfort for the future; perhaps they also feel more secure about the future. In any case, Wong (1985) notes that this group seems to spend more on household goods and other consumer items, even buying on credit. They seek housing that is consistent with their occupational status and income. They often end up in predominantly white neighborhoods and suburbs where, they perceive, schools will be better for their children. Pioneer families who moved into predominantly white areas in the 1960s sometimes encountered prejudice. One mother recalls that her family was the first Asian family to move into a suburban town near Boston. Her children were harassed and called names at school, so she made a special effort to be a good citizen. She got involved in the PTA, scouting, and other community activities to ease her children's acceptance. Her account accords with Wong's observation in New York that American-born Chinese parents tend to participate in organizations such as the PTA. Their participation is eased by their facility in English. The lack of participation by other immigrant parents does not mean that they are less concerned about their children's schooling, but they feel that school policy is the teachers' and administrators' responsibility.

Gender and Generational Relations.   Wives have high rates of labor force participation, either as professionals or white collar workers. Almost one third (31.7 percent) of American-born Chinese women are professionals or managers, and 53.1 percent are technical, sales, or administrative support workers (U.S. Bureau of the Census 1988). Husband and wife are thus coequal breadwinners. One observer claims that gender and generational relations are "American," that is, egalitarian, with husband and wife sharing housework and child care and children being allowed to make their own decisions. However, no systematic study has been done of the actual division of labor.

Although children socialize with non-Chinese peers and thus grow up with attenuated ties to other Chinese, parents still make frequent visits to Chinatown to shop and eat. Parents vary in the degree of concern with maintaining cultural tradition, although American-born Chinese usually do not speak Chinese at home. Parents may try to get their children interested in Chinese culture, even sending them to language school. Children rarely learn the language and are more interested in fitting in with their peers. However, when they reach college, some American-born Chinese experience an "identity crisis." They may go through a search for their ethnic roots by taking courses in Asian American history, getting involved in Asian American social life, or joining political organizations aimed at helping the poor and elderly in Chinatown.

Countering the trend toward "assimilation" among immigrant and American-born professionals has been the huge influx of *new working-class immigrant families* since 1965. About half of the post-1965 immigrants can be classified as working class, having been employed as service workers, operatives, craftsmen, or laborers in Hong Kong. Of those classified as professional or managerial at entry, a significant portion experienced downward mobility into blue-collar and service occupations because of language difficulties or nonacceptance of foreign credentials.

This group consists primarily of families, either immigrating as a nuclear family group or in a relay fashion, with one member immigrating first and sending for the others. A common motive for immigration is the parents' desire to ensure greater educational and economic opportunities for their children. Because of the preference given to relatives under the 1965 act, most immigrants use kinship ties with previous immigrants to gain entry. They in turn sponsor other kin, so that over time an extended kin network is reassembled. Equal weight is given to husband's and wife's ties under this law, thereby negating the traditional emphasis on male lineage. Thus, for example, a couple might be sponsored by the wife's sister. The couple in turn might sponsor the husband's mother, who later sponsors another of her children, and so on in a chain of relations on both sides. Over time an extended family group is reconstituted. Typically, they do not all reside in one household, although several related households may be involved in a family business, such as a restaurant or garment factory (Wong 1985).

For new arrivals, Chinatown is often the first stopping place. Having given up property, businesses, or jobs and having exhausted their resources or even gone into debt to pay for transportation and settlement, working-class immigrants must quickly find a way to make a living. Those who arrive with capital have some choices—they can take time to learn English and perhaps get some job training or buy a small business. For those without resources, language problems and discrimination in construction and craft trades limit options. The most common strategy is for husband and wife to find employment in the secondary labor market, the labor-intensive, low-capital service and small manufacturing sectors. A typical constellation is a husband employed as a waiter, cook, janitor, or store helper, and a wife employed as a stitcher in a garment shop. Although each individual's wages are low, the pooled income is enough to support the family at a modest level. Full-time employment is a new experience for women. Although many were employed in Hong Kong, they usually did so part-time or engaged in piecework at home, sewing garments or assembling plastic flowers. In the United States, they must learn to juggle a full-time job outside the home with housework and child care.

In the dual-earner working-class household, production and reproduction are completely segregated. In contrast to the round-the-clock togetherness of the small producer household, family members spend most of the day apart. Parents' lives are regulated by the demands of the job, whereas children's lives outside school hours are relatively unstructured, usually in the company of peers whose parents also work. Children see mothers more than fathers, mostly because many mothers take children to the factory with them, have their school-age children come to their workplace after school, or go home to cook the evening meal before returning for an evening shift (Chao 1977; Ikels and Shang 1979; Sung 1987). Still, a study by Betty Sung showed that 17 percent of Chinese high school students in New York did not see their mother once during the week. Even less contact occurs between father and children. If they are employed in a restaurant, fathers' hours often prevent them from seeing children at all. The most common shift for restaurant workers is 2:00 in the afternoon until 11:00 or 12:00 at night. Thirty-two percent of the students in Sung's survey did not see their fathers at all during a typical day. This finding accords with student informants in Boston, who reported that they saw their father only on his days off.

Husbands' and wives' responsibilities for production and reproduction tend to be symmetrical: both are responsible for breadwinning. Because it is in the form of wages, women's contribution is highly visible. This contribution constitutes a larger portion of family income than in Hong Kong because of the downward shift of the husband's occupational status. A college student who immigrated with her parents as a young teenager reported that after immigration, relations between her parents were much more equal. The father started helping with housework, and the mother had more say in decision-making.

With two working parents, ties between generations break down. Children complain about the parents' long hours away from home and fatigue when at home. Lack of common experiences leaves little for them to talk about. One young student noted, "We can discuss things, but we don't talk that much. We don't have that much to say." In addition, many parents underwent traumatic experiences from World War II, the Chinese Revolution, or uprooting to Hong Kong that they refuse to discuss. Taboos against certain topics become a barrier to intimacy. Parents in turn complain that they have lost control over their children. They attribute their loss of authority to their children's becoming too Americanized. Because parents are not around much to speak to them in Chinese, the children often lose their ability or willingness to speak Chinese. An immigrant mother lamented,

> Because the family budget is too great, the parents usually have to work and leave the children at home with no one to care for them. That's why our children pick up bad social habits and become Westernized to the point that their own culture gets washed away. Their faces are Chinese but their action and language are all western. How could our children not learn to be bad? (Chinese American Workers: Past and Present 1980:55)

When they reach adolescence, children can find a part-time job, which gives them independence. The absence of close-knit family life among these new immigrants has been blamed for the eruption of youth rebellion, delinquency, and gang violence in Chinatowns during the 1960s and 1970s (Fong 1968; Lyman 1970; Sheu 1986). In addition, adolescents made up a larger proportion of the new immigrants than in previous cohorts; they encounter difficulties in school because of language, and when they leave school, they face unemployment or a low-wage job. Similar difficulties were experienced by earlier immigrants, but they may seem less tolerable in an era when expectations are higher and there is more resentment of institutional racism.

CONTEMPORARY TRENDS

Having discussed the varieties of contemporary Chinese American families, we now turn to demographic, political, and social trends that are affecting Chinese American families as a whole. Probably the most dramatic change has been sheer population growth over the past 25 years. The population of Chinese Americans nearly doubled between 1970 and 1980, rising from 431,583 to 812,178 (see Table 2). It doubled again to 1,645,472 by 1990 (U.S. Census 1992.) Most of the increase was through immigration—of such magnitude as to alter fundamentally the composition of the population. Whereas in 1960, more than 60 percent of the Chinese population were born in the United States, by 1980, the ratio had shifted in the other direction, so that 63.3 percent were foreign-born. Much family communication thus goes on in Chinese. Fully 80 percent of all Chinese persons 5 years and over were reported to speak a language other than English at home. Although speaking Chinese indicates that Chinese American families were retaining traditional culture, the lack of English skills was a serious hindrance for adults. Nearly one third (31.7 percent) of persons 18 years and older said that they spoke English not well or not at all.

Recent immigration has led to the continued "normalization" of family life by evening out the gender ratio. In earlier periods, a skewed ratio made it impossible for many men to form families. Immigrants in the 1940s and 1950s were predominantly women, and immigration after 1965 was made up of family groups. With the aging and dying out of the "bachelor" generation, the gender ratio evened out so that by 1980, it was almost completely balanced at 102 men for every 100 women. (The U.S. population as a whole has 94.5 males for every 100 females.)

Although they now resemble dominant-culture families more than in the past, a composite portrait based on 1980 census data shows that Chinese Americans continue to be distinguishable from white Americans. Furthermore, although they are also distinguishable from blacks, Hispanics, and other Asian–Pacific Island subgroups, they share some interesting commonalities with these historically oppressed minorities.

In terms of household structure, for example, Chinese and other Asians resemble blacks and Hispanics more than they do whites in their propensity to absorb extended kin. Roughly 28 percent of Asian households include extended kin, a percent comparable to that of Hispanics (28 percent) and only slightly lower than that of blacks (30 percent); all three are significantly higher than for whites (18 percent) (Farley and Allen 1989). Thus the average size of households was markedly higher (3.65 persons) than for U.S. households as a whole (3.27 persons). The larger average size is not due to the presence of more children, because the population under 19 is relatively smaller than in the U.S. population as a whole. In other words, without immigration, the Chinese population would not be expected to grow (Jiobu 1988).

TABLE 2.   Selected Social and Economic Characteristics of Chinese Population: 1980

CHARACTERISTICS	TOTAL U.S.	CHINESE
Total persons	226,545,805	812,178
Region		
Northeast	21.7%	26.8%
Midwest	26.0%	9.2%
South	33.3%	11.3%
West	19.1%	52.7%
Age and Gender		
Percent under 5 years old	7.2%	7.1%
Percent 18 years old and over	71.8%	74.1%
Percent 65 years old and over	11.3%	6.9%
Median age	30.0	29.8
Males per 100 females	94.5	102.4
Type of Family		
Families	59,190,133	191,640
Married-couple families	81.8%	86.8%
Female householder, no husband present	13.9%	8.5%
Male householder, no wife present	3.4%	4.7%
Persons per family	3.27	3.65
Nativity, Citizenship, and Language		
Percent foreign-born	6.2%	63.3%
Persons 15 years old and over	175,307,629	640,563
Percent citizen	96.6%	58.9%
Percent of persons 5 years old and over who speak a language other than English at home	11.0%	80.6%
Educational Attainment		
Persons 25 years old and over	132,836,687	494,918
High school graduates	66.5%	71.3%
Four or more years of college	16.2%	36.6%
Labor Force Status		
Males 16 years and over		
In labor force	75.1%	74.3%
Unemployed	6.5%	3.1%
Females 16 years and over		
In labor force	49.9%	58.3%
Unemployed	6.5%	4.1%
Occupation		
Managerial and professional	22.7%	32.6%
Technical, sales, and administrative support	30.3%	30.1%
Precision production, craft, and repair	12.9%	5.6%
Operators, fabricators, and laborers	18.3%	12.7%
Service	12.9%	18.6%
Farming, forestry, and fishing	2.9%	0.5%
Workers in Family in 1979		
No workers	12.8%	7.1%
One worker	33.0%	17.5%
Two workers	41.7%	46.8%
Three or more workers	12.5%	18.7%

TABLE 2.   Selected Social and Economic Characteristics of Chinese Population: 1980 (*con't*)

CHARACTERISTICS	TOTAL U.S.	CHINESE
Income in 1979		
Median family income (dollars)	19,917	22,559
Median income of persons with income		
Persons 15 years and over	8,089	8,133
Male, 15 years and over	12,192	10,797
Female, 15 years and over	5,263	6,064
Per capita	7,298	7,476
Income in 1979 Below Poverty Line		
Families in poverty	9.6%	10.5%
Persons 15 years and over in poverty	12.4%	13.3%

Anecdotal evidence suggests that the propensity to absorb extended kin is not a re-creation of the ideal Chinese "big family," with grandparents, parents, and children under one roof. Rather, a widowed parent may be taken in, or a nephew may be "adopted." The importance of extended family ties cannot be measured solely by common residence. Among Chinese Americans, it is not uncommon for the extended family living in separate households to share some domestic and economic functions (cf. Stack in the case of urban blacks). Immigration laws and the economics of immigration may have reconstructed the extended kin group as a productive unit. Wong (1985) found it not uncommon among Chinese immigrants for family businesses to be owned and operated by a group of relatives, such as a father and his married sons and their spouses. The preference given to relatives by immigration law encourages residents to sponsor relatives and employ them in family business. Because of the difficulties of obtaining loans from banks, many immigrants turn to family sources, pooling assets to finance businesses.

A second characteristic that Chinese share with blacks is women's central economic role. Despite very different images of black and Chinese women, Chinese American women, like their black sisters, historically have had high rates of labor force participation (Glenn 1985). They continue to do so regardless of social class. In 1980, 58.3 percent of Chinese women 16 and over were in the labor force, compared with 49.9 percent of all U.S. women. As in the case of blacks, womanhood has not been defined in terms of a private-public dichotomy or by strict domesticity. Wives are expected to contribute to family income, and their earnings are crucial to the family's economic survival. Again, like their black counterparts, Chinese wives' earnings constitute a higher percentage of family income than is the case among whites. Among U.S. households, women's earnings (including those who worked part-time or part of the year) averaged 43.1 percent of men's, whereas among Chinese households women's earnings averaged 56.2 percent of men's. The discrepancy between men's and women's earnings is smaller for two interrelated reasons: Chinese men are paid less than white men, and Chinese women earn more than white women. We think that this trend is because they more often work full-time and have more continuous work histories and therefore have accrued more seniority. Over three-quarters of employed Chinese American women had a usual work week of 35 or more hours; more than three-quarters worked more than half the year. Whatever success Chinese Americans have achieved economically, it has been because of a corporate effort by husbands and wives. This pattern is similar to that of black middle-class families (cf. Willie 1981).

As noted at the beginning of this chapter, Chinese Americans are widely seen as highly successful, exceeding all other groups, including European Americans, in socioeconomic attainment. Although this finding is true on the average, averages are only part of the story. We need also to consider distribution. Chinese households are characterized by a bipolar distribution on various indices of achievement. That is, they tend to be clustered at the upper and lower ends of the spectrum in education, occupation, and income. Thus the 1980 Census shows that the Chinese exceed the population as a whole at the upper levels of education: 36.6 percent of Chinese Americans 25 years and over had 4 or more years of college, compared with 16.2 percent in the U.S. population as a whole. Despite remarkably high rates of college education, however, 28.7 percent have less than high school, not much less than the U.S. population as a whole (33.5 percent). Moreover, among those with 8 or fewer years of schooling, fully 21.3 percent of Chinese Americans fall into this bottom category. In terms of occupation, Chinese Americans are substantially more likely to be employed in the managerial and professional occupations (32.6 percent) than the U.S. population as a whole (22.7 percent), but Chinese Americans are also more likely to be employed in the low-paid service occupations (18.6 percent) than is true of the U.S. population as a whole (12.9 percent). Overall, Chinese Americans fare well in terms of family income, with a median of $22,559 annually, compared with $19,917 for all U.S. families. However, this higher income was earned by more people in the household working: 65 percent of Chinese households had two or more earners, compared with 54.2 percent of all households; and 18.7 percent of Chinese households had three or more workers, compared with 12.5 percent of all households. At the other end of the spectrum, 10.5 percent of Chinese American households were below the poverty threshold, higher than the 9.6 percent of all American households. Attention to the socioeconomic status of successful Chinese American families has overshadowed interest in the substantial minority that remain in poverty. Furthermore, important regional differences exist: Chinese are not doing uniformly well in all cities. In 1980, Chinese families in New York had a median income nearly 50 percent lower than those in San Francisco–Oakland ($24,409 versus $16,100), and they had a poverty rate nearly 50 percent higher (13.2 percent versus 9.5 percent).

Chinese families continue to differ from both dominant culture and minority families in rates of marital dissolution. Judging by the percentage of divorced persons among Chinese 15 and over in the population (2.5 percent), divorce is still much less common than in the population at large (6.3 percent) (Farley and Allen 1989:427). This is partly an artifact in that immigrants constitute the majority of the Chinese population, and few divorced persons immigrate (Wong 1986). Women are more likely to be divorced than men, reflecting perhaps the smaller opportunity that women have to remarry after divorce. Social workers in Chinatown point out the barriers to immigrant women divorcing even if they wanted to.

Divorced women find it difficult to survive economically and are not readily accepted in the community. As suggested earlier, high suicide rates among women may reflect the lack of choice.

Because of lower rates of marital dissolution, single-headed families are also rarer among Chinese Americans than among U.S. families in general. Of all Chinese family households, 86.8 percent are headed by married couples, compared with 82.8 percent of all U.S. family households. What is unusual is the relatively high percentage of Chinese households headed by men (4.7 percent versus 3.4 percent of U.S. family households). (Another 8.4 percent of Chinese family households are headed by women.) Given the pattern of relay immigration, a significant portion of these male-headed families may be temporary, awaiting the arrival of a wife.

Comparatively speaking, a small percentage of Chinese youth live in single-headed households. Roughly 10 percent of all Chinese under 18 live in households headed by women. This finding suggests the continued presence of parental controls on children. Yet, as noted earlier, in many working-class families, both parents work, and there is little daily supervision of children. Traditionally the Chinese have been noted for their low rates of juvenile delinquency, attributed to strong family controls and adherence to principles of filial piety. Thus, the outbreak of gang violence and delinquency in Chinatown in the 1970s and 1980s generated a great deal of commentary about possible breakdown in family cohesiveness. What few observers noted, however, is that low rates of delinquency in the past were in part due to the small number of youth in the population because of immigration policies. The relatively larger adult population was able to exert control also because they controlled economic opportunities for youth who could not find jobs outside the "Great Wall" of the ghetto (Haynor and Reynolds 1937). Thus the rise of youth crime and gang formation is due to several interrelated changes: the increase in the juvenile population, especially among recent immigrants; the problems that they confront in school; lack of job opportunities; frustrated expectations; parents' absence; and breakdown of community controls, especially because elders of the community no longer control economic life. It might further be added that today's immigrant youth comes from an urbanized, Western background and so is influenced by youth culture and is less willing to put up with limited expectations (Sung 1987; Tsai 1986:165).

Another trend that affects Chinese American families is the increased rate of out-marriage, which was rare in the past. The California antimiscegenation statute remained in force until 1948. Many other states, especially in the South, had such statutes in effect until 1967, when they were declared unconstitutional by the Supreme Court. U.S. Census data for 1980 indicate that about 15 percent of Chinese husbands and 16.8 percent of Chinese women are married to non-Chinese spouses, mainly whites. Systematic studies of intermarriage based on surveys of marriage licenses suggest, however, that the rate of out-marriages among those marrying in the 1970s and 1980s is much higher. Kitano and others' (1984) study of Chinese, Japanese, and Filipinos in Los Angeles found that in 1975, 1977, and 1979, more than 40 percent of all marriages involving a Chinese American were to non-Chinese; Sung (1990) found that 27 percent of all marriages involving a

Chinese American were out-marriages. Out-marriage rates were higher for those with more education and income and higher occupational status; it was also related to generation, with American-born more likely to marry out.

Perhaps the most striking pattern is the difference between male and female rates. Women were more likely to marry out than men (56.3 versus 43.6 percent in Los Angeles, for example). Discussion of the issue with students suggests that racial domination is a factor in this pattern. Weiss (1974) has suggested that Asian women are judged more attractive by white standards of femininity than Asian men by white standards of masculinity. Some Asian female students stated that they liked being associated with white men because in U.S. society, white men have power. However, another factor may ironically be the patriarchal family system that emphasizes male lineage. Chinese American sons may be under more pressure from parents to marry within the group to continue the family line. This interpretation is consistent with the pattern in earlier times in which parents opposed their sons' marrying an American-born Chinese and arranged marriages with Chinese-born women to ensure a docile daughter-in-law.

In one major Asian American group, the Japanese, out-marriage rates approach 60 percent. Because there is little new immigration and the population is not growing, out-marriage could lead to the disappearance of the "Japanese American." Is this likely to happen to the Chinese? We need to keep two factors in mind. First, the rate of out-marriage of minority groups is inversely related to group size; that is, the smaller the minority, the more frequent out-marriage is. Second, rate of out-marriage increases with each generation in the United States. The rate of future out-marriage among Chinese Americans will therefore depend on population growth and immigration. As the Chinese population grows in size, the chances of finding a spouse from within the group increase. As long as immigration continues at a fairly high rate, a substantial segment of the population will marry mainly within the group. On the other hand, there will inevitably be an increase in American-born Chinese, who are more likely to marry out. Overall the rate of out-marriage should increase but stay lower than that of the Japanese for some years to come.[5]

Boundaries and Connections: Family and Community.   The influx of new immigrants has revitalized the major urban Chinatowns in San Francisco, New York, and Boston as a focus for Chinese community life. At the same time, the growing heterogeneity of the population and increasing dispersal beyond the boundaries of Chinatown have altered the role of Chinatown as the center of family life. At one time, when immigrants came from the same districts and spoke a common dialect, clan and other family associations were significant forces. Families turned to them for mutual aid, and social life revolved around the activities of these organizations. These organizations cut across socioeconomic lines, linking affluent merchant and professional families with laundry owners and workers. With the huge influx of new immigrants from many different backgrounds and suburbanization, family associations have lost membership and influence. New immigrants no longer join or turn to them for aid.

In their place have grown a host of municipal and state agencies and voluntary political organizations. These organizations came into being partly through community demands: as the Chinese have grown in numbers and political clout and developed greater political sophistication, they have become more vocal and organized in demanding their share of public services. The influx of new immigrants also coincided with the rise of the War on Poverty, and many new programs were instituted at that time. Although bilingual services are still inadequate, a number of city and country agencies provide medical care, legal advice, counseling services, and other services in the larger Chinatowns. Some see these changes as evidence of the empowerment of what had long been a voiceless, colonized ghetto. The Chinese community increasingly has clout in the city halls of some of America's largest cities. Some, however, lament the loss of the "neighborhood" quality of the old Chinatown, the feeling of belonging to "one big family" (cf. Chao 1977; Sung 1990). The change has meant a lessening of community surveillance that used to reinforce parental controls over children.

The rise of social service agencies and political organizations has also affected gender relations. In contrast to the male-dominated clan organizations, social service agencies employ many women as social workers and administrators. Women also play an active role on the boards of agencies and political organizations. Through their activities they form connections with other women—networking has become the buzzword. Women have thus emerged as centers of community networks and maintainers of community, a role they share with women in other minority communities (Yap 1989). Their emergence as community leaders and activists affects women's position in the family. New immigrant women, who in past times would have been isolated, have some direct access to counseling and other support services. They are therefore less dependent on their husbands or their husbands' associations.

The End of Racism?   Opportunities no doubt have never been greater for Chinese Americans, and current immigration policies facilitate rather than militate against family formation. Docs this status mean that racism is no longer a major factor affecting Chinese American families? Middle-class Chinese may feel relatively safe when they stay in their own environment, but they cannot help but be aware of a rising tide of anti-Asian violence, most of it directed against new immigrants and students. That no one with an Asian face is safe is vividly underscored by the murder of Vincent Chin by an unemployed automobile factory foreman angry at the Japanese; the murderer was let off with a suspended sentence. Children are subjected to name-calling, taunting, and even beatings by white and minority peers. Some immigrant mothers in New York have been called "overprotective" of their children because of fear for their children's safety (Chao 1977). Certainly all Chinese American parents have to be somewhat concerned about their children's safety and well-being. Another lesson that they have to teach them is to try harder than their white peers. Professionals report that they still have to work twice as hard to attain the same recognition as a white, and they are unlikely to rise out of purely technical positions into managerial ones because Asians are not seen as managerial material (Mark 1990).

CONCLUSIONS: REVISIONING THE CHINESE AMERICAN FAMILY

As changes go on in Chinese American families, we need to begin reformulating our approaches to studying the Chinese American family. Just as family sociology itself has been subject to critical revision, so must the sociology of the Chinese American family be rethought.

First, we need to give a more central place to women's experiences in the family. Until recently Chinese and Chinese American women have been largely invisible; where they appeared, they did so in stereotyped, one-dimensional guises. Recent feminist scholarship on the situation of Chinese peasant women suggests that women were not simply passive victims of a patriarchal family system. Although showing that indeed women were oppressed, these studies also reveal that women actively struggled and sometimes resisted victimization. They fought to preserve ties with children and grandchildren and to keep this uterine group together. Women also cooperated across households and sometimes gained considerable power and influence. In the United States, Chinese American women have played active roles in maintaining culture by transmitting folk legends and family histories to children. Ties between women, especially mothers and daughters, are the bonds that hold the family together. And they continue to maintain contact with far-flung family members, to observe traditional celebrations, and to keep track of family news. They were and are the "kin-keepers." As they moved out into the community, they became vital links between the family and schools and ethnic organizations. Women are active in the community, in part because they see this as an extension of their responsibilities as mothers (Yap 1989). They were active in political movements to support China during World War II and in support of the revolution in the 1930s (Yung 1990); today their daughters are active in organizing garment workers and fighting violence against Asian Americans.[6]

Second, just as study of black families has led to questioning the nuclear household as the "normal" mode of family, the study of Chinese American families leads us to question the universality of the nuclear family. In the earlier period, we saw in the split-household forms that income pooling and reproduction may occur between individuals separated by an ocean. In the current period, among new immigrants, domestic sharing and production may involve several related households. Even though extended kin do not reside together, they may cooperate in running a common family business. They may also live nearby, pool income, and share certain domestic functions, such as meals.

Third, we need to overcome the tendency to see the family either as a passive product of outside forces or as an autonomous, self-contained unit operating according to different principles from the "outside" world. To understand the Chinese American family, we must recognize the impacts of racism and economic structure on family formation and intrafamily relations. We must simultaneously recognize the assaults that have been perpetrated on Chinese families by racist immigration policy, a race segregated labor system, and legal and political restrictions on mobility and the active struggle on the part of the Chinese to build family life despite the assaults. The Chinese American family has been a "culture of resistance" (Caulfield 1974).

Fourth, we need to recognize the family not as a monolithic entity with singular interests, but as a differentiated institution. Careful reading of descriptions and personal accounts reveals considerable conflict between generations and between men and women. Power is not equally distributed and shapes relationships among members. Each member has a different position in the division of labor. Therefore, each has a unique point of view. Multiple points of view have been better addressed by fictional sources than by social scientists; for example, Amy Tan's novel, *The Joy Luck Club,* has alternate chapters written from the point of view of daughters and mothers. Much more systematic study is needed of the gender and generational "politics" within the household. Systematic studies of gender politics and generational relations in Chinese American families need to replace impressionistic generalizations.

Finally, we need to develop a concept of Chinese and Chinese American culture as dynamic. Like culture in general, Chinese American culture is not static but is constantly being created. The Chinese culture that recent immigrants bring is not the same as the Chinese culture that nineteenth-century immigrants brought. The interaction and mixing of these influences and varying political, legal, and social conditions of life in the United States have created a rich and diverse Chinese American culture. The family is the crucible within which culture is created, maintained, and passed on.

ENDNOTES

1. This act specifically excluded laborers and their relatives, although it exempted officials, students, tourists, merchants, relatives of merchants, and citizens.
2. A social worker in Boston's Chinatown claimed that children of laundry owners tended to do better in school than children of wage workers because of the constant parental supervision.
3. It is interesting that the literature for the most part focuses on the father-son tie and secondarily on the husband-wife and mother-son ties. The mother-daughter tie has been ignored. Yet, judging from two important literary treatments and a film, the mother-daughter dynamic is emotionally charged. Identification with and differentiation from the other are central to the Chinese American daughter's identity formation, and getting daughter married and perhaps established in a career is seen as crucial to mother's identity (cf. Kingston 1976; Tan 1989). Kingston has said in a talk that she began writing at an early age as a way of making private space for herself in a household where her mother constantly intruded upon and took up most of the psychic space.
4. Many of them, along with visitors and seamen, were stranded by the Chinese Revolution and given permanent resident status by the Displaced Persons Act of 1948. Others were allowed to stay under the Refugee Relief Act of 1953 and a presidential directive in 1962 that permitted refugees from mainland China to enter via Hong Kong (Wong 1988).
5. A number of studies have been done of "mixed" marriages and dual identity of Japanese, but only one so far of the Chinese (Sung 1990). More needs to be done.
6. The neglect of women is being redressed in literary accounts. Whereas memoirs and novels before 1950 (for example, Chu 1979, orig. 1961; Lowe 1943; Wong 1950) focus on the father as the central authority figure and influence, memoirs and novels of the 1970s and 1980s focus on mothers as emotional centers and on the ambivalence of mother-daughter relations (for example, Kingston 1976; Tan 1989).

REFERENCES

Brenner, Johanna, and Barbara Laslett. 1986. "Social Reproduction and the Family." In *Sociology: From Crisis to Science?* Vol. 2, *The Social Reproduction of Organization and Culture,* edited by U. Himmelstrand, 116–131. London: Sage.

Caulfield, Minna D. 1974. "Imperialism, the Family and Cultures of Resistance." *Socialist Revolution* 20:67–85.

Chao, Rose, 1977. *Chinese Immigrant Children.* New York: Department of Asian Studies, The City College, City University of New York.

Chapman, Mary. 1892. "Notes on the Chinese in Boston." *Journal of American Folklore* 5:321–324.

Cheng, Lucie, and Edna Bonacich. 1984. *Labor Immigration Under Capitalism: Asian Immigrant Workers in the United States Before World War II.* Berkeley: University of California Press.

Chinese American Workers. 1980. *Chinese American Workers: Past and Present—An Anthology of Getting Together.* New York.

Chinn, Thomas, H. Mark Lai, and Philip Choy. 1969. *A History of the Chinese in California: A Syllabus.* San Francisco: Chinese Historical Society of America.

Chu, Louis. 1979. *Eat a Bowl of Tea.* Seattle: University of Washington Press (orig. 1961).

Clausen, Edwin G., and Jack Bermingham. 1982. *Chinese and African Professionals in California: A Case Study of Equality and Opportunity in the United States.* Washington, DC: University Press of America.

Coolidge, Mary. 1909. *Chinese Immigration.* New York: Henry Holt.

di Leonardo, Micaela. 1987. "The World of Cards and Holidays: Women, Families and the Work of Kinship." *Signs* 12:440–453.

Dill, Bonnie Thornton. 1986. "Our Mother's Grief: Racial Ethnic Women and the Maintenance of Families." Research Paper, Center for Research on Women, Memphis State University.

Dower, John W. 1986. *War Without Mercy: Race and Power in the Pacific War.* New York: Pantheon.

Farley, Reynolds, and Walter R. Allen. 1989. *The Color Line and the Quality of Life in America.* New York: Oxford University Press.

Fong, Stanley L. M. 1968. "Identity Conflict of Chinese Adolescents in San Francisco." In *Minority Group Adolescents in the United States,* edited by E. B. Brody, 111–132. Baltimore: Williams and Wilkins.

Glenn, Evelyn Nakano. 1983. "Split Household, Small Producer and Dual Wage Earner: An Analysis of Chinese-American Family Strategies." *Journal of Marriage and the Family* 45:35–46.

———. 1985. "Racial Ethnic Women's Labor: The Intersection of Race, Gender and Class Oppression." *Review of Radical Political Economy* 17(3):86–109.

———. 1987. "Gender and the Family." In *Analyzing Gender,* edited by B. Hess and M. Marx, 348–380. Newbury Park, CA: Sage.

Glick, Charles E. 1980. *Sojourners and Settlers: Chinese Migrants in Hawaii.* Honolulu: University Press of Hawaii.

Goldman, Miriam. 1981. *Goldiggers and Silverminers.* Ann Arbor: University of Michigan Press.

Gordon, Milton M. 1964. *Assimilation in American Life: The Role of Race, Religion and National Origin.* New York: Oxford University Press.

Haynor, Norman S., and Charles N. Reynolds. 1937. "Chinese Family Life in America." *American Sociological Review* 2:630–637.

Hirata, Lucie Cheng. 1976. "The Chinese American in Sociology." In *Counterpoint: Perspectives on Asian Americans,* edited by E. Gee, 20–26. Los Angeles: Asian American Studies Center, University of California, Los Angeles.

———. 1979. "Free, Indentured and Enslaved: Chinese Prostitutes in Nineteenth Century America." *Signs* 5:3–29.

Hong, Lawrence K. 1976. "Recent Immigrants in the Chinese American Community: Issues of Adaptation and Impacts." *International Migration Review* 10:509–514.

Hsu, Francis L. K. 1971. *The Challenge of the American Dream: The Chinese in the United States.* Belmont, CA: Wadsworth.

Hunt, C. I., and L. Walker. 1974. "Marginal Trading Peoples: Chinese in the Philippines and Indians in Kenya." In *Ethnic Dynamics: Patterns of Intergroup Relations in Various Societies*, ch. 4. Homewood, IL: Dorsey Press.

Ikels, Charlotte. 1986. "Parental Perspectives on the Significance of Marriage." *Journal of Marriage and the Family* 47:253–264.

Ikels, Charlotte, and Julia Shang. 1979. *The Chinese of Greater Boston.* Interim Report to the National Institute of Aging.

Jiobu, Robert M. 1988. *Ethnicity and Assimilation: Blacks, Chinese, Filipinos, Japanese, Koreans, Mexicans, Vietnamese, and Whites.* Albany: SUNY Press.

Kingston, Maxine Hong. 1976. *The Woman Warrior: Memoirs of a Girlhood among Ghosts.* New York: Knopf.

Kitano, Harry H. L., Wai-Tsang Yeung, Lynn Chai, and Herbert Hatanaka. 1984. "Asian-American Interracial Marriage." *Journal of Marriage and the Family* 46:179–190.

Konvitz, Melvin G. 1946. *The Alien and Asiatic in American Law.* Ithaca, NY: Cornell University Press.

Kung, Shien-woo. 1962. *Chinese in American Life: Some Aspects of Their History, Status, Problems, and Contributions.* Seattle: University of Washington Press.

Kuo, Chia-ling. 1982. *Social and Political Change in New York's Chinatown: The Role of Voluntary Associations.* New York: Praeger.

Kwong, Peter. 1987. *The New Chinatown.* New York: Hill and Wang.

Laslett, Barbara, and Johanna Brenner. 1989. "Gender and Social Reproduction: Historical Perspectives." *Annual Review of Sociology* 15:381–404.

Lee, L. P., A. Lim, and H. K. Wong. 1969. *Report of the San Francisco Chinese Community Citizen's Survey and Fact Finding Committee* (abridged ed.). San Francisco: Chinese Community Citizen's Survey and Fact Finding Committee.

Lee, Rose Hum. 1956. "The Recent Immigrant Chinese Families of the San Francisco–Oakland Area." *Marriage and Family Living* 18 (February):14–24.

Li, Peter S. 1977a. "Occupational Achievement and Kinship Assistance among Chinese Immigrants in Chicago." *Sociological Quarterly* 18(4):478–489.

———. 1977b. "Fictive Kinship, Conjugal Tie and Kinship Claim among Chinese Immigrants in the United States." *Journal of Comparative Family Studies* 8:47–64.

Light, Ivan. 1972. *Ethnic Enterprise in America.* Berkeley: University of California Press.

Light, Ivan, and Charles Choy Wong. 1975. "Protest or Work: Dilemmas of the Tourist Industry in American Chinatowns." *American Journal of Sociology* 80:1342–1368.

Ling, P. 1912. "The Causes of Chinese Emigration." *Annals of the American Academy of Political and Social Sciences* 39:74–82.

Loo, Chalsa, and Paul Ong. 1982. "Slaying Demons with a Sewing Needle: Feminist Issues for Chinatown's Women." *Berkeley Journal of Sociology* 27:77–88.

Lowe, Pardee. 1943. *Father and Glorious Descendent.* Boston: Little, Brown.

Lyman, Stanford. 1968. "Marriage and the Family among Chinese Immigrants to America, 1850–1960." *Phylon* 29(4):321–330.

———. 1970. "Red Guard on Grant Avenue: The Rise of Youthful Rebellion in Chinatown." In *The Asian in the West*, 99–118. Santa Barbara, CA: ABC Clio Press.

———. 1974. *Chinese Americans.* New York: Random House.

———. 1977. "Strangers in the City: The Chinese in the Urban Frontier." In *The Asians in North America.* Santa Barbara, CA: ABC Clio Press.

———. 1986. *Chinatown and Little Tokyo: Power, Conflict and Community among Chinese and Japanese Immigrants in America.* Millwood, NY: Associated Faculty Press.

Mark, Diane Mei Lin, and Ginger Chih. 1982. *A Place Called Chinese America.* San Francisco Organization of Chinese Americans.

Mark, Shirley. 1990. Personal Communication.

McCunn, Ruthanne Lum. 1981. *Thousand Pieces of Gold.* San Francisco: Design Enterprises.

Miller, Stuart Creighton. 1969. *The Unwelcome Immigrant: The American Image of the Chinese, 1785–1882.* Berkeley: University of California Press.

Nee, Victor G., and Brett Nee. 1973. *Longtime Californ'.* Boston: Houghton Mifflin.

Park, Robert. 1950. *Race and Culture.* Glencoe, IL: The Free Press.

Pascoe, Peggy. 1990. "Gender Systems in Conflict: The Marriages of Mission-educated Chinese American Women, 1874–1939." In *Unequal Sisters,* edited by E. C. DuBois and V. L. Ruiz, 123–140. New York: Routledge.

Pfeffer, George A. 1986. "Forbidden Families: Emigration Experiences of Chinese Women under the Page Law, 1875–1882." *Journal of American Ethnic History* 6(2):28–46.

Pruitt, Ida. 1967. *Daughter of Han: The Autobiography of a Chinese Working Woman.* Stanford, CA: Stanford University Press.

Purcell, Victor. 1965. *The Chinese in Southeast Asia.* London: Oxford University Press.

Saxton, Alexander. 1971. *The Indispensable Enemy: Labor and the Anti-Chinese Movement.* Berkeley: University of California Press.

Sheu, Chuen-Jim. 1986. *Delinquency and Identity: Juvenile Delinquency in an American Chinatown.* New York: Harrow and Heston.

Siu, Paul C. P. 1987. *The Chinese Laundryman: A Study of Social Isolation.* New York: New York University Press.

Sollenberger, Richard T. 1968. "Chinese American Child-rearing Practices and Juvenile Delinquency." *Journal of Social Psychology* 74(February):13–23.

Stack, Carol. 1974. *All Our Kin: Strategies for Survival in a Black Community.* New York: Harper and Row.

Sung, Betty Lee. 1967. *Mountain of Gold.* New York: Macmillan.

———. 1987. *The Adjustment Experience of Chinese Immigrant Children in New York City.* New York: Center for Migration Studies.

———. 1990. *Chinese American Intermarriage.* New York: Center for Migration Studies.

Tan, Amy. 1989. *The Joy Luck Club.* New York: Putnam.

Tsai, Shih-Shan Henry. 1986. *The Chinese Experience in America.* Bloomington: Indiana University Press.

U.S. Bureau of the Census. 1985. *Census of Population: 1980.* Vol. 2, *Subject Reports. Marital Characteristics.* PC80-2-4C.

———. 1988. *Census of the Population: 1980.* Vol. 2, *Subject Reports. Asian and Pacific Islander Population of the United States: 1980.* PC80-2-1E.

———. 1992. *Census of the Population: 1990. General Population Characteristics, Urbanized Areas.* Table 3: Race and Hispanic Origin: 1990.

Vernon, Philip E. 1982. *The Abilities and Achievements of Orientals in North America.* New York: Academic Press.

Weiss, Melford. 1974. *Valley City: A Chinese Community in America.* Cambridge, MA: Schenkman.

Willie, Charles. 1981. *A New Look at Black Families.* Bayview, NY: General Hall.

Wolf, Margery. 1972. *Women and the Family in Rural Taiwan.* Stanford: Stanford University Press.

Wong, Bernard. 1978. "A Comparative Study of the Assimilation of the Chinese in New York City and Lima, Peru." *Comparative Studies in Society and History* 20:335–358.

———. 1979. *A Chinese American Community: Ethnicity and Survival Strategies.* Singapore: Chopmen Enterprises.

———. 1982. *Chinatown: Economic Adaptation and Ethnic Identity of the Chinese.* New York: Holt, Rinehart and Winston.

———. 1985. "Family, Kinship and Ethnic Identity of the Chinese in New York City, with Comparative Remarks on the Chinese in Lima, Peru and Manila, Philippines." *Journal of Comparative Family Studies* 16:231–254.

Wong, Jade Snow. 1950. *Fifth Chinese Daughter.* New York: Harper and Brothers.

Wong, Morrison G. 1986. "Post-1965 Asian Immigrants: Where Do They Come From, Where Are They Now, and Where Are They Going?" *Annals of the American Academy of Political and Social Sciences* 487 (September):150–168.

———. 1988. "The Chinese American Family." In *Ethnic Families in America,* edited by C. H. Mindel, R. W. Habenstein, and R. Wright, Jr., 230–258. New York: Elsevier.

Wu, C. 1972. *Chink: A Documentary History of Anti-Chinese Prejudice in America.* New York: Meridian.

Yap, Stacey G. H. 1989. *Gather Your Strength, Sisters: The Emerging Role of Chinese Women Community Workers.* New York: AMS Press.

Young, Michael, and Peter Wilmott. 1973. *The Symmetrical Family.* London: Routledge and Kegan.

Yung, Judy. 1986. *Chinese Women of America: A Pictorial History.* Seattle: University of Washington Press.

———. 1990. "The Social Awakening of Chinese American Women as Reported in Chun Sai Yat Po, 1900–1911." In *Unequal Sisters,* edited by E. C. DuBois and V. L. Ruiz, 195–207. New York: Routledge.

CHAPTER 8

Japanese American Families

Dana Y. Takagi

Sociologists and other social scientists who study the Japanese American experience nearly always turn their attention to the significance of family and kin systems. For example, the Japanese American family and/or kin system has been linked to explanations of Japanese American personality and achievement (Caudill 1952), Japanese American mental health (Sue and Morishima 1982), and the development of ethnic business (Light 1972). Many other writers have also suggested the importance of the family for understanding the Japanese American experience (Glenn 1986; Kitano 1969; Levine and Rhodes 1981; Miyamoto 1972; Petersen 1971; Yanagisako 1987). One very popular line of thinking on the family suggests that what goes on inside Japanese American families is a core reason for Japanese American achievement (Kitano 1969; Petersen 1971). Articles in major media outlets that profile Japanese Americans as a "model minority" invariably refer to the family as the enforcer of cultural norms and ethics responsible for achievement.[1]

The literature contains two major perspectives on the Japanese American family. The first of these, the cultural perspective, emphasizes continuities between traditional Japanese culture and the social practices of Japanese Americans. A major feature of the cultural perspective is that culture is seen as a key variable explaining family experiences, kin systems, and frequently educational achievement as well. The second perspective, which I label the critical perspective, emerged in opposition to culture-based explanations of the Japanese American family. Advocates of the critical perspective suggest that many other variables, such as race relations in the United States, the position of Japanese Americans in labor markets in both the white and the Japanese American community, and historically changing gender and kinship structures ought to be the starting point for the study of the Japanese American family. A key difference between the cultural perspective and the critical perspective is that in the former, culture explains family organization and kin systems, whereas in the latter, historical factors such as the transformation of gender and kin systems explain family organization.

This chapter begins with a brief discussion of cultural and critical perspectives on the Japanese American family, followed by an outline of the historical development of Japanese American families in the United States.[2] Family experiences are considered in two broad historical periods, early immigration, exclusion, and internment (1900 to 1945) and the postwar period (1945 to the present). In each of these periods, two related sets of issues on Japanese American families are discussed. One set of issues concerns how major historical factors such as immigration laws, race relations, and politics have shaped Japanese American family experiences. Such historical factors have had a profound effect on Japanese American experiences of work, community, and family. A second set of issues, partially contingent on the first, concerns what actually goes on inside Japanese American families. The distribution of status, roles, authority, and socialization processes within the family should be examined against the backdrop of the shifting historical landscape of immigration laws, racism, and internment.

These two historical periods have seen three birth cohorts of Japanese Americans and three kinship-defined generations of Japanese Americans—the Issei (first-generation), the Nisei (second-generation), and the Sansei (third-generation). The history of Japanese immigration and the formation of Japanese American communities in the United States was such that most marriages of Issei took place in the early immigration period between 1907 and 1924, thus producing a concentration of births of Nisei prior to World War II. The result was that a large proportion of Nisei marriages occurred during the war and during the early postwar period. The concentration of births and marriages of the Nisei in relatively short periods in turn produced a concentration of births of the third generation. The children of the Nisei, the Sansei, were born mostly between 1945 and 1960. At this writing, a majority of the Sansei generation are in their thirties and forties and are producing a fourth generation, the Yonsei. This chapter focuses on the family experiences of the first three generations—the Issei, Nisei, and Sansei.

CULTURAL VERSUS CRITICAL PERSPECTIVES ON JAPANESE AMERICAN FAMILIES

Culture-based perspectives of the Japanese American family are characterized by two main features. Of most importance, culture is privileged as the main variable that accounts for differences between Japanese and other racial groups. In addition, cultural explanations of the Japanese American experience are typically an extension of an assimilationist bias in the sociology of race relations. A second feature of culture-based perspectives is the tendency to view culture as constant rather than variable through different historical periods and across generations.

To say that culture is a privileged variable means that culture is assigned more explanatory weight in accounting for differences between racial and minority groups and whites than are other historical factors such as socioeconomic and political conditions in the United States. In the case of Japanese American history, culture-based perspectives typically highlight the similarities and differences between traditional Japanese culture and white middle-class culture[3] in America.

The accent on cultural difference or similarity has shifted over time. In the early period of immigration, fierce anti-Japanese activists in California insisted that economic competition and deep cultural differences between whites and Japanese confirmed the undesirable nature of Japanese immigration (Daniels 1962). James Duval Phelan, mayor of San Francisco and passionate anti-Japanese activist, stated at the first anti-Japanese rally in San Francisco in 1900 that the Japanese

> . . . are not the stuff of which American citizens are made . . . Personally we have nothing against Japanese, but as they will not assimilate with us and their social life is so different from ours, let them keep at a respectful distance. (Daniels 1962:21)

Intellectuals couched their beliefs in a more subdued language. For example, sociologist Robert Park, who is well known for his model of a cycle of race-relations—contact, competition, accommodation, and assimilation—believed that with respect to the Japanese, assimilation was an unlikely and a vexing possibility. In his introduction to E. F. Steiner's *The Japanese Invasion*, Park (1950:227) noted that whereas slavery may be seen as one of "those accommodations through which the race problem found a natural solution," such a "solution" was improbable with the Japanese. He explained that

> The Japanese, the Chinese, they too would be all right in their place, no doubt. That place, if they find it, will be one in which they do not greatly intensify and so embitter the struggle for existence of the white man. The difficulty is that the Japanese is still less disposed than the Negro or the Chinese to submit to the regulations of a caste system and to stay in his place. (p. 218)

This passage illustrates Park's racist belief that the Japanese should be relegated to a low caste position in the social order. The assimilationist model first outlined by Park (1950) and later adapted by Gordon (1964) has been criticized for being ahistorical (Takagi 1973) and for drafting a narrow and static notion of culture (Glenn 1983).

After World War II, the bulk of writing on Japanese Americans focused not on the "yellow peril" but rather on the remarkable achievements of the second generation, the Nisei. Once again, as was the case before the war, culture is frequently cited as the key to understanding the Japanese American experience. However, whereas before the war, cultural differences between Japanese and whites accounted for the aggressive, inassimilable nature of the Japanese, culture is currently viewed as the chief reason for Japanese American achievement in the postwar period. The idea that traditional Japanese culture is at the heart of Japanese American achievement was suggested by many writers in the postwar period and continues to be a popular notion today. The most articulate and thoughtful presentation of this perspective has been offered by Caudill (1952).

In an important study of Issei and Nisei, Caudill marveled at the remarkable adjustment of the Japanese to life in Chicago. He suggested that a number of factors contributed to Japanese American adjustment, among them various historical reasons and the scarcity of labor in Chicago during World War II. But according to Caudill, the most insightful hypothesis concerning Japanese American adjustment is that

> . . . there seems to be a significant compatibility (but by no means identity) between the value systems found in the culture of Japan and the value systems found in American middle class culture. (p. 9)

Caudill is careful to point out that although the cultures of Japan and middle America are quite different, the compatible value systems give rise to similar psychological adaptive mechanisms used by Japanese and by whites. In addition, Caudill notes that Japanese and white middle-class Americans share some common values, namely—politeness, respect for authority, filial piety, duty to community, diligence, cleanliness and neatness, and others. Thus, the combination of shared values and similar adaptive mechanisms, both of which spring from compatible cultures, accounts for Japanese American achievement.

Much of the research on the Japanese American family has followed the assimilationist bent in sociology. Several writers suggest that the structure of the Japanese American family follows traditional Japanese family arrangements (Kitano 1969; Miyamoto 1972), and some of these writers go on to suggest that the processes of assimilation and Japanese American achievements have flourished under such family arrangements (Caudill 1952; Kitano 1969; Petersen 1971). For most of these writers, the analysis of the family is considered within the context of attempting to explain the assimilation of Japanese Americans. Kitano (1969) says

> The Japanese have been a markedly well-behaved group and it is widely believed that this is due in large part to the Japanese family—to its structure, to its techniques in socialization and social control, and to its role in mediating the congruent and conflicting demands of the Japanese and American styles of life. (p. 60)

Culture-based perspectives portray the Japanese American family as a strong, cohesive unit that acts as an agent of both socialization of its young and social control of its members. Typical features that characterize the Japanese American family include (1) close family ties between generations indicated by strong feelings of loyalty to the family, (2) low divorce rates, which often are interpreted to be an indicator of family stability, and (3) a complex system of values and techniques of social control including guilt, shame, obligation, and duty, which are transmitted from parents to children. Culture-based perspective authors trace these major features of Japanese American families to traditional Japanese culture (Caudill 1952; Kitano 1969; Petersen 1971).

In contrast to cultural theories of the family, a critical perspective suggests that culture is but one among several variables contributing to an understanding of the Japanese American family. Cultural patterns are acknowledged to play a part in the determination of family life but are not singled out as the principal explanation of family life. Drawn from a variety of disciplines, writers in the critical perspective emphasize the importance of examining patterns of family life within the context of shifting historical arrangements of social, political, and economic conditions in American society (Glenn 1986; Yanagisako 1987).[4]

The critical perspective differs from the cultural perspective in the following three ways. First, advocates of the critical perspective argue for understanding family organization within a historical context. The historical context is set by several interrelated factors, among them, for example, shifting political and legal arrangements, labor market changes, shifts in the gender division of labor, and the extent and manifestation of racism. By situating an analysis of the family within historically changing conditions, advocates of the critical perspective are essentially arguing for a historical and multivariate[5] approach that emphasizes the ways in which several different and changing factors influence family organization. For example, Yanagisako (1987) has detailed the very different family patterns of Issei and Nisei and has suggested that differences between the two illustrate the concept of oppositional categories typical to both gender and kinship analysis. She weaves into her analysis several key variables, including industrial change, shifts in the division of labor, and cultural change.

Secondly, in the critical perspective, the family itself is not necessarily assumed to be a cohesive and stable unit, but rather is seen as a potential site of conflict over power asymmetries between men and women. For example, Glenn (1986), in her study of Issei and Nisei domestics, has suggested that gender politics within the family were related to different economic strategies open to individual members of the family. In other words, Japanese American women face a "concurrent reality" in the family, in that their labor is a means to reproduce the family as an emotional and economic unit, while at the same time their labor is also a vehicle for subordination and oppression within the family (Glenn 1986:193). For Glenn the family represents two sides of a dialectical experience for women: On the one hand, the Japanese American family is a social unit that must struggle against external forces such as racial oppression, and, on the other hand, the family is also an organization that subjugates women.

A third important way in which the critical perspective parts company with a culture-based perspective is that the former does not link an analysis of family organization or family patterns to an assimilationist bias. There is no latent analysis or presumption in the critical perspective to explain Japanese American achievement or assimilation. In fact, followers of the critical perspective are likely to question the appropriateness of the concept of assimilation when referring to the Japanese American family experience. For example, Glenn (1986) explicitly rejects assimilation models in sociology, arguing that such models do not adequately capture important features of the Japanese American experience.

HISTORICAL DEVELOPMENT OF THE JAPANESE AMERICAN FAMILY

At least two broad historical periods mark Japanese American family experiences—early immigration through evacuation, and the postwar resettlement. In each period, the organization of the family is shaped by historical forces external to the family and its members. Several key forces have shaped family patterns among Japanese Americans, among them culture, work, race relations, immigration law, and of course the wholesale evacuation of West-coast Japanese communities during World War II. In the next section we examine each of these periods and then turn to a discussion of current patterns of Japanese American families.

Immigration and Exclusion

In the late nineteenth century, the immigration of Japanese laborers to Hawaii and the mainland began in the wake of Chinese exclusion. Between 1880 and 1924, a sharp and steady rise in the Japanese population occurred in the continental United States, as recorded by the U.S. Census.[6] Daniels (1962) reports that in spite of the rapid growth in the population during immigration, Japanese were still a tiny fraction of the U.S. population, never amounting to more than 0.1 percent of the total. Most of the Japanese immigrants who came to the mainland were young men who left Japan in search of better opportunities for work or study. The class composition of the Issei was quite mixed. Ichihashi (1969:67) finds that for the period from 1886 to 1908, 39.3 percent of the immigrants were laborers, 21.5 percent were merchants, 21.4 percent were students, and 18.1 percent were officials, tourists, and others.[7] Once in the United States, the Japanese immigrants worked as domestics, laborers, cash and tenant farmers, and small entrepreneurial city tradesmen.

Numerous laws were passed against the Japanese to limit their numbers and prevent them from participating in certain occupations. In 1908, under the terms of the Gentlemen's Agreement, Japan stopped issuing passports to Japanese male laborers, and the United States thereafter refused to admit them. Although the intended effect of the law was to curb Japanese immigration to the United States, the net result instead was a shift in the type of immigrants, so that after 1907, an increasing number of women and male nonlaborers entered the United States. The continued immigration of Japanese to the United States infuriated the anti-Japanese movement. Anti-Japanese advocates were particularly frustrated by the arrival of Japanese women because they feared an increase in the Japanese population through births. Virulent anti-Japanese activity in the western states led the Japanese government to voluntarily stop issuing passports to "picture brides" in 1920. The immigration of family members of Japanese already in the United States and nonlaborers continued until the passage of the National Origins Act of 1924, which effectively barred all further Japanese immigration to the United States. After 1924, the Japanese population increased only through births.

Other laws were designed to restrict Japanese activity in certain agricultural pursuits. In California, for example, the state legislature passed a series of Alien Land Laws directed at the Japanese. The first of these, passed in 1913, prevented aliens ineligible for citizenship—the Issei—from owning land or leasing land for the typical 3-year period. The Issei complied with the new law by buying and leasing land in the names of their children, who as citizens could not be prevented from owning land. The state legislature moved in 1920 to amend the Alien Land Law of

1913 so that minor children could not own or lease land. And finally, antimiscegenation laws prohibited intermarriage of Japanese and whites.

Until the turn of the century, Japanese family life was a rarity because very few Japanese women ventured to the continental United States.[8] Ichihashi (1969) reports that the number of passports granted to Japanese women between 1886 and 1908 always constituted less than 20 percent of all passports given out by the Japanese government. In fact, for the first 19 years of Japanese emigration (1886 to 1904), women accounted for less than 10 percent of all passports granted by Japan.[9] Ichihashi found that between 1905 and 1908, the percentage of passports issued to Japanese women climbed to a high of 17 percent. And from 1908 to the passage of the National Origins Act of 1924, which effectively excluded Japanese immigrants from the United States, women and children formed 22.6 percent of the emigrants from Japan (Ichihashi 1969).

We can begin to speak of Japanese family life in the United States around the time of the Gentlemen's Agreement (1908). As with the Chinese immigrants before them, the gender distribution among Japanese immigrants was lopsided. In 1900, women constituted 4 percent of the Japanese population in the United States, 12.6 percent in 1910, and 34.5 percent in 1920. Thus, in this early period of Japanese immigration, there are two subperiods—the first two decades, in which Japanese immigration consisted primarily of men, and, after 1908, a period in which women made up a significant proportion of Japanese immigrants.[10] The difference between these two subperiods is suggested by the dramatic fall in the gender ratio of Japanese men to women, from 25:1 in 1900 to 2:1 in 1920 (Glenn 1986).

Many Japanese women immigrated as "picture brides" (shashin kekkon). Following customary practices in Japan, marriages among the Issei were arranged by a go-between (baishakunin). The formation of Japanese families depended on individual capital and wealth or, in many cases, on the ability of the immigrant to borrow the money to send for a wife. Issei men either returned to Japan to meet their future wives or, with the help of the baishakunin and family in Japan, arranged a marriage through the exchange of pictures. Glenn (1986) found that the Issei women she interviewed remember that they had little choice in the selection of their husbands. And because the marriage arrangements were often conducted through letters and the exchange of pictures, many picture brides were surprised to find that their husbands were quite different from the photographs of the men whom they thought they had married. One of Glenn's (1986) respondents, a Mrs. Yoshida, remembers that

> A lot of people that I came together with said, "I'm going back on this very boat." I told them, "You can't do that; you should go ashore once. If you really don't like him, and you feel like going back, then you have to have a meeting and then go back" . . . Many times the picture was taken twenty years earlier and they had changed. Many of the husbands had gone to the country to work as farmers, so they had aged and became quite wrinkled. And very young girls came expecting more and it was natural.

Many authors have pointed out how the internal structure of Issei families was shaped by cultural tradition in Japan (Glenn 1986; Kitano 1969; Miyamoto 1972).

The household, or "ie," was a basic social unit in nineteenth- and early-twentieth-century Japan (Nakane 1970). The ie included members of the household (family and unrelated individuals living in the household) and acted as an economic unit of ownership, production, and consumption. The ie also acted as the basic unit responsible for organizing social activity in the community. Authority in the household was strictly organized along divisions of gender, age, and insider-outsider status. In an extended household situation, the eldest man was at the top of the authority ladder, whereas outsider women such as a daughter-in-law were at the bottom. The strict lines of hierarchy and authority in the ie clearly prescribed roles and behavior for individual members.

Kitano (1969) likens the Japanese American family to a "traditional family," in which roles, status, and authority are strictly defined. Family cohesion is obtained through rigid application of rules and prescribed obligations rather than through emotional affections. Love as a basis for cohesion in Japanese families was secondary to other means of social control. As Kitano (1969) says,

> Therefore instead of the American prescription—"you'll obey Mother because you love her"; the Japanese child was more apt to hear—"You'll obey Mother because you have to." (p. 66)

Other features of the Japanese family noted by Kitano (1969) included the use of shame and guilt to enforce norms and the consolidation of family ties through feelings of obligation and responsibility. Although Kitano notes many "unfavorable" aspects to Japanese family life, he suggests that regard for Japanese values has had some functional outcomes for Japanese Americans. One of those outcomes has been that Japanese Americans have values compatible with those of middle-class America (Kitano 1969:76).

Glenn (1986) draws a less rosy picture of the Issei family, pointing out that the organization of the family resulted in extensive oppression of Japanese women. Glenn goes on to suggest that the kind of work opportunities available to the Issei enforced a continuity between Issei family organization and traditional family organization in Japan. For example, the organization of Issei entrepreneurial enterprises coincided nicely with authority in the traditional ie. Glenn explains,

> As in Japan the household served as the basic unit of ownership, production, and consumption. The husband was the ultimate authority; he managed the farm or store and oversaw the unpaid labor of wife and children. (p. 206)

According to Glenn, the other major family strategy, the wage-earning family in which both husband and wife worked in low-paying and marginal jobs, was both consistent and contradictory with the Japanese ie system. On the one hand, the fact that Issei women were employed outside the family was consistent with the notion that women were contributing members of an economic unit. On the other hand, women's employment contradicted the traditional ie, in which women were under the economic control of men. Thus, according to Glenn, family organization of Japanese Americans is related to the work strategies of the Issei immigrants.

Life histories collected under the auspices of the Japanese Evacuation and Re-settlement Study (JERS)[11] further bear out "unfavorable" facets of Japanese Issei families mentioned by Kitano (1969) and support Glenn's (1986) contention that the family was oppressive for women. In a sample of 15 case studies reported by Thomas (1952), some remember that there was little love between their Issei parents. Many of the Nisei women have childhood memories of parental alcohol abuse, domestic violence, and long hours working in the family business. Also, several Nisei women recall that their plans for school or work took second place to those of their brothers.

World War II and Internment

The Second World War and internment of Japanese Americans destroyed the pre-war economy of the Japanese community and radically altered the organization of Japanese American families. As the prewar family organization and economic basis of the Japanese community were related phenomena, internment had a devastating impact on both. One important effect of war and internment was that the economic and social basis for Issei authority and Issei security was abruptly taken away with relocation. As Broom and Kitsuse (1956) note,

> Issei security had become dependent upon their ability to influence, directly or indirectly, their children's actions. With their increasing independence however, the Nisei were not easily controlled. (p. 42)

Broom and Kitsuse note that relocation is a stark contrast to the prewar Japanese American community. Under relocation, Issei interests clearly diverge from Nisei interests in the family. For example, the registration process and the so-called loyalty questions pitted the Nisei against their parents.[12]

> A "loyal" response might make possible the drafting of the adult Nisei male and at the same time force the relocation of the rest of the family during his absence.

Parents wanting to keep the family together might urge a disloyal response, whereas a Nisei wanting to avoid stigmatization by his peers was often inclined to answer "loyal." As Broom and Kitsuse (1959) observed,

> The registration program required that each family assess its resources for future adjustments. Changes in policies, rumors, and interpretations of policy were scrutinized for effects on family interests and family resources.
> The issues raised by the registration struck at family unity and control. In facing these problems the family was thrown back upon its internal resources, and strong leadership became an essential condition for the maintenance of family cohesion. (p. 46)

Echoing the concerns raised by Broom and Kitsuse, other writers (such as Osako 1976) have argued that several other factors chipped away at the internal structure of prewar Japanese American families. Issei parental authority concomitant with the family and Japanese prewar economy was further undermined by the loss of status and authority of the "unemployed" Issei in camp, one result of which was that Nisei children were granted more independence in social activities inside camp. In addition, only American citizens were allowed to work in the War Relocation Authority administration jobs in the camps, a fact that further divided the Issei from the Nisei. Finally, the decision of many Nisei to "resettle"[13] to work and live in the Midwestern states further separated the Nisei from the Issei and left a population of Issei parents and very young Nisei in the camps.

Postwar Period

The Nisei, a majority of whom were born between 1915 and 1940, reached young adulthood just before and just after World War II. For many of the Nisei, resettlement was their first opportunity to work and live independently of their parents. The formation of Nisei families during this period symbolizes an important difference between Issei families and Nisei families. This difference centers on a change in the relation between work and family among Issei and Nisei. Whereas for many Issei families, work (production) was closely related to family (reproduction)[14] through a traditional organization of family based on the ie, this was not the case for the Nisei. Generational and cultural differences between Issei and Nisei, along with a shift in work opportunities available to Japanese Americans after World War II, contributed to a separation between work and family for the Nisei.[15]

An important example of how the change in work for the Issei and Nisei has affected the family is detailed by Yanagisako (1987). She begins by noting that among the Issei, spheres of "inside" and "outside," which she describes as gendered domains, were such that female experiences are primarily inside the family, whereas male experiences constitute identity outside the family. One of her insightful observations is that the pattern of "inside" and "outside" domains in Issei families was transformed to be perceived as a division between "family" and "work" among the Nisei. The significance of the change in perception and in discourse about family life from the Issei to the Nisei generation, according to Yanagisako, is that it reflects a change in the relation between family and labor among the Nisei:

> The Issei's metaphor of gender opposition chiefly concerns the relative placement of men and women—their activities, relationships, and orientations—in a hierarch of social space. Men are located physically, socially and motivationally between women and the world outside the home.
>
> The Nisei opposition of "work" and "family/home" constitutes a model of gender based on labor specialization. The central concern here, and the critical difference between men and women, lies in the kind of work they do, that is, in their respective "jobs" or functions. (p. 104)

Yanagisako's core argument is that the change in the organization of the Japanese American family reflects wider historical changes in capitalist-industrial societies, where production is increasingly separated from household and family.[16]

Another significant difference between Issei and Nisei families was that many Nisei insisted upon choosing their own marriage partners. Frequently the subject of marriage was an arena for conflict between Issei parents and their Nisei children. One woman remembers this:

> Before I went to business college, my dad wanted to marry me off to a fellow but I absolutely refused to do. My mother was more sympathetic and she said she would not force me. I didn't even like the fellow and it upset me a great deal when my parents tried to arrange a marriage for me. They meant well but I just couldn't see their point of view. In some Japanese families the girls are forced to get married, even if they don't want it. (Japanese Evacuation and Resettlement Study: Ch. 22, p. 17)

Glenn (1986) has pointed out other differences between Issei and Nisei families in her study of domestic workers. She notes that in addition to the breakdown in traditional family organization due to internment, other historical changes such as geographical dispersion and changes in work have brought about greater affluence and increased leisure time. In addition, she notes a gradual weakening of Issei family organization in the Nisei generation according to age. The eldest in the Nisei cohort retain traditional elements in family life such as hierarchical authority and arranged marriages. In contrast, younger Nisei families are characterized by relative egalitarianism, shared decision-making, and companionship between husband and wife (Glenn 1986:220).[17] These changes in the division of labor in the family should not be overstated. For example, Osako (1980), in a survey of Japanese Americans in Chicago, found that among the middle-aged Japanese American couples, men seldom cooked, did laundry, or washed dishes.

CONTEMPORARY JAPANESE AMERICAN FAMILIES

The change away from traditional family organization exemplified by the ie in nineteenth-century Japan that was started by the Nisei clearly continued with the next generation, the Sansei. For example, the Sansei evidence the gender opposition (Yanagisako 1987) of work and family/home that was apparent among the Nisei. Sansei men *and* women, like their parents, attach great importance to the kind of work they do. Indeed, the Sansei held similar occupational aspirations to their parents. For example, when asked about their future plans in 1967, an overwhelming majority (87 percent of men and 90 percent of women) of the Sansei in the Japanese American Research Project (JARP)[18] study indicated that they desired white-collar occupations (Levine and Rhodes 1981:119). And an analysis of the 1980 census data reveals that the labor force participation of Japanese women continues to outrank that of most other groups in American society (Woo 1985). The occupational characteristics of the Sansei along with the high labor force participation of women suggest that labor or the kind of work that they do forms a critical portion of Sansei identity.

If the Sansei are similar to their parents in occupational achievements, they differ from their parents in other ways. One of the most dramatic differences between Nisei families and Sansei families is the trend toward intermarriage. The lifting of antimiscegenation laws in the 1950s and 1960s resulted in a dramatic rise in out-marriage among Japanese Americans. Kitano and Kikumura (1980) reported that Sansei intermarriage rates were 50 percent compared with rates of 15 percent for the Nisei and 5 percent for the Issei. A three-generation survey of Japanese Americans by the JARP revealed that 40 percent of the married Sansei had wed non-Japanese Americans (Levine and Rhodes 1981:110). It is projected that the overall out-marriage rate of the Sansei generation will be perhaps 60 percent (Levine and Rhodes 1981). Analysis of 1980 census data (Jiobu 1988) confirms that observed rates of Japanese intermarriage are five times the expected rate and that the rate of intermarriage is gender specific. Women are a little over twice as likely to intermarry as men (Jiobu 1988:161). Although the assumption has been that high intermarriage rates are an indicator of assimilation (Gordon 1964; Jiobu 1988; Kitano 1969), such a contention remains somewhat speculative.[19] But the rate of out-marriage among the Sansei clearly bespeaks consideration of a new issue for future research—how we define Japanese American families. If current projections of out-marriage continue, we will not be able to speak much longer of the Japanese American family in the singular. Rather, we will have to consider whether Japanese Americans married to other races constitute a "Japanese American" family.

For example, analysis of 1980 Public Use Microdata Sample[20] shows that 43.2 percent of married-couple households containing at least one Japanese person were headed by a non-Japanese man. The remaining 56.7 percent of households with a Japanese person were headed by Japanese men. But these Japanese male householders were not necessarily married to Japanese wives. Do households with non-Japanese husbands and Japanese wives constitute a Japanese American family? Similarly, shall we label households with Japanese husbands and non-Japanese wives as Japanese American families as well? If current exogamy trends persist, more than 50 percent of married-couple households will contain non-Japanese as either wives or husbands.

Another important feature of contemporary Japanese American families, many of whom are Sansei, is the trend toward greater equality between men and women in the family. Studies suggest a trend toward egalitarianism and less authoritarianism in the family (Osako 1980). However, Osako has noted that in spite of a tendency toward equality, a fairly strict division of household labor remains among the Nisei. Although no empirical evidence is available about the household division of labor in Sansei families, there is little reason to expect that Sansei couples have a more balanced division of tasks than whites.[21] However, we can infer that the high labor force participation of Japanese American women, for example, has had the effect of creating greater economic equality between men and women in the family. In spite of a trend toward greater economic equality, women still lag far behind men in average earnings. For example, the median income for full-time female workers was $11,241, whereas the median income for full-time male workers was $15,450.[22] Greater economic equality between men and women offers women the possibility of more choice in partnerships and less dependence in marriage. This greater economic independence may be one explanation for the higher percentage of divorced Japanese women than men (Table 1).

Several other demographic features of contemporary Japanese American families are worth noting. The marital status of the Japanese population in the United

TABLE 1. Marital Status for Japanese in the United States

	MEN (%)	WOMEN (%)
Single	38.5	24.4
Married	55.7	61.1
Separated	1.0	1.2
Widowed	1.7	8.1
Divorced	3.1	5.1

Source: Adapted from Table 34: Social Characteristics of Japanese Persons 15 Years of Age and Over by Age and Nativity for States and SMSA's with 10,000 or more. U.S. Bureau of the Census 1988.

States is presented in Table 1. Japanese men and women are more likely to be married and less likely to be divorced than white men and women. Although such figures have led to the popular impression that the Japanese family is more stable than others, such conclusions are premature.

Chu's analysis (1988) of Los Angeles County 1980 census data found that Japanese women have lower rates of both divorce and fertility than do white women. In addition, compared with whites, blacks, Chinese, Mexicans, and Vietnamese, Japanese have a very low gender ratio at 86 males per 100 females (Jiobu 1988).[23] This finding represents a reversal from the high male:female gender ratio found in the early twentieth century among Japanese immigrants. One explanation for this reversal is the increased number of immigrants after 1965 who were war brides.[24] The combined result of these characteristics is that the Japanese population in the United States has a relatively small number of young people, which in the long run will make it difficult to maintain the population (Jiobu 1988).

Data from the 1970 and 1980 censuses show that median family income for Japanese was above the U.S. median at $12,515 and $27,354, respectively.[25] Such figures have often been used as evidence for ethnic group success or assimilation. It should be pointed out, however, that considerable debate exists as to whether the demographic and socioeconomic characteristics of Japanese Americans warrant such value-laden titles as the "model minority." Although the popular conception is that the Japanese have "made it," some writers have argued that Japanese Americans do not receive the same economic returns on education as whites (Woo 1985).

In spite of the high marks that Japanese Americans receive at the educational and occupational counter, it should also be pointed out that more diversity exists in the types of Japanese American families today than in the previous two periods. Married couples and female-headed households face different economic realities. For example, the 1980 census revealed that 14.3% of Japanese American family households are headed by women. Table 2 dramatizes the difference between male- and female-headed households. Whereas the median income of married-couple families is $29,292 a year, the corresponding median income for female-headed households is $15,576.

TABLE 2. Types of Japanese Households

HOUSEHOLD TYPE	PERCENT	MEDIAN INCOME
Married couples	85.7	$29,292
Female householder with no husband present	14.3	$15,576

Source: U.S. Bureau of the Census 1988.

Not only are female-headed households poorer than married-couple families, but also female-headed households must make better use of their financial resources than married-couple households. A slightly greater percentage of female-headed households (52.8 percent) have children under 18 than married-couple households (49.8 percent).

CONCLUSIONS

The Japanese American family has undergone important changes since the arrival of Japanese laborers in the late nineteenth and early twentieth centuries. In tracing out a history of the Japanese American family, several themes can be drawn. One is that the formation and maintenance of the family have been profoundly influenced by historical factors. For example, immigration laws restricted the type of immigrants and the timing of immigration to the United States; antimiscegenation laws prevented the Japanese from marrying whites; and internment restructured family organization.

A second theme is that with each birth and kin cohort, important historical changes have occurred in the organization of the family. The family is no longer organized as the ie was, with strict lines of authority and rigidly defined rules for behavior. For example, traditional authority structures in Issei families were no longer viable when faced with a generation of children who were American citizens and the loss of economic and social authority that accompanied internment.

A third theme is that it is now difficult to speak of a singular Japanese American family experience. The racial composition of Japanese American family households as well as the differences between female-headed and married-couple households suggests some diversity in family experiences. One interesting countervailing trend is likely to face all Japanese American families: On the one hand, the evidence from the older cohort of Sansei interviewed by JARP 1967 suggests that the Sansei are interested in "retaining" their Japanese cultural heritage (Levine and Rhodes 1981). But interest in Japanese culture is not necessarily linked to a desire to reinstate the rigid prescriptions for behavior associated with the ie. On the other hand, given the high rate of out-marriage among the Sansei, this resurgence of ethnicity obviously does not apply to the selection of partners. Thus, the very definition of what constitutes a Japanese American family will be at the heart of a discussion of the future of the family for Japanese Americans.

ENDNOTES

1. It should be noted that Japanese Americans are not the only group singled out for such praise. Similar arguments have been made about Chinese American families. For a review and critique of this position, see "Split Household, Small Producer, and Dual Wage Earner: An Analysis of Chinese American Family Strategies" (Glenn 1983).

2. Discussion in this chapter focuses on Japanese American families in the continental United States.

3. A definition of white middle-class culture used by assimilationist writers is often more implicit than explicit. The writers emphasize the values of hard work, respect for authority, emphasis on education, and the ability to defer gratification.

4. As Glenn (1983) has pointed out, the critical perspective is more typical of research on black and Hispanic minority families than of Asian American families. Studies of family organization and family patterns on non-Asian minority groups frequently note the importance of institutional structures in society for understanding minority family life (Gutman 1976; Stack 1974).

5. In sociology, the term *multivariate* is typically associated with quantitative and not historical research. However, the deployment of several variables to explain historical events is also essentially a multivariate approach.

6. Ichihashi (1969) reports the Japanese population in the United States as follows:

YEAR	NUMBER
1870	55
1880	148
1890	2,039
1900	24,326
1910	72,157
1920	111,010
1930	138,834

7. It should be noted that the class character of immigration to the mainland is different from the class character of immigration to Hawaii. See Ichihashi (1969).

8. However, the situation in Hawaii was somewhat different during this early period of immigration. Japanese families were less rare in Hawaii because of the encouragement of female immigration by labor contractors (Ichihashi 1969; Takaki 1983).

9. Ichihashi (1969) notes that in one exceptional year, 1895, 10 percent of passports were issued for Japanese women.

10. Ichihashi (1969) notes that between 1911 and 1920, women constituted about 40 percent of the Japanese immigration to the United States.

11. The Japanese Evacuation and Resettlement Project led by Dorothy Swaine Thomas examined the three stages of internment: evacuation, internment, and resettlement. Included in the voluminous data collected were some 64 life histories gathered by Charles Kikuchi. See Takagi (1988, 1989) for an analysis of the life histories.

12. The loyalty questions refer to questions 26 and 27 on the registration form of the War Relocation Authority in which the internees were asked whether they are loyal to the United States and whether they would be willing to bear arms for the United States.

13. Resettlement refers to a program operated under the War Relocation Authority that allowed Nisei to leave the camps to work and live in militarily safe zones in the interior of the United States.

14. See Glenn (1983) on the separation of work from family for the Chinese.

15. The importance of the separation of work and home for understanding change in an upper Manhattan neighborhood is given by Katznelson (1981).
16. This distinction between work and home has also been looked at by Katznelson (1981) as the distinction between work and community.
17. Osako (1980) made similar findings in a survey of 225 Japanese Americans in Chicago.
18. The Japanese American Research Project headed by Gene Levine was a three-generation survey of Japanese Americans. The results of the survey are reported on by Levine and Rhodes (1981).
19. By this logic, and according to Jiobu's analysis (1988) of the 1980 Public Use Microdata Sample, Filipinos would be the most assimilated of the Asian groups, as they have the highest rates of intermarriage. Also by this logic, Japanese, Chinese, Mexican, Filipino, and Vietnamese women are more assimilated than men. More careful consideration and critique of the concept of assimilation should be prerequisites to such analysis.
20. U.S. Department of Commerce, Public Microdata Use Sample C (1/1,000 nationwide sample). I selected all households with at least one Japanese person (n = 250).
21. See Berk (1985).
22. U.S. Bureau of the Census 1988.
23. Gender ratios: Japanese, 86; blacks, 96; Filipinos, 97; whites, 97; Chinese, 99; Mexicans, 105; Vietnamese, 108; Koreans, 84. (From Jiobu [1988:68].)
24. The term *war brides* refers to Japanese women who married American servicemen during occupation in the 1950s. See Kim (1980), who estimated that between World War II and 1975, more than 200,000 Japanese wives of U.S. citizens immigrated to the United States.
25. U.S. Bureau of the Census 1988.

REFERENCES

Berk, Sara Fenstermaker. 1985. *The Gender Factory*. New York: Plenum Press.

Broom, Leonard, and John I. Kitsuse. 1956. *The Managed Casualty*. Berkeley: University of California Press.

Caudill, William. 1952. "Japanese-American Personality and Acculturation." *Genetic Psychology Monographs* 45:3–102.

Chu, Judy. 1988. "Social and Economic Profile of Asian Pacific American Women: Los Angeles County." In *Reflections on Shattered Windows: Promises and Prospects for Asian American Studies*, edited by Gary T. Okihiro, Shirley Hune, Arthur A. Hansen, and John M. Liu, 192–205. Pullman: Washington State University Press.

Daniels, Roger. 1962. *The Politics of Prejudice*. Berkeley: University of California Press.

Glenn, Evelyn Nakano. 1983. "Split Household, Small Producer and Dual Wage Earner: An Analysis of Chinese-American Family Strategies." *Journal of Marriage and the Family*. February, 45:35–46.

———. 1986. *Issei, Nisei, War Bride: Three Generations of Japanese Women in Domestic Service*. Philadelphia: Temple University Press.

Gordon, Milton. 1964. *Assimilation in American Life*. New York: Oxford.

Gutman, Herbert. 1976. *The Black Family in Slavery and Freedom*. New York: Pantheon Books.

Ichihashi, Yamato. 1969. *Japanese in the United States*. New York: Arno Press and the New York Times.

Japanese Evacuation and Resettlement Study. 67/14 C, (**R, **S) Bancroft Library, UC Berkeley.

Jiobu, Robert M. 1988. *Ethnicity and Assimilation*. New York: SUNY Press.

Katznelson, Ira. 1981. *City Trenches*. Chicago: The University of Chicago Press.

Kim, Bok Lim. 1980. "Asian Wives of U.S. Servicemen: Women in the Shadows." In *Asian Americans: Social and Psychological Perspectives,* Volume II, edited by R. Endo, S. Sue, and N. Wagner, 231–247. Ben Lomond, CA: Science and Behavior Books.

Kitano, Harry H. L. 1969. *Japanese Americans: The Evolution of a Subculture*. Englewood Cliffs, NJ: Prentice-Hall.

Kitano, Harry H. L., and Akemi Kikumura. 1980. "The Japanese American Family." In *Asian Americans: Social and Psychological Perspectives,* Volume II, edited by R. Endo, S. Sue, and N. N. Wagner, 3–16. Ben Lomond, CA: Science and Behavior Books.

Levine, Gene N., and Colbert Rhodes. 1981. *The Japanese American Community*. New York: Praeger.

Light, Ivan H. 1972. *Ethnic Enterprise in America*. Berkeley: University of California Press.

Miyamoto, Frank. 1972. "An Immigrant Community in America." In *East Across the Pacific,* edited by H. Conroy and T. S. Miyakawa, 217–243. Santa Barbara: ABC Clio Press.

Nakane, Chie. 1970. *Japanese Society*. London: Weidenfeld and Nicolson.

Osako, Masako Murakami. 1976. "The Effects of Asian-American Kinship Systems on Women's Educational and Occupational Attainment." In *Conference on the Educational and Occupational Needs of Asian Pacific American Women,* 211–236. (San Francisco, California, 1976). U.S. Department of Education, Office of Educational Research and Improvement, National Institute of Education.

———. 1980. *Aging, Social Isolation and Kinship Ties among Japanese Americans: Project Report to the Administration on Aging*.

Park, Robert E. 1950. *Race and Culture*. New York: The Free Press.

Petersen, William. 1971. *Japanese Americans*. New York: Random House.

Stack, Carol. 1974. *All Our Kin*. New York: Harper Colophon Books.

Sue, Stanley, and James K. Morishima. 1982. *The Mental Health of Asian Americans*. San Francisco: Jossey-Bass, Inc.

Takagi, Dana. 1988. "Personality and History: Hostile Nisei Women." In *Reflections on Shattered Windows: Promises and Prospects for Asian American Studies,* edited by G. T. Okihiro, S. Hune, A. Hansen, and J. Liu, 184–194. Pullman: Washington State University Press.

———. 1989. "Life History and JERS: A Reassessment of the Work of Charles Kikuchi." Forthcoming in an anthology on JERS.

Takagi, Paul. 1973. "The Myth of Assimilation in American Life." *Amerasia Journal* 2:149–158.

Takaki, Ronald. 1983. *Pau Hana*. Honolulu: University of Hawaii Press.

Thomas, Dorothy Swaine. 1952. *The Salvage*. Berkeley: University of California Press.

U.S. Bureau of the Census. 1980. *Census of Population and Housing, 1980*. Public Microdata Sample C.

———. 1985. *Marital Characteristics*. Volume 2: *Subject Reports*. PC80-2-4C.

———. 1988. *Asian and Pacific Islander Population in the United States: 1980*. Volume 2: *Subject Reports*. PC80-2-1E.

Woo, Deborah. 1985. "The Socioeconomic Status of Asian American Women in the Labor Force: An Alternative View." *Sociological Perspectives* 29(3):307–338.

Yanagisako, Sylvia Junko. 1987. "Mixed Metaphors: Native and Anthropological Models of Gender and Kinship Domains." In *Gender and Kinship: Essays toward a Unified Analysis,* edited by Jane Fishburne Collier and Sylvia Junko Yanagisako, 86–118. Stanford: Stanford University Press.

CHAPTER 9

Vietnamese American Families

Nazli Kibria

With the settlement of about 0.5 million refugees from 1975 to 1985, Vietnamese Americans became one of the largest Asian-origin populations in the United States. In 1990, they were estimated to be the sixth largest Asian American group, numbering 593,423. In the decades to come, Vietnamese Americans are expected to be a significant presence, particularly in California and Texas.[1] This chapter provides a descriptive overview of the family life of Vietnamese immigrants in the United States, paying particular attention to the effects of the migration process on Vietnamese American family patterns. Data from historical and demographic studies of Vietnamese refugee families are supplemented with materials from an ethnographic study, based on in-depth interviews and participant observation of Vietnamese refugees in Philadelphia during the mid-1980s (Kibria 1993).

The chapter begins with a brief description of the historical context of Vietnamese settlement in the United States. This is followed by a discussion of the key demographic characteristics of the Vietnamese American population, such as its age and gender composition and rates of marriage, divorce, and childbearing. The next sections of the chapter deal with family and household structures and the dynamics of family roles and authority.

THE VIETNAMESE EXODUS

The exodus of refugees out of Vietnam, which began in 1975 and continued through the 1990s, is a process that has deep and complex roots in the contemporary history of Vietnam, including the military, political, and economic involvement of the United States with South Vietnam. Vietnam was colonized by France in 1883. The French presence in Vietnam continued until 1954, when the country was partitioned across the middle into the "North" and the "South." South Vietnam became closely allied with the West, particularly with the United States, which was interested in supporting the South Vietnamese government's efforts to defeat the Communist regime that had been established in the North. The U.S. military, political, and economic involvement in South Vietnam escalated during the 1960s as the conflict between the two Vietnamese regimes grew in scope. The long war ended in 1975, soon after the military withdrawal of the United States from Vietnam, when Northern forces gained control of the South and the country was reunited under Communist rule. Shortly before the fall of Saigon to Communist rule, about 130,000 Vietnamese were flown into the United States as part of an evacuation effort designed to aid South Vietnamese employees and associates of the U.S. government. Often referred to as the "first-wave" refugees, the 1975 arrivals tended to be from the elite strata of South Vietnamese society, with high levels of education and occupational attainment (Baker and North 1984).[2]

Largely unanticipated by the U.S. government was the continuing flow of refugees out of Vietnam after the 1975 evacuation. These later waves of Vietnamese refugees were driven to leave the homeland by the political and economic policies of the Communist government. Many of these refugees had been persecuted by the new government because of association with the former South Vietnamese government. For example, some were sent to the "reeducation camps" set up by the new government to indoctrinate and punish those associated with the former regime. Those South Vietnamese who had drawn on the urban business and service sectors for their livelihood were also affected by the new government's economic policies, particularly the efforts to nationalize businesses. These policies particularly impacted the Chinese minority in Vietnam, a group that had been prominent in commerce and trading activities. In the late 1970s, the Chinese were also subject to discriminatory policies such as reduced food rations and the forced closure of Chinese-language newspapers and schools. As a result, during the 1978 to 1979 period, the Chinese Vietnamese accounted for about 70 percent of the "boat people" leaving Vietnam (Wain 1981). Another factor that spurred the outflow of people from Vietnam was the compulsory military draft imposed by the Vietnamese government in the late 1970s in order to cope with ongoing military conflicts in the region. Motivated by a desire to escape compulsory military service, young men constituted a large portion of Vietnamese arrivals to the United States during the 1980s.

As a group, post-1975 Vietnamese refugees differ from the 1975 evacuees in a number of ways. Unlike the 1975 evacuees, these later arrivals (often referred to as "boat people") have left Vietnam via covert boat journeys, taking them to nearby asylum countries such as Thailand, Malaysia, and Hong Kong. In the refugee camps that had been set up by those countries, they have waited for resettlement decisions, for periods of time ranging from six months to more than two years. The major countries of Vietnamese resettlement have included Australia, Canada, China, and the United States. In order to cope with the growing number of refugees from Vietnam (as well as Cambodia and Laos), in 1980 the U.S. government instituted the Refugee Act, which specified a set of formal guidelines for the entry, resettlement, and assistance of refugees.

This brief discussion of the history of Vietnamese migration to the United States provides some background for understanding the characteristics of Vietnamese family life in the United States. As suggested by the discussion, Vietnamese refugees are a diverse group. There are, for example, significant differences in the socioeconomic background of the 1975 wave and the later arrivals. Whereas many of the first-wave Vietnamese had held white-collar or high-level military jobs in Vietnam, a large proportion of those who have arrived since 1977 had occupied blue-collar or sales/service positions. Levels of educational attainment and English language proficiency have also been lower for the later arrivals (Rumbaut 1989; Strand and Jones 1985). Furthermore, the Vietnamese refugees include the Chinese Vietnamese, a group that has in many ways a cultural identity and experience distinct from those of the ethnic Vietnamese. In Vietnam, many Chinese had maintained a distinct identity from Vietnamese by living in enclaves and maintaining their own schools and newspapers. We can expect these differences in social class and ethnic background to enter into the family patterns of Vietnamese Americans in important ways.

Besides the diversity of the Vietnamese American population, what is also relevant to understanding the group's family patterns is the fact that migration from Vietnam has, in the recent past, been a selective process. The costly, secretive, and hazardous nature of the boat journeys out of Vietnam has meant that it has not usually been possible for entire family units to migrate. The process of resettlement from refugee camps has also contributed to family disruption, given the greater favor with which resettlement officials have viewed smaller family units (Haines 1988). Since the 1990s, there have been important political changes in Vietnam, easing the ability of Vietnamese nationals to apply through regular immigration channels to come to the United States, often to join family members already present here. However, the migration-related disruptions of family structure just described remain an important part of the Vietnamese American family experience.

DEMOGRAPHIC TRENDS

Age and Gender Composition

Both the age and the gender compositions of the Vietnamese American population have some unusual qualities. The Vietnamese American population has been young, reflecting both the greater proclivity of young persons to undertake the difficult journey out of Vietnam and the high rates of fertility among the group. In 1984, the Office of Refugee Resettlement (1985:10) reported that the median age of all Vietnamese arrivals was 20 years. Data from a longitudinal study of Southeast Asian refugees in San Diego County show that for the 93 Vietnamese households surveyed in 1983, children under 18 years of age comprised 44 percent of the total household members. In 1984, for the same group of households, the percentage of children (42.4 percent) had changed little (Rumbaut 1989). The 1990 census reports a median age of 25.6 years for Vietnamese Americans.

During the 1970s and 1980s, a predominance in the number of men over women was another important characteristic of the Vietnamese American population. In

1975, males composed 49 percent of the general U.S. population. In comparison, 55 percent of the first-wave Vietnamese settlers to the United States were men. The proportion of Vietnamese men to women climbed to 58.4 percent among 1982 arrivals, reflecting in part increasing efforts of young Vietnamese men to escape the compulsory military draft (Baker and North 1984:25). From the study in San Diego, Rumbaut (1989) reported a gender ratio of 120 males to 100 females for the Vietnamese. Evidence also showed the gender ratio to be particularly skewed for Vietnamese Americans aged 12 to 24 years. For example, the Office of Refugee Resettlement (1985) reported that among the Vietnamese who entered the United States in 1984, men outnumbered women by more than two to one in the 12 to 24 year age group.

The 1990 census shows 53 percent (311,858) of the Vietnamese American population to be male, thus indicating a gradual shift away from the sharply male-dominated gender ratio of the 1980s. However, most observers would agree that the "skewed" gender ratio has shaped family life for many Vietnamese Americans. Besides affecting the ability of men in certain age groups to find Vietnamese American marriage partners, the male-dominated gender ratio may also be part of the organization and ideology of gender roles and relations in the group (for a discussion of the effects of gender ratios on gender relations, see Guttentag and Secord 1983). An ethnographic study of Vietnamese refugees, conducted in the 1980s, showed that although married Vietnamese refugee women did not derive benefit from the high gender ratio, young unmarried women did experience greater power in their sexual relationships with men owing to the "shortage" of women in the group (Kibria 1993).

Marriage, Divorce, and Childbearing

Because the marriage and divorce patterns of Vietnamese Americans have not been widely explored, information on this topic is preliminary in nature. There may be some special problems in gathering accurate information on marital dissolution because of the stigma attached to divorce in Vietnamese culture, particularly for women.

In an analysis of data on the 1975 Vietnamese arrivals, Baker and North (1984) report 49 percent of those 15 years or older to be married at the time of arrival. A small number of the group, all women, indicated that they were divorced (0.3 percent) or widowed (0.1 percent). From his survey study in San Diego, Rumbaut (1988) reported the average of age of marriage for Vietnamese Americans as 21.4 years for women and 25.8 years for men. The study also shows extremely low rates of marital dissolution through either death or separation/divorce. For example, of the 157 Vietnamese adults who were surveyed in 1983, none were divorced or separated, and less than one percent indicated that they were widowed. The same respondents were questioned about what their marital status had been in 1975. Sixty-four percent indicated that they were married in 1975, compared with 87.3 percent in 1983. There was little difference in the proportion of widowed and divorced persons in 1975 and 1983. A Bureau of Social Science Research study (Dunning and Greenbaum 1982; Dunning 1986) of 555 Vietnamese refugees (including

Chinese Vietnamese) in the New Orleans, Houston, and Los Angeles areas also reveals fairly low rates of marital dissolution. The study found that of those who had ever been married, 83 percent were with their initial spouse at the time of the study. The 1990 census showed about 40 percent of the eligible Vietnamese American population to be married, and 1.1 percent divorced or widowed.

Far more information is needed to clarify the marriage and divorce rates of Vietnamese Americans and the variations of these patterns within the group due to differences of social class and ethnicity. Contrary to the picture of stability and continuity suggested by the preceding information, a number of qualitative, in-depth studies suggest that there has been a rise in separation and divorce due to the strains on marriages generated by settlement in the United States (Gold 1989; Kibria 1993; Kinzie 1981; Masuda and others 1980).

Fertility rates in Vietnam are significantly higher than in the United States (Rumbaut and Weeks 1986). For Vietnamese Americans, rates of childbearing continue to be high, owing to both the large proportion of persons of childbearing age and traditional values concerning fertility. The 1980 census shows the number of children ever born per 1,000 Vietnamese American women (aged 15 to 44) as 1,785. This figure is close to that recorded for Hispanic (1,817) and African American women (1,806) and higher than that of the general U.S. population (1,429) or that of other Asian American groups (Gardner and others 1985:17). Rumbaut and Weeks (1986) suggest that the 1980 census figures (which provide information mainly on the 1975 arrivals) may underestimate the current fertility rates of the Vietnamese because of the higher socioeconomic background of the 1975 arrivals, a condition that tends to depress rates of childbearing. Using data from a study in San Diego, they report a child-to-woman ratio[3] of 574 children (aged 0 to 4) per 1,000 Vietnamese American women of childbearing age. This figure is somewhat higher than that found for the Chinese Vietnamese (511) and substantially higher than that of the general U.S. population (309). They found the subgroup of 1975 arrivals within their sample of Vietnamese respondents to have lower fertility rates than later arrivals. The authors also found that increased length of residence as well as a higher level of economic and cultural adaptation to the United States significantly lowered childbearing rates. On the basis of these findings, they predict a decline in childbearing over time for Vietnamese Americans. However, given current rates of childbearing, we can expect a large proportion of children and young persons to be an important characteristic of the Vietnamese American population in the near future.

HOUSEHOLDS AND EXTENDED FAMILY

In traditional Vietnamese culture, the family was seen as an extended structure, a group that stretched beyond immediate or nuclear family ties to include a wide range of kin (Haines 1984; Luong 1984; Whitmore 1984). Households, which could include nuclear or extended family members, were enmeshed in a large and an active web of kinship relations in the neighborhood and general vicinity. These relations with kin often functioned as important sources of economic and social support (Hickey 1964).

A number of studies have emphasized the continued significance of extended family ties for Vietnamese in the United States. Data on the size and composition of Vietnamese American households provide some evidence for this idea. The 1980 census reports an average household size of 4.4 for Vietnamese Americans. Other relatives beyond the householder's immediate family (that is, householder, spouse, children) were found to account for 55 percent of total household members. Seven percent of those living in the household were found to be unrelated to the head of household. In comparison, among whites, the immediate family accounted for 94 percent of total household members (Gardner and others 1985:23). A Bureau of Social Science Research study (Dunning and Greenbaum 1982) reports an average household size of 4.5 for Vietnamese refugees. For purposes of comparison, respondents were also asked about the size and composition of their households in Vietnam. Average household size in Vietnam was larger (6.5 persons), and there were also a greater number of three-generational households in Vietnam than in the United States.

From his study in San Diego, Rumbaut (1988; 1989) reports a mean household size of 5.5 for the Vietnamese American sample in 1983. Nuclear family members accounted for about four, and extended family members for one, of all household members. Unrelated persons composed a relatively small proportion (0.43) of total household members. There was little change in these figures in 1984, when the same respondents were questioned again (Rumbaut 1988). Data from this study also show few differences in household size and composition between the first "wave" and later arrivals. However, the average household size of the Chinese Vietnamese sample was somewhat larger than that of the Vietnamese. Further investigation is needed into both the diversity and the processes of change that are most likely occurring in the composition of Vietnamese American households.

The resurfacing of extended family household structures in the United States is in some ways unexpected, given the considerable disruptions to family relations that have been part of the migration process for the group. Studies suggest that the presence of extended family ties in the United States has been made possible by the vigorous efforts of Vietnamese Americans to rebuild their families in the face of the disruption to family ties caused by the migration process (Gold 1989; Kibria 1993). One expression of this family reconstruction process is the heavy secondary migration of Vietnamese Americans within the United States to areas of the country where kin and friends reside. Crucial to this process of reuniting and rebuilding has been the popular Vietnamese conception of family as a large and an inclusive circle of significant kin. In effect, this fluid and inclusive conception has allowed for the incorporation of people into the extended kin network who would perhaps not have been part of it in the past. More specifically, Kibria's (1993) study shows three means by which family networks are reconstructed. First, relationships with distant kin are elevated in importance. In other words, relatives who were previously marginal members of the family circle in Vietnam are incorporated into the network of active kin relations. Second, compared with the past, distinctions based on paternal versus maternal descent or the ties of blood versus marriage were considered less important in determining the closeness of family ties. Third, close friends were incorporated into the family circle and treated as kin members.

The efforts to reconstruct kin networks clearly reflect the cultural importance placed on familial relations by Vietnamese Americans. But in addition, studies have suggested that extended family ties have material significance for Vietnamese Americans, in that they play an important part in the processes by which the group copes with the economic conditions and institutions of U.S. society. Kin are often involved in relations of mutual aid with each other, exchanging goods, services (for example, child care, cooking), and information on how to deal with such U.S. institutions as hospitals and welfare agencies. Family members are often a source of job referrals as well as investment capital for opening small business or purchasing homes (Finnan and Cooperstein 1983; Gold 1989; Haines and others 1981; Kibria 1993).

FAMILY ROLES AND AUTHORITY

The rebuilding of kinship ties highlights the continuities of Vietnamese American family life and the ways in which families may be a source of support in the process of adaptation to U.S. society. At the same time, many aspects of the traditional Vietnamese family, particularly patterns of family roles and authority, are being challenged by the conditions of life in the United States. The following sections explore the effects of migration to the United States on intergenerational and gender relations in the family.

Intergenerational Relations

The traditional Vietnamese ideal of the family, derived from Confucian principles, was of a hierarchical entity in which the young were subordinate to the old, as were women to men. For the young, ideal behavior entailed obedience to the elderly and the submission of individual needs and desires to those of the family collective. These principles were given meaning and legitimacy through the practice of ancestor worship, in which rites were performed to remember and honor the spirits of ancestors. For Vietnamese, the practice of ancestor worship helped to socialize children into ideal family values through its symbolic expression of the unified, sacred, and hierarchical quality of the kin group. Slote (1972) further suggests that traditional modes of child-rearing in Vietnamese families helped to generate qualities of dependence rather than independence in children, thus supporting the prescribed behaviors of obedience and submission to the family collective.

In the United States, these core traditional familial values—the authority of the old over the young and the primacy of the family collective over the individual—continue to be emphasized by the older Vietnamese immigrant generation in their interactions with the young. However, a number of conditions have eroded the ability of parents and other family elders to influence the younger generation. First, there is the youthful age structure of the Vietnamese American population and the small number of Vietnamese elderly in the United States (Eckles and others 1982). And particularly in recent years, many Vietnamese youth have arrived in the United States without older family members. Migration to the United States has thus often created situations in which the elderly are simply not present to enforce their authority over the Vietnamese American young. The growth of Vietnamese American youth gangs is at least partly a reflection of the significant number of young Vietnamese refugees who are in the United States without their parents or other family guardians (Vigil and Yun 1990).

Besides an absence of guardianship, settlement in the United States has also enhanced the economic and social resources of the young compared with those of the old. In a number of Vietnamese American families observed (Kibria 1993), the better language skills, opportunities for education and job training, and familiarity with U.S. cultural norms have placed children in a position of greater advantage than that of their parents in dealing with the institutions of U.S. society, a condition that has eroded parental authority. Along with their diminished power and authority over the young, Vietnamese American parents and other family elders also complain about the cultural assimilation of the young, fostered by such powerful cultural agents as U.S. television, popular music, and schools. Of particular concern to the Vietnamese immigrant generation is the growing individualism of the young. Studies document intergenerational clashes within Vietnamese American families, involving attempts by parents or older guardians to ensure that the young behave in ways that meet traditional Vietnamese cultural expectations (Indochina Refugee Action Center 1980; Kibria 1993; Pennsylvania Department of Public Welfare 1979).

However, to suggest that the intergenerational relations of Vietnamese Americans are characterized solely or even primarily by change and conflict would be misleading. A study by Simon (1983) pointed to the considerable consensus of values and expectations between Vietnamese American parents and their adolescent children. Kibria's study (1993) found considerable attachment among younger Vietnamese Americans to traditional Vietnamese family values, including the collectivist and hierarchical qualities of traditional Vietnamese family life.

Gender Relations

The ideal traditional Vietnamese family, modeled on Confucian principles, was one in which women were subordinate to men in all phases and aspects of their lives. The realities of traditional Vietnamese family life of course deviated from this normative model in many ways. For example, older women often exercised considerable power in their household. As part of their domestic caretaking role, women often controlled the family budget and exerted influence over the family economy. And although men controlled key economic institutions, Vietnamese women did have access to economic resources through their extensive involvement in small business and trading. Even though such activities may have enhanced the resources and power of women in the family, there is little evidence that they weakened fundamental subordination and dependence of women on men (Kibria 1990).

Scholars have observed that migration to the United States has challenged traditional Vietnamese bases of male authority and thus generated a rise in conflicts between men and women. They note how there has been a reversal of traditional male/female roles, a situation that has given rise to conflict. More specifically, Vietnamese American women often assume the "breadwinner" role because service sector jobs are more easily available than the kinds of unskilled blue-collar or professional jobs that men seek. In some cases, the woman economically supports the family while the man undergoes educational or technical training for a skilled job (Gold 1989; Kinzie 1981; Masuda and others 1980).

Although the employment rates of Vietnamese women in the United States are relatively high (see Haines 1986), it is not clear that the economic activities of women have taken on primary significance compared with those of men. The unemployment rate of Vietnamese American women is higher than that of the group (Dunning and Greenbaum 1982; Haines 1987). Perhaps the crucial difference in Vietnamese refugee men's and women's employment is revealed in a comparison of their wages and income. For example, the Bureau of Social Science Research study (Dunning and Greenbaum 1982) showed the wages and income of women to be far less than those of men. Whereas, on average, the income of women constituted 36 percent of total household income, the comparable figure for men was 64 percent. Kibria's (1989) study also showed Vietnamese refugee women to be working in unstable, low-paying jobs, often in the underground or informal economy. In short, the evidence suggests that the elevation of Vietnamese American women's economic activities to primary significance compared with men's activities may be a reality for only a small number of families.

Although migration may not have generated a sharp reversal in the economic roles of Vietnamese refugee men and women, it has certainly resulted in a decline in men's ability to obtain jobs that ensure a middle-class standard of living for their families. By the mid-1980s, those Vietnamese immigrants who had arrived as part of the 1975 evacuation had achieved parity in their household income levels with the general U.S. population (Office of Refugee Resettlement 1988:147). The later cohorts of Vietnamese refugees, however, have had less economic success (Haines 1987). The 1990 census reports 23.8% of Vietnamese American families to be below the poverty level. A 1984 survey of Vietnamese refugees in San Diego found 22.4 percent of respondents to be unemployed and 61.3 percent to have incomes below the poverty level. Of those who were employed, 29.2 percent indicated that they received no fringe benefits at work, and 48.7 percent said that there was no possibility for promotion at their jobs (Rumbaut 1989). Caplan and others (1985) note that although the economic self-sufficiency of Vietnamese American families tends to rise over time, this condition is usually achieved not through a rise in individual wages but through the use of multiple wage-earner household strategies. Tensions concerning traditional conceptions of male authority may become apparent when men who were the sole or primary family breadwinners in Vietnam find themselves dependent on the income of other wage-earners in the household. More generally, we can expect the conditions of economic scarcity and insecurity faced by many Vietnamese American families to be a source of strain on marriages and other family relationships.

Besides economic conditions, other factors have affected gender relations in Vietnamese American families. Kibria's (1993) study shows how the cultural and legal conceptions of male authority that are prevalent in the majority U.S. society may work to challenge and shift Vietnamese American normative attitudes regarding men's and women's behavior. Also important was the expansion of Vietnamese refugee women's homemaking activities beyond such traditional work as child care and housework to include negotiation with social institutions located outside the household, such as schools, hospitals, and welfare agencies. The expanded "intermediary" role played by women is a potentially important source of power for women in their relations with men.

CONCLUSIONS

This chapter provides overview of research on Vietnamese families in the United States. Many studies of Vietnamese American family life have focused on patterns of continuity as evidenced, for example, by the presence of extended family household structures. In these studies, the continued significance of the traditional values and organization of Vietnamese family life in the U.S. context is emphasized. In contrast, other studies have stressed the theme of conflict, or the clashes between traditional expectations of family life and the conditions and orientations of U.S. society. Incorporation of these two themes into a unified perspective may provide a better understanding of ongoing processes of change or the ways in which Vietnamese American families are being shaped and constructed by both the past and the present.

Future research on Vietnamese American families must take into account some distinctive aspects of the Vietnamese experience prior to arrival in the United States. This observation includes not only the group's complex cultural and historical heritage but also the somewhat unusual conditions that have surrounded the migration from Vietnam. For example, the predominance in number of young persons and of men will most likely have important effects on Vietnamese American family life for some time into the future. Also relevant is the considerable disruption of family ties experienced by most Vietnamese refugees. Because of the difficulties of leaving Vietnam, chain migration processes or the gradual migration of entire family units has been less prevalent among the Vietnamese than among many other immigrant groups.

Finally, the diversity of the Vietnamese American population is another important key to understanding the group's family life. As has been discussed, there are significant differences of social class among Vietnamese Americans in terms of both past and current socioeconomic status. Differences between the Chinese Vietnamese and ethnic Vietnamese are also important to consider. In short, rather than viewing Vietnamese Americans as a monolithic population, future research must take into account the differences in social class and ethnic background within the group and the ways in which those differences are affecting family experiences.

ENDNOTES

1. The 1990 census showed California to be home to 45.6 percent of the Vietnamese population in the United States, with Texas following at 11.3 percent.
2. Baker and North (1984) present information on the socioeconomic background of the 1975 arrivals. They found that 19 percent of the adults had had postsecondary (13 to 16

years) education, whereas 51 percent had received secondary (12 years) level education. Twenty-five percent had held professional jobs in Vietnam. Others had held mainly clerical and service sector jobs.

3. Child-to-woman ratio = (Total number of children aged 0–4) / Women of childbearing age × 100.

REFERENCES

Bach, Robert L. 1984. "Labor Force Participation, Household Composition and Sponsorship among Southeast Asian Refugees." *International Migration Review* 20:381–404.

Baker, Reginald P., and Davis S. North. 1984. *The 1975 Refugees: Their First Five Years in America.* Washington, DC: New Transcentury Press.

Caplan, Nathan, John K. Whitmore, and Quang L. Bui. 1985. *Southeast Asian Refugee Self-Sufficiency Study: Final Report.* Ann Arbor, MI: The Institute for Social Research.

Donoghue, John D. 1962. *Cam An: A Fishing Village in Central Vietnam.* Saigon, Vietnam: Michigan State University Vietnam Advisory Group.

Dunning, Bruce B. 1986. "Vietnamese in America: Domain and Scope of Adjustment among 1975–79 Arrivals." Paper presented at the Annual Meeting of the American Association for the Advancement of Science. Philadelphia, Pennsylvania.

Dunning, Bruce B., and J. Greenbaum. 1982. *A Systematic Survey of the Social, Psychological and Economic Adaptation of Vietnamese Refugees Representing Five Entry Cohorts, 1975–1979.* Washington, DC: Bureau of Social Science Research.

Eckles, Timothy J., L. S. Lewin, D. S. North, and D. J. Spakevicius. 1982. *Portrait in Diversity: Voluntary Agencies and the ORR Matching Grant Program.* Lewin and Associates: Office of Refugee Resettlement Report.

Finnan, Christine R., and Rhonda Cooperstein. 1983. *Southeast Asian Refugee Resettlement at the Local Level.* Office of Refugee Resettlement Report.

Gardner, Robert W., Bryant Robey, and Peter C. Smith. 1985. "Asian Americans: Growth, Change and Diversity." *Population Bulletin* 40.

Gold, Steven J. 1989. "Differential Adjustment among New Immigrant Family Members." *Journal of Contemporary Ethnography* 17:408–434.

Grant, Bruce. 1979. *The Boat People.* New York: Penguin Books.

Guttentag, Marcia, and Paul F. Secord. 1983. *Too Many Women? The Sex Ratio Question.* Beverly Hills, CA: Sage.

Haines, David. 1984. "Reflections of Kinship and Society under Vietnam's Le Dynasty." *Journal of Southeast Asian Studies* 15:307–314.

———. 1986. "Vietnamese Women in the Labor Force: Continuity or Change?" In *International Migration: The Female Experience,* edited by R. J. Simon and C. B. Brettell. Totowa, NJ: Rowman & Allenheld.

———. 1987. "Patterns in Southeast Asian Refugee Employment: A Reappraisal of the Existing Research." *Ethnic Groups* 7:39–63.

———. 1988. "Kinship in Vietnamese Refugee Resettlement: A Review of the U.S. Experience." *Journal of Comparative Family Studies* 19:1–16.

Haines, David, Dorothy Rutherford, and Patrick Thomas. 1981. "Family and Community among Vietnamese Refugees." *International Migration Review* 15:310–319.

Hendry, James B. 1954. *The Small World of Khanh Hau.* Chicago: Aldine Publishing Co.

Hickey, Gerald C. 1964. *Village in Vietnam.* New Haven, CT: Yale University Press.

Indochina Refugee Action Center. 1980. *An Assessment of the Needs of Indochinese Youth.* Washington, DC: IRAC.

Kibria, Nazli. 1989. "Patterns of Vietnamese Refugee Women's Wagework in the U.S." *Ethnic Groups* 7:297–323.

———. 1990. "Power, Patriarchy and Gender Conflict in the Vietnamese Immigrant Community." *Gender and Society* 4:9–24.

———. 1993. *Family Tightrope: The Changing Lives of Vietnamese Americans.* Princeton, NJ: Princeton University Press.

Kinzie, J. D. 1981. "Evaluation and Psychotherapy of Indochinese Refugee Patients." *American Journal of Psychotherapy* 35:251–261.

Luong, Hy Van. 1984. "Brother and Uncle: An Analysis of Rules, Structural Contradictions and Meaning in Vietnamese Kinship." *American Anthropologist* 86:290–315.

Marr, David G. 1976. "The 1920's Women's Rights Debate in Vietnam." *Journal of Asian Studies* 15:371–389.

Masuda, Minoru, Keh-Ming Lin, and Laurie Tazum. 1980. "Adaptation Problems of Vietnamese Refugees: Life Changes and Perception of Life Events." *Archives of General Psychiatry* 37:447–450.

Nguyen Long. 1981. *After Saigon Fell: Daily Life under the Vietnamese Communists.* Berkeley, CA: Institute of East Asian Studies, University of California.

Nguyen Van Canh. 1983. *Vietnam under Communism, 1975–1982.* Stanford, CA: Hoover Institute Press.

Office of Refugee Resettlement. 1984. *Refugee Resettlement Program-Report to Congress.* U.S. Department of Health and Human Services.

———. 1985. *Refugee Resettlement Program-Report to Congress.* U.S. Department of Health and Human Services.

———. 1987. *Refugee Resettlement Program-Report to Congress.* U.S. Department of Health and Human Services.

———. 1988. *Refugee Resettlement Program-Report to Congress.* U.S. Department of Health and Human Services.

Pennsylvania Department of Public Welfare. 1979. *National Mental Health Needs Assessment of Indochinese Refugee Populations.* Philadelphia: Office of Mental Health, Bureau of Research and Training.

Rumbaut, Ruben G. 1988. *Southeast Asian Refugees in San Diego County: A Statistical Profile.* San Diego: Indochinese Health and Adaptation Research Project, San Diego State University.

———. 1989. "Portraits, Patterns and Predictors of the Refugee Adaptation Process: Results and Reflections from the IHARP Panel Study." In *Refugees as Immigrants: Cambodians, Laotians and Vietnamese in America,* edited by D. W. Haines. Totowa, NJ: Rowman & Littlefield Publishers.

Rumbaut, Ruben G., and John R. Weeks. 1986. "Fertility and Adaptation: Indochinese Refugees in the United States." *International Migration Review* 20:428–466.

Simon, Rita J. 1983. "Refugee Families' Adjustment and Aspirations: A Comparison of Soviet Jews and Vietnamese Immigrants." *Ethnic and Racial Studies* 6:492–504.

Slote, Walter H. 1972. "Psychodynamic Structures in Vietnamese Personality." In *Transcultural Research in Mental Health,* edited by W. Lebra. Honolulu: University of Hawaii Press.

Strand, Paul J., and W. Jones, Jr. 1985. *Indochinese Refugees in America: Problems of Adaptation and Assimilation.* Durham, NC: Duke University Press.

Ta Van Tai. 1981. "The Status of Women in Traditional Vietnam: A Comparison of the Le Dynasty (1428–1788) with the Chinese Codes." *Journal of Asian History* 15:97–145.

Vigil, James Diego, and Steve Chong Yun. 1990. "Vietnamese Youth Gangs in Southern California." In *Gangs in California,* edited by R. Huff. Beverly Hills, CA: Sage.

Wain, Barry. 1981. *The Refused: The Agony of the Indochinese Refugees.* New York: Simon and Schuster.

Whitmore, John K. 1984. "Social Organization and Confucian Thought in Vietnam." *Journal of Southeast Asian Studies* 15:296–306.

CHAPTER 10

Korean American Families

Pyong Gap Min

The current Korean community in the United States is largely the by-product of the contemporary migration flow that started with the enforcement of the 1965 Immigration Act. Although the fraction of American-born Koreans has increased in recent years, the vast majority of them are the children who live in their families of orientation or young adults who have not established their own families. In fact, the 1990 census shows that only 4 percent of Korean American families were headed by the native-born. Therefore, this chapter on Korean American families devotes much of its space to Korean immigrant families.

This chapter consists of four sections. The first section overviews the immigration and settlement of Koreans with a focus on contemporary immigration. The second section examines demographic and other characteristics of Korean immigrant families largely on the basis of 1990 census reports. The third section focuses on Korean immigrants' marital relations. The fourth section examines Korean immigrants' child socialization patterns and parent-child relations. The third and fourth sections are largely based on results of various studies and on the author's participant observation. The last section compares native- and foreign-born Koreans in basic family characteristics using the 1990 census.

Traditionally, the U.S. media and researchers have depicted Asian immigrants as maintaining strong family ties, and they have emphasized the harmony between husband and wife and that between parents and children. The media have stressed that cultural mechanisms—strong family ties—have facilitated Asian immigrants' socioeconomic adjustments. In reaction to these cultural explanations, a number of researchers have recently tried to examine Asian American families by using a structural approach (Chow 1995; Glenn 1983, 1986; Kibria 1993; Wong 1988). For example, Glenn (1983:35) has focused on the "changing structure of Chinese-American families resulting from the interplay between shifting institutional constraints and the efforts of Chinese Americans to maintain family life in the face of these restrictions." In her ethnographic study of Vietnamese immigrant families, Kibria (1993:22) has argued that "immigrant families must be studied in relation to the external structural conditions encountered by immigrants in the host society."

In line with this newly emerging orientation, this chapter examines the effects of structural factors on Korean immigrant families. In particular, it explains how Korean immigrants' economic structure—their high level of concentration in small, family businesses—has modified their family relations. However, by emphasizing the effects of structural conditions, I do not mean to ignore the role of Korean cultural traditions in shaping immigrant families. If earlier researchers put a one-sided emphasis on the role of family ties and values in facilitating Asian immigrants' adjustments, some revisionist critics of the cultural approach fail to recognize the powerful influence of conservative family ideologies from their home countries in Asian immigrant families. Korean immigrants have brought with them a Confucian family ideology that emphasizes family/kin ties, filial piety, children's education, and an extreme form of patriarchy (I. Park and Cho 1995). This family ideology has wide-ranging effects on Korean immigrant families, particularly on child socialization patterns and intergenerational and marital relations of Korean immigrants. Thus, this chapter intends to examine how structural conditions and Koreans' traditional family ideology mutually influence each other.

IMMIGRATION AND SETTLEMENT

Hawaiian plantation owners decided to bring Korean laborers to Hawaii at the turn of the twentieth century to moderate the monopoly of plantation labor by Japanese workers on the islands. As a result, approximately 7,200 Korean laborers moved to Hawaii to work on sugar plantations between 1903 and 1905, composing the first wave of Korean immigrants to the United States (Patterson 1988). Although plantation owners in Hawaii needed more Korean workers in the first decade of the twentieth century, in 1905 the Korean government was forced by the Japanese government to stop sending any more laborers to Hawaii. Korea became Japan's protectorate after Japan's victory in the Russo-Japanese War in 1905. The Japanese government pressured the Korean government not to send any more immigrants to Hawaii to protect the economic interests of Japanese workers. Before the enforcement of the "Oriental Exclusion" Act of 1924 barred Korean immigration completely, approximately 2,000 additional Koreans moved to Hawaii and the West Coast of the United States. "Picture brides" of the pioneer immigrants in Hawaii and political refugees who engaged in the anti-Japanese movement constituted the vast majority of Korean immigrants between 1906 and 1924.

Beginning with the Korean War in 1950, the United States maintained close military, political, and economic relations with South Korea. The linkages between the two countries helped to resume the immigration of Koreans to the United States. About 15,000 Koreans immigrated to the United States between 1950 and 1964. Korean orphans adopted by American citizens and Korean women married to U.S. servicemen stationed in South Korea composed the vast majority of immigrants during this period. The immigration of the Korean children adopted by American citizens and internationally married Korean women was expanded in the next three decades.

Despite nearly one hundred years of immigration history, the Korean population in the United States before 1970 was negligible. The 1970 census enumerated the Korean population to be less than 70,000. However, Korean immigration has accelerated with the enforcement of the 1965 Immigration Act. In the 1970s, Koreans immigrated to the United States at an average of 25,000 per year. In the 1980s, more than 30,000 Koreans immigrated to the United States annually, composing the third largest immigrant group in that decade, following Mexicans and Filipinos. The prospect for a higher standard of living and better opportunities for children's education in the United States were two major pull factors for the influx of Korean immigrants (Kim and Min 1992; Yoon 1993). The political and social insecurity in South Korea characterized by military dictatorship between 1961 and 1987 also pushed many Koreans to the United States and discouraged American-educated Korean intellectuals from going back to Korea. The military, political, and economic linkages between the United States and South Korea and the consequent American cultural influence in South Korea were the major structural factors for the influx of contemporary Korean immigrants (I. Kim 1987). In the 1990s, Korean immigration has dropped substantially, below the level of 20,000 per year. This recent reduction of Korean immigration has been caused by great improvements in economic and political conditions in South Korea. In the 1970s, when there was a huge gap in living standards between the United States and South Korea, the vast majority of Korean immigrants were from the middle class and the upper-middle class. However, few middle-class Koreans are now motivated to emigrate from South Korea, where per capita income reached the $10,000 mark in 1995. In fact, the expanding South Korean economy has recently attracted many Koreans who completed their professional education in the United States, including second-generation Korean Americans. Politically, in 1987 a civilian government based on a popular election replaced the military government that had pushed many Korean intellectuals out of the country. At the same time that conditions in South Korea have improved significantly, people there are increasingly well informed of the difficulties of Korean immigrants in adjusting to the United States. After the Los Angeles riots, the South Korean people donated five million dollars to help the Korean riot victims. Therefore, at present Koreans do not hold it an attractive prospect to immigrate to the United States. In fact, many Korean immigrants have returned to Korea permanently, giving up their "American dream."

As a result of the influx of Korean immigrants over the last three decades, the Korean population has achieved a phenomenal increase. The 1990 U.S. census enumerated the Korean population to be close to 800,000 (U.S. Bureau of the Census 1993a, Table 23), but this figure seems to be an undercount. The Korean population in 1990 may have reached the one million mark, and we may put it at close to 1.2 million as of 1996. The 1990 census revealed that native-born Koreans composed 28 percent of Korean Americans and that their median age was 8.8

(U.S. Bureau of the Census 1993b, Table 1). It showed that only 4 percent of Korean American families were headed by native-born Koreans (U.S. Bureau of the Census 1993b, Table 2). This finding suggests that Korean American families at present are generally Korean immigrant families, although the proportion of native-born Korean families is likely to increase rapidly in the future.

The Korean immigrants who moved here in the 1970s and the early 1980s generally represented the middle- and upper-middle-class strata of Korean society. A large proportion of them were professionals such as physicians, nurses, schoolteachers, and bankers (Hurh and Kim 1988; Min 1984). Those who immigrated recently represented lower socioeconomic backgrounds than the earlier immigrant cohorts, but they, too, represented slightly higher socioeconomic backgrounds than the U.S. population and substantially higher backgrounds than the population in Korea. The 1990 census indicated that 34 percent of Korean immigrants 25 years old and over completed four years of college, and that 80 percent completed high school (U.S. Bureau of the Census 1993b: 84). By contrast, 20 percent of the U.S. population completed college, and 75 percent completed high school (U.S. Bureau of the Census 1993b, 72).

Another distinctive characteristic of contemporary Korean immigrants is their strong Christian background. Protestantism and Catholicism are the second and third largest religions in South Korea next to Buddhism, with 19 percent of the population affiliated with Protestantism and 6 percent with Catholicism (Park and Cho 1995). Although Christians make up only a quarter of the population in South Korea, more than 50 percent of Korean immigrants in the United States were Christians in Korea (Hurh and Kim 1990). Because Christians in Korea are over-represented among the middle-class segment of the population in large cities and because Korean immigrants were drawn mainly from the same population segment, Christians are overrepresented among Korean immigrants. Many Korean Buddhists or those not affiliated with any religion in Korea have joined a Korean church upon arriving here. Thus, approximately 75 percent of Korean immigrant families are affiliated with Korean churches (Hurh and Kim 1990; Min 1989). Ethnic churches help Korean immigrants to maintain fellowship and Korean cultural traditions (Min 1992a); moreover, they provide all kinds of practical services for Korean immigrants (Min 1992a).

The first wave of Korean immigrants at the turn of the century was concentrated in Hawaii and California. Contemporary Korean immigrants are more widely scattered over the United States, moderating their concentration in the West. But they are still overrepresented in California. The 1990 census showed that approximately 260,000 Korean Americans resided in California, accounting for 32 percent of all Korean Americans. The Korean population in California grew by 150 percent between 1980 and 1990, experiencing a higher growth rate than in the United States as a whole (U.S. Bureau of the Census 1983, Table 3; 1993a, Table 276). Over 180,000 Koreans, 70 percent of the Korean population in the state, lived in Los Angeles and Orange Counties. Since the late 1970s, Koreans in Los Angeles have developed Koreatown, a territorial community comparable to Chinatown, about three miles west of downtown Los Angeles. Koreatown is the residential, business, cultural, and social center for Koreans in Los Angeles.

In 1990, 12 percent of all Korean Americans settled in New York State, a substantial increase from 9.6 percent in 1980 (Min 1996:33). About 100,000 Koreans currently reside in New York City, with about 70 percent in the borough of Queens. Koreans in Queens are heavily concentrated in Flushing, which has gone through a radical ethnic change in the last two decades from a predominantly white area to a multiethnic city. Korean immigrants have developed another overseas Seoul along Union Street in a downtown Flushing area, where several hundred Korean stores with Korean language signs are lined up. According to the 1990 census, another 5 percent of Korean Americans settled in New Jersey, which marked a 200 percent growth rate in the Korean population between 1980 and 1990, higher than any other state (Min 1996:33). The New York–New Jersey metropolitan area, the home to approximately 150,000 Korean Americans, is the second largest Korean population center following Southern California.

It is interesting to note that the Korean population in Hawaii proportionally decreased over the years. In 1990, only 3 percent of Korean Americans settled in the state of Hawaii. In the 1970s and 1980s, Chicago was the third largest Korean center, following Los Angeles and New York. During more recent years, however, Chicago has become less attractive to Korean immigrants and the New York–New Jersey area has become more popular, a preference that is also a general trend in other Asian immigration patterns.

FAMILY CHARACTERISTICS

In general, Korean immigrant families are more Americanized (modern) than families in Korea but more traditional than American families. Thus, to understand better the Korean immigrant families, we need to make a two-way comparison, first comparing Korean immigrant families with families in Korea and then with non-Hispanic, white families (who we believe represent American families in general). Table 1 compares the three groups in family characteristics on the basis of the 1990 U.S. and Korean census reports.

As expected, Korean Americans, on average, have larger households and larger families than white Americans but smaller ones than Koreans in Korea. Korean Americans have a larger household than white Americans partly because they have fewer single-person households. Single-person households compose 15 percent of Korean American households, compared with more than a quarter of white American households. Unmarried Korean adult children, particularly girls, usually live with their parents, unless they go to college in another city, whereas unmarried white American adult children often live separately from their parents. Also, the Korean American population has a smaller proportion of divorced or separated persons, many of whom live alone, than the white American population. Finally, widowed Koreans usually live with their adult children, but few widowed white Americans do so. These three factors have contributed to a larger household size of Korean Americans than of white Americans. Regardless of differential proportions of single-person households, Korean American families are larger than white American families, because Korean American families have more children and nonnuclear kin members than white American families.

TABLE 1. Family Characteristics of White, Korean American, and Korean Populations

	NON-HISPANIC WHITE	KOREAN AMERICAN	KOREAN IN KOREA
Number of Persons per Household	2.5	3.2	3.7
Number of Persons per Family	3.0	3.6	4.0
% of Single-Person Households	25.5	15.2	9.0
Number of Children per Family	1.1	1.9	—
Number of Nonnuclear Family Members per Family	0.1	0.4	—
Number of Divorcees per 1,000 Persons 15 Years Old and Over	74 (Male) 95 (Female)	23 (Male) 54 (Female)	7 (Male) 9 (Female)
% of Married Couple Families	83.5	83.4	—
% of Female-Headed Families	12.3	11.6	—
% of Persons under 18 in Married Couple Families	78.7	86.6	—
% of Women (16 years Old and Over) in the Labor Force	56.4	55.5	44.2*
% of Married Women in the Labor Force	57.9	59.8	25.3*
Number of Children Born per 1,000 Ever-Married Women 25–34 Years Old	1,233	1,067	1,873
Number of Children Born per 1,000 Ever-Married Women 35–44 Years Old	1,849	1,776	3,100

*The nonfarm population.

Source: U.S. Bureau of the Census, 1993a, Tables 40 and 48; 1993b, Tables 41, 44, 105, 108, and 109; Korean Bureau of Statistics, 1993, Tables 2-1 and 2-2; Korean Women's Development Institute, 1994, Tables 2-1-2, 2-2-1, 4-1-1, and 4-1-2.

Table 1 also provides data reflecting marital stability for the three comparison groups. As expected, Korean Americans have a higher divorce rate than the Korean population in South Korea but a lower divorce rate than white Americans. It is, however, surprising that the Korean American population that consists mainly of recent immigrants, is closer in the divorce rate to the white American population than to the population in Korea. This finding suggests that Koreans have experienced a phenomenal increase in the divorce rate since their immigration to the United States. The following three factors seem largely to explain this remarkable increase.

First, a higher divorce rate of 1.5-generation Koreans who immigrated to the United States at early ages inflated the divorce rate of Korean immigrants. Native-born Koreans have a much higher divorce rate than foreign-born Koreans; and 1.5-generation Koreans, who make up a significant proportion of foreign-born Koreans, are likely to have a high divorce rate close to that of native-born Koreans. Second, residence in this country for several years has led to a change in Korean immigrants' attitudes toward divorce. In South Korea, many people continue to maintain unhappy marital relations because custom discourages divorce. In this country, however, divorce is not considered deviant behavior, and thus exposure to this liberal cultural milieu has led many Korean immigrants to make the decision to divorce more easily than they would have done in Korea. Many Korean immigrant women in particular are ready to accept divorce as an alternative either to an abusive or to an unhappy marriage. I recently heard a story of Korean partners who got divorced in their early sixties. The wife, who had been treated imprudently by her husband for many years, got divorced after she acquired a boyfriend. If she had been in Korea, she would not have reacted to her imprudent husband by finding a boyfriend.

Korean American women have a divorce rate 2.5 times higher than Korean American men. Because a high percentage of the marriages between Korean women and American servicemen have terminated in divorce, the divorce rate of Korean American women has inflated. Korean women married to American servicemen generally have a low socioeconomic status, although there are many exceptions (B. Kim 1972; Lee 1989). Many of them were born and raised in rural villages and migrated to Seoul and other large cities in search of urban employment. Their language barrier and lack of assimilation make their adjustments to American society and to intermarriages very difficult (Jeong and Schumm 1990). Moreover, many interracially married American servicemen neglect and even abuse their Korean wives, feeling that the women who provided them with companionship in Korea are no longer valuable to them in this country. For these reasons, an unusually high proportion of the intermarriages between Korean women and U.S. servicemen are known to have ended with divorce, although no hard data are available.

The Confucian ideology prescribes that the wife should stay at home as a full-time homemaker and that the husband's role should be limited to earning a living. Despite significant changes in the Korean family system, this norm about gender role differentiation has not changed much in South Korea. Both role expectations and employment discrimination discourage married women from participating in the labor market. Only 25 percent of married women in urban areas in South Korea participate in the labor force (see Table 1). Many women work outside the home before they get married; however, upon getting married, they quit their jobs—very often involuntarily—to focus on housework, child care, and services to their husbands. The married women who participate in the labor force, usually representing a working-class or a low-class background, do so out of economic needs, with but few women working for career achievements.

The most noteworthy change that the trans-Pacific migration has brought about in the Korean family system is a radical increase in the labor-force participation rate of married women. The 1990 census shows that approximately 60 percent of Korean American married women participated in the labor force, compared with 58 percent of white married women. Korean immigrants are heavily concentrated in small business (Kim 1981; Light and Bonacich 1988; Min 1996). Most Korean married women who participate in the labor force work for the family business as unpaid family laborers or as employees of coethnic businesses (Min 1997a). Many of these women in the ethnic subeconomy are unlikely to report their work either to the Internal Revenue Service or to the census survey. Thus, the 1990 census seems to have underestimated to a great extent the labor-force participation rate of Korean married women. A survey in New York City conducted in 1988 showed that 70 percent of Korean immigrant married women worked outside the home and that 54 percent worked full-time (Min 1992b). Korean immigrant women also work extremely long hours. The New York City survey showed that Korean married women spent an average of 51 hours per week for paid work (Min 1992b), longer hours than those of American married working women, who spent an average of 37 hours per week for paid work (Shelton 1992: 39).

The bottom two rows in Table 3 on page 206 provide data on fertility for two age groups: 25 to 34 years old and 35 to 44 years old. For both age groups, Korean American women have a substantially lower fertility rate than women in South Korea and a slightly lower rate than white American women. Korean American women who have passed childbearing age (35 to 44 years old) have, on average, less than two children, whereas their counterparts in South Korea have approximately three children. Since the vast majority of Korean American women 35 to 44 years old are Korean immigrant women, the low fertility rate of Korean American women in the bottom row of the table indicates the low fertility rate of Korean immigrant women. That Korean immigrant women have a lower fertility rate than women in South Korea is to be expected, but the fact that the Korean immigrant population shows a slightly lower fertility rate than the white American population is surprising.

Two major factors seem to explain the low fertility rate of Korean immigrants. First, their low fertility rate is largely the result of their selective migration. Korean immigrants, particularly those who came to this country in the 1970s, represent the well-educated, middle-class segment of the Korean population. Middle-class couples generally have a lower fertility rate than lower-class couples. Korean immigrants are also a select group in terms of their motives for economic success and social mobility. All immigrants are self-selected in that more progressive, economically aggressive, and achievement-oriented people chose to leave their native country for life in an alien environment (Chiswick 1982). Korean immigrants as a group have a higher level of aspiration for economic success and social mobility than the middle class in Korea has, and this mobility orientation seems to have negative influence on their fertility behavior.

Second, a high labor-force participation rate of Korean married women serves as a restrictive force on fertility. In South Korea, a small proportion of married women work outside the home, although many of them can depend on a cohabiting mother-in-law or a housemaid for child care. By contrast, most Korean immigrant women work long hours outside the home for economic survival, but they usually do not live with an elderly mother or a mother-in-law who can help them with babysitting. Thus, Korean immigrant women have difficulty raising their children while holding their paid work. This fact suggests that many Korean immigrant women have to delay their pregnancy in order to undertake their economic role. Women's economic role and fertility mutually influence each other; but, for immigrant women, their economic role seems to influence their fertility behavior more than the other way around.

MARITAL RELATIONS

As noted before, a significant change that Koreans' migration to the United States has brought about in the Korean family system is a phenomenal increase in married women's economic role. The participation of a wife in the labor force leads to changes in marital relations. First, it usually reduces her homemaker's role and increases her husband's share of household tasks (Huber and Spitze 1983; Ross 1987). How much has the radical increase in a Korean wife's economic role in this country changed her own and her husband's shares of housework in the expected direction?

Survey studies reveal that a Korean immigrant wife's employment or self-employment has not increased her husband's homemaker's role significantly, and that in addition to long hours spent for paid work, the wife bears the major responsibility for housework (Kim and Hurh 1988; Min 1992b). As shown in Table 2, my survey of Korean married women in New York City yields similar findings. Korean working wives' share of responsibility for the four major traditional domestic tasks is substantially lower than that of Korean housewives, but Korean working wives still shoulder most household work except garbage disposal. Moreover, the decrease in the proportion of household work for Korean working women does not result from a significant increase in their husbands' domestic role. Korean working wives can reduce their share of housework mainly because other family members (usually elderly mother and/or daughter) help them at home. As a result, Korean working women spent 12 more hours per week on their job and housework combined than their overworked husbands (Min 1992b). This finding suggests that most Korean immigrant women suffer from overwork, stress, and role strain (Choi 1995).

Another important issue regarding Korean immigrants' marital relations is the extent to which the increased economic role of Korean immigrant women has increased their power and status in the family. The wife's employment usually increases her marital power because it provides her with economic and other resources to bring to the marriage (Blood and Wolfe 1960). However, how much the

TABLE 2. Share of Domestic Tasks by Wife's Work Status (Unit: %)

DOMESTIC TASKS	FAMILIES WITH WIFE NOT WORKING			FAMILIES WITH WIFE WORKING		
	WIFE	HUSBAND	OTHERS	WIFE	HUSBAND	OTHERS
Cooking	94.7	2.8	2.5	78.9	8.4	12.7
Dishwashing	92.8	3.3	3.9	72.7	9.6	17.7
Laundry	93.7	3.7	2.6	63.1	13.3	23.6
Housecleaning	91.4	7.2	1.4	58.9	19.5	21.6
Grocery Shopping	71.9	25.6	2.5	65.2	28.6	6.2
Garbage Disposal	68.1	27.2	4.7	41.8	37.8	20.4

Source: Min 1992b.

employment increases her marital power depends on a particular cultural context that prescribes marital relations (Rodman 1967). The occupational segregation of Korean immigrants in the ethnic subeconomy hinders both husbands and wives from altering the traditional patriarchal ideology brought from Korea. Thus, the employment or self-employment of Korean immigrant women in the conservative cultural milieu will discourage them from bargaining actively to improve their power and status. Also, the participation of most Korean immigrants in a Korean Christian church perpetuates the patriarchal ideology and thus diminishes the positive effects of Korean women's economic role on their power and status (A. Kim 1995; Min 1992a). Furthermore, a significant proportion of Korean immigrant working women work for the family business as unpaid family workers, and the nature of their work is less helpful in increasing their power and influence than regular employment would be. Employed women increase their bargaining power mainly because they have an independent source of income. Korean women who assist their husbands in the family store do not seem to enjoy the economic and psychological independence that most employed American wives seem to enjoy.

My discussion with Korean social workers, my reading of Korean ethnic newspapers, and my participant observations indicate that many Korean immigrant couples have a high level of marital conflicts. There are several factors that have contributed to marital conflicts in these families. First, the great increase in wives' economic role and a concomitant reduction of their husbands' economic resources have contributed to marital conflicts in Korean immigrant families. As we noted before, the engagement of Korean immigrant wives in the ethnic economy, particularly in the family business, compared with American wives' employment, is not effective in increasing their power and status. Nevertheless, many Korean immigrant wives have increased their negotiating power in their marriages, compared with housewives in Korea. Many Korean immigrant husbands are unemployed or underemployed, whereas most Korean immigrant wives have increased their level of contribution to the family economy; in fact, in many Korean immigrant families, the wife plays a more important role in the family economy than her husband. A husband's inability to fulfill his culturally prescribed role as the sole provider threatens his authority and dominant position. In this situation, the husband may react angrily or even violently. It is known that proportionally more Korean immigrant women in Los Angeles and New York become victims of conjugal violence than other Asian immigrant women (Korea Times Los Angeles 1990; Song-Kim 1992). Korean immigrant husbands' sense of psychological insecurity resulting both from their weakened economic resources and from cultural factors related to the patriarchal ideology apparently has contributed to frequent violence against their wives.

Second, both partners' dissatisfaction with their low social status, particularly a husband's frustrations over his low social status, complicates their marital relations. Coming from a Confucian society, Korean immigrants are very conscious of their social status. However, self-employment in a small business or employment in a co-ethnic business does not give Korean immigrants social status comparable to their educational levels (Min 1990). Many Korean husbands try to maintain authority at least at home, but their wives and children challenge their authority.

Third, both partners' long hours of work outside the home and work-related stress are also contributing factors to marital conflicts. In many cases, both the husband and the wife work long hours in the same family business. Two partners' staying together day and night seven days a week increases the chance for arguments and conflicts, particularly so when they work under deplorable conditions.

CHILD SOCIALIZATION AND GENERATIONAL CONFLICTS

As a consequence of the strong Confucian cultural tradition, child socialization in South Korea places a great emphasis on children's obedience to and respect for parents and adults. Korean immigrant parents, the vast majority of whom completed their formal education in South Korea, are more authoritarian than white American parents in child socialization practices, although there are significant class differences. Most Korean immigrant parents try to teach their children Korean customs, including the Korean way of speaking politely to parents and other adults. They usually discourage their children from talking back even when they are wrong. Most Korean immigrant parents use whipping as a means of punishing their children.

Korean parents' authoritarian child socialization practices, which conflict with the more liberal, American child socialization practices, are a major source of generational discord in many Korean immigrant families. In 1989, I conducted a survey in New York in which Korean children and their mothers were asked to report their three most common complaints about each other. The child respondents cited "restricting my freedom too much" and "too strict" as two of the most common complaints about their parents, whereas many mothers complained about their children's "not respecting parents" and "talking back" (Min 1995b). Naturally, Americanized Korean children want to escape parental control and authority, leading to a high level of intergenerational conflicts. Korean parents have some level of control over their children during childhood, but they gradually lose control as their children reach adolescence. A small proportion of Korean parents continue to administer corporal punishment to their children of high school age. However, most parents cannot continue to do so because their adolescent children, too, respond by using physical force. Some Korean parents end up in court when their child or a neighbor reports their use of physical force to the police.

Another core element of Confucianism is emphasis on children's education and social mobility through education. Many Korean immigrants have chosen emigration to the United States to give their children better opportunities for education (Kim 1978: 189). For most of these parents, getting a good education means getting good grades in school and going to a good college; thus, they put a lot of pressure on their children to perform well in school. Korean immigrants have brought with them the Korean practice of giving children after-school lessons to prepare them for admission to specialized high schools and prestigious universities. In Queens, where about 70 percent of New York City Koreans reside, there are about 30 Korean-run private institutes specializing in mathematics and English. In a survey study comparing Korean and Jewish mothers in Queens (Rose and Min 1992), the majority of the Korean secondary school children were found to attend private institutes specializing in after-school programs or to receive tutoring in the previous summer, compared with only 6 percent of Jewish children. The survey also found that Korean mothers pressured their children to study longer hours after school and to get better grades than did Jewish mothers.

Korean parents' overemphasis on their children's good performance in school is another major source of generational conflicts in Korean immigrant families. In the New York survey of Korean children and their mothers, 25 percent of child respondents indicated "putting too much pressure on me to perform well in school" as one of their three major complaints about their parents, whereas nearly half of the mother respondents cited "not studying hard" as one of their three complaints (Min 1995b). Of course, children's unsatisfactory performance in school is a source of intergenerational conflict in many white American families as well. However, it seems to cause a greater degree of conflict in Korean immigrant families because Korean immigrant parents have higher expectations of their children's success in school. Korean children who do very well in school are well rewarded. Unsuccessful Korean children, however, are not rewarded and are sometimes even neglected by their parents, thereby increasing the likelihood that they will spend time on the street.

Korean immigrants are significantly different from the white middle class in gender socialization. Of course, Korean parents practice a more conservative gender socialization than white American parents, treating boys and girls differently. In a survey study of Korean and Jewish mothers (Rose and Min 1992), Korean mothers were found to agree with statements reflecting traditional gender stereotypes to a far greater extent than Jewish mothers. Also, Korean mothers were found to be more traditional than Jewish mothers in assigning housework chores to boys and girls. For example, 63 percent of Korean mothers felt that setting the table should be done only by girls, whereas all Jewish respondents said it should be done by both boys and girls. Although most Korean American high school girls help their mothers with cooking, dishwashing, and laundry, few Korean high school boys undertake these tasks, traditionally considered to belong to "the female domain."

The fact that Korean parents teach different social roles to boys and girls is well reflected in Korean children's extracurricular activities. Korean parents place great emphasis on having their children undertake musical studies; for example, Korean children usually take piano lessons at one time or another in their formative years. However, far more Korean girls than boys take piano or other kinds of music lessons. In a survey of Korean high school students in New York, 47 percent of Korean girls, compared with 29 percent of boys, reported that they were taking either piano or other kinds of music lessons (Min 1997b). The same survey showed that 57 percent of Korean boys, compared with 29 percent of girls, participated in sports as extracurricular activities. There are gender differences not only in the proportion of Korean children participating in athletic activities after school but also in the types of activities. Few Korean girls play soccer or softball, although these are currently accepted as popular sports for American girls. Most Korean parents discourage their daughters from engaging in any sport that involves much action; instead, they encourage their daughters to study music and art.

Korean immigrants consider it very important for their children to learn both the Korean language and Korean customs, but they have difficulty teaching Korean cultural traditions because of limited resources. First of all, they have little time to spend with their children at home because both parents work long hours outside the home. Korean parents attend a Korean church partly because the church usually provides Korean language and cultural programs for their children (Min 1992a), thus offering the Korean immigrants an advantage over other immigrant groups in passing on their cultural traditions to the next generation. However, exposure to a Korean language program for one hour to three hours a week given by a Korean church is not enough for second-generation Korean children to achieve fluency in the language. Although most Korean children understand the Korean language in the way that their parents use it at home, only a small proportion of second-generation Korean children have achieved a high level of proficiency in the language, and they feel more comfortable using English as their everyday language (Hong and Min 1996).

Very often, Korean parents speak in Korean, while their children respond in English. This language barrier, along with value conflicts, creates an unbridgeable distance between Korean parents and adolescent children. In a survey of Korean adolescents and their mothers (Min 1995b), the vast majority of the child respondents complained that their parents are "too traditional" or that their parents "do not understand their situation," whereas the majority of the mother respondents indicated their children's "failure to learn the Korean language and customs" as one of the three most dissatisfying things about their children. Korean parents are embarrassed when they see their children having difficulty communicating with other Koreans in the Korean language. On the other hand, Korean children feel ashamed when they observe their parents' speaking broken English with their teachers. Many Korean children feel that there is a conflict between what they learn in school and what they learn in school and what they learn at home (Min 1991).

GENERATIONAL DIFFERENCES IN THE FAMILY SYSTEM

About 25 years have passed since the contemporary mass migration of Koreans to this country started. Therefore, many second- and 1.5-generation Koreans have already completed their formal education and established their own families. As the annual flow of Korean immigrants has gradually decreased since the late 1980s and will continue to decrease in the future, these younger-generation Koreans will compose an increasingly larger proportion of the adult population in the Korean community. The increase in the size of younger-generation Korean Americans relative to the first-generation immigrants, in turn, is likely to lead to significant changes in the structure of the Korean community and family system.

The segregation of Korean immigrants both in economic activities (concentration in small businesses) and in religious services (affiliation of the vast majority with ethnic churches) has hindered their assimilation into American society. However, there is evidence that the younger-generation Korean Americans are not particularly segregated either in economic activities or in religious services. Native-born Koreans, who are not attracted to labor-intensive small businesses, are finding jobs in the mainstream economy, as their exceptionally low (lower than that of the white population) self-employment rate suggests (Min 1996:52). The ethnic church participation rate of younger-generation Koreans seems to have decreased significantly. Their education in the United States as well as their noninvolvement in an ethnic economy and/or ethnic congregations has facilitated their cultural and social assimilation.

It is likely that the high cultural, social, and occupational assimilation of younger-generation Korean Americans has led to significant changes in their family lifestyles, making their families similar to white American families. Although there is no empirical study that has focused on younger-generation Korean families, the 1990 census provides data that suggest significant differences between native- and foreign-born Koreans in selected family characteristics.

As shown in Table 3, Korean Americans born in the United States have a much higher divorce rate and a larger proportion of female-headed families than foreign-born Koreans. In fact, relevant indicators suggest that native-born Korean families are more unstable than white American families. This characteristic may

TABLE 3. Family Characteristics of the Foreign-Born Korean, Native-Born Korean, and White Populations in the United States

	FOREIGN-BORN KOREAN	NATIVE-BORN KOREAN	WHITE
% of People 25 Years Old and Over Who Completed High School	79.9	87.7	79.1
% of People 25 Years Old and Over Who Completed 4-Year College	34.4	36.5	22.0
Number of Divorcees for 100 Married Men	3.4	14.6	12.5
Number of Divorcees for 1,000 Married Women	8.4	19.6	16.9
% of Married Couple Families	84.4	77.2	83.5
% of Female-Headed Families	11.1	15.1	12.3
% of Women 16 Years and Over in the Labor Force	55.5	56.4	56.4
% of Married Women in the Labor Force	—	—	57.9
Number of Children Born per 1,000 Ever-Married Women 25–34 Years Old	1,088	669	1,233
Number of Children Born per 1,000 Ever-Married Women 35–44 Years Old	1,826	1,747	1,849

Sources: U.S. Bureau of the Census, 1993a, Table 40; 1993b, Tables 41, 42, and 44; 1993c, Tables 1, 2, 3, and 4.

be due partly to the fact that native-born Korean adults consist mainly of young people who are more prone to divorce than people in the middle and older years. Nevertheless, even with age controlled, native-born Koreans are likely to be as divorce-prone as white Americans. Younger-generation Koreans have a much higher divorce rate than Korean immigrants mainly because they are more ready to accept divorce as an alternative to an unhappy marriage than are their parent generation. American-born Korean women in particular are much more ready to escape from an unequal marriage than their mothers. In this connection, it is important to note that native-born Koreans have narrowed a gender gap in education to an almost insignificant level. In 1990, 47 percent of foreign-born Korean men had a four-year college education, compared with 26 percent of their female counterparts, whereas native-born Korean men were ahead of women in the college graduation rate only by 39 percent to 35 percent (U.S. Bureau of the Census 1993c, Table 3).

Native- and foreign-born Koreans do not differ in the labor force participation rate of married women; both native- and foreign-born Korean married women have similarly high labor force participation rates, slightly higher than that of white married women. However, the nature of economic activities differs significantly for native- and foreign-born Korean women. Most of the Korean immigrant women who work outside the home accept traditional gender role stereotypes (Min 1997a), and they are forced to work simply out of economic need. By contrast, most American-born Korean working women seem to participate in the labor force for career achievements, and many engage in the professional occupations, such as accounting, and legal and medical services, areas traditionally dominated by men. Naturally, native-born Korean married women work shorter hours than Korean immigrant women, and thus they feel less harried in juggling paid work and housework.

The last two rows in Table 3 compare native-born Korean, foreign-born Korean, and white married women in fertility rate. For the 25 to 34 age group, there is a marked difference in fertility rates between native-born and foreign-born Korean women. For the native-born Korean population in the 25 to 34 age category, there is a 0.7 fertility rate per woman, compared with 1.1 for the foreign-born. However, for the older women in the 35 to 44 age category, there is virtually no difference in the fertility rate between the native-born and the foreign-born. Two factors seem to be responsible for the marked difference in fertility behavior between the native- and foreign-born Korean populations in the younger age category. First, the native-born younger Korean women seem to have a lower fertility rate than their foreign-born counterparts partly because they delay marriage longer than do the foreign-born Korean women. More Americanized, more highly educated, and thus more career-oriented, native-born Korean women tend to marry at a later age than do Korean immigrant women. Second, a larger gap between marriage and the birth of the first child for native-born Korean women than for foreign-born Korean women also contributes to the significant differential in the fertility rate between the two groups. Because they are more familiar with contraceptives, native-born Korean women tend to delay the birth of their first child longer than do Korean immigrant women.

CONCLUSION

Koreans have experienced significant changes in their family characteristics since immigration to this country. On average, they live in smaller households and have smaller families than their South Korean counterparts. Korean immigrants have a much higher divorce rate than has the population in their home country. Also, they have a much lower fertility rate than their compatriots in South Korea and a slightly lower fertility rate than even the white American population. Korean immigrants' high-class background and Korean immigrant women's active economic roles seem to be the main causes of their significant reduction in fertility rate.

The most significant change that has occurred in Korean immigrants' marital relations is a phenomenal increase in the economic role of married women. Although the economic role of Korean immigrant wives has increased significantly, their husbands' share of traditional housework tasks has not increased. Consequently, Korean immigrant wives suffer from the rigors of overwork—from both paid work and housework—and work-related stress. Moreover, the economic role of Korean immigrant wives is less effective for enhancing their marital power and status than that of American wives in general. This is the case partly because a large proportion of Korean working women work for the family business as "unpaid family workers" and partly because Koreans' concentration in small business hinders their altering the traditional gender role ideology. Korean immigrant families usually have a high level of marital conflicts. Korean husbands' psychological insecurity caused by their wives' increased economic role, both partners' overwork and work-related stress, and their dissatisfaction with low-status jobs seem to be the main causes of their marital conflicts.

Korean immigrants exercise more authority over children and place more emphasis on children's education than do white American families. They also stress their children's learning the Korean language and customs. These aspects of their child socialization practices put the parents in conflict with their children. Korean children often complain that their parents restrict their freedom too much, put too much pressure on them to succeed in school, and do not understand their situation as teenagers in the United States. Korean immigrants practice more conservative gender socialization than do white Americans, treating boys and girls differently.

At present, an overwhelming majority of families in the Korean community are headed by Korean immigrants. Yet, families established by second- and 1.5-generation Korean adults will compose an increasingly larger proportion of Korean-American families in the future. Highly assimilated into American culture and society, younger-generation Koreans are similar to white Americans in family characteristics. Data from the 1990 census show that American-born Koreans have a much higher divorce rate than foreign-born Koreans, a divorce rate that is comparable to white Americans. The data also reveal that native-born younger Korean women (25 to 34 years old) have a much lower fertility rate than their foreign-born counterparts. We can hypothesize that younger-generation Koreans are similar to white Americans in conjugal relations and child socialization practices. To test these and other hypotheses regarding generational changes in the family system, we need research on younger-generation Korean families.

REFERENCES

Blood, R. O., and D. M. Wolfe. 1960. *Husbands and Wives: The Dynamics of Married Living*. New York: Free Press.

Chiswick, Barry. 1982. "The Economic Progress of Immigrants: Some Universal Patterns." In *The Gateway: U.S. Immigration Issues and Policies*, edited by B. Chiswick, 119–158. Washington, DC: American Enterprise Institute for Public Policy Research.

Choi, Helen. 1995. *The Korean American Experience: A Detailed Analysis of How Well Korean-Americans Adjust to Life in the United States*. New York: Vintage Press.

Chow, Esther Nan-Ling. 1995. "Family, Economy, and the State: A Legacy of Struggle for Chinese American Women." In *Origins and Destinies: Immigration, Race, and Ethnicity*, edited by S. Pedraza and R. Rumbaut. Belmont, CA: Wadsworth Publishing Company.

Eu, Hongsook. 1992. "Health Status and Social and Demographic Determinants of Living Arrangements among the Korean Elderly." *Korea Journal of Population and Development* 21: 197–224.

Glenn, Evelyn Nakano. 1983. "Split Household, Small Producer, and Dual Wage Earner: An Analysis of Chinese American Family Strategies." *Journal of Marriage and the Family* 45:35–46.

———. 1986. *Issei, Nisei, and War Brides*. Philadelphia: Temple University Press.

Hong, Joann, and Pyong Gap Min. 1996. "Ethnic Attachment among Second-Generation Korean Adolescents." Paper under review.

Huber, Joan, and Glenna Spitze. 1983. *Sex Stratification: Children, Housework, and Jobs*. New York: Academic Press.

Hurh, Won Moo, and Kwang Chung Kim. 1984. *Korean Immigrants in America: A Structural Analysis of Ethnic Confinement and Adhesive Adaptation*. Madison, NJ: Fairleigh Dickinson University Press.

———. 1988. "Uprooting and Adjustment: A Sociological Study of Korean Immigrants' Mental Health." Final Report submitted to National Institute of Mental Health.

———. 1990. "Religious Participation of Korean Immigrants in the United States." *Journal of the Scientific Study of Religion* 29:19–34.

Jeong, Gyung Ja, and Walter Schumm. 1990. "Family Satisfaction in Korean/American Marriages: An Exploratory Study of the Perceptions of Korean Wives." *Journal of Comparative Family Studies* 21:325–335.

Jushua, Rose, and Pyong Gap Min. 1992. "A Comparison of Jewish American and Korean Immigrant Families in Child Socialization." Paper presented at the Annual Meeting of the American Sociological Association, Washington, DC.

Kibria, Nazli. 1993. *Family Tightrope: The Changing Lives of Vietnamese Americans*. Princeton, NJ: Princeton University Press.

Kim, Ai Ra. 1995. *Women Struggling for a New Life: The Role of Religion in the Cultural Passage from Korea to America*. Albany, NY: State University of New York Press.

Kim, Bok-Lim. 1972. "Japanese and Korean Wives of Americans." *Social Casework* 53:273–279.

———. 1978. *The Asian Americans: Changing Patterns, Changing Needs*. New York: The Association of Korean Christian Scholars in North America.

Kim, Hyun Suk, and Pyong Gap Min. 1992. "Post-1965 Korean Immigrants: Characteristics and Settlement Patterns." *Korea Journal of Population and Development* 21:121–143.

Kim, Illsoo. 1981. *New Urban Immigrants: The Korean Community in New York*. Princeton, NJ: University of Princeton Press.

———. 1987. "Korea and East Asian: Remigration Factors and U.S. Immigration Policy." In *Pacific Bridges: The New Immigration from Asian and the Pacific Islands*, edited by J. Fawcett and B. Carino, 327–346. Staten Island, NY: Center for Migration Studies.

Kim, Kwang Chung, and Won Moo Hurh. 1988. "The Burden of Double Roles." *Ethnic and Racial Studies* 11:151–167.

Korean Bureau of Statistics. 1993. *A Comprehensive Analysis of the 1990 Korean Population and Housing Census (4–3): Korean Household and Family Types.* Seoul: Korean Bureau of Statistics.

Korean Women's Development Institute. 1994. *1994 Statistical Yearbook on Women.* Seoul: Korean Women's Development Institute.

Korea Times Los Angeles. 1990. "Physical Violence against Wife in the Korean Community Has Reached A Severe Level." February 15.

Lee, Daniel. 1989. "Marital Adjustments between Korean Women and American Servicemen." *Korean Observer* 20:321–352.

Light, Ivan, and Edna Bonacich. 1988. *Immigrant Entrepreneurs: Koreans in Los Angeles, 1965–1982.* Berkeley: The University of California Press.

Min, Pyong Gap. 1984. "From White-Collar Occupations to Small Business: Korean Immigrants' Occupational Adjustment." *Sociological Quarterly* 25:333–352.

———. 1988. *Ethnic Business Enterprise: Korean Small Business in Atlanta.* Staten Island, NY: Center for Migration Studies.

———. 1989. "Some Positive Functions of Ethnic Business for an Immigrant Community: Koreans in Los Angeles." Final report submitted to National Science Foundation, Queens College of CUNY.

———. 1990. "Problems of Korean Immigrant Entrepreneurship." *International Migration Review* 24:436–455.

———. 1991. "Children's Education and Problems in the Korean Immigrant Community," in *Koreans in the United States* [in Korean], edited by Pyong Gap Min, 217–248. Seoul: Yurim Publishing Company.

———. 1992a. "The Structure and Social Functions of Korean Immigrant Churches in the United States." *International Migration Review* 26:1370–1394.

———. 1992b. "Korean Immigrant Wive's Overwork." *Korea Journal of Population and Development* 21:121–143.

———. 1995a. "Korean Americans. In *Asian Americans: Contemporary Trends and Issues,* edited by P. G. Min, 199–231. Newbury Park, CA: Sage Publications.

———. 1995b. "The Relationship between Korean Immigrant Parents and Children." [in Korean]. *The Academy Review of Korean Studies* 18:119–136.

———. 1996. *Caught in the Middle: Korean Merchants in America's Multiethnic Cities.* Berkeley: The University of California Press.

———. 1997a. "Korean Immigrant Wives' Labor-Force Participation, Marital Power, and Status," in *Women and Work: Race, Ethnicity, and Class,* edited by E. Higginbotham and M. Romero. Newbury Park, CA: Sage Publications.

———. 1997b. Forthcoming. *Changes and Conflicts: Korean Immigrant Families in New York.* Boston: Allyn and Bacon.

Park, Insook Han, and Lee-Jay Cho. 1995. "Confucianism and the Korean Family." *Journal of Comparative Family Studies* 26:117–134.

Patterson, Wayne. 1988. *The Korean Frontier in America: Immigration to Hawaii, 1896–1910.* Honolulu: University of Hawaii Press.

Rodman, Hyman. 1967. "Marital Power in France, Greece, Yugoslavia, and the United States: A Cross-National Discussion." *International Migration Review* 20:4–20.

Rose, Jushua, and Pyong Gap Min. 1992. "A Comparison of Jewish-American and Korean Immigrant Families in Child Socialization." Paper presented at the Annual Meeting of the American Sociological Association, Pittsburgh.

Ross, Catherine. 1987. "The Division of Labor at Home." *Social Forces* 65:816–833.

Shelton, Beth Ann. 1992. *Women, Men and Time.* New York: Greenwood Press.

Song-Kim, Young I. 1992. "Battered Korean Women in Urban United States." In *Social Work Practice With Asian Americans,* edited by S. M. Furuto, R. Biswas, D. K. Chung, K. Murase, and F. Ross-Sheriff, 213–226. Newbury Park, CA: Sage Publications.

U.S. Bureau of the Census. 1983. *1980 Census of Population, General Population Characteristics, United State Summary* (PC80-1-B1). Washington, DC: U.S. Government Printing Office.

———. 1993a. *1990 Census of Population, General Population Characteristics,* United States (CP-1-1). Washington, DC: U.S. Government Printing Office.

———. 1993b. *1990 Census of Population, Social and Economic Characteristics,* United States (CP-2-1). Washington, DC: U.S. Government Printing Office.

———. 1993c. *1990 Census of Population, Asian and Pacific Islanders in the United States* (CP-3-5). Washington, DC: U.S. Government Printing Office.

Wong, Morrison, 1988. "The Chinese American Family." In *Ethnic Families in America: Patterns and Variations,* edited by C. Mindel, R. Habenstein, and R. Wright, Jr., 230–256. New York: Elsevier.

Yoon, In-Jin. 1993. "The Social Origin of Korean Immigration to the United States, 1965–Present." Honolulu: East-West Population Institute.

CHAPTER 11

Rules, Roles, and Realities: Indo-American Families in the United States

Bandana Purkayastha

A common experience of most nonwhite groups in the United States is how local and national laws have restricted the formation of families. Split households, families by adoption, and bachelor societies are part of the continuum of nonwhite family experience; Indo-Americans share this history of family formation with other racial minority groups in the United States.[1] To many scholars, this statement may sound counterintuitive because Indo-Americans are often projected as the quintessential model minority. Indo-Americans, predominantly recent immigrants, have the highest level of education, very high incomes, and very low poverty rates, and they are characterized by a significant proportion of two-parent families that appear to approximate closely the American ideal.[2] Nevertheless, a closer examination of family formation among this group reveals the hiatus between the image of the elite minority and the reality of struggles and adjustments, within a restrictive set of rules that govern family experiences of Indo-Americans in the United States.

Following recent work by gender and race scholars that questions the separation of spheres (e.g., Espiritu 1997; Ferree 1990; Taylor 1994; Zinn 1994), this discussion of Indo-American families is grounded in how race/gender/class structures affect this relatively affluent group. Much of the work on Indo-American families emphasizes cultural explanations (e.g., Bacon 1996; Helweg and Helweg 1990; Leonard 1997; Saran 1985); in contrast, this chapter emphasizes the interaction of large-scale social structures and cultural expectations in influencing family life among Indo-Americans in the United States. The first section of this chapter describes how immigration and naturalization laws structure who are allowed to form a family, emphasizing the race/class/gender inequalities inherent in the legal framework. The second section focuses on three overlapping aspects of Indo-American family life—creating ideal families, evolving parental roles, and the relationship between immigrant parents and their children—to illustrate the complex dynamics of family life. The data for this chapter are drawn from archival materials and my ongoing research on Indo-Americans.[3]

RULES AND REALITIES: WHO ARE IN A FAMILY?

Whereas a focus of the mainstream family literature has been on real versus ideal families (e.g., Coontz 1992), for nonwhite populations, the question is often more basic: who, in reality, are allowed to make up a family? Most white families[4] in the United States rarely have to consider the question about who is able to form a family; however, for nonwhite groups, this becomes a central issue for understanding the context within which family life is carried out. In order to meet the contradictory need for cheap labor and the political need to maintain a white nation, Indo-American migration historically, like most nonwhite migrations, has been overwhelmingly male.[5] This selection has meant that the immigrant's ability to marry, create a family, or reunite with a family has been dependent on prevalent restrictions such as antimiscegenation laws; periodic bans on Asian migration; country quotas on family reunification; and currently, temporary work permits for skilled workers with few rights or supports for their families. In addition, a host of other laws have curtailed access to the social resources necessary to maintain families; nonwhites have encountered barriers to employment, ownership of property, and support of family members.

The global restrictions imposed by the British to prevent migration of its colonial subjects (except when the colonial power was involved in moving indentured laborers between different colonies) prevented the migration of Indians to the United States in significant numbers until the twentieth century.[6] Nevertheless, by 1910, about 6,000 migrants from India (ex-British-army personnel) were in the United States, having moved to this country from China and/or Canada. This group was, of course, overwhelmingly male. There were 109 females to over 5,000 males, and over half the males were married to women in India (Kitano and Daniels 1995).

The nativists' reaction to "the tide of turban" on the West Coast meant that the local laws that had been crafted to control Chinese Americans and Japanese Americans were soon used against the "Hindoos"[7] (Kitano and Daniels 1995; Simon and Alexander 1993). As the Japanese Americans and Indo-Americans demonstrated some success in agriculture, a series of laws was passed to restrict their ability to engage in a variety of occupations. In addition, the restrictions on citizenship, to which was tied the "privilege" of owning property further eroded the opportunities of these early groups. The 1790 law of naturalization limited citizenship to "free white males," and although that privilege was extended to black males after the Civil War (at least on paper), it left Indo-Americans in an ambiguous position. Some Indo-Americans were able to acquire citizenship through their states. In 1923, the United States Supreme Court set a new standard for defining whiteness (in *United States vs. Thind*) based on the perception of the common person on the street, and Indo-Americans, who had gained citizenship from states, were stripped of those privileges. The next year a worldwide Asian immigration ban was issued preventing the immigration of "Asians" from any part of the world.

The repercussion of these laws on Indo-Americans was immediate and devastating. As noncitizens, they could not own property, nor were they considered to be employable in most occupations (Gonzales 1996; Mazumdar 1989). Thus, not only was their opportunity to earn sufficient money to return to India to their families severely curtailed, but also they could not send for their families because the 1924 Asian Migration Ban was in effect. In addition, strict antimiscegenation laws restricted their ability to marry local women. Many of those who had left families at home lived in split households like the Chinese and the Chicano populations (Dill 1994). Some of these men married women of Mexican origin; at the same time, many of them continued financially to support their families in India (Leonard 1992). This ongoing support of the "other" family often led to the dissolution of marriages contracted in the United States (Kitano and Daniels 1995).

In 1965, the change of laws that followed the Civil Rights Movement instituted two visa categories that supported Asian Indian migration and family formation. First, the need for skilled labor meant that a significant number of highly skilled (overwhelmingly male) professionals were recruited from other countries to work in the United States. Asian Indians and Chinese made up a significant proportion of this group. Second, the family reunification immigration quota meant that these migrants were allowed to sponsor the migration of their families to the United States over several years.[8]

The combined effect of the two new visa categories led to the arrival of a very highly educated group from India, between 1965 and the mid-1980s, along with their families (see Table 1). Between 1965 and the middle of the 1980s, it appeared that the opportunities for forming families in the United States significantly outweighed the restrictions on these "new" immigrants. The more balanced sex ratios (100 females to 116 males in 1990) are testimony to this change (Kitano and Daniels 1995). For the first time in the group's immigration history, males and females were able to migrate; and, given their education along with the post-1965 opening up of labor markets to all race groups, they could access the opportunities in the primary labor market and maintain their families. The high achievement profile of Indo-Americans is determined overwhelmingly by the characteristics of this group (Barringer et al. 1995).

However, since the middle of the 1980s, new restrictions have begun to affect who are able to constitute a family. Although the race-based national quotas were discarded in 1965, new gender/race restrictions have begun to restrict the oppor-

TABLE 1.   Indo Americans: A Profile

	U.S.	WHITE	INDO AMERICAN
4+ years college			
All	20.3	21.5	58.0
Male	23.3	25.0	65.9
Female	17.6	18.4	48.7
Economic characteristics			
Median earnings	$30,056	$37,152	$49,309
% below poverty	10	7	7.2
Family characteristics			
% under 18, living with 2 parents	73.0		91.8
% divorce	8.3		2.1

Source: U.S. Bureau of Census 1990.

tunities for family formation. First, since the late 1980s, spouses of immigrants have to prove nonfraudulent marriages after a couple of years. This requirement has meant that all recent immigrants (overwhelmingly nonwhite) have to meet a far higher standard of marital continuity than is expected of couples in the mainstream. Second, since the 1990s, alternate visa categories are increasingly used to bring highly skilled workers to the United States. Under a category known as H1-B, people with degrees in the specialty occupations are recruited to work in the United States for a period for three to six years. H1-B visas, with their rapidly expanding quotas, are becoming the primary plank for recruiting highly-skilled technical labor from nonwhite countries: Indians make up 40 to 60 percent of this category (U.S. INS 2000). As temporary legal aliens, these migrants can work in the United States, but they are not eligible for any of the social benefits. Of more importance, because of the restrictions on family migration, split households appear to be developing once again among Asian Indians.

These later immigration restrictions have enforced gender distinctions on Indo-American families.[9] First, since the primary migrant is likely to be male, his spouse's fate in the United States depends on her ability to prove, to the satisfaction of the Immigration and Naturalization Service (INS) officials, that she is still married to him (after two years) in order for her to get legal permission to work (her "green card"). In cases of domestic abuse, the sponsored spouse has little recourse to legal remedies[10] and thus is forced to remain in the marriage in order to get the work permit that would allow her the opportunity to support herself. Second, the new H1-B visas allow only the primary migrant to work, leaving the spouse with two options: either she can live in a split household in order to continue her career or she can move to the United States temporarily and becoming a full-time homemaker.

These immigration laws also include a definite class bias. Immigrants sponsoring family members now have to prove to the INS that they are able to support families and personally guarantee that the sponsored member will not become a public charge. Thus, who are able to meet these conditions, as well as for how many family members at any given time, is decided on the basis of the sponsor's class position. Even though less affluent people may feel a great deal of responsibility for, and closeness with, "extended" family, their financial circumstances may militate against their ability to reconstitute families on the basis of emotional ties.

In sum, the "model" image of two-parent families, with low divorce and poverty rates, that appears closely to approximate the American ideal, simply describes a type of family that has developed in response to the selection criteria of the U.S. immigration laws. The data do not indicate other types of families that existed previously or that exist currently, *in other countries,* in response to race/gender constraints on nonwhite immigrants.

FAMILY DYNAMICS

Although Indo-American family life, like that of other minority groups, has been described in terms of the group's traditional culture (e.g., Hines et al. 1997; Saran 1985), a closer look at some overlapping aspects of these families—creating ideal families, evolving parental roles, and the relationship between immigrant parents and their children—reveals that such cultural explanations do not capture the range of conflicts and contradictions that characterize family life among Indo-Americans in the United States. Indo-Americans, like other groups, emphasize selected aspects of their culture in response to the larger social context (Nagel 1994; Swidler 1995). There is often a rational component to what is emphasized as "ethnic-ness." The interaction of race with gender and class remains salient for understanding the dynamic relationship between the macrostructural context and a family's effort to carry out the production/reproduction tasks in the United States.

IDEAL VERSUS REAL FAMILIES

Although the nuclear family—two parents and children—may closely approximate the norm in the United States, this unit is not necessarily the ideal among Indo-Americans. Ethnographic work among Indo-Americans reveals that there is an ongoing acknowledgment of the influence of extended family members on the nuclear family units in the United States (e.g., Bacon 1996; Leonard 1997). Part of the answer may be traced to a different understanding of the concept of a nuclear family in India: the typical urban nuclear family in India is composed of a couple and their children, the male's parents and unmarried siblings, and sometimes also of his married brothers and their families, as well as unmarried aunts and uncles (Seth 1995). Other relatives—married siblings and their families, the wife's family, uncles, aunts, and cousins—who do not live in the same household, are also considered to be part of the family. Indeed, all the major Indian languages indicate intricate and nuanced family relationships that cannot be translated by using English words such as uncle, aunt, cousin, or grandparent.[11] Family care work, especially socialization of the young and care of older members, organizing marriages, and resolution of marital problems, are usually shared by several members of the family. In addition, the lifelong commitment of brothers and sisters adds other networks of responsibilities to the understanding and practice of "family" in India (Knuckolls 1993). Thus, the Indo-American family in the United States represents part of a larger complex family network that may be spread over several countries of the world (Rex 1995; Tatla 1999).

Since legal structures restrict the migration of extended family members, Indo-Americans appear to have used two primary mechanisms to re-create "ideal" families. First, like other nonwhite groups, Indo-American families create a network of fictive kin (Dill 1994; Renteria 1992; Stack 1974). Among the first-generation immigrants, selected coethnics are addressed in terms of family relationships such as older brother, elder sister, and sister-in-law (Purkayastha 1991). These relationships become especially crucial in times of need, for arranging child care, for help during illnesses and catastrophic events, and, in the absence of formal religious organizations among the Hindus, for the collective task of religious socialization. For the second generation, these adoptive relationships are a source of support and of social capital (see also Portes and Sensenbrennar 1993; Zhou and Bankston 1998). As one second-generation person stated, "I can simply pick up the phone and get information on research, medical issues, or corporate life; it is a comfortable entry to white collar careers" (Purkayastha 1999).

The second mechanism used by Indo-American families has been to maintain ties with family members around the world (Rex 1995; Purkayastha 1999). Cheaper telephone calls and airfares, and, increasingly, the rapid spread and use of e-mail facilitates this ongoing communication. Although family ties withered away in previous eras because of the difficulty of staying in touch, preliminary data indicate that even second-generation Indo-Americans stay directly in touch with selected family members in other countries (Purkayastha 1999). The exact nature of communication depends on the class position of specific Indo-American families; for instance, the more affluent families tend to have e-discussion lists or log onto chat rooms at preappointed times over the weekend. Less affluent families tend to rely on telephone calls to selected family members. Regular remittances of money for supporting the extended family for elder care; for family events such as marriages, rite-of-passage rituals, and illnesses; as well as increasing property and expanding businesses form a significant part of these connections (Tatla 1999). Depending on the financial position of the family, frequent visits to India, as well as visits by relatives from India to the United States, also facilitate the process of maintaining meaningful connections with family members. Indeed, Rex (1995) argues that the needs of family-based networks are becoming more important determinants of the nature of ethnic group life in any particular country than the restrictions imposed by states.

PARENTAL ROLES

The distribution of tasks between fathers and mothers within any family tends to follow a gender division. In examining the life of Indo-Americans, many scholars have explained these divisions with reference to traditional gender roles in India (Hines et al. 1997; Saran 1985). However, structural conditions such as who is allowed to work (the male or the female or both migrants), what are the work place norms about the number of hours expected of male white-collar professionals, and the restricted educational and occupational opportunities women can access, also enhance the gender division of labor within households.

Scholars who describe the division of labor in Indo-American families in terms of cultural traditions point to the separation of female and male spheres in India. However, the selection of which tasks are considered appropriate for the male and which ones appropriate for the female varies significantly by marital and age status, class, region, and availability of other family members collectively to carry out the tasks of production and reproduction. A case in point is the socialization and care of children, since grandparents, uncles, and aunts often have a significant role to play within families. For middle-class women, the ability to hire household help also affects the nature of the responsibilities that are considered to be those of the mother. When couples move to the United States, both the unavailability of the family support network and structural constraints extant in society lead to recreation of "traditional" gender roles within Indo-American families.

The long hours of work expected of white-collar professionals (Acker 1990) mean that Indo-American fathers, like other mainstream white-collar professionals, are usually not at home to share in family tasks. Thus, the role of the male in a marriage often gets defined in terms of the family provider. The tasks of reproduction (that is, all the tasks that are required for sustaining family life other than economic production) become the woman's responsibility. This arrangement is especially true when the female has few options in the labor market even if she has advanced degrees.

A closer look at the mother's position vis-à-vis the mainstream illustrates the race/gender structures that enforce the immigrant woman's "traditional" role. The ability of the female to find a job in the primary labor market is often severely restricted. In the case of the post-1965 migrants who are legal residents or citizens, although the primary migrants are often recruited to niche jobs such as informational technology or medicine on the basis of their foreign training, their wives have to contend with nonacceptance of their foreign degrees in the primary labor market.[12] Women who wish to acquire higher education, find themselves classified as "foreign students" by universities, their degrees are devalued, and they face the need to spend years (and considerable sums of money) reacquiring the "right" degrees. Several highly skilled women have described how they end up acquiring several degrees similar to those they already have to prove their competency in the workplace (Radhakrishnan 1999). Given these difficulties in building a career, many highly educated females whose credentials are devalued retreat to underemployment or full-time motherhood. Spouses of H1-B professionals, who are not legally permitted to work, share the same difficulties about getting a higher education. Among less affluent families, women have to work to financially support the family. Yet, given the emerging Indo-American norm based on the upper-middle-class lifestyle of the first group, her work is often defined as an extension of her mother role and secondary to the breadwinning role of the father.

Other constraints affect the Indo-American women's roles in families. Although many middle-class Indo-American women can afford day care, the protracted cross-cultural negotiations involved in arranging child care—methods of child care and discipline, or agreement about appropriate foods for the child who may be vegetarian or may not eat beef or pork—means that child-rearing devolves primarily on mothers (Bacon 1996; Radhakrishnan 1999). Often women also have to take on the task of negotiating the social location of their children in the school system. The demands on immigrant families (particularly the English-speaking immigrants such as Indo-Americans) to provide "enriching" multicultural experiences within public school education become an additional task of mothering in the United States. At the same time, women often become involved in combating the racism and violence that their children experience in schools.[13] In addition, kinwork—the tasks involved in creating and maintaining relationships that support the ideal Indo-American families—imposes additional demands on the women's time.

The structural constraints that influence gender roles among Indo-American families, are paralleled by two overlapping ideologies that attempt to define how Indo-American families are to be understood, relegating them to "special cultural cases" (Zinn 1994: 305). A conservative ideology about ideal Indo-American families (which are "different" from the "other minority" families), where women are devoted to their mother roles and fathers provide for the family, has emerged among some sections of the ethnic group (Leonard 1997; Shah 1997). This conservative rhetoric assigns a changeless "Indian cultural" role to women as mothers and men as heads of families. This rhetoric in the ethnic group is paralleled in the mainstream with recurring stories of wife abuse and traditional Indian women. Although these ideologies are resisted and contested (see Dasgupta and Dasgupta 1997; Purkayastha, Raman, and Bhide 1997), they represent, at the level of the ethnic group, attempts to recapture some of the masculine privileges that the conservative leaders, as racial minority men, lack in larger society (see Messner 1997). The ideology in the mainstream is part of the history of labeling minority men as inappropriate (in this case as "wife abusers") and women as lacking initiative and agency ("too subordinate").

ROLES AND REALITIES BETWEEN GENERATIONS

The nature of intergenerational relations offers another glimpse into the complex ways in which race/class/gender structures affect minority families. An ongoing cause of conflict and negotiation arises from the differential experiences and understanding of race structures among the two generations. First-generation parents often emphasize class advantages as a way of minimizing the effects of race structures, while their children, who understand and experience racial marginalization in more direct ways, emphasize fitting in with the peer crowd as a way of adapting to prevailing structures. Ironically, the second generation appears to end up using some of the same strategies as their parents and create transnational webs of network and support to combat racial discrimination.

Parental emphasis, particularly in middle-class and affluent Indo-American families, is on a high level of achievement. Using their class-based experiences as *the* Indian cultural norm, first-generation families encourage their children to work toward selective white-collar careers, especially in medicine, information technologies, law, and research. Indeed, a great deal of family resources, including financial support through college and professional schools, is devoted toward making these expectations possible. For first-generation immigrants, race is often interpreted as national origin, a factor that makes it appear as though acquiring class advantage would offset the initial barriers encountered by recent immigrants (Kibria 1998). These parental expectations, however, are often in direct conflict with how their children try to adjust to racial structures that they encounter in schools. Second- generation youth often recount their sense of marginalization in schools as they fail to meet the standards of "whiteness" set by their peers (Bacon 1996; Bose 1999; Mediratta 1999). For the more affluent Indo-Americans, who are likely to be among the handful of minority students in mostly white schools, this tendency often means trying to fit into white youth masculinities and femininities, that is, adopting the right (white) fashions, playing the right (white) sports, and fitting into the racial hierarchy.[14] For the second generation, this situation means always remaining outside the norm, having "strange and unpronounceable" names, eating "odd foods," having "weird" parents, and practicing "mysterious and suspect" religions (Shah 1994). Thus, having to follow the path as "nerds" appears to be an insurmountable additional burden imposed by parents. Although many of these youth become high achievers, most of them recount the high cost of being caught in the contradictory set of expectations of fulfilling the American dream and remaining socially marginal.

Although most youth talk about a phase of rejecting their ethnic-ness, during college, it appears that many rediscover their culture. Racial marginalization remains a part of everyday interactions. For instance, many youth recount how others of their ethnic group are described as unacceptable; for instance, "My roommate said that she would never consider dating an Indian guy." However, in the presence of a larger number of coethnics, it is possible to form or join their own "cultural" groups. In addition, for the first time, some youth are able to take academic courses that discuss race/gender issues. The process of ethnic rediscovery often involves constructing a panethnic identity (Indo-Americaness) that is neither the culture practiced by their parents, nor the "traditional" culture valorized at ethnic events around the United States (Mukhi 2000). What emerges, in the context of what is feasible in U.S. colleges, is a new Indianness, or a new "Asian-Americanness." Those in the second generation sift through the cultural repertoires available through family networks, ethnic communities, businesses, and mainstream America in order to pick "tools" that help them to establish networks with others like themselves. Contrary to the whiteness adopted during adolescence, this emerging *desi* culture (Indian ethnicity constructed by the second generation) is based on an amalgam of Indian folk cultures and black and white cultures prevalent in the United Kingdom and the United States (Maira 2000). Conscious examination of racial position emerges as a central axis of this emerging ethnicity.

Ironically, this ongoing construction of culture draws on the transnational networks established by parents in their search for "ideal" families. An increasing number of youth are choosing to visit families in India and other countries, travel to India on their own, and organize a part of their professional, especially medical, training in India. Many are choosing to get married amid their family in India (Bose 1999; Purkayastha 1999). Organizing these practices involves drawing on family, including fictive kin networks, for support and information.[15]

The conflicts and negotiations that structure intergenerational relations reveal the continuing significance of race. The U.S. racial structure, which is based on a white-black-yellow framework, forces Indo-American families to adopt different racial positions over their lifetime. Nevertheless, the context of marginalization remains unchanged, and Indo-Americans use their class position to create identities by drawing on more than one nation.

CONCLUSION

Even a brief look at Indo-American families reveals that, contrary to popular assertions about model minority cultures, intersections of race/gender/class structures remain very relevant in order to understand the experiences of Indo-Americans. The rhetoric about "model families," whether in the mainstream media or among sections of the ethnic community, serves to gloss over the extent to which these families are simply an adjustment to the prevailing restrictions in the United States. Many Indo-Americans are forced to maintain split households, despite their achievement profiles. Given the extra restrictions against immigrant women in the United States, women disproportionately continue to bear the burden of maintaining families as well as of creating and sustaining the support networks necessary for carrying out family-related tasks. Similarly, the questions of social location and achievement, a core area of conflict between the two generations, are a response to the race structures in the United States. The active effort on the part of Indo-Americans of both generations to maintain transnational connections appears to be a class-based adaptation to the marginalizing structures in the United States. Thus, the interaction of entrenched rules and possible roles within everyday realities in the United States form the structure of the family experience of Indo-Americans.

ENDNOTES

1. The terms *Indo-Americans* and *Asian Indians* are often used interchangeably. There is a long social history of the other terms that have been used to describe migrants whose roots are in India (see Purkayastha 1999b). Here I use Asian Indian to talk about persons migrating from India and Indo-Americans to allude to the established ethnic group in the United States.

2. This is an average description of Indo-American families. Since the mid-1980s, more Asian Indians with lesser qualifications have arrived in the United States, although the average profile still shows high levels of human capital. The latter group does not work in the white-collar niches occupied by the earlier group but are more likely to be taxi drivers, newspaper kiosk attendants, or small-business owners. In this chapter, I will focus on the experience of the more affluent group in order to show that class position does not mitigate the effect of racial structures in the United States.

3. Part of the data on second-generation Indo-Americans is drawn from my current research on transnational ties among the new second generation. The quotations in this chapter are from that database.

4. I am restricting this discussion to heterosexual families. Obviously, gays and lesbians of all races have to contend with these structures as well.

5. Although historical records indicate that immigrants from India have been in the United States since 1798 (see Chandrasekhar 1982), I am focusing on the period when there were significant numbers of people.

6. See Sanjek 1990 or Peach 1994 for a discussion on indentured Asian Indian laborers around the world.

7. The majority of the early migrants were not Hindus; rather, they practiced Sikhism. Since 1965, the majority of the migrants have been Hindus.

8. However, it is important to note that *family* has been defined primarily as the nuclear family: the spouse and children are considered to be part of the nuclear family; parents and unmarried siblings are considered to be extended family and have to wait for longer periods. The waiting period of any family member varies by country depending on the quota established by the United States. On average, the waiting period for Indian spouses of legal residents is a couple of years, for siblings the waiting period is about ten years, and for parents between two and ten years.

9. Actually, this is an interaction of immigration laws with the gendered structure of education. The sciences are still significantly male dominated. Few of the women who graduate from the top technical institutes of India are recruited directly by multinational corporations. They are more likely to come to the United States for higher studies and then find job openings (Kurien 1999).

10. This requirement has been eased since 1998 after lobbying by several organizations. Nevertheless, as a member of a South Asian support network in Connecticut, I am very much aware of the problems faced by a spouse who returns to her natal family in another country or another state in the United States. Attorneys who deal with these matters are divided on this issue for divorce in Connecticut, and the laws vary by states, making the dissolution of a marriage an extremely complicated process for newer immigrants.

11. For instance, any child would address her aunts and uncles in ways that indicate whether they are their father's or mother's siblings such as *mama* or *pishi;* whether they are older or younger than their parents such as *jetha* or *kaka;* and often in terms that indicate degrees of emotional closeness such as *pishi* or *pishimoni* or *pishibhai.*

12. As discussed in the earlier section on immigration laws, most of the primary migrants among Asian Indians are male. Thus, this discussion on parental roles is based on the general pattern of males as breadwinners and females as spouses. The restrictions described here would also apply to the opposite case where females are primary migrants, and their male spouses migrate as dependents.

13. The harmful effects of this emphasis on strict parenting roles is often apparent among older women, who find that once they have successfully supported their spouse's career and helped their children to go to Ivy League schools, they are left with no role to play during the remaining half of their lives (Purkayastha, Raman, and Bhide 1997).

14. This process appears to be more difficult for the males. The prevailing ideology about females as small (or at least smaller than males physically), sultry, and docile or bubbly (see Espiritu 1997), provides a template into which Indian females might find a niche. The males, on the other hand, never match up to the "normal" desired male physical characteristics. Thus, this racial construction of desire maintains the hegemonic position of white youth within social circles.

15. However, the emerging practices of Indo-Americanness should not be interpreted as a simple reversion to traditional culture (and the extension of that argument about the success of model families to instill Indian norms among their children). Several types of evidence complicate the picture. First, data on marriages indicate that Indo-American females, who are apt to be more embedded in the transnational networks directly, also have a very high rate of marriage to white men (Fong 1998). Second, many of these global practices may be grounded in economically rational reasons—it is simply less expensive to organize a wedding in India that would meet the highest standards of "ethnic chic." As the selling and consumption of cultures have emerged as a significant industry in the United States (Zukin 1995), the practices described before also indicate the extent to which these youth fit in with upper-middle-class ways of life in the United States.

REFERENCES

Acker, J. 1990. "Hierarchies, Jobs, Bodies: A Theory of Gendered Organizations." *Gender and Society* 4:139–158.

Bacon, J. 1996. *Life Lines: Community, Family and Assimilation among Asian Indian Immigrants.* New York: Oxford University Press.

Barringer, H., R. Gardner, and M. Levin. 1995. *Asians and Pacific Islanders in the United States.* New York: Russell Sage Foundation.

Bose, M. 1999. "Multiple Identities." In P. Min and R. Kim (eds.) *Struggle for Ethnic Identity: Narratives by Asian American Professionals.* Walnut Creek: Altamira Press.

Chandrasekhar, S. 1982. *From India to America: A brief history of immigration, problems of discrimination, admission and assimilation.* La Jolla: Population Review.

Coontz, S. 1992. *The Way We Never Were.* New York: Basic Books.

Dasgupta, S. and S. Dasgupta. 1997. "Bringing up Baby: Raising a Third World Daughter in the First World." In S. Shah (ed.) *Dragon Ladies: Asian American Feminists Breathe Fire.* Boston: South End Press.

Dill, B. 1994. "Fictive Kin, Paper Sons and Compadrazgo: Women of Color and the Struggle for Family Survival." In M. Baca Zinn and B. Thornton Dill (eds.) *Women of Color in U.S. Society.* Philadelphia: Temple University Press.

Espiritu, Y. 1997. *Asian American Women and Men.* Thousand Oaks: Sage.

Ferree, M. 1990. "Beyond Separate Spheres: Feminism and Family Research." *Journal of Marriage and Family* 54:866–876.

Fong, T. 1998. *The Contemporary Asian American Experience: Beyond the Model Minority.* Upper Saddle River: Prentice Hall.

Gonzalez, J. 1996. *Racial and Ethnic Groups in America.* Dubuque: Kendall Hunt Publishing.

Helweg, A., and U. Helweg. 1990. *The Immigrant Success Story: East Indians.* Philadelphia: University of Pennsylvania Press.

Hines, P., N. Garcia-Preto, M. McGoldrick, R. Almeida, and S. Weltman. 1997. "Intergenerational Relationships Across Cultures." In. A. Skolnick and J. Skolnick (eds.) *Family in Transition.* New York: Longman.

Kibria, N. 1998. "The Racial Gap: South Asian Racial Identity and the Asian American Movement." In L. Shankar and R. Srikanth (eds.) *A Part, Yet Apart: South Asians in America.* Philadelphia: Temple University Press.

Kitano, H., and R. Daniels. 1995. *Asian Americans: Emerging Minorities.* Englewood Cliffs: Prentice Hall.

Knuckolls, C. (ed.) 1993. *Siblings in South Asia: Brothers and Sisters in Cultural Context.* New York: Guilford.

Kurien, P. 1999. "Gendered Ethnicity: Creating a Hindu Indian Identity in the United States." *American Behavioral Scientist* 42:648–70.

Leonard, K. 1992. *Making Ethnic Choices: California's Punjabi Mexican Americans.* Philadelphia: Temple University Press.

———— 1997. *The South Asian Americans.* Westport: Greenwood Press.

Maira, S. 1999. "Ideologies of Authenticity: Youth, Politics, Diaspora." *Amerasia* 25:139–149.

Mazumdar, S. 1989. "A Woman Centered Perspective on Asian American History." In Asian Women United of California (eds.) *Making Waves: An Anthology By and About Asian American Women.* Boston: Beacon Press.

Mediratta, K. 1999. "How Do You Say Your Name?" In P. Min and R. Kim (eds.) *Struggle for Ethnic Identity: Narratives by Asian American Professionals.* Walnut Creek: Altamira Press.

Messner, M. 1997. *Politics of Masculinities: Men in Movement.* Thousand Oaks: Sage.

Mukhi, S. 2000. *Doing the Desi Thing: Performing Indianness in New York City.* New York: Garland Publishing.

Nagel, J. 1994. "Constructing Ethnicity: Creating and Recreating Ethnic Identity and Culture." *Social Problems* 41:152–176.

Peach, C. 1994. "Three Phases of South Asian Emigration." In J. Brown and R. Foot (eds.) *Migration: The Asian Experience.* Oxford: St. Martin's Press.

Portes, A., and J. Sensenbrennar. 1993. "Embeddedness and Immigration: Notes on the Economic Determinants of Economic Action," *American Journal of Sociology* 98:1320–50.

Purkayastha, B. 1991. "A Sense of Place in the Act of Immigration." *Proceedings, NESTVAL,* Vol. XXI.

Purkayastha, B., S. Raman, and K. Bhide. 1997. "Empowering Women: Sneha and Multifaceted Activism." In S. Shah (ed.) *Dragon Ladies: Asian American Feminists Breathe Fire.* Boston: South End Press.

Purkayastha B. 1999. "Maintaining Meaningful Connections: Second Generation Asian Indians and Ties with the 'Old Home.'" Paper presented at the American Sociological Association Conference, Chicago, IL.

——— 1999b. Asian Indians in Connecticut. Storrs: Asian American Studies Institute.

Radhakrishnan, M. 1999. "Ethnicity, Gender and Class: Personal Histories and Multifaceted Activism of Sneha Members." Unpublished M.A. thesis. University of Connecticut.

Renteria, T. 1992. "The Culture of Mexican American Professionals Today." Unpublished Ph.D. dissertation. Department of Anthropology, Stanford University, Stanford, CA.

Rex, J. 1995. "Ethnic Identity and the Nation State: The Political Sociology of Multicultural Societies." *Social Identities* 1:21–34.

Sanjek, R. (ed.) 1990. *Caribbean Asians: Chinese, Indian, and Japanese Experience in Trinidad and the Dominican Republic.* Asian American Center at Queens College/CUNY.

Saran, P. 1985. *The Asian Indian Experience in the US.* Cambridge, MA: Shenkman.

Shah, P. 1997. "Redefining the Home: How Community Elites Silence Feminist Activism." In S. Shah (ed.) *Dragon Ladies: Asian American Feminists Breathe Fire.* Boston: South End Press.

Shah S. 1994. "Presenting the Blue Goddess: Towards a National, Pan Asian Feminist Agenda." In K. Aguilar San Juan (ed.) *The State of Asian America: Activism and Resistance in the 1990s.* Boston: South End Press.

Seth, M. 1995. "Asian Indian Americans." In P. Min (ed.) *Asian Americans: Contemporary Trends and Issues.* Thousand Oaks: Sage.

Simon, R., and Alexander, S. 1993. *The Ambivalent Welcome: Print Media, Public Opinion and Immigration.* Westport, CT: Praeger Press.

Stack, C. 1974. *All Our Kin: Strategies for Survival in a Black Community.* New York: Harper and Row.

Swidler, A. 1995. Culture, Power and Social Movements. In H. Johnston and B. Klandermans (eds.) *Social Movements and Culture.* Minneapolis: University of Minnesota Press.

Tatla, D. 1999. *The Sikh Diaspora: The Search for Statehood.* Seattle: University of Washington Press.

Taylor, R. (ed.) 1994. *Minority Families in the United States.* Englewood Cliffs: Prentice Hall.

U.S. Bureau of Census, 1990 Census of Population, Asians and Pacific Islanders in the United States. Washington, DC: Government Printing Office 1993.

U.S. Immigration and Naturalization Service. 2000. H1-B Frequently Asked Questions. Available at: www.ins.gov.

Zhou, M., and C. Bankston. 1998. *Growing Up American: How Vietnamese Youth Adjust to Life in the U.S.* New York: Russell Sage Foundation.

Zinn, M. 1994. "Feminist Rethinking of Racial-Ethnic Families." In M. Baca Zinn and B. Thornton Dill (eds.) *Women of Color in U.S. Society.* Philadelphia: Temple University Press.

Zukin, S. 1995. *The Cultures of Cities.* Boston: Blackwell.

PART IV

Native American Families in the United States

The term "Native American" (or "American Indian") pools together under a single label tribes or ethnic groups with a diversity of languages, lifestyles, religions, kinship systems, and political organizations, whose histories predate those of other racial ethnic populations in the United States. By some accounts, when the first Europeans arrived in this country during the late fifteenth century, between 2 and 18 million Native Americans were living north of Mexico, speaking as many as 300 different languages and representing hundreds of cultures. Their numbers had declined dramatically by the early 1800s, and by the end of the nineteenth century had been reduced to an estimated 250,000. By the early 1900s, the Native American population reversed its decline, and it has grown significantly throughout this century. For example, between 1950 and 1970, the American Indian population increased by more than 100 percent, from 357,499 to 792,730; and from 1970 to 1980, by 72 percent, to 1.4 million. The 2 million American Indians, Eskimos, and Aleuts living in the United States in 1990 represented an increase of 38 percent over the 1980 total. By 2000, the American Indian population, including Eskimo and Aleut, was estimated at 2.4 million, constituting 0.9 percent of the total population. Thus, the American Indian population is one of the fastest growing and youngest subpopulations in the United States. Because of their relatively small numbers and high concentration in rural areas, American Indians are one of the country's least visible minority groups. One-fifth, or 437,000, of all American Indians (including Eskimos and Aleuts) lived on 314 reservations and trust lands (i.e., areas with boundaries established by statute, treaty, court, or executive order) in 1990. Moreover, nearly half of all American Indians are found west of the Mississippi River, mainly in such states as Arizona, California, New Mexico, Oklahoma, and Washington.

As Michael Yellowbird and C. Matthew Snipp observe in their chapter on American Indian families, the body of work on such families is relatively small compared with the large volume of research on other racial ethnic groups in the United States. Consolidating what is known about Native American families, they begin by reviewing the available demographic data with respect to household composition, marriage and divorce, family structure and economic well-being, labor force participation and education, and patterns of intermarriage. Following their review of the empirical record, they examine the literature on Native American families, giving special attention to qualities that make American Indian families unique in the social landscape. While noting changes in the status and authority enjoyed by Indian elders and in the relationships between men and women in Native American families, Yellowbird and Snipp emphasize the continuing importance of certain "core" family values that have enabled American Indians to preserve important aspects of native culture. They conclude that although many Native American family practices have changed, one of the enduring features of American Indian families is that they have a great capacity to change and adapt to a changing social environment.

CHAPTER 12

American Indian Families

Michael Yellowbird and C. Matthew Snipp

Without question, the family is a preeminent institution in American Indian and Alaskan Native cultures. In an earlier era, family organization made physical survival possible through mutual defense and economic cooperation. In such circumstances, estrangement from one's family was almost certain to produce extreme physical hardship. Among contemporary American Indians, the family perhaps plays a smaller role in ensuring physical survival, yet family networks continue to make up the fabric of social organization in modern American Indian communities.

Compared with what is known about other groups in American society, not much is known about American Indian families. Because American Indians are small in number and often live in remote rural areas, they are one of this nation's least visible minority groups. The 1980 census recorded approximately 1.5 million American Indians, about one-half of whom resided outside of metropolitan areas. American Indians and Alaskan Natives represent about 0.5 percent of the total U.S. population—341,000 families. Consolidating what is known about American Indian families, this chapter first surveys the available demographic data and then reviews the literature on American Indian families.

THE DEMOGRAPHY OF AMERICAN INDIAN FAMILIES

Before the demographic data about American Indian families and households is presented, it is important to note the precise definition that the U.S. Bureau of the Census uses to describe family and household characteristics. According to the Census Bureau, a family consists of "two or more persons, including the householder, who are related by birth, marriage, or adoption, and who live together as one household" (U.S. Bureau of the Census 1983). Note that not all households have families and that no household contains more than one family. For example, either persons living alone or two or more unrelated individuals in a single dwelling would constitute households without families. Furthermore, a second family in the household would not, by Census definitions, be considered a family if those individuals were not related to the householder. Instead, these individuals are counted as "unrelated household members" despite the fact that they belong to a second family in the same household.

One of the most significant problems posed by this view of families is that it obscures the existence of extended family relationships. Extended families might be regarded as groups of individuals related by birth, marriage, or adoption who function as an economic unit by sharing economic resources such as rent or groceries. When extended families reside in a single household, they are enumerated as members of subfamilies related to the householder. However, extended families involving large numbers of individuals may not reside in single living quarters, although they may reside in close proximity to one another. For example, an extended family that functions as a single economic unit might nonetheless reside in several separate dwellings, perhaps all within a few hundred yards of each other. Yet by Census procedures, this family would not be recognized as a single entity but instead as independent households. Another perhaps more common situation is parents or grandparents residing in a dwelling such as a mobile home near children or grandchildren. Again, this type of family relationship would not be captured by Census procedures.

Another potential problem arises from cultural conceptions of family relationships that differ in meaning from those intended by the Census Bureau. For example, an Indian "grandmother" may actually be a child's aunt or grandaunt in the Anglo-Saxon use of the term. In another instance, extended families may form around complex kinship networks based on clan membership instead of birth, marriage, or adoption. The term "cousin" also may have a variable meaning, not necessarily based on birth or marriage. To make these matters even more complex, definitions of family relationships vary from one tribal culture to another. The lesson to be taken from this variability is that the categories used by the Census Bureau to describe family relationships are not uniformly consistent and unambiguous when applied to American Indians. They are, however, useful approximations and the best information available about American Indian families.

Household Composition

Table 1 shows the composition of households occupied by blacks, whites, and American Indians. The data in the first two rows are for "nonfamily" householders—persons who live alone or with persons with whom they have no family relationship, at least not in the sense that the Census Bureau uses the term. It is easy to see that such persons make up a very small part of the total population and that there are few differences between men and women or between blacks, whites, and American Indians.

Among householders residing with family members, blacks, whites, and Indians are appreciably different. Compared with the white population, nearly 24 percent of which are male family householders, American Indians and blacks have substan-

TABLE 1. Percent Distribution of Household Types and Family Relationships among Blacks, Whites, and American Indians and Alaskan Natives

	BLACKS	WHITES	AMERICAN INDIANS
Nonfamily householder			
Male	4.2	4.1	3.5
Female	4.7	5.9	3.3
Family householder			
Male	14.0	23.7	17.0
Female	9.8	3.8	6.0
Spouse	13.2	23.6	16.8
Child	41.1	33.1	41.5
Other relative	9.5	3.3	7.6
Nonrelative	3.5	2.5	4.3
TOTAL	100.0	100.0	100.0
Persons per household	3.05	2.68	3.30
Persons per family	3.69	3.19	3.83

Source: 1980 Census of Population, General Social and Economic Characteristics, *U.S. Summary.*

tially smaller percentages of their populations in this role, 17 and 14 percent, respectively. On the other hand, Indians and blacks have noticeably higher percentages of female householders than the white population has. In this respect, blacks and Indians have considerably more in common with each other than they do with whites.

The differences among American Indian, black, and white householders are the same for nonhouseholders. Predictably, American Indians and blacks have smaller percentages of persons as spouses, just as they have fewer male householders. In fact, the percentages of spouses and male householders are about the same for all three groups. For example, 17 percent of American Indians are male householders, and 16.8 percent are spouses. Again, blacks and Indians are relatively similar and clearly different from whites. Indian and black households also have significantly more children than white households.

The distribution of black and Indian household composition is similar in a number of ways, but there are some important differences. American Indians typically live in larger households and families than either blacks or whites. This circumstance is not because Indians have more children or more nonrelatives and extended family members. On the contrary, blacks and Indians have almost the same percentages of children, and Indians have 1 percent less of their number residing in households as "other" or nonrelatives. The most obvious explanation for why Indian households and families are larger than those of blacks is that American Indians have larger percentages of persons who are male householders and spouses and smaller percentages of female householders, who typically live in smaller households. This finding means that American Indians are more likely than blacks to live in husband-wife family units, but with about the same number of children, relatives, and nonrelatives as in black households (see Table 3).

TABLE 2.   Percent Distribution of Marital Status and Median Age at First Marriage for Blacks, Whites, and American Indians and Alaskan Natives Age 15 and Over

	BLACKS		WHITES		AMERICAN INDIANS	
	MALES	**FEMALES**	**MALES**	**FEMALES**	**MALES**	**FEMALES**
Single	41.1	34.4	28.2	21.2	37.3	28.9
Married except separated	42.6	35.1	62.5	57.4	49.6	48.0
Separated	6.1	8.6	1.4	1.8	2.9	4.1
Widowed	3.8	12.8	2.5	12.6	2.5	8.9
Divorced	6.4	9.1	5.4	7.0	7.7	10.1
TOTAL	100.0	100.0	100.0	100.0	100.0	100.0
Median age at first marriage	23.3	20.7	23.2	20.8	22.3	19.7

Source: 1980 Census of Population, General Population Characteristics, *U.S. Summary; 1980 Census of Population, Subject Report,* Marital Status.

Marriage and Divorce

Marriage and divorce rates for blacks, whites, and American Indians and Alaska Natives are shown in Table 2. For all of these groups, women are more likely than men to be separated, widowed, or divorced. On average, American Indians tend to get married about a year earlier than either blacks or whites, and Indians are more likely than blacks but less likely than whites to have been married. A particularly curious finding in Table 2 is that unlike other women, American Indian women are more likely to exit their marriage through legal proceedings than through the death of their spouse. Among black and white women, widowhood is more common than divorce, but the opposite is true for American Indian women.

FAMILY STRUCTURE AND ECONOMIC WELL-BEING

Many different types of families and households exist. It should be remembered, however, that in Census data, all families reside in households but not all households include families. This discussion deals mainly with married couples and with families headed by single women. Collectively, these family and household types represent approximately 67 percent of the households occupied by American Indians; most of the balance reside in nonfamily households.

Table 3 shows the distribution of family types among blacks, whites, and American Indians. White households are most likely to contain a married-couple family (63.3 percent). About 55 percent of American Indian households include a married couple, which is a smaller percentage than for white households but significantly larger than the percentage of black households with married couples. Similarly, American Indian households have a smaller percentage of single female householders than black households, 17.5 percent and 27.0 percent, respectively,

TABLE 3. Percent Distribution of Households with Families and Nonfamilies among Blacks, Whites, and American Indians and Alaskan Natives

	MARRIED COUPLES	FEMALE HOUSEHOLDER, SPOUSE ABSENT	MALE HOUSEHOLDER, SPOUSE ABSENT	NONFAMILY HOUSEHOLD	TOTAL
Blacks	41.4	27.0	4.2	27.4	100.0
Whites	63.3	8.0	2.1	26.6	100.0
American Indians	55.4	17.5	4.2	22.9	100.0

Source: 1980 Census of Population, General Social and Economic Characteristics, U.S. Summary.

and both of these groups are substantially above the 8 percent of white households with single female householders.

American Indians occupy a position about midway between blacks and whites in terms of their propensity to live as married couples or as single female householders. However, another way of viewing this finding is that American Indians are noticeably less likely than either blacks or whites to live singly or with unrelated individuals in nonfamily households. About 23 percent of American Indian households consist of nonfamily units, compared with approximately 27 percent for blacks and whites, suggesting that American Indians have a somewhat stronger tendency than blacks or whites to reside in a family environment, either as married couples or as single family householders.

Children and Family Structure

One of the primary reasons for family formation is the care and rearing of children. By the traditional norms of American society, children are best raised in the stable environment of a married-couple household. Rearing children in households where a spouse is absent is considered undesirable for a number of reasons. One belief is that the absence of a spouse deprives children of important role models for socialization and development. A second belief is that homes with single parents provide a less stable social environment for the upbringing of children. A third belief is that single parent familes, especially those of single women with young children, are economically marginal and more likely to be subject to economic hardships.

Whether single-parent homes are intrinsically unstable or whether absence of role models causes lasting harm cannot be studied with the demographic data available from the Census Bureau. However, the economic status associated with different types of families can be examined in detail. Before looking at the economic characteristics of different types of families, a good place to begin is with data for the distribution and age of children. Table 4 shows the presence and age of children for different types of families and households. Among married couples, about one-third have children age 6 to 17 years, and another third have no children in their households. This finding does not necessarily mean that these couples are childless but only that there are no children living with them. Among the remaining third of couples, about half (16.1 percent) have young children under the age of 6, and the other half (16.6 percent) have children over and under the age of 6.

Single Female Householders

Single female householders are not very different from married couples in terms of the presence and ages of children in their households, except in one very apparent way. These women are substantially more likely than other types of householders to have children age 6 to 17 living with them, about 42 percent compared with about 31 percent for single male householders and 33 percent for married couples. This finding is undoubtedly the result of marital disruptions—divorce and separation—which occur within a few years after childbirth, combined with legal and social traditions that typically assign child custody to mothers. As one sociologist has noted, "the typical outcome of a marital breakup is that the man becomes single, while the woman becomes a single parent" (Pearce 1982). American Indians, it appears, are not very different from other parts of American society in this respect. This also is consistent with the statistic that single female householders also are the *least* likely to be in a household without children, 28 percent.

The fact that, nationwide, about 18 percent of Indian households are headed by a single female householder (see Table 3), combined with the fact that more than 70 percent of these women are caring for children under 18 years of age (see Table 4), underscores the importance of information about the socioeconomic conditions of these households, especially in relation to other types of households. This situation occurs because single female householders responsible for the care of their children frequently experience economic hardship and limited opportunities, for themselves and their children.

Education

The figures in Table 5 show that about 48 percent of single female householders have less than 12 years of schooling. In contrast, 39 percent of the householders in married couples and 38 percent in nonfamily households have an equally low level

TABLE 4.   Percent Distribution of the Presence and Age of Children in American Indian and Alaskan Native Households

	MARRIED COUPLES	FEMALE HOUSEHOLDERS, SPOUSE ABSENT
Families with children under age 6 only	16.1	15.4
Families with children age 6 to 17	32.6	42.1
Families with children age 0 to 17	16.6	14.3
Families without children	34.7	28.2
TOTAL	100.0	100.0

Source: U.S. Bureau of the Census. Public Use Microdata Sample, 5 Percent A File.

TABLE 5. Percent Distribution of Educational Attainments by American Indian
and Alaskan Native Householders by Household Type

YEARS OF EDUCATION	MARRIED COUPLES	FEMALE HOUSEHOLDERS, SPOUSE ABSENT	NONFAMILY HOUSEHOLD
0–8	21.0	23.9	23.0
9–11	17.9	23.7	15.4
12	32.2	29.1	27.5
13–15	19.1	18.6	22.0
16 and over	9.8	4.7	12.1
TOTAL	100.0	100.0	100.0

Source: U.S. Bureau of the Census. Public Use Microdata Sample, 5 Percent A File.

of education. Especially significant is that about 24 percent of single female householders are high school dropouts with 9 to 11 years of schooling. This finding is
significant because other data show that American Indians with 8 years or less of
schooling tend to be older, whereas high school dropouts are younger (Snipp
1989). Younger single female householders with less than 12 years of schooling
may have dropped out of school to become mothers.

Labor Force Participation

The limited education and the child care responsibilities of single female householders predictably translate into a marginal attachment to the labor force. As
the data in Table 6 show, 47.2 percent of single female householders do not participate in the labor force, and only 46.1 percent are employed. These figures
are especially striking compared with those for the householders in married couples. Only about 21 percent of this group are not in the labor force, and 72 percent are employed. The only group that even distantly approaches the marginal
labor force attachment of single female householders are householders in nonfamily households, with 38 percent of their number not in the labor force. A

TABLE 6. Percent Distribution of Labor Force Participation of Civilian American Indian
and Alaskan Native Householders by Household Type

	MARRIED COUPLES	FEMALE HOUSEHOLDERS, SPOUSE ABSENT	NONFAMILY HOUSEHOLD
Employed	72.0	46.1	54.8
Unemployed	7.3	6.7	7.0
Not in labor force	20.7	47.2	38.2
TOTAL	100.0	100.0	100.0

Source: U.S. Bureau of the Census. Public Use Microdata Sample, 5 Percent A File.

clear indication of the marginal economic status of single female householders is that 33.5 percent of these women received public assistance income in 1979 (Table 7). In comparison, only 6 percent of the householders in married couples required public assistance. The differences between these households are equally dramatic for the incidence of poverty. About 17 percent of married-couple householders reported incomes below the official poverty threshold in 1979. This figure is slightly higher than the poverty rate for the nation as a whole, but it also is well below the figures for single female Indian householders. Among these women, 47 percent are poverty stricken. This statistic is even more alarming by recalling that nearly three-fourths of these women have child care responsibilities.

In terms of other kinds of income, the situation of single female householders is no different, and married-couple households are decisively ahead of other household types. Focusing on median family and household income, the gap between married-couple households and the households of single female householders is substantial. For instance, the median family income of married households ($18,005) is more than twice the median family income of single female householders. The largest disparity between these household types is with respect to family income. The median incomes of the families of married couples is 2.3 times larger than the incomes of the families of single women. One reason why the income gap between these households is slightly greater for family income than for household income is that single women may share their residences with persons outside their immediate family to generate additional income for household expenses, thereby raising their household but not their family incomes.

TABLE 7.   Characteristics of Income Received by American Indians and Alaskan Natives in 1979 by Household Types

	MARRIED COUPLES	FEMALE HOUSEHOLDERS, SPOUSE ABSENT	NONFAMILY HOUSEHOLD
Percent of householders receiving public assistance	6.0	33.5	12.9
Percent below poverty	16.7	47.3	31.3
Median wages and salaries of householders	$12,005	6,005	8,505
Median total income of householders	$11,165	5,005	6,305
Median household income	$18,005	8,610	8,845
Median family income	$17,870	7,710	NA[a]

[a]*NA: Not applicable.*

Source: U.S. Bureau of the Census. Public Use Microdata Sample, 5 Percent A File.

MARRIAGE WITH NON-INDIANS

Not all American Indians choose other American Indians as their spouses; they also marry persons with black, Asian, Hispanic, or white backgrounds. The racial characteristics of the spouses of American Indians are significant from at least two perspectives. In one respect, the extent to which American Indians are selected by non-Indians as marriage partners is an important indicator of racial discrimination. Discriminatory practices and prejudicial beliefs reduce intermarriage by making numbers of particular racial or ethnic groups unacceptable as potential marriage partners. From another standpoint, intermarriage represents an important form of cultural diffusion. As Indians marry non-Indians, they are likely to become more active in mainstream American culture, and by the same token, some non-Indians who marry Indians become incorporated into the tribal cultures of their spouses.

Patterns of Intermarriage

Patterns of intermarriage are usually cast in terms of endogamy and exogamy. Endogamous marriages result when persons of the same race marry. Racially exogamous couples involve persons with different racial backgrounds. Table 8 shows patterns of racial endogamy and exogamy among blacks, whites, and American Indians and Alaskan Natives. As the statistics in this table make amply clear, American Indians have extraordinarily high rates of exogamy compared with blacks and whites. Among married American Indian men and women, only about 47 percent are married to other Indians; or alternatively, 53 percent are married to non-Indians. In contrast, marital endogamy is close to 99 percent among whites and nearly 98 percent for blacks.

A number of explanations are possible for why American Indians have such remarkably high rates of intermarriage. The most readily apparent reason is that American Indians are perceived, especially by whites, as socially acceptable marriage

TABLE 8. Percent Distribution of Racial Endogamy and Exogamy among Blacks, Whites, and American Indians and Alaskan Natives

	WHITES	BLACKS	AMERICAN INDIANS
Wife's Race			
White	98.0	0.8	48.0
Black	0.2	98.8	2.1
American Indian	0.3	0.1	4.3
Asian[a]	0.3	0.3	0.5
Other	0.4	0.5	2.5
TOTAL	100.0	100.0	100.0

[a]*Includes Japanese, Chinese, and Filipinos.*
Source: 1980 Census of Population, Subject Report, Marital Characteristics.

partners. Among American Indian men, 48.0 percent were married to white women. Similarly, 48.3 percent of Indian women were married to white men. It is interesting that Indian men resemble white men in being slightly less likely than their female counterparts to choose a black person as a spouse. Among American Indian women, about 2 percent have black husbands, whereas only 1 percent of Indian men are married to black women. Very clearly, American Indians are more likely to have white than black spouses.

Assimilation and Intermarriage

The extraordinarily high level of racial intermarriage for American Indians provides a good reason to expect that growing numbers of American Indians and their descendants will choose non-Indians for spouses and, to a greater or lesser degree, become absorbed into the dominant culture. Some of these Indians will abandon their cultural heritage altogether, whereas others may make only minor accommodations as the result of having a non-Indian spouse. This probability raises a question that is extremely controversial within many quarters of the American Indian community. Namely, are American Indians assimilating so quickly through racial intermarriage that they will eventually, in the not too distant future, marry themselves out of existence?

For most of this century, anthropologists and other social scientists have predicted that American Indians as a distinctive ethnic group would vanish in the wake of poverty, disease, and the demands of Western civilization (Linton 1963). By the mid-1950s, many of these anthropologists began revising their predictions about the inevitable extinction of American Indians (Vogt 1957). However, the data on marriage patterns raise the prospect that Indians, through their spousal choices, may accomplish what disease, Western civilization, and decades of federal Indian policy failed to achieve.

Predicting the future viability of the Indian population is a risky and difficult, if not inadvisable, venture. However, recently published data from the U.S. Office of Technology Assessment provide some interesting insights into the impact of racial exogamy on the Indian population. "Blood quantum" is a measure of Indian ancestry in which, for example, a "full blood" is someone who is entirely descended from American Indians and has no non-Indian ancestors. One-half blood quantum might denote a non-Indian father and a full blood Indian mother, or some other large number of possible combinations. Although it is not necessarily so, persons with say, three-fourths or full blood quantum are typically less assimilated and more committed to traditional Indian lifestyles than persons of one–thirty-second or one–sixty-fourth blood quantum. With this idea in the background, the Office of Technology Assessment (OTA) published a number of population projections showing the changing distribution of blood quantum within the Indian population through the year 2080 (U.S. Office of Technology Assessment 1986).

Some of the OTA projections were based on patently unreasonable assumptions—for instance, that American Indians do not marry non-Indians or that all Indians are full bloods. However, one projection in particular is interesting because it is based on Bureau of Indian Affairs data for the distribution of blood quantum and takes into account the prevalence of racial intermarriage among Indians, using data from the 1980 Census. The results from this OTA projection (referred to as Scenario II in the original report) are limited to the 32 states with reservations served by the Bureau of Indian Affairs; these data are shown in Table 9. These projections predict, not surprisingly, that in relative numbers, the percentages of persons with one-half or more Indian blood quantum will decline continuously throughout this and the next century, dropping precipitously from 87 percent to 8 percent in the next 100 years. The percentage of persons with one-fourth to one-half Indian blood quantum is predicted to grow from about 10 percent of the Indian population in 1980 to a peak of 40 percent in the year 2040 and then decline to 33 percent in 2080. However, the percentage of persons with less than one-fourth Indian blood quantum is expected to increase from 4 percent to 59 percent in the 100 years following 1980.

The changing distribution of blood quantum shows that persons with one-half blood quantum or more will shrink, if not disappear, as a significant segment of the American Indian population. Does this finding mean that persons with predominantly American Indian ancestors are drifting toward numerical extinction? This question is best answered with absolute rather than relative numbers. In viewing these numbers, it is easy to make two conclusions. One is that the OTA projections forecast massive growth in the American Indian population of the 32 states that it covers, from 1.3 million Indians in 1980 to 15.8 million in 2080. Most of these persons, over 90 percent, will have a minority of Indian ancestors—less than one-half blood quantum—but the number of persons with one-half or more Indian blood quantum is projected to be 1,292,911 in 2080, only slightly less than the total Indian population, including all blood quantum, residing in reservation states in 1980: 1,295,450 persons. The OTA forecasts predict that the 50 percent blood

TABLE 9. Office of Technology Assessment Population Projections by Blood Quantum, 1980 to 2080*

	PERCENT BLOOD QUANTUM			
YEAR	50.0 AND ABOVE	25.0 TO 49.9	LESS THAN 25.0	TOTAL
1980	1,125,746	123,068	46,636	1,295,450
	(86.9)	(9.5)	(3.6)	(100.0)
2000	1,722,116	345,309	146,092	2,213,517
	(77.8)	(15.6)	(6.6)	(100.0)
2020	2,119,717	1,106,345	465,084	3,691,144
	(36.1)	(39.9)	(24.0)	(100.0)
2060	1,866,738	3,971,782	4,090,935	9,929,455
	(18.8)	(40.3)	(41.2)	(100.0)
2080	1,292,911	5,187,411	9,286,884	15,767,206
	(8.2)	(32.9)	(58.9)	(100.0)

Based on 32 states with federal reservations. Percent of population in parentheses.

Source: U.S. Office of Technology Assessment, 1986. Indian Health Care. Washington, DC: U.S. Government Printing Office.

quantum group will grow and then decline over the next 100 years. In any event, persons with a majority of Indian ancestors certainly are not expected to disappear, according to these predictions.

Racial exogamy is hardly a new phenomenon in the American Indian population; a long history exists of relations with non-Indians, especially among tribes from the eastern United States that had very early contact with white immigrants. Among Indians enumerated from the 1910 Census, only 56.5 percent reported full blood quantum. Full blood Indians were most likely undercounted in this census for a variety of reasons, yet this statistic indicates a surprising degree of racially mixed marriages at a time when American Indians were still highly isolated from the mainstream of American society.

STUDIES OF AMERICAN INDIAN FAMILIES

The data for American Indian families are sparse, and studies of Indian families are no more abundant. In the balance of this chapter, we turn from the empirical record to published studies detailing the lives of American Indian families. In this discussion, we give special attention to qualities that make American Indian families unique in the social landscape.

Traditional versus Nontraditional Lifestyles

A great deal of the American Indian family literature has focused on sociocultural behavior such as the use of Native language, values, and beliefs, and the acculturation of non-Native family practices (Lewis 1970; Miller 1979; Price 1976; Red Horse 1980; Red Horse and others 1978; Wagner 1976). A typology of Native American families constructed on an acculturation framework classifies American Indian families on a sociocultural continuum ranging from "traditional" to "nontraditional" practices (John 1987).

Price (1976) investigated the cultural practices of four North American Indian groups and one Eskimo group and found that, although the impact of European culture on American Indians has reduced the linguistic, racial, and cultural diversity among various groups, many still maintain traditional family practices. However, as Price makes clear in these case studies, practices vary from tribe to tribe according to the contact and acculturation experienced by each group. For example, Price maintains that the Hopi of Northern Arizona have enjoyed more "continuity" and "homogeneity" in their culture than most other Indian tribes in the United States. To this end, Price asserts that the Hopi is an

> . . . Indian society that has had sufficient autonomy from Euro-American pressures to gradually evolve a modern culture with a consistently high level of internal integration. Wage work, Western education, automobiles, electrical appliances, Western dress, weekend supermarket shopping, etc., are now being accepted practices, but the aboriginal language is being retained as second language to English, and the Hopi religion has never been replaced by Christianity. (p. 262)

Miller (1979), in a three-part longitudinal study, examined 120 American Indian families living in Oakland, California, and the surrounding area to determine the socialization and adaptation of these families to the city. Her findings identified several "modes of adaptation," which were grouped in the following four classifications:

> Traditional, in which the person clings to Indian values and behaviors; Transitional, where the individual adapts to white means and ends and leaves traditional values and behaviors behind; Bicultural, in which the person is able to hold onto Indian values and means and is also able to adapt to white ends without considering them primary value structure; and Marginal, whose individuals are anomic in both worlds, with ends and means neither Indian nor white. (p. 479)

Miller also describes families in each classification as having distinct sociocultural characteristics and levels of well-being:

> The Bicultural Family . . . have a sense of harmony having retained the use of their native language and the practice of many of their beliefs while making it in the city . . . The Traditional Family . . . know and use their native tongue, practice Indian ways, and have close relationships with other Indian families who also live much as they did on the reservation . . . The Transitional Family [are] moving toward the adoption of white means and ends, letting their Indian language and values slip away . . . The Marginal Family have lost their native language and show no evidence of having known Indian ways, or white ways either, seeming to be maladapted in both. (pp. 479–481)

Miller hypothesized that each of these family types would display distinctive patterns of adjustment and adaptation to urban living. The "Traditional" family would make only a "minimal adjustment" to urban living, and the children of these families would experience only "minimal" psychological problems. The "Transitional" family would be the most likely to become assimilated by joining the white lower class. Next, the "Bicultural" family would be able to make the most successful "social" and "psychological" adaptations and adjustment. Finally, the "Marginal" family would suffer the greatest social and psychological adjustments.

Comparing her hypotheses with empirical data, Miller found that her expectations for the Bicultural group appeared to be valid, but that the Transitional and Traditional groups "seem to be merging largely into the Bicultural group." The Marginal group continued to be "transient" between the reservation and the city.

Red Horse and others (1978) also have examined the sociocultural class status of Native American families, using an acculturation framework. In a study of family behavior among urban Chippewas in Minneapolis, they found three distinct lifestyles:

> (1) a traditional group which overtly adheres to culturally defined styles of living, (2) a non-traditional, bi-cultural group which appears to have adopted many aspects of non-American Indian styles of living, and (3) a pan-traditional group which overtly struggles to redefine and reconfirm previously lost cultural styles of living. (p. 69)

However, they argue that differences in acculturation should not be considered "valid criteria" for gauging "Indianness." Other studies (they cite Hallowell [1967] and Krush and others [1969], for example) suggest that American Indian "core values are retained and remain as a constant regardless of family lifestyles patterns." Red Horse and others (1978) also point out that the data used for this analysis were taken from one program and "point to significant variability" among family networks.

ROLE, STATUS, AND AUTHORITY IN THE FAMILY

As these studies suggest, the role, status, and authority structures among Indian families are highly differentiated and continually evolving. Unfortunately, few studies have carefully examined the changing social dynamics within Native American families, and we are therefore left with only a partial picture of what may actually be occurring. In one of the most extensive literature reviews on the Native American family, Robert John (1987:328) complains that "even though studies of various aspects of Native American family life have increased during the last 15 years, these studies do little to clarify precisely what is occurring with Native American families as a whole."

Elders' Roles

Historically, elderly American Indians have occupied a special role in the decision-making of American Indian families. Often, this practice has been accomplished by elders' meeting and directing the spiritual, social, and cultural needs of the family and community. Red Horse (1980) presented a model of three life-span phases to explain the formal organization of relationships in the family and the way that each is acted out. With respect to elders, Red Horse explains that they have entered the "assuming care for" stage, wherein they are seen to be an important stabilizing social and cultural force in the "extended family." He maintains that American Indian elders transmit "wisdom" and "order" within the "extended family" system:

> Proactive roles as an elder with family responsibilities to transmit a world view derivative from a wisdom of years serves as a life goal in the extended family. (p. 464)

Red Horse also states that "an elder's role 'to assume care for' often goes beyond the natural family to include a broader community" (p. 466). Therefore, Indian elders preserve the heritage of and provide strength to members of their own extended family and to the members of the tribal community as well.

Edwards (1983) reiterates the importance of the social role and cultural authority of elders in Native American families, but in a more historical context:

> They performed a variety of important and beneficial roles, including instructing the young and helping care for children. They also maintained responsibility for remembering and relating tribal philosophies, myths, traditions, and stories/events peculiar to their tribal groups.

Edwards (1983) notes, however, the older American Indians, similar to the rest of the Indian population, continue to face "periods of transition" that are limiting the roles and responsibilities that they once performed in their tribal communities. Data from the National Indian Council on Aging (NICA) and U.S. Bureau of the Census show economic conditions, health status, and poor housing to be major impediments to the well-being of aged American Indians. For example, in 1969, the median income for people of all races 45 years and older was $3,959, but American Indians in this same category had an income of only $2,117. In addition, a 1981 NICA study stated that

> . . . older American Indians suffer from inadequate housing with income inadequate to cover their necessities of life. Overcrowding is also a condition in which many older Indian people live. Plumbing and other modern conveniences are not available to many American Indian elders. (Edwards 1983:79)

Despite the tenuous economic conditions under which many American Indian elderly live, they maintain social and cultural obligations to their families. For example, the NICA reported that 26 percent of Native American elderly had taken charge of caring for at least one grandchild and that 67 percent of all aged Indians resided within 5 miles of family, on whom they depend for socialization, chores, and routine obligations (Edwards 1983).

John (1985) also examined the NICA data and found that aged American Indians face a more marginal economic lifestyle within the Native American family. He summarized his findings with this statement:

> . . . reservation residents are poorer, have greater financial concerns, support more people on less income, have fewer social contacts, have somewhat lower life satisfaction, and are in poorer health than urban Indians. (p. 245)

John attributes the poor social and economic condition of elderly American Indians to a decline in the integration of the "extended family," which was once the "traditional source of support" for this population.

Indeed, American Indians, like the general population, live in a highly diverse and vacillating social and economic environment in which the needs of the elderly population are often overlooked. However, the higher poverty, poorer economic conditions, and lack of resources among Native Americans suggest a more vulnerable elderly Indian population. Such conditions threaten the social and economic roles, status, and authority enjoyed by Indian elders, and they may also undermine the cultural authority that they hold in the family.

Men's Roles

Like other subjects, empirical research about the sociocultural role, status, and authority that American Indian men assume within contemporary Native American families is very scarce. However, the traditional positions once held by men within tribal families seem to have been greatly altered. In a study of acculturation, child rearing, and self-esteem among Miccosukee and Seminoles, Lefley (1976) found that the absenteeism and the altered role of Seminole fathers in this matrilineal tribe tended to lower the status of male children within the tribal families. Lefley maintains that the Seminole father's role disintegrated when traditional dwellings were replaced by individual houses that dispersed the families. Previously, under traditional tribal kinship structure, fathers served as the primary "sex-role modeling" figure for male children.

Price (1976) reported that men in the matrilineal Hopi tribe join their wives' households following marriage and support them economically. However, he noted that the men retain greater leadership, ritual, and disciplinary roles within their natal households by providing discipline to their sisters' children. In the households of their wives, they maintain only a "passive role." Under this arrangement, Eggan (1966) found a high divorce rate among the Hopi as a result of these conflicting roles. In contrast, Miller (1979:451) maintains that within the patrilineal urban Sioux, the self-concept of the man may suffer more intensely because of his inability to provide for his family "than his counterpart from a tribe that is not so bound by patrilocal culture."

One of the most prevalent ways that Indian men have continued to maintain a traditional status and authority within the family and community has been through service in the military. More than any other racial or ethnic minority, American Indians have had the greatest proportion of their men serving in this country's armed forces during wartime. As early as 1917, when many American Indians were not yet citizens of the United States, 17,000 served during World War I, with about two-thirds of this number being volunteers (Hale 1982). Before the Japanese attack on Pearl Harbor, 4,481 Indians were serving in the military, and by June 1, 1942, more than 7,500 had enlisted (Collier 1942). Perplexed by the earnest response of the Indians to serve the country that had mistreated and ignored them, John Collier, the Commissioner of Indian Affairs under President Roosevelt (1942:30), wrote,

> One might be inclined to attribute the eagerness of the Indians to have a part in the conflict to their traditional love of fighting. But it runs far deeper than that . . . it is a life and death struggle for the survival of those things for which they have been unceasingly waging an uphill fight for many generations. This has been a fight to retain their cultural independence, the right to their native religions, and the right to local democracy. It has been a struggle against the totalitarian concept of a super-race dominating, absorbing, and reducing to serfdom the small minority group of a different culture . . . it may be that they see victory of the democracies a guarantee that they too shall be permitted to live their own lives.

During the Vietnam War, American Indian men again served in proportionally greater numbers than any other group in this country. A total of 62,100 Indian Vietnam era veterans served during the war (Veterans Administration 1985). With few exceptions, Indian men who are veterans of military services have been granted special status and roles within tribal society. Most powwows and ceremonials begin by honoring the tribe's veterans. In addition, Indian veterans' fraternities such as the Old Scouts Society of the Arikara, the Kiowa Black-leggings Warrior Society, the Red Feather Society of the Sioux, and many others offer a special status to young men who have served in the military. In many plains tribes, only the Indian veteran is granted special authority to pick up the sacred eagle feathers that may be accidentally dropped on the ground during a powwow.

Women's Roles

The growing number of single-parent female-headed families among American Indians has undoubtedly been the most significant role change in recent times. From 1970 to 1980, families headed by women increased by 28 percent (U.S. Department of Commerce 1984) and made up 23.4 percent of all Native American families (U.S. Department of Health and Human Services 1986). This increase of female-headed families in the Indian population means that Indian women now take on greater authority and status within the Indian family structure, at least within traditionally patriarchal tribes. Indeed, they have assumed this role most often with limited economic resources and social support. In 1979, 68 percent of female-headed families with no husband present on Indian reservations were living below 125 percent of the poverty level, compared with 49 percent of all U.S. female-headed families (U.S. Department of Health and Human Services 1986). Almost 70 percent of these families had children under 18 years of age (U.S. Bureau of the Census 1983), suggesting that a very large proportion of Indian children on reservations are living in poverty.

Miller (1979) also found a sizable number of single female parent Indian families in a sample of 120 urban Indian families living in Oakland, California, and the surrounding area; one-third of her sample were families headed by single women. However, the proportion of female-headed families between different tribal groups varied significantly. Single female-headed Navajo families were fewer in number than single female Sioux families. Miller attributed this finding to the different cultural values of the tribes. She explained that because the Navajo have closer ties to an extended family and their home reservation, they receive stronger support than Sioux women. She also believes that Navajo matrilocal culture has made Navajo women better able to sustain their families as the holders of status and wealth than the patrilocal culture of the Sioux.

On the basis of individual case studies of five Indian women, Hanson (1980) concludes that the role of many Indian women is also moving from "homemaker" to "breadwinner" through their participation in the arenas of politics, higher education, and administration. She attributes this movement to a shortage of Indian men and increased educational opportunities for Indian women. Although moving into these leadership positions means greater role conflicts for Indian women, Hanson asserts that they continue to "find support systems and maintain their cultural heritage while living in two worlds" (p. 482).

Family Values and Socialization

Values. Tribal identity is one of the most significant and ubiquitous values among American Indians. Identity as a tribal member denotes involvement in numerous family, social, religious, and political functions. In some tribes, identity is specifically linked to clans, whereas in others, it is linked to the tribe itself. On a more global scale, identity as an American Indian also may be connected with the precepts of "Pan-Indianism" (Ablon 1964; Price 1976; Red Horse 1980; Thomas 1970). As the name suggests, Pan-Indianism means that tribal identification is subordinate to ethnic identification with American Indians from all tribes.

Tribal identification has been a focal point in sustaining the federal/Indian relationship. Although more than 300 federally recognized Indian tribes in the United States are eligible for federal services, another 100 tribes do not have federal recognition (Porter 1983). Many of these unrecognized tribes are now petitioning for federal recognition under regulations for "Federal Acknowledgment." The criteria under this process, however, are not easily met, nor have they resulted in a "speedy determination" of which tribal groups should or should not be recognized (U.S. Office of Technology Assessment 1986).

Many "core values" among American Indians continue to be held and practiced by tribal families. For example, the concepts of "time," "cooperation," "leadership," "sharing," and "harmony with nature" are often viewed quite differently from those of the dominant culture. The temporal orientation of the Pueblo Indians is that time is always with us, as opposed to Anglo-American society, in which "clock-watching" dominates (Trimble 1976; Zintz 1963). In a sample of 84 Rosebud Sioux, Dana and others (1984:22) found the following value orientation profile:

> . . . simultaneously past and present oriented but polarized in extremes of feelings concerning the present. Human nature is seen as good, capable of change, and one should not condemn others, or be wary of them. In the rational sphere, one should make up one's own mind but accept advice from elders and work primarily in groups.

Lewis and Gringerich (1980) examined the perceptions of "leadership" qualities between 37 Native Americans and 40 non-Indian graduate social work students and found that different perceptions of leadership existed between these groups. The Indian students indicated that the "kind of person a leader is" is more important than the person's skills or knowledge, but the non-Indian sample held an opposite view. The American Indian students viewed the role of a leader as a more sacred, more humanistic, more person-oriented, more honest, more intuitive, and less ambitious position than did the non-Indian students. Furthermore, the American Indian group perceived the role of leadership as one of servitude, as opposed to a view of leadership as more assertive and aggressive held by non-Native students.

Socialization.   Throughout history, American Indian families have been subjected to a United States federal Indian "family policy" of civilization and assimilation into Euro-American society. As a matter of public policy, American Indians have had their family values and practices systematically attacked by federal legislation for the purpose of socializing them into the dominant culture. Although less oppressive than in the past, federal policies remain one of the dominant socializing forces for today's American Indian family.

The federal government's education of American Indians in formal school settings has been one of the most salient methods of socialization for Indian children. Until the nineteenth century, Indian education was the domain of missionary organizations. Beginning in 1802, the Trade and Intercourse Act paved the way for federal involvement in Indian education. From this point forward, the education of Indians was synonymous with the loss of tribal culture and values.

In 1933, John Collier, as the Commissioner of Indian Affairs in the Roosevelt administration, began the first efforts to reverse the federal government's antagonistic policies towards tribal culture, especially in its educational programs. Under his administration, Indian history and tribal culture, which had previously been prohibited in government and Christian Indian schools, were slowly made part of the curriculum. However, it was not until 1975, under the Indian Self-Determination and Education Assistance Act, that most tribes had an impact on the education and socialization of their children. Under this legislation, many tribes assumed control of their children's education by implementing curriculum programs that teach the traditional values, beliefs, and language of their tribe.

In 1986, 38,475 Indian students were enrolled in Bureau of Indian Affairs–funded schools (Office of Indian Education Programs 1988). Since the Self-Determination and Education Assistance Act of 1975, Indian students attending bureau-funded schools are more likely to receive a bicultural education that socializes the student to both Anglo-American and American Indian beliefs and practices. However, this group represents slightly less than 10 percent of the Indian student population, suggesting that the overwhelming majority of Indian students are still socialized and educated in a predominantly Anglo-American environment.

Socialization in many tribes still continues to be the province of the clan, band, or tribe. Cultural initiation and control of family members into different societies, organizations, or stages of life are often accomplished along matrilineal or patrilineal descent lines or through extended family members. Most recent research, however, has focused primarily on the socialization process and behavioral response of individual family members.

Among many Indian tribes, members are socialized to show respect for authority figures by use of good listening skills. Often this response takes the form of nonverbal communication. Basso (1970) found silence to be the usual response to role ambiguity among the Western Apache. In the classroom, Dumont (1972) maintains that the silence of Indian children is a common response in their learning behavior. In general, many American Indians who are reared with a sense of traditional values use the passive response in new situations (Edwards and Edwards 1980).

Ignoring inappropriate behavior of children is a discipline practice sometimes used by Indian parents. The individual rights and choices of Indian children in some tribes are preserved under the concept of "noninterference" (Good Tracks 1970). In return for this autonomy, the child also learns to respect and not to interfere with others. Among Indian families, Lewis (1981) maintains that limited physical punishment of children is due to the respect that each person has in his or her relationship with all others, starting especially with the children's relationship with the family. After observing Indian families who were participants in the "Alternative to Foster Care" Program, Ishisaka (1978:304) concluded that the parents of the children tended to be permissive, seldom insisting that the children comply with parental wishes. But when children violated standards of behavior consistent with their Indian cultural backgrounds, the parents assumed a direct and forceful role in guidance.

Of all the members in the extended family, the role of elders in the discipline and teaching of Indian children continues to be regarded as the most important (Cross 1986; Edwards 1983; Red Horse 1980; Red Horse and others 1978). Elders are primary providers of child care; at the same time, they link children with their tribal heritage. Elders also are seen as a resource for young parents to assist them in understanding traditional roles of discipline and child rearing (Cross 1986).

CONCLUSION

From the arrival of Columbus in 1492 until late in the nineteenth century, American Indians and American Indian families declined in number (Dobyns 1983). By 1900, most observers expected the American Indian population to disappear entirely. Contrary to this expectation, the American Indian population reversed its decline into extinction and has grown significantly throughout this century.

The twentieth-century resurgence in the American Indian population has meant, of course, a parallel increase in the number of American Indian families. The structure and organization of American Indian families vary greatly from one tribe to another, yet one constant is the importance of the family in daily social life.

The diversity of American Indian families should not be underestimated, however. That diversity is not always emphasized in studies of American Indians, and it is frequently overshadowed in statistical data. Yet the diverse tribal cultures found within the American Indian population are host to an array of different systems of family organization: some patrilocal, others matrilocal; some with distantly extended networks, others more nuclear; some with many functions, others with many obligations; the list of possible differences is lengthy.

Besides this diversity, another enduring feature of American Indian families has been their dynamic quality. American Indian families have sustained the Indian population and made possible their resurgence in this century. It seems almost certain that the sustaining power of the American Indian family has been its dynamic ability to change and adapt to a changing social environment.

The arrival of Europeans, the emergence of the United States, and rapidly changing social conditions have had a profound impact on the social organization and culture of American Indians. Surviving these changes meant being able readily to adapt existing social institutions to the demands of a newly emerging social environment. American Indian families have been able to perpetuate the American Indian population, sustain tribal organization, and preserve native culture precisely because they were capable of changing to meet the needs of the population. It should surprise no one that American Indian families today are as different from their ancestors of 100 years ago as those Indians were different from their ancestors another 100 years earlier.

From this perspective, it also should not be surprising that the American Indian family of tomorrow will be different from that of today. The literature clearly indicates that Indian families are changing, but within this change, elements of tradition are retained. For example, the roles of men, women, and the elderly appear to be in transition, but these changes are certainly shaped by traditions rooted in the past. What may be necessary for successfully anticipating the future will be to understand better how the ways of the past are fused with the needs of the moment to create new modes of family organization and living. Certainly more single women are trying to rear a family, but in the context of tribal traditions with strong matriarchal roles, these developments have very different implications for American Indians than for either blacks or whites. Nonetheless, such knowledge should be useful for understanding the dynamics of family organization across the spectrum of race and ethnicity.

REFERENCES

Ablon, Joan. 1964. "Relocated American Indians in the San Francisco Bay Area: Social Interaction and Indian Identity." *Human Organization* 23:296–304.

Axtell, James. 1985. *The Invasion Within: The Contest of Cultures in Colonial North America.* New York: Oxford University Press.

Basso, K. H. 1970. "To Give Up on Words: Silence in Western Apache Culture." *Southwestern Journal of Anthropology* 26:3.

Collier, John. 1942. "The Indian in a Wartime Nation." *Minority Peoples in a Nation at War.* (September) 6:29–35.

Cross, Terry L. 1986. "Drawing on Cultural Tradition in Indian Child Welfare Practice." *Social Casework: The Journal of Contemporary Social Work.* (May) 67:283–289.

Dana, Richard H., and others. 1984. "Local Norms of Personality Assessment for Rosebud Sioux." *White Cloud Journal* 3:2.

Dobyns, Henry F. 1983. *Their Numbers Become Thinned: Native American Population Dynamics in Eastern North America.* Knoxville: University of Tennessee Press.

Dumont, R. V., Jr. 1972. "Learning English and How to Be Silent: Studies in Sioux and Cherokee Classrooms." In *Functions of Language in the Classroom,* edited by C. B. Cozden and others. New York: Teachers College Press.

Edwards, E. Daniel. 1983. "Native American Elders: Current Issues and Social Policy Implications." In *Aging in Minority Groups,* edited by R. L. McNeely and J. N. Colen, 74–82. Beverly Hills, CA: Sage.

Edwards, E. Daniel, and Margie E. Edwards. 1980. "American Indians: Working with Individuals and Groups." *Social Casework: The Journal of Contemporary Social Work.* (October) 61:498–506.

Eggan, Fred. 1966. *The American Indian: Perspectives for the Study of Social Change.* Chicago: Aldine.

Good Tracks, Jim G. 1970. "Native American Non-Interference." *Social Work* 17:11.

Hale, Duane K. 1982. "Forgotten Heroes: American Indians in World War I." *Four Winds.* (Autumn) 4:39–41.

Hallowell, Irving A. 1967. "Ojibway Personality and Acculturation." In *Beyond the Frontier,* edited by P. B. and F. Plog. New York: The Natural History Press.

Hanson, Wynne. 1980. "The Urban Indian Woman and Her Family." *Social Casework: The Journal of Contemporary Social Work.* (October) 61:476–483.

Ishisaka, Hideki. 1978. "American Indians and Foster Care: Cultural Factors and Separation." *Child Welfare* 57:299–308.

John, Robert. 1985. "Service Needs and Support Networks of Elderly Native Americans: Family, Friends, and Social Service Agencies." In *Social Bonds in Late Life,* edited by W. A. Peterson and J. Quadagno. Beverly Hills, CA: Sage.

———. 1987. "The Native American Family." In *Ethnic Families in America: Patterns and Variations,* edited by C. H. Mindel and R. Habenstein, 325–362. New York: Elsevier.

Krush, Thaddeus P., and others. 1969. "Some Thoughts on the Formation of Personality Disorder: Study of an Indian Boarding School Population." In *Hearings Before the Special Subcommittee on Indian Education of the Committee on Labor and Public Welfare, United States Senate—Part 5.* Washington, DC: U.S. Government Printing Office.

Lefley, Harriet P. 1976. "Acculturation, Child-Rearing, and Self-Esteem in Two North American Indian Tribes." *Ethos* 4:385–401.

Lewis, Claudia. 1970. *Indian Families of the Northwest Coast: The Impact of Change.* Chicago: University of Chicago Press.

Lewis, Ronald. 1981. "Patterns of Strength of American Indian Families." In *The American Indian Family: Strengths and Stresses,* edited by J. Red Horse, A. Shattuck, and F. Hoffman, 101–106. Isleta, NM: American Indian Social Research and Development Associates.

Lewis, Ronald, and Wallace Gingerich. 1980. "Leadership Characteristics: Views of Indian and Non-Indian Students." *Social Casework.* (October) 61.

Linton, Ralph. 1963 [1940]. "Introduction." In *Acculturation in Seven American Indian Tribes,* vii–xi. Gloucester, MA: Peter Smith.

Miller, Dorothy. 1979. "The Native American Family: The Urban Way." In *Families Today: A Research Sampler on Families and Children,* edited by E. Corfman, 441–484. Washington, DC: U.S. Government Printing Office.

Office of Indian Education Programs. 1988. "Report on BIA Education: Excellence in Indian Education through the Effective Schools Process." Final Review Draft, Bureau of Indian Affairs, March.

Pearce, Diana. 1982. "Women in Poverty." In *The American Promise: Equal Justice and Economic Opportunity.* New Brunswick, NJ: Transaction Books.

Porter, Frank W., III (ed.). 1983. *Nonrecognized American Indian Tribes: An Historical and Legal Perspective.* Paper of the McNickel Center for the Study of the American Indian, No. 7. Chicago: Newberry Library.

Price, John A. 1976. "North American Indian Families." In *Ethnic Families in America: Patterns and Variations,* 2nd ed., edited by C. H. Mindel and R. W. Haberstein, 248–270. New York: Elsevier.

Prucha, Francis P. 1975. *Documents of United States Indian Policy.* Lincoln: University of Nebraska Press.

Red Horse, J. G., R. Lewis, M. Feit, and J. Decker. 1978. "Family Behavior of Urban American Indians." *Social Casework* 59 (February): 67–72.

Red Horse, John. 1980. "Family Structure and Value Orientation in American Indians." *Social Casework* 61 (8):462–467.

Snipp, C. Matthew. 1989. *American Indians: The First of This Land.* New York: Russell Sage Foundation.

Thomas, Robert. 1970. "Pan-Indianism." In *The American Indian Today,* edited by S. Levine and N. Lurie, 128–140. Baltimore: Penguin.

Trimble, Albert. 1976. "An Era of Great Change: A Single Decency Is Goal for Ogalala Sioux." *Wassaja* 4(May):5.

U.S. Bureau of the Census. 1983. *General Population Characteristics: United States Summary.* Washington, DC: Government Printing Office.

————. 1985. *Ancestry of the Population by State: 1980.* Washington, DC: U.S. Department of Commerce: April, PC80-S1-10.

U.S. Department of Commerce. 1984. *American Indian Areas and Alaska Native Villages: 1980.* Washington, DC: U.S. Government Printing Office.

————. 1985. *American Indians, Eskimos, and Aleuts on Identified Reservations and in Historic Areas of Oklahoma (Excluding Urbanized Areas),* Part 1. Washington, DC: U.S. Government Printing Office.

U.S. Department of Health and Human Services. 1986. *Indian People in Indian Lands, 1980: Profiles of American Indian and Alaskan Populations in Various Settings.* Washington, DC: U.S. Government Printing Office.

U.S. Office of Technology Assessment. 1986. *Indian Health Care.* Washington, DC: U.S. Government Printing Office.

Veterans Administration. 1985. "Statistical Brief: Native American Veterans." Office of Information Management and Statistics, October.

Vogt, Evon. 1957. "The Acculturation of American Indians." *Annals of the American Academy of Political and Social Science* 311:137–146.

Wagner, Jean K. 1976. "The Role of Intermarriage in the Acculturation of Selected Urban Indian Women." *Anthropologica* 18(2):215–229.

Zintz, Miles V. 1963. *Education across Cultures.* Dubuque, Iowa: William C. Brown, p. 175.

PART V

Minority Families and Social Change

During the 1960s and 1970s, major changes in the nature and forms of American family life led some observers to predict the demise of the family system in the United States. A number of social trends seem to lend support to such predictions: rising divorce rates, delays in marriage and childbearing, dramatic increases in the number of female-headed households, the escalation of women's labor force participation, the institutionalization of cohabitation and single living, the rise of voluntary childlessness, and the growing number of individuals of all ages who live alone. However, many of the recent changes in American family life are perceived by other analysts simply as a continuation of long-term social trends that began decades earlier and as signs of evolution rather than erosion or disintegration of American families. In accounting for these trends, they point to structural changes in the economy among other major developments that are restructuring the nature of work, gender roles, and relationships across classes and racial ethnic groups. In short, the "traditional" family has given way to a diversity of family forms and household arrangements—from dual-wage-earner families and single-parent households to nonmarital cohabitation and lesbian/gay collectives.

How minority families have been affected by recent structural shifts in the economy and associated trends is assessed in the concluding chapter. Ronald L. Taylor argues that although minority families, like other American families, are greatly affected by national economic and social trends, these families tend to respond to such trends in ways that reflect their differential access to economic opportunity structures and resources and their respective social biographies in the United States. As Taylor observes, assessing the effects of recent structural shifts in the economy and other national social trends on minority family patterns is complicated by recent changes in the racial ethnic composition of American society, resulting from the massive influx of immigrants from Latin America, Asia, and other Third World countries during the past two decades, whose traditional family lifestyles and values are sources of both stability and change in minority communities. The substantial increase in international migration has been more consequential for trends in marriage and family structure among some racial ethnic groups (such as Asians and Hispanics) than among others (such as African Americans and American Indians), altering the age and gender composition of these groups and their prospects for further socioeconomic advancement. He notes that observed differences among minority families in family structure and practices are not only a function of unique demographic and ancestral backgrounds, cultural histories, economic origins, and statuses, but also are the products of contemporary social, political, and economic forces of the larger society to which they are continually exposed. He concludes with some observations on the contribution of persons of "mixed race" to the shift in the racial ethnic composition of the U.S. minority population and the need for research on the growth and adaptation of second generation children of the post-1965 immigration era, since it is among the second generation that the long-term consequences of immigration, including the resilience of traditional family forms, will be decided.

CHAPTER 13

Minority Families and Social Change

Ronald L. Taylor

The past three decades saw substantial changes in patterns of marriage, family, and household composition in the United States. During this period, divorce rates doubled, marriage rates declined, fertility rates fell to record levels, and the proportion of children raised in female-headed households rose dramatically (Cherlin and Furstenberg 1983; Levitan and Belous 1981). These trends, in concert with sharp increases in the labor force participation rates of housewives and mothers and shifts in sexual mores and social attitudes toward premarital sex, illegitimacy, and cohabitation, have caused some observers to conclude that the American family is disintegrating (Espanshade 1985). Other analysts, however, contend that these changes are not necessarily to be equated with decline, immorality, or a general deterioration of American families (Eshleman 1991; Westoff 1983). On the contrary, they argue, it is more reasonable to interpret recent strains and changes in American family life as signs of evolution (Norton and Glick 1979). As Levitan and Belous (1981:vii) assert, "American families are changing, but they are not eroding," becoming more diverse or pluralistic in both form and function.

To be sure, a diversity of family types has always existed in the United States, encouraged by such factors as social class, urban-rural residence, racial and ethnic membership, religious affiliation, and age. Thus, to speak of the changing or disintegrating American family as if such families were uniform entities is misleading (Eshleman 1991). Rather, observers have in mind the traditional or "ideal" family, consisting of a working father, full-time housewife, and one or more dependent children when they speak of family change or decline. But such families now represent only a fraction of all families in the United States. For example, in 1990, only a quarter of all families in the United States fit the traditional model, and in 2000, 23.5 percent (New York Times 2001), whereas the living arrangements of the remaining majority took other family forms. By the end of the 1990s, the majority of married couples had both spouses in the labor force (63 percent), and more than two-thirds of married women with children were employed (U.S. Bureau of the

Census 2000a). Moreover, in 1988, for the first time, the proportion of childless families exceeded the number of families with children in the home (Wilkie 1991), a trend that continued through the 1990s. In addition, single-person households increased sharply during this period, as did the number of couples living in non-marital relationships. Over the decade, the fastest-growing family type was the household maintained by a woman with no husband present. In short, Americans today are living in a larger number of family and household arrangements—from dual-worker families and single-parent households to nonmarital cohabitation and extended kinship units—than was the case two generations ago. As a result, it has become more difficult for proponents of just one family form to contend that it is the ideal form or norm.

Although recent changes in family and household arrangements among middle-class white Americans are often described as the new lifestyles of the main-stream, many are in fact variants of family patterns and living arrangements that have long characterized African American and other minority communities but that were cited in the past as evidence of cultural deviance or pathology when ob-served in such families (Baca Zinn 1990). However, these alternative family struc-tures and living arrangements are best interpreted as responses to structural changes in the economy and other social trends, which are restructuring the na-ture of work, gender roles, and relationships across classes and racial ethnic groups in society (Eitzen and Baca Zinn 1989; Thorne 1982). As Gerstel and Gross (1987:7) observe, "The shifting economy produces even demands diverse family forms, including, for example, female-headed households, extended kinship units, dual-career couples, and lesbian collectives."

The recent transformation of the economy, marked in part by the emergence of new technologies and the shift from an economy based on the manufacture of products to one based on information and services, brought women into the work force in record numbers. In 1960, for example, little more than a third of all women aged 16 years and over held jobs outside the home; by the beginning of the 1990s, two-thirds worked at paid jobs (U.S. Department of Labor 2000). In fact, since 1950, labor force participation rates have increased substantially for women in every age group except those over the age of 65. This trend has been especially strong among women of childbearing age and among married women with chil-dren, whose rate of labor force participation has nearly quadrupled (Hartmann 1989). These changes in the job-holding patterns of women are directly related to shifts in the economy, particularly the expansion of the service sector. Two-thirds of the jobs created since 1975 have been filled by women, and "it is precisely this increase in women's paid work that has been a primary factor in the rise of service jobs" (Eitzen and Baca Zinn 1989:12).

Among the more visible consequences of the increased labor force participation of women have been postponement of marriage and childbearing until later ages, lower fertility and higher divorce rates, and increases in the number of women liv-ing alone or as heads of their own families (Hartmann 1989). Since 1973, the me-dian age at first marriage increased from 21 years to 24.8 years for women and from 23.3 years to 27.1 years for men, the highest levels since the early 1900s (U.S. Bureau of the Census 1989; 1998a). Although more women today are having children, "they are having them later and closer together and are having fewer of them" (Hartmann 1989:299). From 1960 to the late 1970s, the median interval between a first marriage and the birth of the first child increased from about 15 months to over 2 years, and the fertility rate (number of births per adult women) for wives 18 to 34 fell sharply, from 3.1 children in 1965, to 1.8 children in 1980, and 2.1 children in 1994 (U.S. Bureau of the Census 1994), just at the rate (2.1) necessary for population replacement (Bianchi and Spain 1984; Levitan and Belous 1981).

Although the preponderance of adult Americans continue to marry, the divorce rate since the mid-1960s has more than doubled. The number of divorced mothers increased at an average rate of 9 percent a year in the 1970s (New York Times 1991a), and by 1979, there was one divorce for every two marriages. It has been estimated that half of all first marriages in the 1980s will probably end in divorce (Cherlin and Furstenberg 1983). The divorce rate is higher among employed married women and among those with postgraduate degrees, in part, perhaps, because employed and better-educated women "are more likely than housewives to have the financial and other resources to end a relationship they are not satisfied with" (Wilkie 1991:151). Whatever the case, the high divorce rate has been a significant factor in the large increase in the proportion of women as heads of their own households or living alone during the past two decades. In 1970, female-headed families accounted for only 10 percent of all families. Marital dissolution (divorce and separation) and premarital births have combined to double the proportion of single-parent households since 1970. Nearly 13 million families were headed by women in 1998, accounting for almost 18 percent of all families in the United States (U.S. Bureau of the Census 1999).

Although the effects of increased labor force participation among women have not been uniform across all racial ethnic groups and classes in the United States, the broadened employment opportunities for women, in tandem with other forces transforming the economy, have "produced new relations among individuals, families and labor systems that have had profound effects on family development throughout American society" (Baca Zinn 1990:75).

How have minority families been affected by these recent trends? Given the nature of their relationship to the economy and their distinct and cumulative social histories in the United States, it might be anticipated that the recent structural shifts in the economy and associated trends have had a differential impact on marriage patterns, gender relations, living arrangements, and other family characteristics of these groups. To some extent, assessing the effects of recent economic developments on minority family patterns is complicated by the dramatic shift in the racial ethnic composition of the United States as a result of the massive wave of immigrants from Latin America, Asia, and other Third World countries during the past three decades. The influx of these groups in such large numbers has been a source of both stability and change in minority communities, as many who come with more traditional family lifestyles and values seek to adjust to new social situations and cultural influences (Time 1985). The strains and changes that have accompanied the absorption of these new arrivals must be taken into account in assessing the effects of recent economic and social trends on patterns of marriage, family, and household behavior among minority populations in the United States.

Because many of the recent trends in family structures and living arrangements among the major minority populations in the United States have already been examined in the various chapters of this volume, the following sections highlight and summarize these trends, noting the impact of recent changes in immigration patterns on family life in minority communities and the implications of these trends for the future of these groups in the United States.

MINORITY FAMILIES: CHANGE AND ADAPTATION

Minority families, like other families in the United States, are greatly affected by trends in the national economy—from deindustrialization to high rates of unemployment—and respond to such trends in ways that reflect their differential access to economic opportunity structures and resources and their respective social biographies in American society (Mullings 1986; Steinberg 1981). Prevailing discrepancies in economic opportunities between white and racial ethnic families predictably affect family structures and household behavior by, for example, increasing the economic pressures that encourage dual-wage-earner families, marital instability, and female-headed households (Cherlin and Furstenberg 1983; Levitan and Belous 1981). Differences in demographic characteristics and ecological processes can likewise affect family patterns in important ways. For example, differences in the gender ratios and age distribution between majority and minority populations may help to account for differential trends in marriage and household formation, out-of-wedlock births, and single-parent families (Glick 1988; Wilson 1984). Similarly, such ecological factors as regional location and concentration can affect family income and household behaviors (Jiobu 1988). That is, the regional location and concentration of minority populations "can affect family members' occupational opportunities and thus the economic security of the household." (Wilkinson 1987:89)

In addition to these factors, changes in immigration patterns can have a major effect on marriage, family, and household behaviors among racial ethnic groups and influence the trajectory of trends in these areas over time. In fact, because of declining fertility rates in the United States during the past two decades, international migration has become an important source of the nation's population growth, increasing from 16 percent in the 1960s to more than 30 percent in the 1990s (Population Reference Bureau 1999; U.S. Bureau of the Census 2000b). This increase has been more consequential for the family and community life of some racial ethnic groups than for others.

Prior to the passage of the new Immigration Act of 1965, which abandoned the quota system that for nearly 50 years had preserved the overwhelmingly European character of the nation, approximately 80 percent of the migrants who legally entered the United States came from European countries. Immigrants from the Americas, including Canada, accounted for about 15 percent of the total, while 3 percent arrived from Asia, and less than 1 percent were admitted from Africa and

Australia combined (Farley and Allen 1989). The new law dramatically altered the mix of international migration and invited the largest wave of immigrants from Latin America, Asia, and other Third World countries since the turn of the century. Between 1965 and 1980, for example, immigration from Europe declined to just over 20 percent of the total immigration population, while immigration from the Americas increased to nearly 50 percent, and the Asian share grew almost tenfold to 28 percent of the total (Bean and Tienda 1987; Farley and Allen 1989; Wong 1986). Blacks from the West Indies and Africa also increased their share of immigration, accounting for slightly less than 10 percent of all immigration to the United States since 1969 (Time 1985). By 1996, 27 percent of immigrants came from Mexico, 27 percent came from Asia and the Pacific Islands, 17 percent came from Europe, and 12 percent came from Central and South America. In 1999, foreign-born residents accounted for 9.7 percent of the U.S. population, or 26.4 million. Of that number, 34 percent came from Central America, 10 percent from the Caribbean, 7 percent from South America, 16 percent from Europe, 27 percent from Asia, and 6 percent from other countries (U.S. Bureau of the Census 1998a; 2000a).

The rate of growth of the minority population was almost twice as fast in the 1980s as in the previous decade, and much of that increase was among those of Asian and Hispanic ancestry. In fact, between 1980 and 1998, almost three-quarters of all immigrants entering the United States came from Asia and Latin America, about 20 percent from Europe, and about 4 percent from Africa. Since 1980, the Asian population in the United States has increased by more than 200 percent and tripled from 3.5 million in 1980 to more than 10.9 million in 1999 (U.S. Bureau of the Census 2000a). Similarly, the Hispanic population grew by nearly 8 million people (53 percent) over 1980, and between 1990 and 2000, increased by 50 percent to 32.8 million (U.S. Bureau of the Census 2000a). Although their rate of growth since 1980 has been less dramatic, blacks and American Indians increased their numbers by significant amounts over the past two decades: for African Americans, their numbers grew from 26.1 million in 1980, to 35.4 million in 2000; the American Indian population grew from 1.3 million in 1980 to an estimated 2.4 million in 2000 (New York Times 1991b; O'Hare and others 1991; U.S. Bureau of the Census 2000b).

Clearly, such rapid growth in the minority population due to recent immigration has important implications for current and future trends in marriage, family, and living arrangements in minority communities, especially because such large increases have the potential for altering the age and gender composition of some minority populations and their prospects for further advances in socioeconomic achievement (Jiobu 1988).

AFRICAN AMERICANS AND THE DIVERSIFICATION OF FAMILY LIFE

Current trends in marriage, family, and household behavior among African Americans have been affected less by the recent surge in international migration than by structural shifts in the economy and other demographic changes in the African

American community. Although the flow of foreign-born blacks to the United States has increased significantly during the past two decades, the numbers are small compared with the size of other foreign-born groups. There are, for example, seven times as many foreign-born Hispanics in the United States as blacks and nine times as many foreign-born whites (Farley and Allen 1989; Population Reference Bureau 1999). The Census counted 1.3 million foreign-born blacks in the United States in 1990, and nearly 1.5 million in 1998, representing about 5 percent of the total black population. Immigration from the Caribbean and Africa accounts for about 20 percent of the growth of the African American population between 1990 and 1997. About 95 percent of the foreign-born black population comes for the Dominican Republic, Haiti, Jamaica, Trinidad and Tobago, and other West Indian and Latin American countries. Immigrants from African countries accounted for less than 4 percent of U.S. immigrants between 1981 and 1998, but there are indications that the flow of immigrants from Africa may increase in the near future. In 1998, about 560,000 Americans were born in Africa, up from 360,000 in 1990, and nine times the number in 1970 (Population Reference Bureau 1999). Because these groups are concentrated in only a few large cities and regions of the country (for example, New York, Chicago, Miami, and Washington, D.C.), their increasing numbers have had little apparent impact on trends in family structure and household arrangements among African Americans.

Since the mid-1960s, changes in labor market conditions and national social policies have had both beneficial and adverse effects on the socioeconomic positions and family life of African Americans. The rapid growth of the economy and the enactment of major civil rights legislation eliminating many of the more overt forms of racial discrimination during the 1960s made it possible for a substantial number of African American families to improve their incomes and living standards and enter the mainstream of American life. Today, African Americans are better educated, earn higher incomes, work in more prestigious jobs, and are better represented in city, state, and federal legislative bodies (Jaynes and Williams 1989; O'Hare and others 1991). Although they still lag behind whites on nearly every measure of socioeconomic status, their quality of life has greatly improved over the past three decades.

Despite overall progress, improvements in the economic status of African Americans over the past quarter century have been uneven, creating greater diversity in African American communities and accentuating differences in socioeconomic status. That is, whereas some segments of the African American community made dramatic economic gains relative to whites during this period, others fell further behind (Farley 1984). Thus, some analysts contend that African Americans are increasingly divided into two groups—a growing affluent middle class, composed mainly of younger, better educated individuals who are moving into high-status occupations that guarantee economic security and a prosperous lifestyle, and a relatively small but significant "underclass" of individuals and families concentrated in the inner cities and mired in a vicious circle of poverty, intermittent employment, and welfare dependency (Auletta 1982; Wilson 1978, 1987). Although analysts disagree over the appropriateness of the term "underclass" in describing the economic position of the vast majority of African American families in poverty, they generally agree that the African American community has become more economically polarized as more of its members have moved into the economic mainstream.

The increasing disparity in economic position among African Americans is most clearly evident in the growing economic polarization by family type. During the past three decades, income levels have risen much more rapidly in black married-couple families than in households headed by women. As a result, incomes in families headed by black women have fallen further behind husband-wife families in both absolute and relative terms (Farley 1984). Whereas income in families headed by black women was 63 percent of that of husband-wife families in 1959, its declined to 50 percent in 1981. By 1998, married-couple black families had incomes 2.5 times that of families headed by black women—$45,372 compared with $17,962 (U.S. Bureau of the Census 2000b). Thus, an important aspect of the polarization in incomes of African American families has been the growth of female-headed households since the 1960s, which pulled a larger proportion of black families into the lowest income groups. In summarizing the divergent trends in family income among African Americans, Jaynes and Williams (1989:275–276 observe,

> While some female-headed families are middle-class just as some two-parent families are poor, it is not an exaggeration to say that the two most numerically important components of the black class structure have become a lower class dominated by female-headed families and a middle-class largely composed of families headed by a husband and wife.

The sharp increase in female-headed households among African Americans in recent decades is the result of a combination of demographic and economic factors. As recently as the mid-1960s, three-fourths of all African American households were husband and wife families, while female-headed families accounted for 25 percent. By 1990, the proportion of black married-couple households had fallen to about half of all African American families, while female-headed households nearly doubled to 45 percent (O'Hare and others 1991). By 1998, the proportions were 46.5 percent and 46.7 percent respectively (U.S. Bureau of the Census 2000b). To be sure, the proportion of women who head their own families has risen for all racial categories since the 1960s, but the increase has been greater for African American women (Jaynes and Williams 1989; Wilson 1987). Whereas the increase in female-headed households among whites is attributed to disrupted marriages (that is, divorce and separation), the increase among African Americans is linked to declining marriage rates and the increasing economic marginalization of African American men (Norton 1985; Wilson and Neckerman 1986).

Although African Americans have traditionally married at younger ages than whites, this pattern was reversed during the 1960s, as blacks exceeded whites in the percentages of young adults never married. By 1970, 43 percent of black women aged 20 to 24 were never married, compared with 36 percent of white women in this age cohort. By 1993, the percentage had increased to 81 percent for black and 64 percent for white women in this age group; in 1998, 85 percent of black women and 67 percent of white women in this age group were never married (U.S. Bureau of the Census 1998b). Trends in marital status for African American women have paralleled trends among African American men, except that increases in the percentage of black men never married have been more dramatic among those aged 16 to 19 and 20 to 24 (Mare and Winship 1991). Among black teenage males (16 to 19), marriage has virtually disappeared; 99 percent of black males in this age group were unmarried in 1998, the same as in 1993. The percentage of never-married black men in the 20 to 24 age category increased from 57 percent in 1970 to 92 percent in 1998, up from 90 percent in 1993 (U.S. Bureau of the Census 1994, 1998b).

Among the major factors contributing to the rapid decline of marriage rates among African Americans in recent decades have been changes in school enrollment trends and high rates of black male joblessness (Glick 1988; Mare and Winship 1991; Wilson 1987).

Because young men and women enrolled in school have lower rates of marriage than nonstudents, in part because they are less likely to be employed, and if employed have lower incomes, Mare and Winship (1991) examined the effects of the significant increase in school attendance among African Americans on their marriage rates between 1960 and 1980, the period when most of the decline in marriage rates occurred. For young men, they found that increased school enrollment had little effect on marriage rates, "except among Black teenagers, for whom increased school enrollment explain[ed] about 12 percent of the decline in their marriage rates since 1960" (Mare and Winship 1991:177). However, for black women under age 24, increased school enrollment accounted for 13 to 29 percent of the decline in marriage rates. They conclude that increased school enrollment accounted for only a modest portion of the decline in marriage rates among African Americans between 1960 and 1980.

According to some analysts, the precipitous decline in employment opportunities among African American men largely accounts for the low marriage rate and growth in female-headed households among African Americans in recent decades (Norton 1985; Staples 1988; Wilson and Neckerman 1986). William J. Wilson, a leading proponent of this view, has shown that as rates of employment and labor force participation for young African American men declined during the past two decades, the proportion of attractive potential marriage partners for African American women also declined. The decrease in the ratio of employed black men to women of the same age since the 1960s is cited as evidence of the relationship between the employment status of black men and marriage rates, both of which declined gradually in the 1960s and rapidly in the 1970s. Moreover, "when the factor of joblessness is combined with high black male mortality and incarceration rates, the proportion of black men in stable economic situations is even lower than that conveyed in the current unemployment and labor force figures" (Wilson and Neckerman 1986:253). Thus, the shortage of African American men with the economic resources to support a family has made it necessary for many African American women to leave a marriage or to forgo marriage altogether. The need to adapt to these and other structural conditions has left many African American women disproportionately separated, divorced, and solely responsible for their children (Baca Zinn 1990:78).

Whether formed through divorce, separation, or out-of-wedlock childbearing, the rise in female-headed households in recent decades has been an important source of the widening gap in family income and the high incidence of poverty in African American communities (Farley 1984; Mare and Winship 1991). Black female-headed households rank at the bottom of the income distribution, with a medium income of $13,000 in 1998 compared with more than $15,000 for white female-headed households (U.S. Bureau of the Census 1998b). Moreover, such families constitute a growing proportion of the poverty population. In 1999, 53 percent of all poor families and 82 percent of all poor black families were female-headed (U.S. Bureau of the Census 2000d).

Female-headed families not only are more likely to be poor but also are more likely than male-headed families to be poor for long periods. Although most individuals and families who become poor endure poverty for only 1 or 2 years, a considerable number remain poor for sustained periods (Duncan 1984). African American households headed by women are overrepresented among the long-term poor, accounting for 62 percent of the persistently poor between 1969 and 1978. More recently, 28 percent of whites who were poor in 1985 moved out of poverty within a year, whereas only 17 percent of poor black female-headed families escaped poverty during that year (U.S. Bureau of the Census 1990a; Wilson and Neckerman 1986). Nonetheless, changes in black family structure per se have not been a major source of continuing high poverty rates over the past two decades. As Jaynes and Williams (1989:281–282) report: "Rather than family structure, it is low earnings that have led to increased poverty since the 1970s. Many intact black families are poor because the two adults heading them have very low earning capacities. Likewise, many single-parent families would remain poor if there were two adults present."

Much of the concern about the growth of female-headed households is related to concerns about the welfare of children. The living arrangements and well-being of children have been most affected by recent changes in marital status and family composition of African American households. Beginning in the 1960s, changes in the family living arrangements of children, according to Jaynes and Williams (1989), have divided most of the African American community into two groups: "those living in families with one adult head—overwhelmingly poor—and those living in families with two adult heads—largely middle-class" (p. 36). For example, the proportion of African Americans under 18 living with two parents declined from 58 percent in 1970 to 36 percent in 1998 (U.S. Bureau of the Census 1998a). More than half (55 percent) of black children lived in single-parent households in 1998, 51 percent with their mother (U.S. Bureau of the Census 1998b). In contrast, 74 percent of white children under 18 were living with two parents (the proportion was 79 percent in 1990), and 18 percent were living with mother only (U.S. Bureau of Census 1998b).

In the course of their childhood, more than twice as many African American children as white children are likely to spend some time in a single-parent household, and much of it in poverty (Levin and Ingram 1988). In fact, 48 percent of black children under 18 who lived in female-headed households in 1998 were being brought up in poverty, more than twice the percentage (21 percent) of white children in such households (Joint Center for Political and Economic Studies 1999). Regardless of family structure, African American children are nearly four times more likely to be poor as are their white counterparts. (U.S. Bureau of the Census 1998b). Taking family assistance and other government transfer into account, twice as many black children as white children lived in poor households in 1998. (U.S. Bureau of the Census 1998a). But the situation is considerably worse when comparisons of pretransfer resources are considered:

> . . . especially for children in the decisive and vulnerable first 10 years of life. While a large majority of white children raised during the 1970s escaped poverty in their first 10 years, two-thirds of black children were not so fortunate. And 5 of 10 black children were poor for 4 of their first 10 years; only 1 of 12 white children knew that much poverty during the 1970s. One black child in 3, but only 1 white child in 33, was poor at least 7 of the 10 years. (Jaynes and Williams 1989:279).

By comparison, the 4.1 million African American children residing in two-parent families (in 1998) fare considerably better:

> Their parents are more educated, earn nearly four times as much money, and are more than twice as likely to own their own home. These stark differences highlight the two separate worlds inhabited by poor and middle-class black children, and suggest that the African American population will become more polarized as these children mature. (O'Hare and others 1991:20)

In sum, the past three decades have seen major changes in the marriage and family patterns of African Americans, including higher rates of marital dissolution, lower rates of marriage, rapidly rising proportions of female-headed households, and increasing proportions of children being raised in single-parent families. Although such changes are in tune with the changes in other American families, these trends have been more pronounced for blacks than for whites, suggesting possible differences in causal circumstances. For example, as Jaynes and Williams (1989:512) observe, "the growth in the number of white and black poor families headed by women results from different behaviors: among whites, disrupted marriages; among blacks, a decrease in marriage rates." Thus, although black and white women are increasingly likely to end up as single parents, race tends to create different routes to this family form (Baca Zinn 1990).

Current patterns of marriage, divorce, and female headship among African Americans, combined with other demographic and economic trends, suggest greater diversity in family forms, living arrangements, and socioeconomic status in the African American community as America enters the twenty-first century. Between the late 1980s and the year 1998, the total number of African American families increased by 17 percent, from 7.2 to 8.4 million. Whereas married-couple households rose by about 5 percent during this period, female-headed families increased by 19 percent. Thus the number of female-headed African American families increased three times as fast as the number of married-couple families between 1988 and 1998, increasing the proportion of black households headed by women from 44 to 47 percent of all African American families (U.S. Bureau of the Census 2000a). Among whites, the number of families headed by women increased more than four times as fast as married-couple families during this period (14 percent versus 3 percent). In 1998, 29.4 percent of all households (family and nonfamily) were female-headed, and 33 percent of those had children under 18 at home (U.S. Bureau of the Census 2000d).

Although economic instability and high unemployment were major contributors to family instability and the increase in alternative living arrangements among African Americans during the 1970s and 1980s, labor market opportunities for male and female heads of black families and for black youth were expected to improved over the 1990s. The U.S. Department of Labor (1988a) projected an increase of 34 percent in labor force participation of black men aged 25 to 54 during the decade, double the 16 percent increased protected for white men, and a 42 percent increase for black women in this age category, compared with 33 percent for white women. However, labor force participation rates for all men declined during the 1990s. Among black men aged 16 and older, labor force participation rates fell by 2.0 percent from 1988 to 1998 (from 71.0 to 69.0 percent) and among white men by 1.3 percent (from 76.9 to 75.6 percent) during this period (U.S. Dept. of Labor 2000). Among women, labor force participation rates increased by 3.3 percent over the decade. Among black women aged 16 years and older, labor force participation rates improved by 5 percent, from 58 percent in 1988 to 62.8 percent in 1998, and by 3 percent among white women (from 56.4 percent in 1988 to 59.4 percent in 1998). Although the state of the economy over the next decade will determine the quality and quantity of employment opportunities available to all workers, regardless of race, demographic projections suggest that by 2008, if not before, African American families will experience more favorable job opportunities. For example, the black labor force is expected to grow by 20 percent between 1998 and 2008, twice as fast as the 10 percent growth rate for the white labor force (U.S. Dept. of Labor 2000).

Although declining competition from whites is expected to improve the employment prospects of African Americans during the next decade, some analysts suggest that increased competition from Hispanic and Asian immigrants—whose numbers have been growing more than twice as fast as those of African Americans—may imperil black economic advancement in the near future and beyond (O'Hare and others 1991). Writing a decade ago, Hill (1989:50) observed that

> Hispanics obtained the same number of new jobs created between 1975 and 1980 as blacks, although they were about half the size of the black population, while Asians secured half as many new jobs as blacks, although they were only one-fifth the size of the black population. Clearly, the extent of legal and illegal immigration over the next decade will be an important determinant of the economic status of black families by the year 2000.

Some results from the 2000 census and other sources confirms Hill's observations (Borjas 1998; U.S. Bureau of the Census 2000b).

HISPANIC MINORITY FAMILIES: STRUCTURE AND PROCESS

The term *Hispanic* refers to a highly diverse population, composed to individuals who share ancestral ties to Spain and/or the Latin American countries. Although their common ancestral ties and use of the Spanish language may imply a shared cultural heritage, persons of Mexican, Puerto Rican, Cuban, and Central or South American origin—who represented 94 percent of the Hispanic population in 2000—differ considerably in "their immigration histories—in where they came from, in when they arrived, and in how favorably they were received when they got here" (Bean and Tienda 1987:398). They also differ in their demographic and economic characteristics. Under the umbrella term *Hispanic,*

> We find individuals whose ancestors lived in the country at least since the time of independence and others who arrived last year; we find substantial numbers of professionals and entrepreneurs, along with humble farm laborers and unskilled factory workers; there are whites, blacks, mulattoes, and mestizos; there are full-fledged citizens and unauthorized aliens; and finally, among the immigrants, there are those who came in search of employment and a better economic future and those who arrived escaping death squads and political persecution at home. (Portes and Truelove 1987:360).

Because of the diversity of national origins, distinct immigration histories, and the absence of a firm sense of collective identity among the segments of this population, some scholars challenge the use of the term *Hispanic* as an ethnic label in referring to the Spanish-origin population (Bean and Tienda 1987; Portes and Truelove 1987). Rather than consolidated minority, the Hispanic population is "a group in formation whose boundaries and self-definition are still in a state of flux" (Portes and Truelove 1987:359).

As recently as 1950, fewer than 4 million residents on the mainland of the United States were counted as Hispanic by the census, representing 2.7 percent of the total population. The number increased to 14.6 million in 1980, to 22.3 million in 1990, and to 32.8 million in 2000, accounting for 12 percent of the total U.S. population. Of the nearly 33 million Hispanics in 2000, 66 percent were of Mexican ancestry, 9 percent were Puerto Rican, and 4 percent were Cuban. The remaining 21 percent were made up of sizable contingents of Dominicans, Columbians, and other Central and South Americans, each with its own distinct history, characteristics, and patterns of adaptation.

Although persons of Spanish origin are found in every state, nearly 70 percent are concentrated in just four times—California (33.4 percent), Texas (19.4 percent), New York (8.7 percent), and Florida (7.5 percent). More than half (53 percent) of U.S. Hispanics live in California and Texas alone (U.S. Bureau of the Census 2000b). The regional concentration of the major Hispanic groups reflects their point of entry into the United States. Mexican Americans are concentrated in California and Texas, whereas the Puerto Ricans are heavily clustered in the New York metropolitan area. The bulk of Cuban Americans reside in Florida, the point of entry for refugees fleeing the Castro regime in the 1950s and 1960s. Other Hispanic groups, including those from Central and South America, are also concentrated in these regions, but large communities also exist in eastern and midwestern urban areas such as Boston, Washington, D.C., and Chicago (Valdivieso and Davis 1988). Although the major Hispanic groups continue to be regionally concentrated and relatively geographically isolated from one another, their rapid growth during the past two decades has had an increasing impact on the sociodemographic, economic, and ethnic features of the United States.

The extensive social, economic, and ethnic diversity among Spanish-origin groups in the United States and the relative shortage of empirical studies on some of these groups suggest the need for care in generalizing about recent trends in family and household structures among Hispanics as a single population. As Portes and Truelove (1987) observe, some subgroups of the Hispanic population "are not yet 'settled,' but continue expanding and changing in response to uninterrupted immigration and to close contact with events in the home countries" (p. 361). This tendency implies continual reinforcement of traditional patterns of family organization that prevail in their country of origin, whereas family patterns among groups with a longer history of settlement and acculturation in the United States are more likely to reflect trends in family and household structures characteristic of the population at large (Bean and Tienda 1987; Vega 1990).

One of the most persistent generalizations in the social science literature about Hispanic Americans is their strong familistic orientation, or adherence to familistic values, that is, values that "give overriding importance to the family and the needs of the collective as opposed to individual and personal needs" (Bean and others 1977:759). In their review of the empirical literature on Mexican American families, Ramirez and Arce (1981:45) observe that the structure and function of these families are characterized by (1) a strong and persistent familistic orientation, (2) the prevalence of highly integrated extended kinship systems even among families who are three or more generations removed from Mexico, and (3) the consistent preference for relying on the extended family as a primary means of support for coping with emotional stress. However, this characterization of Hispanic families is controversial and is regarded by some analysts as stereotypical and, as such, a source of "many of the pejorative images that have beset discussions of the Hispanic family" (Vega 1990:1018). In fact, familism as a defining characteristic of Hispanic families has been used to account for the high fertility and marriage rate among Hispanics, as well as their high levels of marital stability (Frisbie and others 1985; Glick 1969). However, the research literature in this area is inconsistent and reflects a "mixed bag of assumptions, approaches, findings and interpretations" (Baca Zinn 1982–83:225).

In their comprehensive review and analysis of 1980 census data, Bean and Tienda (1987) assess the extent to which Hispanic groups exhibit demographic behaviors consistent with familistic orientations, including marriage and household behaviors. They argue that if family relationships assume greater importance among Hispanic groups than non-Hispanic whites, such an orientation should be reflected in differential patterns of marriage and marital instability, in the composition of households, and in other forms of family and household behavior.

Examining first the current status distributions (for example, percent married, never married, divorced, separated) within the various populations of Spanish-origin persons aged 14 and over in 1980, Bean and Tienda found only small variations in rates of marital disruption between non-Hispanic whites, Mexican Americans, and Cuban Americans, although they did find higher rates of marital instability among Puerto Ricans than among the other groups. Their findings, however, are at odds with findings from earlier studies of marital stability among Mexican Americans reported by Frisbie and others (1985), who found lower rates of instability among Mexican Americans compared with non-Hispanic whites and African Americans living in five southwestern states. But as Bean and Tienda point out, findings based on data from the southwestern states alone appear likely to derive from demographic characteristics of the non-Hispanic white population peculiar to that region, and that when separation is included in marital disruption, such observed differences largely disappear. Of greater significance than the negligible variations in rates of marital disruption between non-Hispanic whites and the Spanish-origin groups, Bean and Tienda (1987:186) conclude,

> . . . is the fact that the Hispanic groups have followed the same trends of increasing instability characteristic of non-Hispanic whites since 1960. Among Puerto Ricans and other Hispanics the increases have been substantial, resulting by 1980 in levels of instability substantially higher among females than those of the remaining Spanish-origin groups. In summary, the national data examined here on levels of instability, together with the trends observed toward increasing instability among the Hispanic groups, do not provide a very strong basis for concluding that cultural orientations among Hispanics increase the likelihood of marital stability. If anything, instability is little different or even greater than that observed among non-Hispanic whites.

Although the data on marital instability among Spanish-origin groups may not support the idea that these groups are more familistic in orientation than non–Hispanic whites, other features of Hispanic families do seem to favor this interpretation. The prevalence of extended household structures and kin networks among Hispanic populations is interpreted by some observers as evidence of greater familistic emphases among Hispanic groups (Becerra 1988; Markides and others 1983). Although the trend among all American families has been a decline in the average size of households, Hispanic households are typically larger than the households of non-Hispanic whites and include a larger number of adult relatives as well as children (U.S. Bureau of the Census 2001; Valdivieso and Davis 1988). In 2000, for example, 31 percent of Hispanic family households consisted of five or more people, in contrast to 12 percent of non-Hispanic white family households (U.S. Bureau of the Census 2001). According to data reported by Bean and Tienda (1987), Hispanic households are considerably more likely than non-Hispanic white households to contain adult relatives, especially adult relatives other than children. Whereas Mexicans and Central and South Americans are more likely than other Spanish-origin groups to have other related adults living with husband-wife families, among all Hispanics the percentages exceed those for non-Hispanic whites. Although the most common household type among Hispanic groups is nuclear-centered, "the norm is geographic propinquity and strong kinship ties among family units, especially in times of need" (Wilkinson 1987:193). In addition to its instrumental function, the kinship network is seen as a major source of emotional support for its members and "as the main outcome of familism" (Vega 1990:1019) among Hispanic groups.

With respect to other features of family and household structures, Hispanic groups are characterized by many of the same trends that affect the situation of non-Hispanic whites. Among Spanish-origin populations over the past four decades, social forces have "decreased the percentage of husband-wife families, increased the percentage of other families (the vast majority of which are female-headed) and increased the percentage of non-families" (Bean and Tienda 1987:191). For example, among Mexican Americans and the category "other Hispanic," the percentage of husband-wife households declined from 76 percent in 1960 to 66 and 58 percent, respectively, in 1980. Among Puerto Ricans, the decline in the proportion of such households was even more dramatic, falling from 72 percent in 1960 to 49 percent in 1980. By 1990, 60 percent of Mexican American and 57 percent of Central and South American households were married-couple families, compared with 46 percent of Puerto Rican households (U.S. Bureau of the Census 1991). However, the 1990s saw a reversal of the downward trend in the percentage of husband-wife families. By 1999, 70 percent of Mexican American and 67 percent of Central and South American households were married-couple families, compared with 57 percent of Puerto Rican and 62 percent of "other Hispanic" households (U.S. Bureau of the Census 1991; 2000c).

The percentage of households headed by women among Hispanic groups has also grown during the past three decades. In 1980, only 14 percent of non-Hispanic white families were headed by a woman, while the percentage of such families among Hispanic groups ranged from 16 percent among Cuban Americans to 37 percent among Puerto Ricans. The percentage of female-headed households among Mexican Americans, who represent the majority of all Hispanics, was 19 percent in 1980, or about half that of Puerto Ricans. Indeed, by 1988, the percentage of Puerto Rican families headed by single women had increased to 44 percent, double the Hispanic average of 23 percent and nearly triple the non-Hispanic average of 16 percent (Bean and Tienda 1987; Valdivieso and Davis 1988). By 1999, 24 percent of all Hispanic family households were female-headed, compared with 13 percent for non-Hispanic white family households. The proportion of such households was highest among Puerto Ricans, 37.3 percent, Central and South Americans, 23.7 percent, Mexicans, 21.3 percent, and Cubans, 17.0 percent (U.S. Bureau of the Census 2000c). The high proportion of female-headed households among Puerto Ricans is accounted for in part by the overrepresentation of disrupted families from Puerto Rico among recent migrants to the mainland, the tendency among second-generation families to cohabitate, and the labor market problems of Puerto Rican men (Bohon 2001; Muschin and Meyers 1989; Vega 1990.)

Divorce and separation were a significant source of the larger percentage of female-headed households among Spanish-origin groups than among non-Hispanic whites through the 1980s, accounting for more than 40 percent of such households among Central and South Americans and Puerto Ricans and for more than a third among Mexican and Cuban Americans. Among non-Hispanic whites, widowhood was the major contributor to female headship, whereas divorce and separation accounted for 28 percent of such households. In 1998, more than half of female-headed households among Hispanics were the result of divorce (28 percent) or separation (25 percent) (U.S. Bureau of the Census 1999, Table 82). As Bean and Tienda pointed out a decade earlier, these results do not accord well with the familistic hypothesis: "If familistic emphases are comparatively strong among Hispanics, they apparently are not strong enough to ward off the forces making for these increases in families without father" (1987:191).

The growing proportion of Hispanic families headed by women parallels increases in poverty rates among subgroups of the Hispanic population during the past two decades. As in the case of African Americans, low earnings rather than family structure per se have been mainly responsible for increased poverty among Spanish-origin groups since the 1970s (Sandefur 1988; Valdivieso and Davis 1988). In fact, for Hispanics as a whole, the poverty rate increased by 33 percent between 1979 and 1985, whereas rates for non-Hispanic whites and African Americans actually declined during that period. The number of poor Hispanics rose from 2.9 million in 1979 to 5.5 million in 1987, an increase of 90 percent in less than a decade. Among subgroups, Puerto Ricans and Mexican Americans were the most likely to be in poverty (38 and 26 percent, respectively), whereas Cubans and Central and South Americans were the least likely (14 and 19 percent, respectively). More than double the proportion of Hispanic families were living in poverty in 1989 (23.4 percent) than non-Hispanic families (9.2 percent). Among single-parent households headed by a Hispanic female, nearly half (48 percent) were below the poverty line in 1989, identical to the proportion of African American families headed by a single woman in poverty (48 percent) in 1990 (U.S. Bureau of the Census 1990a; 1991). However, among subgroups, two thirds (64.4 percent) of Puerto Rican families maintained by a woman without a spouse present were in poverty in 1990. However, the rate of poverty among Hispanics actually decreased during the 1990s, mirroring the national trend for all groups except whites. In 1996, 30.3 percent of Hispanics were in poverty (U.S. Bureau of the Census 1998a). By 1999, 25.6 percent of the Hispanic population were in poverty (U.S. Bureau of the Census 2000c). Among subgroups, Puerto Rican and Mexicans experienced the highest levels of poverty, 30.9 and 27.1 percent respectively, whereas Cubans and Central and South Americans experienced the lowest (13.6 and 19.9 percent respectively). Moreover, by 1999, the percentage of single-parent households headed by females living below the poverty line had fallen to 43.7 percent (from 48 percent in 1989), compared with 29.9 percent of all female-headed households (U.S. Bureau of the Census 2000c).

The poverty of Hispanic children in particular is striking: 34.4 percent of Hispanic children lived in poor households in 1999. The comparable figure for non-Hispanic white children was 9.4 percent. Among subgoups, the highest rate of child poverty is found among children in Puerto Rican households, with 44 percent living in poverty. Among children of Mexican, Central and South American, and other Hispanic origin, the poverty rate was considerably less: for Mexicans it was 35 percent, for Central and South Americans, 27 percent, and for other Hispanics, 32 percent. With a child poverty rate of 16.4 percent, Cuban-origin households had the smallest proportion of children living in poverty in 1999 (U.S. Bureau of the Census 2000c). Although Hispanic children represented 16.2 percent of all children in 1999, they constituted 29 percent of all children in poverty (U.S. Bureau of the Census 2001).

High rates of unemployment and low family incomes have often encouraged the disadvantaged members of minority populations to compensate for their relatively inferior economic position by the incorporation of supplemental earners within the household (Angel and Tienda 1982; Bean and Tienda 1987; Stack 1974). This strategy is apparent among African Americans and Spanish-origin groups in the United States. As noted before, Hispanic households contain larger numbers of nonnuclear adult family members than non-Hispanic white households, and more actual or potential contributors to household income. This finding may help to explain relative improvements in household incomes for some subgroups of the Hispanic population during the past two decades. Whereas only 15 percent of non-Hispanic white households contained three or more adults in 1980, more than a quarter of all Cuban, Mexican, and Central and South American households did. Moreover, as Bean and Tienda report, regardless of household or family type (for example, husband-wife, single-parent), the percentages of households containing three or more adults are greater among Hispanics than among non-Hispanic whites, and

> . . . to the extent that such adults provide supplemental source of income, it is interesting that Puerto Ricans and other Hispanics are the least likely of the various Spanish origin groups to contain three or more adults in households of any type. Whatever economic deficiencies might be incurred by the Puerto Rican population, they are less likely to be overcome through the presence of supplemental earners in the household. (Bean and Tienda 1987:195)

In their study of Hispanic and non-Hispanic households containing multiple adult earners, Angel and Tienda (1982) found that the contributions of nonnuclear family members were greatest in female-headed households. However, such contributions are rarely sufficient to raise the income of these households above the poverty level, although they are important in alleviating some of the hardships of poverty. Moreover, in the absence of such strategies to compensate for the inadequate earnings of household members, the degree of income inequality between Hispanics and non-Hispanic white households would be even greater (Baca Zinn and Eitzen 1990).

Table 1 presents a summary of descriptive statistics on the major Spanish-origin populations drawn from recent census data. These data highlight some of the disparities among Hispanic groups and between these subpopulations and the U.S. population as a whole.

As might be anticipated, given the diversity of the population involved, the Hispanic groups differ considerably in such demographic and socioeconomic characteristics as age, level of education, employment, and income. Overall, Puerto Ricans fare worse than the other Spanish-origin groups with respect to income, employment, poverty, and the proportion of households headed by women. Mexi-

TABLE 1. Selected Characteristics of Spanish-Origin Groups, 1998

VARIABLES	MEXICAN	PUERTO RICAN	CUBAN	CENTRAL/SOUTH AMERICAN	OTHER HISPANIC
Number (in millions)	19.8	3.1	1.3	4.4	2.0
Median age (years)	24.1	25.7	38.9	28.1	28.5
Percent high school graduates[a]	48.3	63.8	67.8	64.9	72.2
Percent with 4+ years of college[a]	7.5	11.9	22.2	17.4	16.0
Percent in labor force	68.8	60.0	61.3	72.9	65.3
Percent unemployed	7.3	8.3	6.0	6.1	7.8
Median family income	$27,088	$23,729	$37,537	$32,030	$30,130
Percent married-couple families	72.1	53.9	80.8	67.6	59.8
Percent female-headed families	20.0	37.7	15.1	23.2	34.0
Percent of all families below the poverty level	25.8	31.5	15.6	18.4	25.0
Percent of female-headed families below poverty level	46.9	48.0	25.3	31.6	42.5

[a]*Persons 25 years of age or older.*
[b]*Persons 16 years of age or older.*
Source: U.S. Bureau of the Census 1999.

can Americans occupy an intermediate position, exhibiting higher levels of labor force participation, higher median income, and fewer families in poverty or headed by women compared with mainland Puerto Ricans. The socioeconomic situation of Cubans and Central and South Americans comes closest to, and in some cases exceeds, the averages for the U.S. population as a whole. Of all of the Spanish-origin groups, the Cubans and the Central and South Americans have the highest percentage of college graduates, the highest median fmaily income, the lowest unemployment levels, and the lowest incidence of poverty. Cubans also have the highest proportion of married-couple families, whereas Central and South Americans have the highest proportion of individuals in the labor force.

In accounting for differences between these groups in such characteristics as labor force participation, income, family structure, and poverty, researchers offer several explanations. Portes and Truelove (1987), for example, point to the distinct "mode of incorporation" of Mexican, Puerto Rican, and Cuban populations as a major source of the current economic and social condition of these groups. "Mode of incorporation" refers both to the average individual characteristics of each of these groups and to the social and economic context in which its successive cohorts are received. Although Mexican and Puerto Rican communities were created under different circumstances in the United States, as Portes and Truelove show, certain similarities between them are important to understanding the contemporary socioeconomic position of the two groups. For instance, because of their low average levels of education and modest socioeconomic origins, Mexican immigrants and new Mexican American entrants into the labor market are forced into a rural economy of the Southwest and Midwest, where Mexican laborers have traditionally supplied the bulk of unskilled, seasonal labor. Moreover,

> . . . social networks within the ethnic community tend to direct new workers toward jobs similar to their co-ethnics, a pattern reinforced by the orientation of employers. Lacking a coherent entrepreneurial community of their own or effective political representation, Mexican wage workers are thus thrown back into their own individual resources, "discounted" by past history and present discrimination against their group. Because many Mexican workers are immigrants and a substantial proportion are undocumented, they continue to be seen by many employers as a valuable source of low-wage pliable labor. This employer "preference," which may account for the relatively low average rates of Mexican unemployment, creates simultaneous barriers for those with upward mobility aspirations. (Portes and Truelove 1987:368)

Like the Mexicans in the Southwest, Puerto Ricans in the Northeast have fulfilled a similar function for industry and agriculture. However, they entered labor markets in the Northeast that were highly unionized, and this fact, together with the legal protection against the threat of deportation afforded them by virtue of their U.S. citizenship, "combined over time to make Puerto Rican workers a less pliable, more costly, and better organized source of labor" (Portes and Truelove 1987:368). Eventually employers shifted their preference toward other immigrant groups (for example, West Indians, Columbians, and Dominicans), especially undocumented workers.

Lacking an entrepreneurial community to generate their own jobs and shunted aside by new pools of "preferred" immigrant labor in the open market, Puerto Ricans on the mainland confronted a difficult economic situation. Record numbers have migrated back to the Island during the last two decades, while those remaining in the Northeast continue to experience levels of unemployment and poverty comparable only to those of the black population. (Portes and Truelove 1987:368)

In short, geographical and economic differences explain the divergent experiences of Puerto Ricans and Mexican Americans. The decline of the industrial sectors of the economy in the Northeast, together with the shift in the geographical location of jobs from the central cities to the suburbs, have left many Puerto Rican families living in a bleak ghetto economy, whereas Mexican Americans living in the Southwest, where many industries still depend upon cheap, unskilled labor, have not experienced the same degree of economic dislocation (Moore 1988). In fact, as Baca Zinn and Eitzen point out, the incidence of poverty and female-headed households among Hispanics is greatest in the Northeast, where the most significant declines in the economy have occurred:

High rates of structural unemployment have led to poverty and female headship rates among Puerto Ricans that are steadily converging with, and in some cases exceeding, the rates of Blacks. This supports the structural argument that societal conditions rather than deficient racial ethnic cultures create family forms associated with poverty. (Baca Zinn and Eitzen 1990:124)

The circumstances under which Hispanics of Cuban origin entered the United States were much more favorable. As Bean and Tienda (1987) point out, "Until the Cuban refugees arrived, no other immigrant group in this hemisphere has been so advantaged in terms of socioeconomic background and country acceptance (p. 29). The first refugees from Cuba in the late 1950s and early 1960s were members of Cuba's business and professional elite rather than laborers, who brought their entrepreneurial skills and other resources to start new enterprises in the United States after a brief period of adjustment (Portes and Truelove 1987). Unlike Mexican and Puerto Rican immigrants, Cuban refugees were the recipients of extensive aid and resettlement provisions, including "job training, professional re-certification, assistance in securing employment, reimbursement to public schools for costs incurred by the entrance of Spanish-speaking Cuban children, and funds for special research and teaching opportunities for Cuban scholars" (Bean and Tienda 1987:29). Although later waves of Cuban refugees were more diverse in education, skills, and socioeconomic background, the enthusiastic public response to the first immigrant cohorts created a more favorable context of reception for subsequent arrivals.

Moreover, the adaptation of successive waves of Cuban immigrants was greatly facilitated by the emergence of an ethnic enclave economy in South Florida, which provided jobs for the new arrivals and opportunities for self-employment and upward mobility (Wilson and Portes 1980). By the late 1970s, for example, nearly a third of all businesses in the Miami area were Cuban-owned, 75 percent of the workforce in construction was Cuban, and 40 percent of the industry was

Cuban-owned. Cuban-owned businesses have continued to grow since the 1970s, such that by 1984, "five of the ten largest Hispanic-owned firms in the country and four of the ten largest banks were part of the Cuban enclave, at a time when this group represented barely 5 percent of the Spanish-origin population" (Portes and Truelove 1987:370). By the late 1980s, "there were 61,000 Hispanic-owned firms in Miami with gross receipts of $3.8 billion, the largest by far of any city in the United States" (Portes and Stepick 1993:129). Thus, the more advantaged position of Cubans relative to other Hispanic groups can be accounted for in large measure by the more favorable circumstances under which they were incorporated and by the resources derived from their socioeconomic background (Gonzalez 2000).

The impact of recent structural changes in American society on familism, gender roles, and family structure among Hispanic subpopulations is not easy to assess, given the heterogeneity of the groups involved, the diversity of their economic and social condition, and the shortage of empirical research in these areas. However, on the basis of trends in marital instability and other indicators, it may be assumed that Hispanic households are being modified and family stability is being threatened by forces in American society "that are transforming its economy, redesigning and redistributing jobs, exacerbating inequality, and reorganizing cities and regions" (Eitzen and Baca Zinn 1989:2). Because of their more tenuous position in the economy and labor market, minority groups tend to be more severely affected by new technologies and industrial restructuring. According to Eitzen and Baca Zinn (1989:131–134), the effects of these changes are most evident in three areas: (1) the changing distribution and organization of jobs, and the tendency for newly created jobs to be low paying, (2) the trend toward women's rising rates of labor force participation, and (3) the trend toward poverty and unemployment. Each of these trends is related to industrial restructuring and has created problems for families.

As noted earlier, the effects of macrostructural shifts in the national economy on labor market opportunities of Hispanics have not been uniform but have affected subgroups in different ways. The shift in the geographical location of jobs from the traditional manufacturing cities of the Northeast to the Sunbelt regions of the South and Southwest has had the most serious impact on Puerto Rican families, increasing rates of poverty, welfare dependency, and unemployment to unprecedented levels. Although Spanish-origin groups in the Southwest, especially Mexicans, have benefited from such regional shifts in employment, "most of the newer Sunbelt industries offer either high paying jobs for which few Hispanics are trained or low paying ones that provide few opportunities for advancement" (Moore 1988:8). Hence, despite higher rates of labor force participation and employment, Mexican Americans are only slightly less likely to live in poverty than their Puerto Rican counterparts. On the other hand, because the majority of Cuban Americans work and live in an enclave economy, which generates many of their own jobs, recent shifts in the national economy appear to have had little impact on their employment structure.

However, as the process of industrial restructuring reorganizes work, women of all Hispanic subgroups are being drawn into the labor force (see Baca Zinn and Pok, this volume). Although women of Spanish origin have historically had relatively low rates of labor force participation, the percentage of Hispanic women employed outside the home has increased steadily over the past two decades (Population Reference Bureau 2000). In 1990, 53 percent of Mexican American women, and 57 percent of Cuban and other Hispanic women were in the civilian labor force, a percentage identical to that for the U.S. population as a whole. However, the percentage of Puerto Rican women in the labor force in 1990 (41.4 percent) remained virtually the same as it was in 1980 (40.1 percent), a finding that probably reflected declining employment opportunities in the Northeast during this period, where the majority of this group is concentrated. In 1998, 56 percent of Hispanic women 16 years of age and older were in the labor force, nearly the same as in 1990 (Joint Center for Political and Economic Studies 1999). Even so, for women of some Hispanic subgroups, "entering the labor force remains a culturally anomalous behavior, requiring constant negotiation, conflict, and justification" (Vega 1990:1020). As is the case among other groups, the employment of Hispanic women outside the home has begun to undermine the economic and cultural bases of male power in the family. But even as gender role expectations change and as more and more Hispanic couples adopt modern and egalitarian role relationships, they may still adhere to ethnic customs in other areas of family life (Baca Zinn 1980).

ASIAN AMERICAN FAMILIES: PATTERNS AND VARIATIONS

Like Hispanic Americans, the Asian American population includes a number of diverse groups who differ in language, culture, and recency of immigration. The 1990 census reported more than 30 subgroups of the Asian population, with the Chinese, Filipino, Japanese, Asian Indian, Korean, and Vietnamese representing 95 percent of the total (U.S. Bureau of the Census 1990b). Other Asian groups with sizable numbers included Laotian, Thai, Cambodian, Pakistani, and Indonesian. In 2000, the designation "Asian" included approximately 30 Asian and 25 Pacific Islander subgroups. With the passage of the Immigration Act of 1965, Asian immigration to the United States skyrocketed and increased the ranks of the Asian population from 1.4 million in 1970 to 5.1 million in 1985, representing 2.1 percent of the total U.S. population (U.S. Bureau of the Census 1990b). By 1990, the Asian population reached 7.2 million, or 3 percent of the total U.S. population, a 107 percent increase since 1980, making it the fastest-growing and third-largest minority group after African Americans and Hispanics (U.S. Bureau of the Census 1996). By 1999, there were 10.9 million Asian Americans in the U.S., accounting for 4 percent of the population (U.S. Bureau of the Census 2000d). The size of the Asian American population is expected to increase to 15.2 million, or 5 percent of the total U.S. population by 2010 (U.S. Bureau of the Census 2000b).

The rapid growth in the Asian population has been accompanied by equally dramatic changes in its composition. Japanese Americans, the largest of the Asian subgroups in the United States since the 1920s, fell to third place in 1990, with a share of 12 percent, surpassed by the Chinese at 24 percent and the Filipinos at 20 percent. Asian Indians and Koreans ranked fourth and fifth among Asian groups, with 11 and 10 percent shares of the population, respectively. The Vietnamese, among the latest wave of refugees from Indochina, with little representation in the United

States before the 1960s, was the sixth largest Asian subpopulation in 1990, accounting for approximately 8 percent of the population. However, the number of Vietnamese refugees to the United States increased by more than 150 percent between 1980 and 1985, from 245,000 to an estimated 634,200 (Gardner and others 1985).

Although Asian Americans are found in every region of the country and are more dispersed today than a decade ago (U.S. Commission on Civil Rights 1992), they remain more highly concentrated in the West, particularly in California and Hawaii, which together were the home of 71 percent of the Japanese, 63 percent of the Filipinos, and 47 percent of the Chinese population in 1980. California also ranked first in the number of Vietnamese (35 percent) and Koreans (29 percent). By contrast, the 1990 census found only 19 percent of all Asian Americans living in the Northeast, where 19 percent of Chinese, 35 percent of Asian Indians, and 23 percent of Koreans resided. A total of 16 percent of Asian Americans were found in the South (especially Texas, Louisiana, and Virginia), with the Vietnamese share (27 percent). By 1999, 17.6 percent of Asian Americans were found in the northeast, 9.5 percent in the Midwest, 19.8 percent in the South, and 53.1 percent in the West (U.S. Bureau of the Census 2000d).

Not only are Asian Americans more concentrated geographically than the general U.S. population, but they are also more urbanized. More than 90 percent of the six major subpopulations were living in large metropolitan areas in 1990, in contrast to 75 percent of the total population. In the Northeast and the West, the proportions were even higher, 96 and 93 percent, respectively. For the total population, the proportions were 85 percent in the Northeast and 84 percent in the West. And in 1994, 95 percent of these subgroups lived in metropolitan areas; 52 percent of both Asians and whites lived in suburbs of the large cities, but Asians were twice as likely to be in central cities than were whites (42 percent versus 23 percent) (U.S. Bureau of the Census 1998a). Recency of arrival is the major reason for the high concentration of Asian Americans in urban areas because immigrants have historically flocked to cities. With a longer period of residence, subsequent generations tend to be distributed more evenly.

As a group, Asian Americans vary widely in their characteristics, according to their cultural origins and the time when they arrived in the United States. Because the Japanese and Chinese have been coming to the United States for more than a century, these groups are more generationally diverse and less culturally distinct in some of their characteristics than Asian American groups who have entered the United States in more recent decades (Lieberson and Waters 1988). For example, only 32 percent of the Japanese population were foreign-born in 1990, in contrast to 64 percent of Filipinos, 76 percent of Asian Indians, 73 percent of Koreans, and more than 80 percent of the Vietnamese and other refugees from Southeast Asia. Overall, 38 percent of Asians in the six major groups counted in the 1990 census reported immigrating to the United States since 1980 (U.S. Bureau of the Census 1990b). The large proportion of recent immigrants among Asian Americans is shown to have important implications for family organization, community dynamics, and other social characteristics of Asian American populations (Wong 1986).

Table 2 presents some of the social and demographic characteristics of the major Asian American groups and the corresponding figures for the U.S. popula-

TABLE 2. Selected Characteristics of Asian American Population, 1990

VARIABLE	CHINESE	FILIPINO	JAPANESE	ASIAN INDIAN	KOREAN	VIETNAMESE	TOTAL (U.S.)
Number (in thousands)	1,648	1,419	847	815	798	614	248.7
Percent foreign born	69.3	64.4	32.4	75.5	72.7	79.9	8.0
Median age (years)	32.3	31.3	36.5	29.4	29.1	25.6	32.8
Median family income (1989)	$41,316	46,698	51,550	49,309	33,909	30,550	35,400
Percent of children under 18 living with two parents	87.6	80.9	86.1	91.8	89.0	76.6	72.5
Percent of female-headed households	9.4	15.1	14.4	4.4	11.2	15.9	12.0
Percent of all families below poverty level (1989)	11.1	5.2	3.4	7.2	14.7	23.8	12.0

Source: U.S. Bureau of the Census, 1990b.

275

tion. On the whole, Asian Americans are younger than the U.S. population, although the Japanese exceed the national median. Most striking is the low median age of the Vietnamese (25.6 years), which was lower than the median age of the black (27.7) and Hispanic (31.8) populations in 1990. The age structure of the Vietnamese population reflects the effects of recent immigration. Recent analyses have shown that the more recent the period of immigration, the greater the proportion of young immigrants (Gardner and others 1985; Wong 1986). In 1999, 29 percent of Asians and Pacific Islanders were under 18 years of age compared with 24 percent of the non-Hispanic white population in the United States, and only 7 percent were 65 years of age or older, compared with 14 percent of whites (U.S. Bureau of the Census 1999).

The implications of the low mean age of the Vietnamese population are summarized by Gardner and others (1985), who observe that "The large number of Vietnamese in or about to enter the prime childbearing ages of the twenties and early thirties portend a large number of Vietnamese births in the near future and a rapid increase in the number of Vietnamese Americans, especially since the birth rate of Vietnamese women is relatively high . . ." (p. 16). Likewise, the relatively low mean ages of the Korean and Filipino populations suggest that these groups will grow more rapidly in the near future than will the native-born Japanese and Chinese. Indeed, the high median age of the Japanese population (36.5 years) is likely to pose a problem for this group in the future because the Japanese are not immigrating to the United States in large numbers. As Gardner and others (1985:16) point out,

> When the relatively small number of Japanese Americans who were children and teenagers in 1980 grow older, they may have to support a much larger number of elderly Japanese who were aged 20–34 in 1980. This problem mirrors that of the total U.S. population when the baby-boom generation retires. Moreover, the relationships of native-born children and their elders are not always smooth because of the clash of cultures. Here the situation of Vietnamese is probably the extreme. There may be turbulent times ahead for the families of America's newest Asian arrivals.

Thirty-seven percent of adults aged 25 and older in the six major Asian American groups had completed 4 or more years of college in 1990, compared with 25 percent of white adults (U.S. Bureau of the Census 1992). By 1999, these percentages had increased to 42 percent and 28 percent, respectively (U.S. Bureau of the Census 1999). Equally impressive is the number of Asian Americans who are high school graduates. Overall, 81 percent of all Asian Americans aged 25 and older were high school graduates in 1990, compared with 79 percent of white adults. However, by 1999, a slightly smaller proportion of Asians and Pacific Islanders (85 percent) than of non-Hispanic whites (88 percent) had completed a high school education or more. The percentage of Asian American men who were high school graduates was even higher. Eighty-four percent of all Asian American men aged 25 and older in 1990 were high school graduates, in contrast to 79 percent of white men. Asian American women lagged behind Asian American men in high school completion (77 versus 84 percent) and behind white women (79 percent) as well.

However, 49 percent of all Asian American men and 40 percent of all Asian American women were college graduates in 1990, in contrast to 25 percent of white men and an equal percentage of white women (U.S. Bureau of the Census 1992). By 1999, the percentage of college graduates among Asian American men and women declined slightly to 46 percent and 39 percent, respectively (U.S. Bureau of the Census 1999).

Such high rates of school completion reflect in part the selectivity among recent Asian immigrants. That is, many young Asian adults who immigrated to the United States in recent decades were likely to have completed high school before they immigrated; others immigrated to the United States with additional education as an objective. For example, Gardner and others (1985) report that "all men and women aged 25–29 in 1980 who had migrated from the Philippines or Korea to the U.S. were much better educated than those in the same age group who remained behind—by a wide margin" (p. 25). They conclude that except for the more recent, less-educated refugees from Southeast Asia, the United States is receiving the best-educated people of the sending countries. Nonetheless, it should be noted that many impoverished Asian American families have members with less than a high school education. By 1999, the percentage of Asian with a sixth-grade education or less had fallen slightly to 5 percent (U.S. Bureau of the Census 2000b).

Labor force participation rates (i.e., the percentage of persons working or looking for work) among Asian Americans are associated with such factors as level of education, recency of arrival, and proficiency in English. In general, Asian American men and women had labor force participation rates as high as or higher than those of white men and women in 1990. However, among foreign-born Asian men, the employment situation was quite different. Although most foreign-born Asian men were employed at some point during 1989 (the year that these data were collected for the 1990 census), the proportion who worked full-time during the year ranged from 77 percent for Filipinos to 53 percent for men born in Japan. The comparable figure for white men was 77 percent. In addition, unemployment at some time during the year was relatively high among immigrant Asian men, ranging from 3 percent for men born in Japan to 12 percent for the Vietnamese, among the most recent arrivals in the United States. Although the labor force participation rate for white women was 57 percent in 1990, the rates for Asian American women were 73 percent for Filipino women, 59 percent for Chinese and Asian Indian women, and 56 percent for Japanese, Korean, and Vietnamese women. Even Asian women with children under 18 years of age have high rates of labor force participation. Only among women with little or no proficiency in English are rates of labor force participation low. The same pattern holds for Asian American men as well, although their rates were higher than those for women in all cases in 1990. In 1999, there was no statistical difference in the proportion participating in the civilian labor force for Asian and Pacific Islanders and non-Hispanic white men (74 percent) and women (60 percent). Similarly, there was no statistical difference in the proportion unemployed for Asian and Pacific Islanders and non-Hispanic white men (4 percent each) or in the proportion of women unemployed (4 percent and 3 percent, respectively) (U.S. Bureau of the Census 1999).

Partly as a result of their high level of education and high rates of labor force participation, Asian American families have incomes that exceed the median incomes of American families in general and white families in particular. The 1990 census reported a median family income[1] of $50,666 for the six Asian American groups who make up 95 percent of the Asian population, in contrast to a median income of $35,400 for all American families and $42,996 for white families (U.S. Bureau of the Census 1996). By 1999, these figures were $56,316 for the six Asian American groups, $48,950 for all American families, and $51,224 for white families (U. S. Bureau of the Census 1999). But these figures are misleading and mask significant differences within the Asian American population. For example, the median income of a Hmong American family in 1990 (the latest year for which data are available) was $14,276, compared with $51,550 for a Japanese family and $49,309 for Asian Indian families.

The income advantage of Asian American families can in part be accounted for by the greater number of workers per household. For example, whereas just under 60 percent of white families in 1990 contained two workers or more and 12 percent at least three, among Asian American families the comparable figures were 63 percent and 17 percent (U.S. Bureau of the Census 1992). A report by the U.S. Commission on Civil Rights (1988), using data from the 1980 census, found that the earnings of family members other than the husband made up a larger share of the total family income in Asian American families than in white families. For example, more than 30 percent of family income in native-born Chinese, Filipino, Japanese, and Korean families was generated by members other than the husband, compared with 25 percent among native-born white households. The proportions were even greater among foreign-born Asian American families, in which the combined labor income of wives, children, and other relatives accounted for 42 percent of Filipino family income, 37 percent of Vietnamese family income, 32 percent of Chinese family income, and 29 percent of Korean family income. The comparable figure for foreign-born white families was 23 percent. Next to husbands, wives were the largest contributors to Asian American family income, contributing between 9 and 34 percent of total family income. Except for the earnings of foreign-born Japanese wives, whose contribution to family income was only 9 percent, the earnings of women across all Asian American groups made up a larger share of family labor income than in white families, which amounted to 20 percent for native-born white families in 1980 and 17 percent for the foreign-born (U.S. Commission on Civil Rights 1988).

A common practice among Asian American families is to pool resources for housing, schooling, and a variety of other needs, particularly during the first years of settlement in the United States. This pattern is reflected in census data on household structure or living arrangements among recent Asian American immigrants, which show that the households of recent arrivals include a much larger proportion of nonnuclear family members than the households of white and native-born Asian Americans (Gardner and others 1985; Wong 1986). In addition to immigration history, childbearing behavior and cultural background are other important influences on household composition among Asian American groups. Some Asian countries (for example, Vietnam and the Philippines) have a traditional preference for large families; and this preference, as with other family values, is likely to be reflected in their household composition. Japanese Americans, among the oldest of the Asian groups, are shown in the 1990 census to have relatively small households, averaging 2.7 persons—identical in size to white households—and just 8 percent of all Japanese households were found to contain nonnuclear family members or persons unrelated to the family, slightly higher than the 6 percent for white households. Chinese and Asian Indian households were also small, averaging 3.1 and 2.9 persons, respectively, although Chinese American households contained a larger percentage (12 percent) of relatives and persons unrelated to the family. Household size among the remaining groups was larger, containing more children, relatives, and nonrelated persons per household. With an average of 4.4 persons, Vietnamese households were the largest and had the highest percentage of children (42 percent), other relatives (14 percent), and unrelated persons (6 percent) of any of the six major Asian American groups (Gardner and others 1985).

Marital stability and strong family ties are often cited as major underlying factors in the educational, occupational, and economic success of Asian Americans. According to historian David Bell (1985), family stability among Asian Americans "contributes to success in at least three ways. First, it provides a secure environment for children. Second, it pushes those children to do better than their parents . . . And, finally, it is a significant financial advantage (p. 30). In fact, recent studies have shown that, in contrast to U.S. families as a whole, Asian American families tend to be more stable, to have lower divorce rates, and to have fewer families with female heads (U.S. Bureau of the Census 1998; U.S. Commission on Civil Rights 1988).

The stability of Asian American families is reflected in the proportion of households headed by women and the proportion of children living with two parents. In 1990, the proportion of non-Hispanic white households headed by women was 13 percent, and 12 percent for the U.S. population as a whole. Among Asian American groups, the proportion of female-headed households ranged from a low of 4 percent among Asian Indians to 16 percent among the Vietnamese. The proportions of female-headed households among Japanese (14 percent), Chinese (9 percent), and Koreans (11 percent) were at or close to the proportion for white families, but in some cases exceeded the proportion for the U.S. population as a whole. The proportion of children under 18 living with both parents is also greater among Asian American groups than among whites. In 1990, 80 percent of non-Hispanic white children under 18 years of age lived with two parents. The comparable figures for Asian American groups were 92 percent for Asian Indians, 89 percent for Koreans, 88 percent for Chinese, 86 percent for Japanese, and 81 percent for Filipinos. Only among the Vietnamese was the proportion of children living with both parents (77 percent) below that of the white population in 1990. In 1998, 82 percent of Asian American households were married-family households, and 12 percent were female-headed families (U.S. Bureau of the Census 2000d).

However, when rates of family dissolution (that is, divorce and separation) among Asian American groups are considered, a somewhat more complex pattern emerges. Although family dissolution rates are generally lower among Asian

American groups than among non-Hispanic whites, divorce and separation rates among *native-born* Asian Americans differ little from the rates for native-born whites (U.S. Commission on Civil Rights 1988). Data from the 1980 census show that, among American-born women aged 25 to 64, family dissolution rates were higher for Filipino (16 percent), Korean (16 percent), and Asian Indian (14 percent) women than for white women (13 percent). Somewhat smaller proportions of Chinese women (12 percent) and Japanese women (9 percent) were divorced or separated than was the case for white women. However, among foreign-born groups, Asian women were less than half as likely to be divorced or separated as their American-born counterparts. For example, family dissolution rates among foreign-born Asian women aged 25 to 64 ranged from 3 percent for Asian Indian women to a high of 10 percent for Japanese women. Except for foreign-born Japanese women, divorce and separation rates were lower among all foreign-born Asian American groups than among whites (U.S. Commission on Civil Rights 1988). Data from the 1990 census on rates of family dissolution among Asian groups, both native and foreign-born, are generally consistent with patterns and trends observed among these groups a decade earlier, and show a downward trend in rates of divorce and separation for all groups (U.S. Bureau of the Census 1992).

The low rates of divorce and separation among Asian American groups may help to account for the relatively low proportion of such families with incomes below the poverty level reported by the 1990 census and more recent data (U.S. Bureau of the Census 2000a), because family breakups resulting in female-headed households are a major cause of poverty and lower family income. The percentage of non-Hispanic white families below the poverty level in 1990 was 9 percent, and 12 percent for the population as a whole. Among Asian groups, the percentage of families below the poverty level ranged from lows of 3 percent and 5 percent for Japanese and Filipinos, respectively, to a high of 24 percent for the Vietnamese, many of whom are recent arrivals with lower education and less proficiency in English than other recent immigrants. The percentage of Korean American families (15 percent) below the poverty level exceeded the percentage of white families with incomes below the poverty level, whereas Chinese families were close to the percentage for the population as a whole.

When only the foreign-born are considered, the percentage of Asian American families with incomes below the poverty level in 1989 was generally lower than the overall percentages for the six major Asian American groups, except for those families with household heads born in China. For example, the proportion of families headed by immigrants arriving from China (Taiwan and Hong Kong) during the period 1980 to 1990 who had incomes below the poverty level was 20 percent—more than twice the percentage of white families. For Vietnamese families who arrived during this period, the figure was 33 percent. As high as the proportion of Vietnamese families in poverty was in 1990, the 33 percent figure "considerably understates the economic and social problems that recent Indochinese refugees face (Gardner and others 1985:35). As Gardner and others observe, many of the recent immigrants from Southeast Asia "are less proficient in English, less educated, less experienced at holding jobs in urban occupations, and generally less familiar with

Western culture" (p. 35). Hence, taking recency of immigration into account helps to explain why foreign-born Asian families in some groups have higher poverty rates than white immigrant families.

As might be expected, given the overall low rate of poverty and high median family incomes, the proportion of Asian American households reporting income from public assistance (Aid to Families with Dependent Children, General Assistance, and other sources) is relatively low compared with other minority group populations and non-Hispanic whites. In their analysis of the extent of participation in welfare programs among Asian Americans, based on data from the 1980 census, Gardner and others (1985) found lower rates of participation in public assistance programs among Japanese (4 percent) and Asian Indian (5 percent) households than among non-Hispanic white households, where the percentage was 6 percent. The percentages of Korean and Chinese households receiving transfer payments were only slightly higher, 6 and 7 percent, respectively, whereas the proportion of Filipino households with income from public assistance (10 percent) was nearly double the percentage for whites. The proportion of Vietnamese households receiving assistance was 28 percent—more than four times the percentage for whites and higher than the proportion of African American (22 percent) and Hispanic (16 percent) households.

As in the case of census data on poverty, the data on public assistance understate the magnitude of welfare dependency among recent immigrants from Southeast Asia.[2] A 1982 survey in five areas across the United States of 1,384 Indochinese households whose members had arrived in the 4-year period 1978 to 1981 found that nearly all of Southeast Asian refugees begin life in the United States on welfare (Caplan and others 1985). Sixty-five percent of the households were receiving public assistance at the time of the survey in 1982, and the figure remained as high as 50 percent for families in the United States for 3 years or more. But the refugees of Southeast Asia are the extreme case among Asian American groups, whose recent arrival in such large numbers has created difficulties of adjustment not unlike those experienced by earlier European immigrants with similar background characteristics.

The speed with which some Asian Americans have surmounted barriers to raise their level of education and family income, their relative success as entrepreneurs, their strong family ties, and their low dependency on public assistance have led some analysts to refer to them collectively as a "model minority" (Kitano and Sue 1973; Petersen 1971) Enviable though it may seem, the "model minority" label is a stereotype of Asian Americans that masks great disparities between groups in terms of problems that they experience with respect to discrimination, underemployment, poverty, and social adjustment (Gardner and others 1985; U.S. Commission on Civil Rights 1988). These problems can be severe among some of the most recent arrivals from Asia, particularly Vietnamese refugees, as noted before. As Lee (1990) has pointed out, the stereotype of Asian Americans as uniformly successful "hurts those Asian Americans who need the most help, because the success of some is used as an excuse to deny benefits to all" (p. 13). Moreover, focusing on success stories and averages

. . . misses an equally striking case of Asian "over-representation" at the bottom of the bar-rel. Although Asian Americans are three to five times as likely as whites to be engineers and doctors, they are also two to four times as likely to work in food services or textiles. Many of the poorest Asian Americans are undocumented or paid under the table at sweat shops or restaurants . . . And offsetting their high educational attainment as a group is the fact that 6 percent of Asian Americans have not completed elementary school—three times the rate for whites. (Lee 1990:13)

In addition to obscuring significant differences within the Asian American pop-ulation, the model minority label implies an invidious comparison between Asian Americans and other minority groups that tends to exacerbate racial tensions and resentments. Such a comparison often ignores major differences in the structural conditions under which Asian Americans and other racial ethnic minorities (such as African Americans and Hispanics) have been incorporated into American soci-ety, as well as differences in background and other group characteristics that serve to facilitate or hinder group progress (Takaki 1987). Like their Cuban counter-parts, Japanese and Chinese immigrants have benefited from the existence of an enclave economy that serves to facilitate cultural adaptation and create opportuni-ties for employment and upward mobility (Jiobu 1988; Light 1972). Moreover, un-like the more recent immigrants from Southeast Asia, the 1965 to 1975 wave of Asian immigrants was largely made up of highly educated, financially solvent pro-fessionals, and these characteristics have been important contributors to overall improvements in the educational, occupational, and economic status of Asian Americans during the past two decades (U.S. Commission on Civil Rights 1988; Wong 1986).

Despite the image of Asian Americans as a monolithic minority group whose members are uniformly successful, the various subgroups of the Asian American population differ markedly in their demographic and socioeconomic characteris-tics and in their responses to the larger forces of social change in American society. Because of their longer tenure in the United States, Japanese and Chinese Ameri-cans have been subjected to greater changes, modifications, and adaptations in their family systems than have more recent immigrants. Although certain cultural styles of family behavior have been retained by Japanese and Chinese families, oc-cupational, housing, and social mobility, and increasing acculturation, especially by generation, have undermined the traditional foundation of family organization.

One of the most noteworthy changes in recent years has been the dramatic in-crease in the incidence of interracial marriages, particularly with whites, of the younger generation (Staples and Mirande 1980; Wong 1988). By some estimates, 60 percent of marriages among third-generation Japanese Americans and a third of Chinese and Korean marriages are interracial (Kitano and others 1984; Wong 1988). Intermarriage is regarded by many analysts as an index of the degree of social integration (or conversely, the degree of social distance) of racial ethnic populations, and high rates of intermarriage "reveal that intimate and profound relations between members of different groups and strata are more or less socially acceptable" (Blau and others 1984:591). In the case of Asian Americans, particu-larly Japanese, Chinese, Koreans, and Filipinos, the growing incidence of intermarriage also signals the loss of family control over marital choices, increasing opportunities for social mobility outside the Asian American community, and changing attitudes toward interracial unions on the part of Asian Americans and the larger society (Kitano and Yeung 1982; Wong 1988). For the Vietnamese and other recent immigrants from Southeast Asia, the incidence of intermarriage is negligible, in part because of the traditional stigma attached to out-marriages (Van Tran 1988) and because the majority have come to the United States as family groups whose family heads were already married upon arrival (Jiobu 1988).

Although increasing labor force participation among Asian American women has led to some modifications in the traditional marital-role differentiation in the family and more egalitarian decision-making (Hong 1982), Asian American families are still largely characterized "by a hierarchy of authority based on sex, age and generation, with young women at the lowest level, subordinate to father-husband-brother-son" (Chow 1987:286). About half of all Asian American women are foreign born (U.S. Bureau of the Census 1990b) and continue to adhere to many of the traditional family values and norms of their homelands. And although immigration to the United States has weakened the control of men over economic and social resources and enabled women to exert greater informal power in the family, "at the same time, the precarious economic environment has heightened the salience of the family system and constrained the possibilities for radical change in gender relations" (Kibria 1990:21). Given the relative social isolation and concentration of many foreign-born Asian Americans in ethnic enclaves (for example, "Little Tokyo," Chinatown, "Little Saigon") and the reinforcement of traditional family values through new immigration, changes in traditional patterns of family organization and gender relations are likely to be slow and uneven (Chow 1987).

On the other hand, as the proportion of Asian American families whose members are native-born continues to grow, the characteristics of Asian American households are more likely to resemble those of the white population; that is, the "average household size will decline, households will contain fewer children and fewer relatives beyond the immediate family should be needed to make ends meet" (Gardner and others 1985:38). In short, Asian American families, like families in general, will continue to change, adapt, and reorganize according to the ebbs and flows of societal forces and the constraints and expansion of opportunities in American society (Wong 1988).

NATIVE AMERICAN FAMILIES: PATTERNS OF ADAPTATION AND CHANGE

The situation of Native Americans, or "American Indians," is unique among the various racial ethnic minorities in the United States because of a history that predates the arrival of the first European immigrants during the late fifteenth century and because of their special status for a time as "wards" of the state. For generations, the term *American Indian* was a pejorative category that pooled together under a single label tribes or ethnic groups with a diversity of lifestyles, languages, religions, kinship systems, and political organizations. It has been estimated that at the time of contact with European immigrants, between 2 and 18 million Native Americans lived north of Mexico, speaking as many as 300 different languages, and representing hundreds of cultures (Denevan 1976). By 1800, however, the Native American population had declined to about 500,000, and by the end of the nineteenth century, it had been reduced to approximately 250,000 (Driver 1969).

Since the 1950s, the Native American population has grown significantly, although the precise numbers are difficult to determine because of shifts in racial identification. Between 1950 and 1970, the Native American population increased by more than 100 percent, from 357,499 to 792,730; and from 1970 to 1980, it increased by 72 percent to 1.4 million (U.S. Bureau of the Census 1980). By 1990, the American Indian population had grown to 2.1 million and by 1998, to 2.4 million and nearly 1 percent of the U.S. population (U.S. Bureau of the Census 2000e). These increases reflect, in part, higher fertility rates among Native American women and greater efforts to count accurately the American Indian population (Lieberson and Waters 1988). They also reflect changes in census enumeration procedures in 1980 that allowed for self-identification by race and by ancestry. Whereas 1.4 million people identified themselves as Native American by race in 1980, an additional 6.7 million people claimed some American Indian ancestry but functioned in society as white. Excluding this latter category, the American Indian population is the third-fastest-growing and youngest subpopulation (median age of 27.8 years in 2000) in the United States (U.S. Bureau of the Census 2000b).

The Bureau of Indian Affairs recognizes more than 450 tribal groups in the United States (Bureau of Indian Affairs 1976). However, 10 of these tribal groups constitute 57 percent of the American Indian population, with Cherokee being the largest, with 16.4 percent, and Navajo being second, with 11.7 percent (U.S. Bureau of the Census 2000e). Although small populations of Native Americans can be found in nearly every state from coast to coast, a substantial number of the 2.4 Native Americans in the 2000 Census lived on or near the 317 reservations and other locations maintained in federal trusteeship for Indians, Aleuts, and Eskimos (Aguirre and Turner 1995; U.S. Bureau of the Census 2000e). The largest of the reservations are found in the western part of the United States. In fact, nearly half of all Native Americans live west of the Mississippi River, with four states—Arizona, California, Oklahoma, and New Mexico—each having more than 100,000 Native American residents, which together account for 70 percent of the total (U.S. Bureau of the Census 2000d).

Although Native Americans remain the most rural of racial ethnic populations in the United States, an increasing number have moved to urban areas in recent decades. More than 600,000 Native Americans were located in central cities in 1980. By 1990, over half of American Indians resided in urban areas (Snipp 1997). Unlike other groups, there are few cities where there are a large concentration of Native Americans. Flagstaff, Arizona, where 28.4 percent of the population is American Indian, and Knoxville, Tennessee, where they constitute 6 percent of the population, are exceptions (U.S. Bureau of the Census 2000e). In 1997, the largest concentrations of American Indians were found in Los Angeles (113,000), Phoenix (67,000), the New York City/New Jersey area (62,000), and Tulsa

(51,000). Other urban areas with significant Native American populations are San Francisco, Oklahoma City, Seattle, Albuquerque, and the Dallas–Ft. Worth area (U.S. Bureau of the Census 2000b). Although large cities tend to attract Native Americans from a variety of tribes and reservation communities throughout the country, Native American populations in smaller or medium-sized cities tend to be more homogeneous in cultural background and are more likely to be found in ethnic enclaves (Spicer 1980). In general, however, the distinctive geographical distribution of American Indian populations reflects the resettlement patterns associated with the establishment of federal reservations and the efforts of Native Americans to escape the encroachment of white American society (Lieberson and Waters 1988).

Historically, the primary sources of Native American identity have been "the family, the kindred or descent group, and the locality of their birth" (Jarvenpa 1988:34). Thus, the externally imposed category of "Indian" as a collective identity for Native Americans was largely irrelevant to individuals who lived their lives as Navajo, Cherokee, Choctaw, or Sioux. Although the common experience of the reservation system, beginning during the 1800s, helped to crystallize a feeling of shared oppression and fate among the diverse groups of Native Americans who were collectively treated as "Indians," only recently has the beginning of a collective Indian identity, referred to as "pan-Indianism," emerged as a unified response to the pressures of acculturation and assimilation (Jarvenpa 1988; Lurie 1971). Although pan-Indianism as a social movement remains segmented and decentralized, it has the potential to transform "diverse tribal societies into an *ethnic group* by mobilizing a shared history" (Jarvenpa 1988:42) Despite considerable cultural differences and factionalism among tribal troops, "the notion of a shared past of intense suffering and broken agreements becomes a quasi-mythic structure that defines important cultural elements in pan-Indian identity" (Jarvenpa 1988:42).

Despite increased exposure to the assimilating forces of the larger society, distinctive family patterns persist among Native Americans. According to Driver (1969), nearly all of the principal variants of marriage and family practices can be found among Native American groups, including arranged marriages and betrothal; bride price and dowry; adoptive and interfamily exchange marriages; trial marriages; monogamy, polygamy, and temporary polyandry; patriarchy and matriarchy; premarital and extramarital sexual relations; divorce; and patrilocal, matrilocal, and bilocal residence patterns (John 1988). Although the range and diversity of Native American family patterns have been reduced by increased rates of urban residence, education, and interracial marriage, continuing high levels of spatial segregation and longstanding cultural differences from American society have enabled Native Americans to retain a high degree of cultural distinctiveness in their family practices from the American cultural mainstream (Jarvenpa 1988; John 1988; Red Horse 1980).

Despite tribal differences as well as urban versus rural residential distinctions, "the extended family network" is said to be a universal cultural feature among Native Americans, regardless of family lifestyle patterns (Red Horse and others 1978). According to Red Horse and others, these family networks are structurally open and include several households of significant relatives and sometimes nonkin as extended family members, who engage in obligatory mutual aid and actively participate in life-cycle events. This characterization of Native American households, however, has been challenged. For example, John (1988) contends that although the extended family was a fair description of Native American households in the past, it is far less characteristic of contemporary groups: "Although extended families remain the cultural ideal among Native Americans, in reality, extended families are not universal, and within families that exhibit extended family characteristics, there are prodigal sons and daughters who have moved outside the sphere of routine, extended family operations" (p. 357). According to John, the claim that extended families are the norm among Native Americans is largely derived from anthropological studies published during the post–World War II period that have continued to influence contemporary descriptions of Native American family life. Moreover, John concludes, even recent studies are limited and "do little to clarify precisely what is occurring within Native American families as a whole" (p. 328).

Although John and other analysts (for example, Manson and Pambrun 1979) concede that Native American families are more firmly based on interdependence than white American families, and that the *modified extended family* form best characterizes the family life of many Native American households, they contend that increasing urbanization and acculturation of young Native Americans have weakened the integrity of the family and familial support networks (Metcalf 1979). In fact, the disruption of the family network system occasioned by the process of urbanization is seen as an important source of family problems among Native Americans in central cities. For example, from her study of Native American families in the San Francisco Bay area, Miller (1979) concluded that the absence of the extended family system created significant emotional problems for family members. She writes,

> Adjustment from the complexity and interdependency of the extended family life on or near the reservation to the constriction of an isolated nuclear, or conjugal, family life in a city is possibly the most difficult adjustment the recently urbanized Native American must make. (p. 458)

Child abuse and neglect (Metcalf 1979), premarital pregnancies among Native American teenagers (Red Horse 1982), and high rates of suicide and other psychological disturbances (Bynum 1972; Westermeyer 1977) have also been associated with the disruption of the familial support network among Native American families in urban areas (see also Guillemin 1975), as has drug and alcohol abuse.

Declines in extended family structures among Native Americans have paralleled declines in marital stability and the rise in the incidence of Native American households headed by females in recent decades (Snipp 1989). The proportion of American Indian women separated or divorced from their spouse increased from 11 percent in 1970 to 14 percent in 1980, higher than the rate for white women (9 percent) in 1980 but lower than the percentage of black women (18 percent in 1980) who were separated or divorced (Snipp 1989; U.S. Bureau of the Census 1973; 1993). The rate was even higher among Native American women in metropolitan and nonreservation areas, where 16 percent were divorced or separated in 1980.

Trends in divorce and separation among Native Americans are reflected in the growing incidence of female-headed households. The 1980 census reported a 28 percent increase in the incidence of American Indian families maintained by women between 1970 and 1980, from 18 percent to 23 percent of all Native American families (U.S. Bureau of the Census 1984). However, the incidence of female-headed households increased by only 13 percent between 1980 and 1990, from 23 percent to 26 percent. Although an increase in female-headed families also occurred among white women, the percentage for Native American women was twice as large. Moreover, as Snipp (1989:171) has observed,

> . . . single female householders in the American Indian population represent a highly disadvantaged group within an already disadvantaged minority. These women are the most likely to be high school dropouts and the least likely to have completed high school and/or attended college. They are most likely to be out of the labor force, and if they are working it is most likely in clerical and technical jobs or service work. In view of their concentration in low-paying occupations and marginal attachment to the labor force, it is hardly surprising that American Indian women who are single householders have lower family and household incomes, more poverty and more dependence on public assistance than any other Indian household type.

Thus, more than half of single female householders among American Indians had less than a high school education in 1990, and 43 percent were not in the labor force (Sandefur and Liebler 1997).

The limited education and marginal attachment to the labor force among single-parent families headed by an American Indian woman are reflected in their relatively low median income, poverty rate, and dependency on public assistance. For instance, the median income of married-couple Native American families was more than double the income of female-headed families in 1980 ($17,870 versus $7,710). The differences between these households are equally striking for the incidence of poverty; 47 percent of households with female heads had incomes below the poverty threshold in 1979, in contrast to only 17 percent of married-couple households (Snipp 1989). The poverty rate for female-headed households on American Indian reservations is considerably higher—57 percent in 1980 (U.S. Bureau of the Census 1986). As a consequence, 34 percent of female-headed households received public assistance income in 1979, in contrast to only 6 percent of married-couple families (Snipp 1989). Such economic hardship is particularly alarming when it is considered that 72 percent of female-headed households among Native Americans contain children under 18 years of age.

The increase in female-headed families among Native Americans has been at the expense of other family forms. Although married-couple families are still the most common type of household arrangement among American Indians, the proportion of such households decreased from 77 percent in 1970 to 71 percent in 1980. In 1990, about 6 in 10 of American Indian families were married-couple families, compared with about 8 in 10 of all families (U.S. Bureau of the Census 1990b). However, the decline in married-couple households is consistent with marital trends among other racial ethnic groups and the population as a whole.

The high incidence of intermarriage has also changed the institutional context of Native American family life. Whereas only 1 percent of marriages in the United States are between couples from different racial groups (Lieberson and Waters 1988), a study of interracial marriages among six racial groups found that Native Americans were the least likely to practice racial endogamy (Clayton 1978). In 1970, about 60 percent of American Indian men and women were married to other Indians, and the remainder were married to persons of a different race. However, by 1980, interracial unions had increased by nearly 20 percent, to about 53 percent (Snipp 1989). By contrast, marital endogamy was 98 percent among whites and 99 percent among African Americans in 1980 (Lieberson and Waters 1988). Between 1970 and 1990, less than half of American Indian men and women married other American Indians. Among American Indian males, only 41 percent married Indian women; among American Indian women, the figure was 40 percent (Sandefur and Liebler 1997). A number of explanations for the extraordinarily high incidence of interracial marriage among Native Americans have been suggested: increased frequency of contact with other ethnic groups as a result of migration to urban areas; higher educational status and new occupational opportunities; and an increased desire for and perception of the possibility of assimilation (Snipp 1989; Wilkinson 1987). No doubt a major reason for the high rate of interracial marriage is the increased social acceptability, especially among whites, of Native Americans as potential marriage partners. The issue is not without controversy within many quarters of the Native American community and raises the question, "Are American Indians assimilating so quickly through racial intermarriage that they will eventually, in the not too distant future, marry themselves out of existence?" (Snipp 1989:165).

Although interest in the multiple roles of American Indian women as wives, mothers, and workers has grown in recent years (Green 1975; Williams 1980), relatively little is known about husband-wife interactions or gender-role behaviors among Native Americans. Among many American Indian tribes, the descent of children and the ownership of property are traced through the mother's lines (Wilkinson 1987). To the extent that rules of matrilocal residence are observed, American Indian women are granted positions of authority and independence in family matters. The relative positions of the husband and wife under a matrilineal familial system are described by Queen and others (1985) for Hopi Indians but are common among other Native American groups as well:

> The husband is a guest in his wife's household, his closest connections being with his mother's household. The wife, however, remains in the house in which she was reared and in the event of a family quarrel is backed by a solid wall of kin. Perhaps as a result of this difference in position, the Hopi husband often acts toward his wife with seeming formality, if not brusqueness. In general, however, the bond between husband and wife is variable and depends largely on the character of the individuals concerned. (p. 39)

According to Queen and others (1985:49), "loose marriage ties" is a longstanding trait of Hopi Indians, resulting in part from "the lack of authority of the husband in the matrilineal family."

John (1988) contends that the traditionally rigid gender roles that have long characterized Native American cultures are being modified by younger American Indians toward the androgynous norms of the larger society but notes the continuing disagreement among scholars over whether the roles of men or women have changed the most. For example, some observers of the Navajo (such as Christopherson 1981), the largest of Native American tribes, contend that the gender roles of men have changed more than the roles of women because the latter continue "to exercise economic power in subsistence residential units that have been the basis of the Navajo tribal economy for over a century" (John 1988:351) Other scholars (Blanchard 1975) emphasize the greater role change for women, who are forced to compensate for the loss of prestige and influence that has accompanied economic changes in Native American communities. On the basis of his own research, John (1988) concludes that changes in gender roles, on balance, have been greater for men.

The status of American Indian families remains in a state of transition, as pressures continue to increase to modify various family practices toward the normative patterns of the American mainstream. The desire for a better life has attracted more and more Native Americans to urban centers in recent decades, increasing contacts between them and mainstream institutions, hastening the process of assimilation, and undermining their ability to preserve many of the distinctive features of Native American family life. In fact, as Snipp (1989:316) observes, "rural-urban migration and residence are closely linked to significant social and economic divisions within the Indian population." He notes that although Native Americans living on rural reservations and in cities experienced significant improvements in their standard of living during the past two decades, largely as a result of federal programs that increased the education and employability of some American Indians, rural Indians remain poorer and less educated than their urban counterparts, "creating yet another division within the American Indian population based on social class" (Snipp 1989:318). Such economic divisions may be expected to grow as Native Americans in urban areas take advantage of opportunities and the economic growth in America's cities, thereby generating other differences between rural and urban Indians (Snipp and Sandefur 1988).

Moreover, continuing high rates of intermarriage are creating another dimension of diversity within the Native American population—two relatively distinct populations of individuals with Native American backgrounds. According to Snipp (1989:310), one group

> . . . is a core population of individuals strongly connected to their American Indian heritage. In terms of their residence, lifestyle, socioeconomic characteristics, and even appearance, this group constitutes a population easily identifiable as American Indian. Members of this group are most likely to speak a native language, live on a reservation, have knowledge of their traditional culture, and participate in a community that identifies itself as American Indian . . . A second population consists of persons who can recall,

legitimately, some amount of Indian ancestry but have little knowledge of Indian culture and in most respects do not resemble the core population of American Indians.

As the 1990 census indicates, the second population is already larger than the first and is likely to continue to grow as increasing numbers of American Indians who marry non-Indians enter the mainstream of American culture and abandon their cultural heritage. These developments are likely to complicate further the ambiguity over who is and who is not an American Indian, both for purposes of official enumeration and for ethnic identification.

For now, however, the identity of most Native Americans is still "firmly anchored in a combination of distinctive cultural traditions, racial characteristics and social structural relations, including membership in legally defined tribal groups" (Jarvenpa 1988:39) and is likely to remain so for some time to come. In order to survive the destructive contact with Anglo-European cultures and various forms of economic hardship and deprivation, Native American families have had to be flexible, pluralistic, and adaptive. These same qualities will likely prove critical in preserving what remains of their cultural heritage and unique family practices in the future.

CONCLUDING REMARKS

It is apparent from the preceding discussion that minority families in the United States differ widely in structure, size, composition, patterns of residence, socioeconomic characteristics, bonds of kinship, and relationship to the network of institutions of the larger society. Yet it is essential to stress that despite differences in form and functioning, families remain the central types of social organization for African Americans, Hispanic Americans, Asian Americans, and American Indians (Wilkinson 1987). Differences among these groups in family practices and living arrangements are the result not only of "unique demographic and ancestral backgrounds, cultural histories, ecological processes, and economic origins and statuses" (Wilkinson 1987:204) but of historical and contemporary social, political, and economic forces of the larger society (Baca Zinn and Eitzen 1990).

"Diversity" is the word for the future of families in the United States (Cherlin and Furstenberg 1983). Such diversity will be reflected not only in the range of alternative family structures (such as single-parent households, nonmarital cohabitation, commuter marriages, and gay and lesbian households) but in the racial ethnic composition of the United States. Current trends in immigration and birth rates are altering the distribution of whites and minority populations in the United States. As Baca Zinn (1990) points out, "In many cities and communities, Blacks, Hispanics, Asians, and Native Americans outnumber the white population. Their families are distinctive not only because of their ethnic heritage but because they reside in a society where racial stratification continues to shape family resources and structures in important ways" (p. 69). By some estimates (Henry 1990), over the next quarter of a century, the number of U.S. residents who are nonwhite or Hispanic will more than double, to more than 115 million, while the white population will increase hardly at all. It is projected that between 2000 and 2010, the Hispanic population will grow by 31 percent, the Asian population by 36 percent, the black (non-Hispanic) population by 12 percent, and the white (non-Hispanic) population by 3 percent. By the period 2030 to 2040, the white population is expected to have a negative growth rate (−0.2 percent), with the Hispanic population continuing to grow at a rate of about 20 percent (U.S. Bureau of the Census 2000e). According to Schwartz and Exter (1989), 38 percent of Americans under the age of 18 will be African American, Hispanic, or Asian, or belong to other minority groups by the year 2010. By the year 2035, over half (51 percent) of all children under the age of 18 will be either Asian, Hispanic, African American, or American Indian (O'Hare 1992). In the largest states—California, New York, Texas, and Florida—minority children will be the majority by the end of the first decade of twenty-first century. As Schwartz and Exter put it, "Our children may show us the future even before they become adults" (p. 37)

Up until a generation ago, the overwhelming majority of this nation's racial and ethnic majorities were African American. Although still the largest of these groups, African Americans now represent less than half of all minorities, and their share is declining (O'Hare 1992). The Asian and Hispanic populations (the "new minorities," as these groups are sometimes called) are growing at a much greater rate than African Americans and American Indians. The number of persons of "mixed race" is also increasing, contributing to the shift in the racial and ethnic composition of the U.S. minority population. In addition to higher levels of immigration from Asia and Latin American countries, higher fertility among minority populations contributed to the rapid growth in their numbers during the past decade. Although minority populations made up only 28 percent of the total population in 1997, they accounted for 40 percent of the 3.9 million births in the United States that year (Population Reference Bureau 1999). The differences in fertility rates between minorities and non-Hispanic whites are in part accounted for by the larger proportion of minority women in their childbearing ages, but many of the differences are due to the fact that minority women have more children than white women.

The varied patterns of immigration and rates of fertility among racial ethnic minorities in the United States over the past several decades have significantly shaped their age and sex profiles. For example,

[t]he ratio of men to women among Hispanics is unusually high . . . reflecting an immigration stream dominated by men whose economic circumstances cause them to leave their families behind. In contrast, African Americans have a slightly lower ratio of men to women, most noticeably among young adults, which is thought to reflect both the undercount of African-American men in large cities and the relatively high mortality among young black men. (O'Hare 1992:17)

On the whole, minority populations are younger than the non-Hispanic white population and as a result have proportionately more women of childbearing age than does the white population. O'Hare (1992) concludes that even if the United States "accepted no more immigrants before the middle of the next century, the higher fertility rates among minorities, combined with their younger age structure, would still increase the share of the minority population from 25 percent in 1990 to 38 percent in 2050" (p. 18). Hence, a young age structure, high fertility rates, and large immigration flows of minorities will continue to make the U.S. population more racially and ethnically diverse in the future, with implications for public schools, the workforce, and family patterns.

In addition to age, immigration, and fertility as sources of the growing racial and ethnic diversity of the population, Americans of mixed-race parentage are also contributing to this diversity. In 1991, mixed-race marriages, that is, those involving partners who are married to someone outside their own race, accounted for about 2 percent of the 53 million married couples in the United States (O'Hare 1992). However, this small percentage masks the dramatic growth in the number of interracial marriages during the past quarter century. Between 1970 and 1998, for example, the number of interracial couples rose from 300,000 to 1.4 million. The number of Hispanics married to non-Hispanics rose from 600,000 to 1.7 million. By 1998, about 5 percent of U.S. married couples included spouses of different races, or a Hispanic married to a non-Hispanic (Population Reference Bureau 1999). Marriages involving black and white partners accounted for about 7 percent of all interracial unions in 1991, whereas 25 percent of those of other races (largely Asian Americans) were married to someone outside their own race. The percentage of interracial marriages involving black and white partners increased to 9 by 1998. According to O'Hare (1992), the "high intermarriage rates of Hispanics and Asians, coupled with their growing numbers, has led to a baby boom of mixed-race children" (p. 14). By some estimates, roughly 2 million children are currently growing up in multiracial households (Edmonston, Goldstein, and Lott 1996), and the absolute number of children with such mixed background is likely to increase in the years ahead. In fact, an estimated 118,000 babies were born to parents of different races in 1989—nearly four times the number reported two decades earlier. The number increased to 159,000 in 1997, accounting for about 5 percent of births.

As the number of multiracial children has grown, so has the pressure for the introduction of a multiracial category to the U.S. census schedule that validates the existence of these children and their families (Root 1992). Under great pressure from advocacy groups, the federal government added the option of choosing more than one race on the 2000 census form, offering 126 categories and combinations. However, the government rejected the proposal to add a new "multiracial" category. Pressure to add the new category will undoubtedly continue, and it is likely that current "racial" categories will give way to new measures and definitions of race which include recognition of those persons who define themselves as multiracial (Taylor 1997).

Likewise, the growth and adaptation of second-generation children of the post-1965 immigration era is also emerging as an area of interest and research among students of American families, since it is among the second generation where such issues as the growth or decline of racial ethnic intermarriage, the resilience of traditional family forms and values, among other familial issues, will be permanently decided (Portes 1996). Moreover, as Portes observes, study of the second generation is the key to establishing the long-term consequences of immigration, but the course of its adaptation is uncertain at present . . . [the] puzzle is whether today's children of immigrants will follow their European predecessors and move steadily into the middle-class mainstream or whether, on the contrary, their ascent will be blocked and they will join children of earlier black and Puerto Rican migrants as part of an expanded multiethnic underclass. As the deteriorating conditions of life in American cities suggest, the question is of more than passing significance for the future of American society. (p. 634)

These changes in the racial ethnic composition of American society are changing the way scholars think about families and their relationship to wider social forces. In fact, recent years have seen revisions in scholarship on American families in general and racial ethnic families in particular. Both feminist scholarship and revisions in scholarship on minority families have produced alternative perspectives, approaches, and explanations of the nature of family life in America. For their part,

> . . . feminists have challenged the monolithic ideology of the family that elevated the contemporary nuclear family with a breadwinner husband and a full-time homemaker wife as the only legitimate family form. We now give equal weight to the varied family structures and experiences that are produced by the organization of the economy, the state, and other institutions. (Baca Zinn 1990:70)

Similarly, revisionist scholarship on racial ethnic families has challenged the tendency to interpret differences in family patterns of these groups as deficits, arguing instead that alternative family patterns are associated with but not responsible for the status of these families in American society: "Revisionist approaches have emphasized the structural conditions giving rise to varied family forms, rather than the other way around. Differences in family patterns have been reinterpreted as adaptations to the conditions of racial inequality and poverty, often as sources of survival and strength" (Baca Zinn 1990:71–72).

However, these two streams of revisionist family scholarship have yet to be integrated in a manner that enhances understanding of race and gender as "interacting hierarchies of resources and rewards that condition material and subjective experiences within families" (Baca Zinn 1990:73). The synthesis of these two streams of research remains a challenge but a necessary first step in the development of theories of American family life that inform our perceptions of family diversity.

ENDNOTES

1. Family income is the sum of earnings from all family members; this includes the earnings of the husband, wife, all children living with the family, and all relatives living with the family who are related by birth or marriage.
2. Because the census data on income from public assistance are derived from self-reports and some Asian Americans are reluctant to admit to dependence on welfare, the "true" rate of welfare dependency for the various Asian groups is likely to be higher than the census data reflect. On this point, see Gardner and others (1985).

REFERENCES

Aguirre, Adalberto, and Jonathan Turner. 1995. *American Ethnicity.* New York: McGraw Hill.

Angel, Ronald, and Marta Tienda. 1982. "Determinants of Extended Household Structure: Cultural Pattern or Economic Need?" *American Journal of Sociology* 87:1360–1383.

Auletta, Ken. 1982. *The Underclass.* New York: Random House.

Baca Zinn, Maxine. 1980. "Employment and Education of Mexican American Women: The Interplay of Modernity and Ethnicity in Eight Families." *Harvard Educational Review* 50:47–62.

———. 1982–83. "Familism among Chicanos: A Theoretical Review." *Humbolt Journal of Social Relations* 10:224–238.

———. 1990. "Family, Feminism, and Race in America." *Gender and Society* 4 (March):68–82.

Baca Zinn, Maxine, and Stanley Eitzen. 1990. *Diversity in Families,* 2nd ed. New York: Harper and Row.

Bean, Frank D., Russell L. Curtis, and John P. Marcum. 1977. "Familism and Marital Satisfaction among Mexican Americans: The Effects of Family Size, Wife's Labor Force Participation, and Conjugal Power." *Journal of Marriage and the Family* 39:759–767.

Bean, Frank D., and Marta Tienda. 1987. *The Hispanic Population of the United States.* New York: Russell Sage Foundation.

Becerra, Rosina M. 1988. "The Mexican American Family." In *Ethnic Families in America,* 3rd ed., edited by C. Mindel, R. W. Habenstein, and R. Wright, Jr., 141–159. New York: Elsevier.

Bell, David A. 1985. "The Triumph of Asian-Americans." *The New Republic* (July 15):30.

Bianchi, Suzanne M., and Daphne Spain. 1984. *American Women: Three Decades of Change.* Special Demographic Analysis CDS-80-8. Washington, DC: U.S. Government Printing Office.

Blanchard, Kendall. 1975. "Changing Sex Roles and Protestantism among the Navajo Women in Ramah." *Journal for the Scientific Study of Religion* 14:43–50.

Blau, Peter, Carolyn Beeker, and Kevin M. Fitzpatrick. 1984. "Intersecting Social Affiliations and Intermarriage." *Social Forces* 62 (March):585–605.

Bohon, Stephanis. 2001. *Latinos in Ethnic Enclaves.* New York: Routledge.

Borjas, George. 1998. *Heaven's Door: Immigration Policy and the American Economy.* Princeton, NJ: Princeton University Press.

Bureau of Indian Affairs. 1976. "You Asked about . . . Facts about American Indians and Alaskan Natives." Washington, DC: U.S. Government Printing Office.

Bynum, Jack. 1972. "Suicide and the American Indian: An Analysis of Recent Trends." In *Native Americans Today: Sociological Perspectives,* edited by H. M. Bahr, B. A. Chadwick, and R. C. Day, 375. New York: Harper and Row.

Caplan, Nathan, John K. Whitmore, and Quang L. Bui. 1985. *Southeast Asian Refugee Self-Sufficiency Study: Final Report.* Department of Health and Human Services. Ann Arbor: Institute for Social Research, University of Michigan.

Cherlin, Andrew J., and Frank F. Furstenberg, Jr. 1983. "The American Family in the Year 2000." *The Futurist* 17 (June):7–14.

Chow, Esther Ngan-Ling. 1987. "The Development of Feminist Consciousness among Asian American Women." *Gender and Society* 1 (Sept.):284–299.

Christopherson, Victor A. 1981. "The Rural Navajo Family." In *The Family in Rural Society,* edited by R. T. Coward and W. M. Smith, Jr., 105–111. Boulder, CO: Westview Press.

Clayton, Richard R. 1978. *The Family, Marriage, and Social Change,* 2nd ed. Lexington, MA: D.C. Health.

Denevan, William M. (ed.). 1976. *The Native Population of the Americas in 1492.* Madison: University of Wisconsin Press.

Driver, Harold E. 1969. *Indians of North America,* 2nd ed. Chicago: University of Chicago Press.

Duncan, Greg J. 1984. *Years of Poverty, Years of Plenty.* Ann Arbor: Institute for Social Research, University of Michigan.

Edmonston, Barry, Joshua Goldstein, and Tamayo Lott (eds.). 1996. *Spotlight on Heterogeneity: The Federal Standards for Racial and Ethnic Classification.* Washington, DC: National Academy Press.

Eitzen, D. Stanley, and Maxine Baca Zinn (eds.). 1989. *The Reshaping of America: Social Consequences of the Changing Economy.* Englewood Cliffs, NJ: Prentice-Hall.

Eshleman, J. Ross. 1991. *The Family,* 6th ed. Boston: Allyn and Bacon.

Espanshade, Thomas J. 1985. "Marriage Trends in America: Estimates, Implications, and Underlying Causes." *Population and Development Review* 11(2):193–245.

Farley, Reynolds. 1984. *Blacks and Whites: Narrowing the Gap.* Cambridge, MA: Harvard University Press.

Farley, Reynolds, and Walter Allen. 1989. *The Color Line and the Quality of Life in America.* New York: Oxford University Press.

Frisbie, W. Parker, Wolfang Opitz, and William R. Kelly. 1985. "Marital Instability Trends among Mexican Americans as Compared to Blacks and Anglos: New Evidence." *Social Science Quarterly* 66 (Sept.):587–601.

Gardner, Robert W., Bryant Robey, and Peter C. Smith. 1985. *Asian Americans: Growth, Change, and Diversity.* Washington, DC: Population Reference Bureau.

Gerstel, Naomi, and Harriet Engle Gross (eds.). 1987. *Families and Work.* Philadelphia: Temple University Press.

Glick, Paul C. 1969. "Marital Stability as a Social Indicator." *Social Biology* 16(3):158–166.

———1988. "Demographic Pictures of Black Families." In *Black Families,* 2nd ed., edited by H. P. McAdoo, 111–132. Beverly Hills, CA: Sage.

Gonzalez, Juan. 2000. *Harvest of Empire: A History of Latinos in America.* New York: Viking.

Green, R. 1975. "The Pocahontas Perplex: The Image of Indian Women in American Culture." *The Massachusetts Review* 16:698–714.

Guillemin, Jeanne. 1975. *Urban Renegades: The Cultural Strategy of American Indians.* New York: Columbia University Press.

Hartmann, Heida I. 1989. "Changes in Women's Economic and Family Roles in Post–World War II United States." In *The Reshaping of America,* edited by D. S. Eitzen and M. Baca Zinn, 296–318. Englewood Cliffs, NJ: Prentice-Hall.

Henry, William. 1990. "Beyond the Melting Pot." *Time* (April 9):28–31.

Hill, Robert B. 1989. "Critical Issues for Black Families by the Year 2000." In *The State of Black America, 1989,* edited by J. Dewart, 41–61. New York: National Urban League.

Hong, Lawrence K. 1982. "The Korean Family in Los Angeles." In *Koreans in Los Angeles,* edited by E. Y. Yu and others, 99–132. Los Angeles: California State University.

Jarvenpa, Robert. 1988. "The Political Economy and Political Ethnicity of American Indian Adaptations and Identities." In *Ethnicity and Race in the U.S.A.,* edited by R. Alba, 29–48. New York: Routledge.

Jaynes, Gerald D., and Robin M. Williams (eds.). 1989. *A Common Destiny: Blacks and American Society.* Washington, DC: National Academy Press.

Jiobu, Robert M. 1988. *Ethnicity and Assimilation.* Albany: SUNY Press.

John, Robert. 1908. "The Native American Family." In *Ethnic Families in America,* edited by C. H. Mindel, R. Habenstein, and R. Wright, Jr., 325–368. New York: Elsevier.

Joint Center for Political and Economic Studies. 1999. *Family and Household Structure: Fact Sheets: Living Arrangements of Children; Trends in Poverty; Single Parent Families.* Washington DC: Website. (July).

Kibria, Nazli. 1990. "Power, Patriarchy, and Gender Conflict in the Vietnamese Immigrant Community." *Gender and Society* 4(March):9–24.

Kitano, Harry H. L., and A. Kikumura. 1980. "The Japanese American Family." In *Asian-Americans: Social and Psychological Perspectives*, edited by R. Endo, S. Sue, and N. Wagner. Palo Alto, CA: Science and Behavior Books.

Kitano, Harry H. L., and Stanley Sue. 1973. "The Model Minorities." *Journal of Social Issues* 29:1–9.

Kitano, Harry H. L., and Wai-Tsang Yeung. 1982. "Chinese Interracial Marriage." *Marriage and Family Review* 5:35–48.

Kitano, Harry H. L., Wai-Tsang Yeung, Lynn Chai, and Herb Hatanaka. 1984. "Asian American Interracial Marriage." *Journal of Marriage and the Family* 46:179–190.

Lee, Thea. 1990. "Trapped on a Pedestal: Asian Americans Confront Model-Minority Stereotype." *Dollars and Sense* (March):12–15.

Levin, Daniel, and Linda Ingram (eds.). 1988. *Income and Poverty Statistics: Problems of Concept and Measurement*. Washington, DC: National Academy Press.

Levitan, Sar A., and Richard S. Belous. 1981. *What's Happening to the American Family?* Baltimore: Johns Hopkins University Press.

Lieberson, Stanley, and Mary C. Waters. 1988. *From Many Strands: Ethnic and Racial Groups in Contemporary America*. New York: Russell Sage Foundation.

Light, Ivan. 1972. *Ethnic Enterprise in America*. Berkeley: University of California Press.

Lurie, Nancy O. 1971. "The Contemporary American Indian Scene." In *North American Indians in Historical Perspective*, edited by E. B. Leacock and N. Lurie. New York: Random House.

Manson, Spero M., and Audra M. Pambrun. 1979. "Social and Psychological Status of the Indian Elderly: Past Research, Current Advocacy, and Future Inquiry." In *The Continuum of Life: Health Concerns of the Indian Elderly*. Albuquerque, NM: National Indian Council on Aging.

Mare, Robert D., and Christopher Winship. 1991. "Socioeconomic Change and the Decline of Marriage for Blacks and Whites." In *The Urban Underclass*, edited by C. Jencks and P. E. Peterson, 175–204. Washington, DC: Brookings Institution.

Markides, Kyriakos S., Sue K. Hoppe, Harry W. Martin, and Dianne M. Timbers. 1983. "Sample Representativeness in a Three-Generation Study of Mexican Americans." *Journal of Marriage and the Family* 45:911–916.

Metcalf, Ann. 1979. "Family Reunion: Networks and Treatment in a Native American Community." *Group Psychotherapy, Psychodrama, and Sociometry* 32:179–189.

Miller, Dorothy. 1979. "The Native American Family: The Urban Way." In *Families Today: A Research Sampler on Families and Children*, edited by E. Corfman, 441–484. Washington, DC: U.S. Government Printing Office.

Moore, Joan W. 1988. "An Assessment of Hispanic Poverty: Does a Hispanic Underclass Exist?" *Tomas Rivera Center Report* 2:8–9.

Mullings, Ruth. 1986. "Anthropological Perspectives on the Afro-American Family." *The American Journal of Social Psychiatry* 6(Winter):11–16.

Muschin, Clara, and George C. Myers. 1989. "Migration and Household Family Structure: Puerto Ricans in the United States." *International Migration Review* 23:495–501.

New York Times. 1991a. "Only One U.S. Family in Four Is 'Traditional.'" *New York Times* (Jan. 30):A19.

———. 1991b. "Census Shows Profound Change in Racial Makeup of the Nation." *New York Times* (March 11):1.

———. 2001. "The Changing American Family." *New York Times* (May 18):A1.

Norton, Arthur J., and Paul Glick. 1979. "Marital Instability in America: Past, Present, and Future." In *Divorce and Separation*, edited by G. Levinger and Oliver C. Moles. New York: Basic Books.

Norton, Eleanor H. 1985. "Restoring the Traditional Black Family." *The New York Times Magazine* (June 2):43, 79, 93, 96, 98.

O'Hare, William P. O., Kelvin M. Pollard, Taynia L. Mann, and Mary Kent. 1991. *African Americans in the 1990s.* Washington, DC: Population Reference Bureau.

———. 1992. "America's Minorities—The Demographics of Diversity." *Population Bulletin* 47 (Dec.):1–46.

Petersen, William. 1971. *Japanese Americans.* New York: Random House.

Population Reference Bureau. 1999. "America's Racial and Ethnic Minorities." *Population Bulletin* 54, No. 3.

———. 2000. "American's Diversity and Growth: Signposts for the 21st Century." *Population Bulletin 55,* No. 2.

Portes, Alejandro, and Alex Stepick. 1993. *City on the Edge: The Transformation of Miami.* Berkeley: University of California Press.

Portes, Alejandro, and Cynthia Truelove. 1987. "Making Sense of Diversity: Recent Research on Hispanic Minorities in the United States." *Annual Review of Sociology* 13:359–385.

———. 1996. "Introduction: Immigration and Its Aftermath." *International Migration Review* 28:632–639.

Queen, Stuart A., Robert W. Habenstein, and Jill S. Quadagno. 1985. *The Family in Various Cultures,* 5th ed. New York: Harper & Row.

Ramirez, Oscar, and Carlos Arce. 1981. "The Contemporary Chicano Family: An Empirically Based Review." In *Explorations in Chicano Psychology,* edited by A. Baron. New York: Praeger.

Red Horse, J. G., R. Lewis, M. Feit, and J. Decker. 1978. "Family Behavior of Urban American Indians." *Social Casework* 59 (Feb.):67–72.

Red Horse, John. 1980. "Family Structure and Value Orientation in American-Indians." *Social Casework* 61 (8):462–467.

———. 1982. "Clinical Strategies for American-Indian Families in Crisis." *Urban and Social Change Review* 15(2):17–19.

Reid, John. 1982. *Black America in the 1980s.* Washington, DC: Population Reference Bureau.

Root, Maria (ed.). 1992. *Racially Mixed People in America.* Newbury Park, CA: Sage.

Sandefur, Gary. 1988. "Blacks, Hispanics, American Indians, and Poverty—and What Worked." In *Quiet Riots: Race and Poverty in the United States,* edited by F. Harris and R. W. Wilkins, 46–74. New York: Pantheon Books.

Sandefur, Gary, and Carolyn Liebler. 1997. "The Demography of American Indian Families." *Population Research and Policy Review* 16:95–114.

Schwartz, Joe, and Thomas Exter. 1989. "All Our Children." *American Demographics* (May):34–37.

Snipp, C. Matthew. 1989. *American Indians: The First of the Land.* New York: Russell Sage Foundation.

———. 1997. "The Size and Distribution of the American Indian Population: Fertility, Mortality, Migration, and Residence. *Population Research and Policy Review.* 16:61–93

Snipp, C. Matthew, and Gary Sandefur. 1988. "Earnings of American Indians and Alaska Natives: The Effects of Residence and Migration." *Social Forces* 66:994–1008.

Spicer, Edward H. 1980. "American Indians." In *Harvard Encyclopedia of American Ethnic Groups,* edited by S. Thernstrom. Cambridge, MA: Harvard University Press.

Stack, Carol. 1974. *All Our Kin: Strategies for Survival in a Black Community.* New York: Harper and Row.

Staples, Robert. 1988. "The Black American Family." In *Ethnic Families in America,* edited by C. Mindel, R. Habenstein, and R. Wright, Jr., 303–324. New York: Elsevier.

Staples, Robert, and Alfredo Mirande. 1980. "Racial and Cultural Variations among American Families: A Decennial Review of the Literature on Minority Families." *Journal of Marriage and the Family* 42(4):157–173.

Steinberg, Stephen. 1981. *The Ethnic Myth.* Boston: Beacon Press.

Takaki, Ronald. 1987. "Reflections on Racial Patterns in America." In *From Different Shores: Perspectives on Race and Ethnicity in America,* edited by R. Takaki, 26–37. New York: Oxford University Press.

Taylor, Ronald L. 1997. "The Changing Meaning of Race in the Social Sciences: Implications for Social Work Practice." *Smith College Studies in Social Work:* Special Issue *Theoretical, Policy, Research and Clinical Perspectives for Social Work Practice with African Americans* 67(June):277–298.

———. 2000. "Diversity within African American Families." In *Handbook of Family Diversity,* edited by D. Demo, K. Allen, and M. Fine, 232–251. New York: Oxford University Press.

Thorne, Barrie. 1982. "Feminist Thinking on the Family: An Overview." In *Rethinking the Family: Some Feminist Questions,* edited by B. Thorne and M. Yalom, 1–24. New York: Longman.

Time. 1985. "Immigrants." Special Issue. *Time* (July 8): Entire issue.

U.S. Bureau of the Census. 1973. "American Indians." Subject Report. *Current Population Reports.* Washington, DC: U.S. Government Printing Office.

———. 1980. *Census of Population,* Vol. 1, *General Social and Economic Characteristics,* pt. 1. U.S. Summary. Washington, DC: U.S. Government Printing Office.

———. 1981. *1980 Census of Population: Supplementary Reports.* Washington, DC: U.S. Government Printing Office.

———. 1984. *American Indian Areas and Alaska Native Villages: 1980.* Washington, DC: U.S. Government Printing Office.

———. 1986. *American Indians, Eskimos, and Aleuts on Identified Reservations and in the Historic Areas of Oklahoma (Excluding Urbanized Areas),* pt. 2, Sections 1 and 2. Washington, DC: U.S. Government Printing Office.

———. 1988. "The Hispanic Population of the U.S.: March 1988:" Advance Report. *Current Population Reports* (April). Washington, DC: U.S. Government Printing Office.

———. 1989. "Marital Status and Living Arrangements: March 1989." *Current Population Reports* (June). Washington, DC: U.S. Government Printing Office.

———. 1990a. "Household and Family Characteristics, March 1990 and 1989." *Current Population Reports.* Washington, DC: U.S. Government Printing Office.

———. 1990b. *Census of the Population.* Vol. 1, *General Social and Economic Characteristics.* Washington, DC: U.S. Government Printing Office.

———. 1991. "Marital Status and Living Arrangements: March 1990." *Current Population Reports* Washington, DC: U.S. Government Printing Office.

———. 1992. *The Asian and Pacific Islander Population in the United States: March 1991 and 1990.* Washington, DC: U.S. Government Printing Office.

———. 1993. "We the Americans: Asians 1993." *Economics and Statistics Administration.* Washington, DC: U.S. Government Printing Office.

———. 1994. "Marital Status and Living Arrangements: March 1993." *Current Population Reports* (May). Washington, DC: U.S. Government Printing Office.

———. 1995. *Statistical Abstract of the United States: 1995.* Washington, DC: U.S. Government Printing Office.

———. 1996. *Statistical Abstract of the United States: 1996.* Washington, DC: U.S. Government Printing Office.

———. 1998a. *The Official Statistics: Population Profile of the United States, Special Reports P23-194.* Washington, DC: U.S. Government Printing Office.

———. 1998b. "Household and Family Characteristics." *Current Population Reports.* Washington, DC: U.S. Government Printing Office.

———. 1999. *March 1999: Current Population Survey.* Washington, DC: U.S. Government Printing Office.

————. 2000a. *Current Population Survey, March 1999.* Washington, DC: U.S. Government Printing Office.

————. 2000b. *Current Population Survey, March 2000.* Washington, DC: U.S. Government Printing Office.

————. 2000c. *Current Population Survey, March 1999.* Ethnic and Hispanic Statistics Branch. Internet Release date 5/5/00.

————. 2000d. *Statistical Abstract of the United States: 1999.* Washington, DC: U.S. Government Printing Office.

————. 2001. "The Hispanic Population in the United States." *Current Population Reports* (March). Washington, DC: U.S. Government Printing Office.

U.S. Commission on Civil Rights. 1988. *The Economic Status of Americans of Asian Descent: An Exploratory Investigation.* Washington, DC: U.S. Government Printing Office.

————. 1992. *Civil Rights Issues Facing Asian Americans in the 1990s.* Washington, DC: U.S. Government Printing Office.

U.S. Department of Labor, Bureau of Labor Statistics. 1988a. "Projections 2000." *BLS Bulletin,* No. 2302. Washington, DC: U.S. Government Printing Office.

————. 1988b. "Twenty Facts on Women Workers." *Office of the Secretary. Women's Bureau.* Washington, DC: U.S. Government Printing Office.

————. 2000. "Highlights of Women's Earnings in 1999." *Report 243* (May 2000). Washington, DC: U.S. Government Printing Office.

Valdivieso, Rafael, and Gary Davis. 1988. *U.S. Hispanics: Challenging Issues for the 1990s.* Washington, DC: Population Reference Bureau.

Van Tran, Thanh. 1988. "The Vietnamese American Family." In *Ethnic Families in America,* edited by C. H. Mindel, R. W. Habenstein, and R. Wright, Jr., 276–299. New York: Elsevier.

Vega, William A. 1990. "Hispanic Families in the 1980s: A Decade of Research." *Journal of Marriage and the Family* 52 (November):1015–1024.

Westermeyer, J. 1977. "The Ravage of Indian Families in Crisis." In *The Destruction of American Indian Families,* edited by S. Unger. New York: Association on American Indian Affairs.

Westoff, Charles F. 1983. "Fertility Decline in the West: Causes and Prospects." *Population and Development Review* 9:99–104.

Wilkie, Jane R. 1991. "Marriage, Family Life, and Women's Employment." In *Marriage and Family in Transition,* edited by J. N. Edwards and D. H. Demo, 143–164. Boston: Allyn and Bacon.

Wilkinson, Doris Y. 1987. "Ethnicity." In *Handbook of Marriage and the Family,* edited by M. B. Sussman and S. K. Steinmetz, 183–210. New York: Plenum.

Williams, A. 1980. "Transition from the Reservation to an Urban Setting and the Changing Roles of American Indian Women." In *Conference on the Educational and Occupational Needs of American Indian Women.* National Institute of Education. Washington, DC: U.S. Department of Education.

Wilson, Kenneth, and Alejandro Portes. 1980. "Immigrant Enclaves: An Analysis of the Labor Market Experiences of Cubans in Miami." *American Journal of Sociology* 86:295–319.

Wilson, William J. 1978. *The Declining Significance of Race: Blacks and Changing American Institutions.* Chicago: University of Chicago Press.

————. 1984. "The Urban Underclass." In *Minority Report: What Has happened to Blacks, Hispanics, American Indians, and Other Minorities in the Eighties,* edited by L. W. Dunbar, 75–117. New York: Pantheon.

————. 1987. *The Truly Disadvantaged: The Inner City, the Underclass, and Public Policy.* Chicago: University of Chicago Press.

Wilson, William J., and Kathryn Neckerman. 1986. "Poverty and Family Structure: The Widening Gap between Evidence and Public Policy Issues." In *Fighting Poverty: What Works and What Doesn't,* edited by S. H. Danziger and D. H. Weinberg, 232–259. Cambridge, MA: Harvard University Press.

Wong, Morrison, 1986. "Post-1965 Asian Immigrants: Where Do They Come From, Where Are They Now, and Where Are They Going?" *Annals of the American Academy of Political and Social Science* 487 (Sept.):150–168.

———. 1988. "The Chinese Family." In *Ethnic Families in America,* edited by C. H. Mindel, R. W. Habenstein, and R. Wright, Jr., 230–257. New York: Elsevier.

Index

G

Gardner, Robert W., 276–281, 283
Genovese, Eugene, 22–23
Gerstel, Naomi, 253
Glazer, Nathan, 4
Glenn, Evelyn Nakano, 166, 168, 170–172, 174, 178
Glick, Paul, 29, 94, 255
Gordon, Milton, 166
Gringerich, Wallace, 244
Griswold, del Castillo, Richard, 83–84, 94–95
Gross, Harriet Engel, 253
Gutman, Herbert, 22–24

H

Haitian American families
  and generational change, 74–75
  and household management, 67–69
  and immigration history, 63–65
  and microeconomic theory of the firm, 63
  and poverty, 75
Hallowell, Irving, 240
Hanson, Wynne, 243
Hatchett, Shirley, 35–38, 41–42
Hayes-Bautista, David, 91
Heer, David, 11
Hernandez, Roberto, 127
Hispanic, defined, 77, 79–80
Hispanic American families: 77–78, 263–273
  and child poverty, 267
  comparison of sub-group, 263–264
  and female-headed households, 266
  and kinship networks, 266
  and multiple earner households, 267–268
  and the economy, 268–272
  and poverty, 267
  and residency, 263–264
  and women's labor force participation, 272
  See also Cuban American families; Mexican American families; Puerto
  Rican American families

I

Ichihashi, Yamato, 170
Immigration, and minority family structures, 253–255
  and population growth, 255–256
Immigration Act of 1865, 7, 256
Indian Self-Determination and Education Assistance Act, 245
Indo-American families: defined, 221
  and the Asian Migration Ban 214
  and child socialization, 216
  and class, 219
  desi culture, 220
  and divorce, 214

  and economic characteristics, 214
  and family dynamics, 215
  and family networks, 217
  and female employment, 218
  and gender roles, 218
  ideal vs. real families, 216–217
  and immigration, 213–215
  and poverty, 214
  and parental roles, 217
  and racial discrimination, 219
  and restrictions on citizenship, 213
Industry Restructuring, 251
  and effects on minority groups, 271–272
  See also Economy, national
Institutional Discrimination, 80
Ishisaka, Hidecki, 246

J

Japanese American families: cohesion and social control
  and the critical perspective, 171–172
  and the cultural perspective, 165–168
  diversity of, 177
  organization of, 177
  and female oppression, 172–173
  and gender roles, 171–172, 175
  and generational change, 173–174
  immigration and exclusion, 169–171
  and immigration law, 169–170
  and intermarriage, 174–175
  and internment, 172–173
  marriage and divorce, 175–176
  and "picture brides," 170, 173–174
  and postwar period, 173–174
  and single-parent households, 176–177
  and socioeconomic status, 176–177
  and women's labor force participation, 174–175
Jaynes, Gerald D., 40, 257–258, 261
Jiobu, Robert, 5–6
John, Robert, 240–241, 286–289

K

Kibria, Nazli, 181, 184, 186–189, 193–194
Kingston, Maxine Hong, 141–142
Kitano, Harry H. L., 155
Korean American families
  and areas of settlement, 189–193
  and child socialization, 203–205
  and the church, 196, 205
  and divorce, 198–199
  and education, 196
  and fertility, 200, 206
  and gender role differentiation, 199
  and gender socialization, 205